Interest
Rate
Futures

INTEREST RATE FUTURES

by

Allan M. Loosigian

DOW JONES-IRWIN
Homewood, Illinois 60430

Published by Dow Jones-Irwin
1818 Ridge Road, Homewood, IL 60430

Copyright 1980 by Dow Jones & Company, Inc.

Printed and bound in the United States of America

3 4 5 6 7 8 9 0 K 5 4 3 2 1

Library of Congress Cataloging in Publication Data

Loosigian, Allan M   1938-
  Interest rate futures.

  Bibliography: p.
  Includes index.
  1. Interest rate futures. I. Title.
HG6024.5.L66   332.8'2   79-21762
ISBN 0-87128-579-7

Dedication:
To My Family

TABLE OF CONTENTS

Part Two: The Prices

Part Three: The Users

ACKNOWLEDGMENTS

A book of this sort is by its nature as much a job of reporting as one of original exposition. While the task of writing it fell to me, its contents are a distillation of the knowledge and experience of many people. Some of these market participants are named in Chapter Twelve, while others preferred to offer their ideas without attribution. The contributions of yet a third group were so significant as to demand explicit recognition at the outset.

In the first instance, it was my good fortune to have as an editor John A. Prestbo of Dow Jones & Company, one of the rare individuals I encountered during a year of research who are equally well versed in the futures and securities markets. The price records and other resources of the Chicago Board of Trade were placed at my disposal by Noel C. Ogan, Manager of Market Information, and by members of that exchange's Financial Instruments Committee. Comparable data were provided by Frank J. Jones, Chief Economist of the Chicago Mercantile Exchange. Among the investment firms, a number of charts and statistical exhibits were supplied by Merrill Lynch, Pierce, Fenner and Smith Inc., and Salomon Brothers made available its *Analytical Record of Yields and Yield Spreads*.

Finally, a most emphatic word of thanks is reserved for Mr. Sidney Homer, a long-time partner in the latter firm and the principal architect of that invaluable research source. Not only did his numerous other published works on interest rates and fixed-income securities comprise the models and points of departure for this book, but his personal encouragement and generous advice during its writing became sorely-needed guideposts for what otherwise was in many respects a foray into uncharted territory.

AML

FOREWORD

More than six years have passed since a liquid market for common stock call options was created amidst speculation that such a market would not be a long-term viable exchange. Call/put options were often dismissed by professional money managers and institutional investors as "speculative" with minimal appeal beyond individual investors. Those skeptics of six years ago have been proven wrong. The opportunities to use listed call/put options have enhanced investing in common stock to the extent where today and in the future I find it difficult to imagine a properly constructed institutional common stock portfolio that excludes the use of options. Investment strategies for individuals through the use of options are even more advanced today than those afforded the institutional market.

Today's interest in financial futures is a repeat of the chain of events that is now leading to widespread acceptance and use of listed stock options. Financial futures, although in their infancy, offer the same opportunity of defining and allocating risk, reward, and return as stock options. The potential use of financial futures is enormous. Whereas, institutional use of stock options is generally limited to common stock investors, the use of financial futures is virtually unlimited. The one common medium in the business world is money. Financial institutions, industrial companies, service organizations, and utilities all have a need to use, invest, borrow and plan their money requirements. Essentially, financial futures have the potential for use by anyone dealing with money. The risk-adverse can hedge, the risk-oriented can speculate, but all need education in this emerging and complex market of financial futures. This book helps provide that education and insight for present and potential users of the rapidly growing market for financial futures.

Kenneth A. Drucker
Assistant Treasurer
Stauffer Chemical Company
Westport, Connecticut

Introduction

Soon after hanging out my shingle as a "specialist in financial futures" in early 1976, I called on an archetypical New England savings banker. The improbable purpose of my visit was to persuade him that investing his depositors' money in the commodity futures market was a prudent thing to do. After delivering my well-rehearsed presentation, I paused to give my skeptical prospect an opportunity to ask any one of three dozen questions for which I had prepared equally well-rehearsed answers. His first question, the obvious one which I had unaccountably overlooked, concerned my credentials and experience to dispense such advice. Grasping the first plausible justification that came to mind, I loftily replied that because I had been active in the interest rate futures market since its inception, there was no one better qualified to assess it than myself. I felt compelled to add in a somewhat subdued voice that the market itself was then only six months old.

If it is true that a realization of how little you know marks the onset of wisdom (and there is nothing like a few trading losses to bring you to that point rather quickly), I can at least claim to have grown with the market during the ensuing three years.

The interest rate futures market is exciting, fascinating and all too often confounding. It is also a place where money is made or lost very quickly. If you have invested your money in this book with the expectation of finding a blueprint to riches by an expert who is magnanimously inclined to share his secrets, you had best return it for a refund. If you more realistically read it as a record of trial and error by someone who earns his living in the market, you will find the material of value. Don't waste your time turning pages in search of a magic formula or system. There is none. Rather, I have set down the various means by which I have managed to make money more often than lose it. Both are part of the game.

Earning money consistently is never easy, whether it be by swinging a pickax or trading futures. But as there is a way of swinging the ax to obtain maximum leverage and performance, there are also ways to trade futures to obtain maximum rewards while controlling the ever-present element of risk.

I can't sell you any secrets because most of the relevant information is readily available, perhaps more so than in the case of the stock market. The vital statistics are released regularly, publicly and without charge by the U. S. government. What I am offering is a system of organizing the plethora of data pertaining to interest rates and a method of evaluating it to survive and prosper in the market place.

The book addresses two general groups of readers, labeled in futures terminology as speculators and "the trade." The speculators might be individuals who have already traded for their personal account such traditional commodity futures as soybeans or copper and who seek to enhance their understanding of the money markets. Or they might be people inexperienced in futures trading of any type who feel a greater affinity for investment securities than for agricultural products or metals. The common objective of the seasoned futures trader and the novice speculator is to buy one of the several interest rate contracts before interest rates decline or a consensus develops that they are about to decline, which causes the contract's value to increase; and, conversely, to sell (short) futures before a perception that interest rates are about to increase becomes widespread enough to cause them to fall in price.

Please consider for a moment and retain for later discussion in some detail this principle: A trader who thinks interest rates will fall would *buy* futures; if he thinks rates will rise, he would *sell* futures. This inverse relationship between price and yield is central to a grasp of this market, and is a cause for some confusion to those approaching it for the first time.

"The trade" consists of professional money managers employed by corporations and financial institutions of various types, such as banks, savings and loan associations, insurance companies, pension funds, etc. They are not paid to speculate with funds placed under their supervision but to invest them as judiciously as possible. In some instances their objective is to borrow money on the most advantageous terms, which usually means at the lowest possible cost. As either prospective investors or borrowers, the purpose of these professional managers is not so much to profit by rising or falling interest rates as to protect their firms' capital from the adverse consequences of such rate changes. In this regard, they are termed "hedgers," whose goal is to avoid or reduce exposure to risk. To illustrate, the market value of a bond portfolio decreases as long-term interest rates rise, in keeping with the principle cited above. A hedger might therefore protect his portfolio from such price depreciation by entering into a futures transaction that generates profits as rates increase—that is, by selling contracts short.

Although the objectives of speculators and hedgers apparently are contrary, in that one group courts risk while the other seeks to avoid it, all operate in the same arena and deal with the same prices. Indeed, the two camps are not so much opposed as they are complementary. Hedgers could not function without speculators in the market and vice versa.

While this book adopts the conventional practice of treating speculators and hedgers separately in light of their different goals, I believe that a successful trader must understand his market fully, which includes having insight into the motives and techniques of his contraparty. Buying invariably drives prices up and selling pushes them down. Whether the buying or selling is done for speculative or hedging motives, the winning trader must recognize the different forces at work and program them into his personal trading plan.

The book is organized to correspond with this duality of emphasis. Since speculators and hedgers do business in the same trading arena and utilize the same instruments, we will begin with a description of the commodity exchanges where interest rate futures are traded, the specifics of the several contracts which comprise the financial instrument group, the different types of exchange members who populate the trading floor and the mechanics of buying and selling futures contracts.

Part Two turns to the theoretical side of the subject by appraising the dynamics of interest rate movements and the pattern of comparative rates known as the yield curve. There is a multiplicity of interest rates taken both by the length of time money is lent and the types of debt instruments which certify the borrowing transaction. The successful financial futures trader must have a view not only of an individual rate vis-a-vis its past and possible future level, but the relationship of each rate to those on comparable fixed-income securities. There are valid reasons why U.S. Treasury bills, say, offer a lower yield than prime commercial paper with the same maturity. The alert futures trader seeks to profit by taking the appropriate market action when he observes the differential between the two interest rates diverge from the customary relationship.

This section also identifies the principal forces within the overall economy that affect the level of interest rates to aid the reader in shaping his own forecasts amidst the ongoing stream of business and economic news. An important, indeed often decisive, adjunct to the economic environment is government policy, particularly as reflected in the actions of the

Federal Reserve System in tightening or easing credit conditions to restrain or stimulate the pace of economic activity at any given time.

Part Three describes how the theory is put into practice by the principal market participants. We revert to the speculator-hedger distinction, although the line dividing them often becomes blurred. A typical speculative trading plan is presented and evaluated. Several hedging strategies which should be of particular interest to investment managers and corporate financial officers are discussed in some detail. I have devoted a chapter to spreading and arbitrage, two overlapping categories of futures trading which together comprise what is probably the most advanced, and certainly the most intriguing, aspect of the subject. Although these somewhat involved techniques also fall principally within the domain of the professional, I see no reason why an adept and diligent part-time trader cannot adapt them to fit his own situation. To this end, the book concludes with a survey of the professional services in the financial futures area offered by brokerage firms, banks and investment advisors to private individuals and institutional managers.

One of the intellectual attractions of interest rate futures is the opportunity they offer determined amateurs to attain a level of financial sophistication normally reserved to professional investment managers. Now that I and the markets have extended our joint longevity six-fold from six months to three years, I hope that the experience distilled in this book will help the newcomer to reap the possible rewards while surviving the pitfalls. I don't say avoid, because they cannot all be avoided. If, along the way, I have managed to provide my fellow practitioners with some fresh insights, that is fair exchange for the help they have given me.

Allan M. Loosigian
Stamford, Conn.

Part One

The Markets

Chapter One

The Exchanges

The traditional image of a market place is one of a common site where buyers and sellers meet to display or inspect the merchandise and to transact their business. In this age of electronic communications, the physical site may have dissolved into a network of telephone or Telex lines, obviating the need for a face-to-face meeting of the participants. The markets with which we are concerned represent a fusion of the old and the new.

Interest rate futures are bought and sold on a trading floor, or "pit," like other commodity contracts, so this study of them begins with a description of the futures exchanges, much like an introduction to chess starts with a diagram of the board. This analogy is appropriate because the futures game involves "pieces," i.e., futures contracts, and players on and off the floor who employ a variety of strategies to win profits. The expression "game" is used advisedly because futures trading is a competitive undertaking. Unlike chess, however, the markets are all too often capricious and impervious to analytic reasoning—or so it seems when you are on the losing side. Yet it is precisely this irrational quality that triggers the price volatility which lures speculative players and reflects the risk hedgers are seeking to offset.

Development of Futures Trading

Though a history of the evolution of futures trading falls outside the limits of this book, a backward glance at its early development in the United States provides a useful framework for understanding the nature of commodity markets and the operation of the exchanges.

The use of advance pricing arrangements has been a common trade practice since the days of antiquity. Reference is made to forward contracting for commodities in the commercial annals of ancient Greece and Rome and the method was refined considerably by the time of the medieval trade fairs in France and England. The risk inherent in such dealings gained considerable notoriety in the aftermath of the ruinous tulip craze in 17th century Holland, which is cited to this day as the inevitable consequence when speculative avarice is inflamed by mob psychology.

The adoption of such techniques in the United States is associated most directly with the Anglo-American cotton trade and the shipment of grain into Chicago during the mid-1800s. Chicago was the railroad and waterway hub of the Midwest by 1850 and as such quickly became the country's leading grain terminal. Established in 1848 for the purpose of promoting the commerce of the city, the Board of Trade of the City of Chicago was designated the official agency for the measurement, weighing and inspection of grain shipments into the terminal market. The development of quality standards and efficient inspection procedures during this early period facilitated the physical handling of grain and the acceptance of warehouse receipts as evidence of ownership, a precondition for the creation of the transferable contracts which evolved into futures contracts.

During that same decade, the difficulties which farmers and the local dealers to whom they sold their crops encountered in moving grain to market when prices were favorable made the improvisation of a system of advance pricing almost inevitable. Even if flooded or frozen dirt roads from the country could be traversed after the fall corn harvest, inadequate storage and lakefront harbor facilities in the city caused those supplies which did arrive to glut the market, depressing prices to giveaway levels. Rather than assuming the price risk of storing their corn in local elevators and cribs through the fall and winter, country merchants would travel to Chicago and contract to sell it at firm prices for spring delivery.

The seasonal crop pattern for wheat made its marketing cycle somewhat different from that of corn. Wheat normally would be moved immediately upon harvest to the Chicago terminal, where it was stored awaiting shipment to the Eastern millers and export markets. Whereas the Chicago grain merchants normally would be buyers of forward corn contracts from country merchants, they were the ones who were encumbered with inventory and financing risks in the case of wheat, which they sought to reduce by selling forward wheat contracts to the Eastern millers and exporters.

These so-called time, or forward, contracts came to be regarded as valid collateral by Chicago bankers in advancing loans to merchants to purchase grain from farmers. The availability of credit allowed the merchants in turn to offer more attractive prices to farmers, since their profit was assured through the sale of forward contracts. Thus, the incipient system of forward pricing allowed all of the participants in the flow of trade to work with a greater measure of price protection and thereby alleviated the pricing and financing problems of everyone involved.

Similar developments were taking place in the cotton trade. During the several months' interval between the time their agents purchased raw cotton in the United States and the sale of the finished goods in England and on the Continent, English importers were at risk of ownership while the cotton was being shipped and processed. To offset the risk implicit in widely fluctuating prices, merchants in Liverpool began selling their consignments on a "to-arrive" basis while the cotton was still at sea.

From specifying a shipment scheduled to make port aboard a particular vessel, the practice evolved of writing contracts covering any cotton of the requisite grade to reach Liverpool within a designated month. This modification hastened the progression from "to-arrive" to "futures" contracts. A flourishing trade in contracts for future delivery developed in the Liverpool market, leading to the establishment of the Liverpool Cotton Exchange with full-time brokers dealing in the contracts under a commonly accepted set of rules and regulations. During the same years and for similar reasons, exchanges for trading cotton contracts for immediate and future delivery were organized in New York and New Orleans.

With the development of these markets, merchants had recourse to a mechanism for transferring the risk of owning cotton. By selling futures contracts, they were protected from a drop in the price of cash cotton during shipment and manufacture. As was the case in the Chicago grain market, dealers with fixed sales contracts in hand were able to guarantee the banks' crop loans to the growers and make rational purchase bids related to a sale price already set through a futures transaction.

The antecedents of the Chicago Mercantile Exchange, the parent organization of the International Monetary Market, also evolved during those years. A produce exchange was formed in 1874 as a market for butter, eggs, poultry and other perishable agricultural products. The butter and egg dealers withdrew to establish their own market, which was reorganized as the present exchange in 1919.

While the Chicago Board of Trade became the country's principal grain market, the Chicago Mercantile Exchange and its predecessor organizations assumed a leading role as a livestock and produce market. Keenly competitive and alert to the possibilities of innovative applications of the principle of risk transfer, the two exchanges independently pioneered the concept of futures contracts for interest-bearing securities with which this book is concerned.

Hedgers and Speculators

The early recourse to forward pricing marked the beginning of the practice of hedging in this country, with the attendant benefits to purchasing, inventory management and credit extension. The underlying rationale of hedging is that commodity prices, then and now, often fluctuate widely and capriciously. The principal parties involved in the production, trade and processing of various crops spontaneously contrived the futures markets as a means of insulating their business operations from unpredictable and potentially damaging price changes. A market mechanism to transfer risk will not meet the test if there is no one with an incentive to accept it. Certainly the grain and cotton merchants were not interested in passing risk back and forth among themselves like a financial hot potato. To perform its economic function, a futures market must have an abundance of risk-takers, namely speculators.

Numerous factors, many of which defy consistent and accurate prediction, interact in the determination of a commodity's price in the market place. To pursue the example of the grain markets, an incomplete list of the forces affecting supply and demand would include: weather conditions, acreage planted (itself a function of past and present prices), insect and disease damage, crop yield, prices and supplies of competing crops, personal disposable income, domestic consumption, foreign prices and demand, cost and availability of transportation and, in the recent past, the effect of government price support programs.

Swift and often sharp price changes triggered by

actual or even suspected revisions of these determining elements are viewed by "the trade" as disruptive risks rather than profit opportunities. To conduct their business on a rational basis, producers, merchants, processors and creditors prefer price stability. This desired stability is lacking when the price of wheat, for example, is capable of fluctuating anywhere from $1.50 to $4.50 a bushel between the time a new crop is planted and when it is brought to market. Without a system of forward pricing to offset such wide price swings, it would be futile to attempt any manner of business planning in the grain or other commodity trades.

Forward pricing through the use of futures contracts does not eliminate price risk. The device merely makes it possible to transfer unwanted risk to a receptive party. As the futures markets evolved into the form we recognize today, the risk-bearing role came to be assumed by individuals who, contrary to "the trade," saw changing prices as profit opportunities. They certainly were not unaware of the risk involved, but were prepared to take it on for the chance of a quick gain.

The early speculators were much the same sort who trade commodity futures today—businessmen in other lines, professional people, stock market operators and diverse individuals drawn to speculative activity (not to say gambling) of any sort. And despite the theoretical dividing line, there was nothing to prevent a member of the trade from crossing the line to buy or sell for purely speculative reasons. As the principal *cash* markets (the purchase and sale of commodities for immediate delivery), the newly established exchanges became the logical organizations to handle the flourishing trade in the related futures contracts. The futures exchanges, then, are sites where several objectives are pursued simultaneously: competitive pricing, risk shifting, equity financing and speculation. Regrettably, though perhaps understandably, it is the last characteristic which has entered the public consciousness to the near exclusion of the others.

Speculators arrived on the scene in pursuit of their own self-interest but also in response to a need by the trade to offset price volatility. But cause and effect have reversed themselves in the popular mind to the extent that speculators are often blamed for exaggerating commodity price fluctuations, if not for instigating them, to derive ill-gotten gains at the public's expense. The President of the United States voiced this view in 1947 when he charged that "the cost of living in this country must not be a football to be kicked about by gamblers in grain."

Certainly the history of futures (as well as stock) markets is sufficiently replete with speculative excess and trading abuses to give some credence to the rapacious speculator theory. The disruptions of trade which occurred during the Crimean and American Civil Wars were the cause of sharply rising grain prices and of feverish speculation. Contemporary literature and newspaper reports made frequent reference to "manipulation" and "corners" on the organized exchanges.

The Illinois Legislature in 1867 passed a bill providing that "all contracts for the sale of grain for future delivery, except in cases where the seller is the owner or agent of the owner of such grain at the time of making of the contract and in actual possession thereof, are hereby declared void and gambling contracts, and all money paid in settlement of differences of any such contracts may be recovered back in the same manner as other money lost in gambling." Though the law was held to be constitutional, it was repealed at the next session of the Legislature.

During the late 1870s at least two Presidents of the Chicago Board of Trade were suspended from office for failure to meet their financial obligations. Between 1880 and 1900 there were frequently attempted corners in a number of commodities where prices rose and fell with dizzying speed, substantial amounts were made and lost, and defaults on contractual obligations were common.

The most blatant abuses occurred in the non-member "bucket shops," where the proprietors bet against their customers on market prices without making any actual transactions on their behalf. By the time they were suppressed by the registered exchanges and legitimate commission firms, bucket shops had proliferated outside Chicago to other major cities in the Midwest and East. The same operators also purportedly provided stock brokerage services to customers who were unable to differentiate between them and reputable firms.

To quote Professor Thomas A. Hieronymus, an expert on the theory and practice of futures trading, the markets at the turn of the century were

> ... beset with problems of rigging, manipulation, power plays, financial failures, and technical problems of delivery. And for a very long time, there was a limited desire or inclination to correct the procedures. For every bit of new speculative blood that flowed in there was someone waiting to lap it up. The exchange members recognized that they had a good thing going when they could control and work the technicalities of the game. They were by nature opposed to rules that circumscribed their behavior, a fiercely independent bunch of swingers.[1] They not only stood ready to devour the outside participants but fought great battles among themselves. The readiness with which they forgave defaults on indebtedness and restored culprits to good standing makes one wonder if they were not more interested in the game itself than in making money.[2]

---

[1] They still are.

[2] Thomas A. Hieronymus, *Economics of Futures Trading,* New York: Commodity Research Bureau, Inc. 1971, p. 74.

This laissez faire conduct eventually yielded to the same public demands for reform that touched other segments of American business during the "trust-busting" years of the early 1900s. The exchanges were faced with the alternatives of exercising more stringent self-regulation or accepting some form of government supervision. They eventually adapted to both.

Today's Futures Exchanges

Despite the tighter regulations governing members' conduct and the penalties to which violators are subject, it would be naive to believe that futures markets today, unlike the rest of the world, are pristine and totally free of abuses. On the other hand, it also would be naive to accept the muckraker line that they are legitimized casinos without economic purpose whose members lay in wait to snare an equally greedy but less knowledgeable public.

The daily price quotations in the financial press underscore the diversity of commodities traded on contemporary futures markets. Listed by product groups, the tables include contracts for grains and feeds, livestock and meat, foods, metals, fibers, forest products and financial instruments. The financial group currently consists of foreign currencies and five interest rate contracts—Government National Mortgage Association pass-through certificates, 90-day and one-year U. S. Treasury bills, long-term U. S. Treasury bonds, and 90-day commercial paper. These contracts, along with the dozen or so awaiting regulatory approval, are collectively the subject matter of this book.

The principal commodity exchanges of North America (including Canada) are: The Chicago Board of Trade, the Chicago Mercantile Exchange and International Monetary Market, Kansas City Board of Trade, Minneapolis Grain Exchange, Winnepeg Commodity Exchange, New York Cocoa Exchange, New York Mercantile Exchange, New York Coffee and

Sugar Exchange, New York Cotton Exchange and the Commodity Exchange, Inc. The latter four New York exchanges, which until recently occupied separate sites, recently amalgamated their operations into a common trading facility in the World Trade Center while each retains its separate organization and identity.

The two Chicago exchanges developed and introduced the concept of interest rate futures and other marts, including the New York Stock Exchange and the American Stock Exchange, have followed suit. However, the Board of Trade and International Monetary Market will occupy most of our attention as the original and primary markets.

The physical layout and operating procedures of the Board of Trade and the IMM are sufficiently alike to allow their description jointly in general terms. Both trading floors contain several "pits," which are octagonal structures with three or four steps rising or, in the case of the IMM, descending from floor level. Each commodity is traded in a designated pit, much like a stock exchange post, as members stand in the center or on a certain step according to the delivery month of the contract they are trading. Treasury bill futures are traded in the center pit at the IMM, while the Board of Trade's three interest rate contracts, GNMA certificates, Treasury bonds and commercial paper occupy an annex to the main trading floor.

All contracts are traded in a continuous auction, meaning that all bids (to buy) and offers (to sell) are made by open outcry, giving every other broker in the pit an equal opportunity to respond. When a bid or offer is made, the first person to accept it becomes the other party to the trade. The market hours for the individual contracts generally conform to the hours during which their underlying securities are traded in the cash market.[3]

During active trading, the shouting becomes so

---

[3]See Appendix E.

vociferous that hand signals are used to transmit bids and offers. A trader holds his palm toward his body to indicate he is buying, thrust outward to indicate he is a seller. Fingers are held vertically to signal the number of contracts, then turned horizontally to show the fraction above or below the most recent price at which the bid or offer is made.

Brokers are obliged to record and make public the price at which each trade is made. Exchange employees acting as observers stand in raised pulpits above each pit, reporting each transaction into the exchange's computer system, which relays the price information for display on the electronic wallboards over the trading floor, over the ticker network, and on terminals in brokerage offices throughout the country and abroad.

Customers' orders are wired or telephoned to the trading floor from branch offices of member brokerage firms, carried by messengers to the brokers in the pit and, as the trades are executed, reported back to the originating offices via the same communication system. Meanwhile, there is a continuous flow of relevant information carried to the floor by news service tickers.

When trading is relatively inactive on the International Monetary Market, bids and offers are listed on a blackboard. Under this system of board trading, a transaction takes place and the appropriate price information is recorded in the regular manner when a written bid and offer coincide.

It is difficult for an uninitiated visitor to discern any order in what often is a chaotic scene. That the system produces competitively set prices, equal access for all traders and instantly available price information proves that there nevertheless is a reasoned purpose underlying the tumult.

Professor Hieronymus captures the color of the spectacle:

> The trading floor is two stories high and the size of a football field. On an ordinary day some six

hundred people are present, a few are sitting at telephones but most are on their feet and in motion, some walking and some running. There are several dense concentrations of people standing on steps that form hexagonal pits.[4] Here, the action is frantic with as many as 300 men shouting, waving their arms, and signaling with their fingers simultaneously. In isolation, as on a television camera, one trader bellows at the man next to him with such vigor that his face turns red, and waves both hands, a trading card and a pencil in his face. The other reciprocates, both write quickly on cards, and turn to repeat the whole process to other traders or to the pit in general. A few feet away messengers run from telephones and other communications machines to the pits and back. Incongruously, there are other people, apparently participants who stroll about chatting with other people similarly engaged or quietly watching, oblivious to the din surrounding them. High on the end walls there are huge electronic scoreboards with flashing numbers that seem to relate to a multiplicity of scores somehow ascertained from the action in the pits. But nothing is shown about which team has the ball. The visitor is told that the players do know what they are doing and the action somehow relates to the real world of commerce in grains, oil seeds, cattle and chickens. The visitor shakes his head and walks away. It *is* possible for one who has seen and heard to be more mystified than one who has not.[5]

The Clearing System

Although the trading floor is the scene of the purchase and sale of commodity contracts totaling mil-

---

[4]Actually, they're octagonal.
[5]Hieronymus, p. 3.

lions of dollars daily, no money changes hands there. As can be inferred from the foregoing description, any attempt to "pay as you go" in the pit would bring trading to a standstill. Moreover, no contract is any better than the financial integrity of both parties to it.

The Board of Trade and the IMM both follow the practice of other commodity exchanges in utilizing a clearing arrangement for the settlement of transactions made on the trading floor. Organized as separate entities for legal and fiscal reasons, but for all practical purposes integral parts of their respective exchanges, the clearing corporations reconcile all trades, manage the payment and receipt of funds and guarantee all contracts. They perform the latter function by interposing themselves between each buying and selling broker, thereby assuming the opposite side of every transaction. Although exchange members trade among themselves in the pit for their own accounts or those of customers, the seller of a contract looks to the clearing house for payment and the buyer is expected to remit funds to it. By this method the proper settlement of each contract is guaranteed by the clearing house and its collective membership. In dealing with the clearing house via his member broker, a speculator or hedger need not be concerned with the possibility of the other party to a trade "reneging," either inadvertently through insolvency or deliberately to avoid a loss.

Another advantage of a clearing system to exchange members is the elimination of individual money settlement for each of the thousands of transactions made daily. Total buys (money owed) and sells (funds due) are offset by each member at the close of the trading session. To simplify the settlement process further, all members group their net balances with other members with whom they traded that day and make or receive one payment from the clearing house before the opening the following morning.

These payments and receipts are made on the basis of a daily settlement price set for each delivery month of every contract. The settlement price may be the closing price, or if a particular contract closes within a range of final prices as frequently occurs at the end of an active session, the settlement will normally be the price at which the last sizable transaction took place.

Members of the clearing corporation also must be exchange members, although the reverse does not necessarily apply. Since it is the collective backing of the clearing members which serves to guarantee all contracts, their financial requirements are more stringent than those of regular trading members. As a result, clearing memberships are generally held by the larger brokerage firms, which are required to purchase stock in the clearing corporation and to deposit an additional amount into its guarantee fund. All other exchange members must clear their transactions through a clearing member.

Over and above their stock investment and guarantee deposits, clearing members must make daily margin deposits to the clearing house for all net positions carried for customer accounts. If a clearing firm buys for the accounts of its non-clearing member and public customers 20 GNMA contracts for a particular delivery month and sells ten similar contracts for other accounts, it must deposit margin for the balance of ten purchased contracts on the grounds that they constitute the market risk for those combined positions. The profit or loss from the ten remaining purchased contracts will be offset as the market moves up or down by the ten contracts that were sold. Clearing members in turn require margin deposits from customers for whose accounts they hold the positions.

Market positions are computed on a daily basis, requiring members to make additional margin deposits on positions that go against them and allowing them to withdraw from the clearing house excess funds if the market moves in their favor. Declining prices

signify losses for a long position (consisting of purchased contracts); higher prices conversely mean
losses for a short position (consisting of sold contracts).
The actual computation of gains and losses and margin
requirements for individual traders are considered at
some length in Chapter Four. If all requirements are
met, the clearing broker is not at risk since all positions are margined by customers whereas the member
is required to deposit margin only on the net position
carried.

The clearing house itself is at any time subject to
the aggregate dollar risk of one day's price fluctuations
since all positions are recomputed daily and additional
margin is posted by clearing members as required. On
an overall basis, any loss on one position is matched
by an equivalent profit in another member's account.
Aside from a small clearing fee, the clearing house
pays out as much as it receives. It is to the credit of
the system and the two Chicago futures exchanges
that no buyer or seller of futures has ever suffered a
financial loss through default on a transaction cleared
through either clearing house.[6]

Organization of Exchanges

Though much of the rough and ready individual-
ism of the last century endures in the trading pit, the
rules of today's exchanges ensure that business is conducted with greater regard for the public interest. The
stated objectives of the Board of Trade and IMM,
among other exchanges, are to: (1) establish equitable
business conduct among members; (2) provide an organized market place and establish the time of trading; (3) provide uniform rules and standards for the
conduct of trading; (4) establish uniformity of contract

---

[6]This claim could be made of all futures exchanges up to 1976, when
default by two large traders in Maine potato futures severely damaged the
credibility of that contract and that of the New York Mercantile Exchange,
where it continues to be traded albeit under a cloud.

size and trade customs regarding quality and its establishment, time and place of delivery, and terms of payment; (5) collect and disseminate price and market information to members and the public; (6) provide a mechanism for the adjustment of disputes among members; and (7) provide machinery to guarantee the settlement of contracts and the payment of financial obligations in connection with trading among members, i.e., the clearing house system described above.

The exchanges are headed by boards of directors elected by and from the membership and operated through a number of committees appointed by the directors and also comprised of members. The committees deal with such specific exchange functions as arbitration, business conduct, clearing house, contract specifications, floor brokers, floor practices, margin, membership, nominating, public relations and rules.

On a daily administrative level, each exchange is managed by a president, several vice-presidents and a professional staff, which is generally structured along the lines of the principal committees.

Like the clearing corporations, the exchanges are non-profit organizations. Their operating costs are financed through investments (including ownership of the buildings in which they are situated), dues and fees from providing price quotations, the sale of market literature and the like.

Members must qualify and pay for the privilege of conducting business on the trading floor. Because a membership—the futures equivalent of a stock exchange seat—cannot be held in the name of a corporation, many members are nominees representing large brokerage firms while others trade solely for their own accounts and perhaps those of a few clients. The various categories of floor members, characterized by their function and style of trading, are discussed at some length in Chapter Three.

There are two main incentives to own a membership: Only members are allowed to trade in the pit, and they alone are entitled to a reduced commission rate (floor rate) even if they do not personally buy and sell on the floor.

There currently are about 1,400 members of the Chicago Board of Trade and 650 of the International Monetary Market, although all members of the parent Chicago Mercantile Exchange are entitled to trade the financial instrument contracts (interest rate and foreign currency futures) listed on the IMM.

New applicants must satisfy the membership committee's criteria for good character and minimum financial requirements. The latter are not personally applied in the case of company memberships since it is the firm's, and not its representative's, financial condition which is the determining factor. After the application is passed by the membership committee and posted for general comment, the board of directors makes the final determination. Upon election, the candidate has a stated period of time during which he must negotiate the purchase of his membership from a current member at a competitively determined price. At both the Board of Trade and the IMM, the number of memberships is fixed according to the exchange charter, but is subject to an adjustment by the directors if a change is considered warranted.

Since its establishment in 1972 as a division of the Chicago Mercantile Exchange (before the advent of interest rate futures) the number of IMM memberships has been increased four-fold to accommodate the burgeoning volume in the financial futures markets, while the negotiated membership price was bid up from the initial $10,000 to $150,000, roughly twice the value of a New York Stock Exchange seat in late 1978. A special financial instrument membership at the Board of Trade, of which there currently are 100, limits the holder to trading interest rate futures and not any of the other commodity contracts. That membership appreciated from $10,000 when initially offered in 1977 to $40,000 a year later.

Given the energetic pace of trading on both exchanges, legitimate disputes regarding individual trades, their prices, quantities and circumstances under which they were made are bound to occur. An important function of exchange operation is the arbitration of such disputes without recourse to the courts. Parties to a dispute present their arguments before the arbitration committee, which has the authority to subpoena members and hear testimony. A recently passed Federal law requires that all claims and grievances amounting to less than $15,000 be voluntarily submitted to the exchanges' settlement procedure, and that the parties involved agree in advance to be bound by the committee's decision.

A member who refuses or otherwise fails to perform the obligations of an exchange contract, including proper payment, will be suspended until the contract is performed or the debt satisfied. If the member denies such default, the matter is referred to arbitration.

Criteria for Futures Contracts

We stated at the beginning of this chapter that futures markets evolved in response to problems of financing and holding inventories of certain seasonal crops. The original "to-arrive" and forward contracts, and later standardized futures contracts, offered producers, merchants and processors a measure of protection against widely fluctuating prices. Venturous individuals discovered in the new futures markets opportunities for rapid profits unequalled elsewhere, and the essentially unplanned bargain to transfer price risk from the hedger to the speculator was struck.

It might appear that any commodity in widespread use and with a history of volatile prices would be a candidate for futures trading. Yet contracts for products that apparently lend themselves to forward pricing such as propane gas and frozen skinned hams

(which are not to be confused with the highly successful pork bellies contract) have on occasion been introduced, only to be discontinued after they failed to
achieve the expectations of their sponsors.

There are no theoretical or empirical criteria for
predicting with assurance whether and to what extent
a new futures contract will be accepted by the principal suppliers and users of a particular commodity.
After the detailed surveys and feasibility studies to
determine the need for a new contract have been completed, the final decision to proceed is largely a matter
of educated guesswork, followed by a period of hopeful
waiting for the market to render the conclusive judgement.

In their *Commodity Exchanges and Futures Trading,* J. B. Baer and O. G. Saxon listed the following
characteristics which, in their opinion, make a commodity conducive to futures trading:[7]

1. Homogenous units. Each unit of the commodity
must be interchangeable with all other units.
2. Readily standardized and graded. Even if all units
are not identical, they can be grouped in a particular
grade and related to other grades by recognized increments of quality or price.
3. Dispersed supply and demand. To assure competi
tive pricing, no dominant group can be capable of cor-
nering the supply or manipulating demand.
4. Natural flow to market. The commodity must move
from producer to consumer free from government restriction or private marketing agreements, i.e., car-
tels.
5. Supply and demand uncertainty. Such uncertainty
is a primary cause of price changes, and the ensuing
risk which is the underlying rationale of a futures
market.
6. Limited perishability. The commodity must be capable of being stored for delivery several months from
the time of its production.

---

[7]New York, Harper and Row, 1947.

Over the past two decades, both Chicago exchanges have expanded their contract lines from the traditional grain, livestock, meat and poultry products list to include lumber and plywood, while the New York Cotton Exchange in 1966 introduced a contract for frozen orange juice concentrate. Yet all of the new contracts to that date conformed to the popular conception of a commodity as a mined or agricultural product.

The breakthrough in giving the term "commodity" futures a wider connotation occurred in 1972 when the International Monetary Market was established for the purpose of trading futures contracts for silver coins and foreign currencies. By the time the Board of Trade pioneered the original GNMA contract three years later, both exchanges had acknowledged that the new "financial commodities" comprised a major innovation in futures trading by creating separate divisions to accommodate their development. Some people maintain that money is unique only insofar as it is an intangible commodity. Others, including me, believe that these futures, in bridging the security and commodity markets, have added a new dimension—futurity—to investment management.

Financial Futures

It might help to dispel any difficulty conceiving of futures for anything other than physical commodities by reiterating that all contracts are themselves financial instruments whose underlying assets happen to consist of soybeans, pork bellies or some other product. In the financial market place, intangible assets are as real as physical products, and modern commodity markets have more in common with security markets than with feedlots or grain elevators. In the present context, the term "commodity" is perhaps a misnomer or at least not fully descriptive of the diverse products for which futures markets exist. Until such time as the traditional label may be superseded by a broader term, such as "asset futures," the exchanges have adopted the expression "financial futures" to emphasize the distinctive nature of these contracts, although strictly speaking all futures contracts are financial instruments.

Like the long-established contracts, the utility of financial futures from the hedger's perspective lies in the protection they afford from losses associated with depreciating assets or appreciating liabilities. A more precise if less wieldy designation for interest rate futures would be "interest-rate sensitive, fixed-income securities futures." But since marketing plays at least as vital a role in the investment world as strict analysis, we are bound to accept the abbreviated label and make an effort to comprehend its meaning to the initiated.

Short- and long-term debt instruments (one year is the accepted division between them) vary in price in inverse relation to their prevailing interest rates. The relationship of these various rates to one another and their movement over time constitute the heart of the matter and are discussed at length in Part Two. It is sufficient to appreciate at this opening stage that interest rate fluctuations entail capital price changes and vice versa. Price and yield are two different ways of expressing the same market condition.

Bonds are called fixed-income securities because their issuers make the same semi-annual interest payments over the life of the security. A 6% corporate bond, for example, will pay its holders $60 per $1,000 bond every year until it reaches maturity. The $60 coupon payments are the fixed-income to which the name refers. Should the level of interest rates on that type and quality of bond rise to 8%, new bonds being offered on the market will pay $80 annually per $1,000 face value. Bond investors, usually institutional bond portfolio managers and traders, will continue to sell the 6% coupon bond (depressing its price and increasing the yield—remember the inverse relationship) until it offers a yield equal to the 8% bond at par, which it will do at a price of $750, quoted by bond dealers in percentage terms at 75.

$$\frac{\$60}{\$750} = \frac{\$80}{\$1,000} = 8\%$$

If rates on comparable bonds instead dropped to 5%, the 6% coupon bond would rise to the price where $60 would constitute a 5% return, namely, $1,200 or 120.

$$\frac{\$60}{\$1,200} = \frac{\$50}{\$1,000} = 5\%$$

The fundamental concept, then, is that on outstanding bonds, whether corporate, U. S. government or municipal, *rising interest rates depress prices and falling rates cause prices to appreciate*. Whoever owns bonds during a period of rising interest rates, therefore, incurs price depreciation in his bond portfolio, while anyone who defers the purchase of bonds during a period of declining rates will later pay higher prices. That's another way of saying he will obtain a lower rate of return on his investment. Given the inverse relationship between price and yield, the significance of futures contracts for bonds and other fixed-income securities begins to emerge, and their designation as interest rate futures becomes more comprehensible.

Looking at the same relationship from a somewhat different perspective, it is often to the advantage of a company which plans to invest (or borrow) a sizeable amount of money by a specified future date to know what it will receive (pay) in interest over the term of the investment. The difference between borrowing $20 million for 20 years at 6% and at 8%, for example, is $400,000 annually, or a total additional borrowing cost of $8 million, noncompounded. The effect of such increments on a company's operating results can be considerable, and again, the logic of employing futures to predetermine investment return or borrowing cost becomes evident.

One of the characteristics cited earlier in the chapter which makes a particular asset, or commodity if you will, suited to futures trading is price volatility. Low volatility entails limited price risk, which in turn means limited reason to hedge or incentive to speculate. The justification for initiating futures trading in such a commodity would therefore be questionable. Until the recent past, any proposal to devise a contract that is sensitive to interest rates would most likely have been rejected on the grounds that there was little need for it. For more than 25 years following World War Two, both short- and long-term interest rates generally moved within a fairly limited and predictable range between 2% and 6%.

As a result of an accelerating inflation rate and other economic dislocations, the 6% ceiling was pierced during the credit crunch of 1973-74, as long-term interest rates reached 9%, and short-term rates soared for a brief period to a previously unheard of 12% on 90-day commercial paper.

In the first instance, this unprecedented rate (and price) volatility imposed severe strains on companies whose operations were geared to the earlier parameters. Doing business in the money market became increasingly difficult as the old yardsticks gave way to new unknowns.

On a broader basis, the abnormally high level of interest rates caused sharp curtailments in such key sectors of the economy as construction. Not only were businesses directly involved in building activity and its financing severely affected by the credit crunch, but the depressing effects of a near stoppage of construction rippled throughout the economy. The adverse impact of soaring interest rates and general nonavailability of credit can be gauged by the statistics of business casualties during the 1973-74 period. By that time, the concept of futures contracts for fixed-income securities, particularly those relating to the mortgage market, was no longer the farfetched idea it may have seemed during the 3%-to-6% days, and the arguments in support of hedging interest rate risks were suddenly of more than academic interest.

The GNMA Contract

Even prior to the 1973-74 credit crunch, staff members at the Chicago Board of Trade, in cooperation with the Center for Real Estate and Urban Economics at the University of California and officials of the Federal Home Loan Mortgage Corporation, had considered the feasibility of a futures contract based on residential mortgages. Since the mortgage market is notably fragmented and diverse, the major difficulty in devising such an instrument was the basic problem of product homogeneity and standardization. Their solution lay in the mortgage-backed certificate guaranteed by the Government National Mortgage Association. Though not representative of all private mortgages made throughout the country, the advantage of GNMAs, or Ginnie Maes, as they were known by the mortgage fraternity, is their uniformity as a contract grade, wherein the only variables are price and yield. The actual specifications and technical details of GNMA futures, as well as the other interest rate contracts, are presented in the following chapter.

Introduced to trading on the Board of Trade in October 1975, the GNMA contract, as the first of the current family of interest rate futures, has become the most successful new futures contract in terms of volume growth. A newly introduced contract is generally regarded to be successful if it attains a weekly volume of 3,000 contracts by the end of its first year. GNMAs reached that level by June 1976, barely a half-year following its inception. The contract continues to flourish, regularly surpassing previous records.

The 90-Day Treasury Bill Contract

The International Monetary Market initiated its first interest rate contract for three-month U. S. Treasury Bills in January 1976 after an equally lengthy period of study and planning. The three-month "T-bill" is a basic money market instrument, and its yield a widely used barometer of all short-term interest rates. As a short-term instrument, the three-month (or 90-day) T-bill occupies a different place in the fixed-income spectrum than the long-term GNMA certificate. Hedgers in each market, therefore, would comprise distinct groups of market participants, at least so far as their investment criteria and objectives are concerned. The T-bill contract also has been a successful innovation.

Climbing on the Bandwagon

The successful launching of the Ginnie Mae and 90-day T-bill contracts prompted the development of similar contracts, first by the two Chicago exchanges to broaden their product lines, and then by other securities and futures exchanges in an effort to secure a share of what they perceived to be a major new market. Some of the proposed new contracts essentially duplicated ones already in existence. Others were based upon different money market instruments and government securities.

The Ginnie Mae contract was designed specifically to facilitate mortgage financing. But this specialized application limited its utility in hedging other fixed-income securities. Because bond and mortgage market interest rates follow similar though not identical paths, the Board of Trade determined that a government bond futures contract would appeal to investors and dealers engaged in that segment of the long-term debt market. Such a contract was accordingly introduced in October 1977. It, too, proved to be successful as trading volume increased even more rapidly than for the Ginnie Mae contract at a comparable stage in its growth.

In the short-term sector, the same problem of correlation—the extent to which interest rates on different kinds of securities behave differently—made the T-bill contract less than an ideal instrument to be used by companies that wish to hedge the rate at which they issue commercial paper. To serve that particular market, the Board of Trade launched a 90-day commercial paper contract shortly after it introduced its government bond contract.

Approximately a year later, in September 1978, the IMM added its second interest rate contract, one-year T-bills, to supplement its original 90-day bill futures. Like bonds and Ginnie Maes or T-bills and commercial paper, bills with varying maturities exhibit somewhat different yield behavior. The one-year bill contract, therefore, offered an alternative to investors active in the longer maturity range.

At about the same time the American Stock Exchange, eager to gain a foothold in this burgeoning market, established its affiliated American Commodity Exchange, or ACE, and commenced trading a Ginnie Mae contract. The principal distinction between the Board of Trade and ACE contracts was that the former involved the transfer of collateralized depository receipts as delivery instruments, while the latter provided for the delivery of the actual pass-through certificates. This apparently technical difference between the two contracts was important to mortgage bankers and other institutions accustomed to receiving and delivering securities rather than depository receipts in the normal course of their business.

The Board of Trade, unwilling to accept passively a competitive challenge by a stock exchange, responded by introducing its own certificate delivery Ginnie Mae contract, which was traded alongside the original CDR contract.

The Commodity Futures Trading Commission, or CFTC, is the federal agency which has regulatory jurisdiction over the futures industry. The commission's responsibilities include examining and approving new contracts before they may be traded. By December 1978, no less than 12 additional interest rate contracts had been submitted for approval by four exchanges. The Board of Trade proposed to establish contracts for four- to six-year U.S. Treasury notes, Eurodollar certificates of deposit and 30-day commercial paper. The IMM also wished to introduce a four-year Treasury note contract. In New York, ACE proposed to step up its competitive challenge to the Chicago marts with additional contracts for 90-day T-bills and domestic CD's, Treasury notes and long-term bonds. Yet another entry, the Commodity Exchange, Inc., or Comex, also applied for authorization to trade bill, note and Ginnie Mae contracts.

Most significant of all was the announcement in early 1979 by the New York Stock Exchange that it, too, proposed to deal in financial futures. If there were any remaining doubts about the Wall Street establishment's acceptance of interest rate futures, they were dispelled by the unprecedented move by the august Big Board into the realm of futures trading.

This bandwagon aura and the consequent proliferation of existing and proposed contracts became a cause of concern to the CFTC and other agencies in-

---

The CFTC approved in mid-1979 applications by four exchanges to commence trading in additional interest rate contracts. The Amex Commodities Exchange (ACE) and the Commodity Exchange, Inc. (Comex) were each cleared to trade 90-day T-bill futures. The two Chicago exchanges were both authorized to introduce Treasury note contracts with a four-year maturity by the I.M.M. and four-to-six years by the Board of Trade.

To restrain proliferation and excessive duplication of contracts, the Commission stipulated different delivery months for similar contracts traded on the respective exchanges. Moreover, provisions were included for the substitution of comparable securities or cash reimbursements in the event of supply and delivery problems in response to the above-mentioned concerns expressed by the Federal Reserve Board and the Treasury Department.

volved in the regulation and supervision of the capital markets. The Treasury Department, SEC and Federal Reserve expressed fears that the entire phenomenon was getting out of hand, and urged the commission to adopt a "go-slow" policy in approving additional contracts until the impact of futures trading on the underlying securities could be more thoroughly determined.

Chapter Two

Cash Markets and Futures Contracts

Futures contracts aren't financial assets in the same way stocks and bonds are. Although the market value of a futures contract will appreciate or depreciate from day to day, the instrument doesn't necessarily represent possession of an underlying commodity, nor does its purchase or sale denote any immediate change in a commodity's ownership.

In commodity trading, the term "contract" adheres to the dictionary definition of a commitment. It is an agreement between seller and buyer that the former deliver to the latter on a designated date a precise quantity of a particular commodity that conforms to the quality and delivery standards established by the exchange on which the contract is traded. The buyer is obligated to receive the delivery and pay the contracted price. As was noted in the previous chapter, buyer and seller part company for good after their respective floor brokers make the initial trade, and each deals through his broker with the clearing corporation so long as he remains a party to the contract. At the appropriate time, the seller, known as the "short," will make his intention to deliver known to the clearing house, which in turn will designate the previous buyer, called the "long," who will receive whatever evidence of ownership that constitutes good delivery.

All shorts and longs have the choice of avoiding this procedure by liquidating their contracts before the delivery date, an option which most futures traders do in fact exercise.

Other provisions of the contract include the commitment to make additional margin deposits with the broker if a certain amount of loss is incurred, and the right to withdraw from the trading account whatever profits that accrue. The margin and liquidation features of the contract, rather than the delivery procedure, are the key provisions for most hedgers and speculators. The image of thousands of bushels of wheat dumped over the front lawn (or, in the less picturesque case of the financial instruments, a bank transfer of $1 million in Treasury bills) is pure fiction. In most instances, a futures trader confronted with an unwanted delivery notice has made a mistake and his broker was remiss in performing his job. Even then, there are procedures for disposing of the commodity or securities short of paying in full and taking physical possession.

Before proceeding to buy or sell any futures contract, a trader should become thoroughly familiar with its specifications. New entrants to the market, having been told that it is unlikely they will ever find themselves making or taking delivery, invariably are perplexed by the constant references to the quantity, quality, location and method of delivery as well as the allowable deviations from the deliverable grade and consequent price adjustments. All they would like to know is how to buy low and sell high. Although more than 95% of all futures transactions are liquidated by an offsetting purchase or sale rather than by delivery of the so-called "cash" commodity, the precise terms of delivery are what make the contract a viable financial instrument that can be used for either risk management or speculative purposes. Like any tool, one must know its characteristics to use it properly.

A working knowledge of the Chicago Board of

Trade's wheat futures contract, for example, presupposes a grasp of the forces that determine the immediate price of wheat in the cash market. The same reasoning applies to contracts to deliver Treasury bills, commercial paper, government bonds and mortgage-backed securities. Before considering the salient points of each of these interest rate contracts, then, some attention should be given to the fixed-income securities themselves, their composition, methods by which they are priced, the conditions under which they are traded, and by whom.

Prospective hedgers, of course, do not require an introduction to the cash fixed-income market inasmuch as their involvement in it is what's prompting their use of futures. Since considerable portions of Parts Two and Three of this book are devoted to tracking and evaluating the relationship between interest rates in the two markets, however, the following review may serve as a familiar point of departure for new territory.

The speculator whose sole objective is to capture favorable price fluctuations of the futures contracts, and who may never have occasion to operate in the cash market, must nevertheless be aware of developments there because that is where he will begin his quest for profit.

U.S. Treasury Bills

Treasury bills are short-term obligations of the U.S. government with maturities of either three months, six months or one year from their date of issue. They are sold to institutional and private investors at weekly and monthly competitive auctions conducted by the Federal Reserve Banks. Unlike coupon instruments which bear a stated interest rate, bills are traded at a discount from their face value. The return to the investor is the difference between the discounted price and the par value at which they always mature.

As of Dec. 31, 1978, there were outstanding bills with 40 separate maturities totaling nearly $170 billion. Daily trading volume in the secondary market is usually between $3 billion and $4 billion. Treasury bills have become an important medium for the investment of short-term funds since their introduction in 1929. From the government's side, they have emerged as a principal instrument of debt management and monetary policy.

Because of the market's great size and liquidity, the Treasury is able to raise on a regular basis large amounts of fresh money quickly at minimum expense without causing undue price changes through the sheer volume of its offerings. Any attempt to raise comparable sums through the sale of long-term bonds would severely disrupt the market. Size and liquidity are mutually reinforcing in the bill market since it is the ability to buy and sell securities in substantial amounts without excessive price concessions that attracts the large institutional investors. Purchases running in some cases into the hundreds of millions of dollars are routinely made at or near the same price. Though bills are redeemable at their face value on maturity, institutions must sometimes sell them earlier to raise cash. They can be readily liquidated in the secondary dealer market, again with a minimum effect on their price.

Like other direct government obligations, Treasury bills are backed by the full faith and credit of the United States, which excludes possibility of default or failure of the government to pay the full face amount at maturity. The short maturities, the size and liquidity of the market and the absence of credit risk are the characteristics which give Treasury bills the sobriquet of "near money."

That bill holders are assured of payment at maturity does not mean their investment is absolutely riskless. Individual bills can and do fluctuate in price between the dates they are issued and when they mature. It is even possible that they are sold for a loss, although that cannot occur when the bills are held until they mature. These price fluctuations are solely a function of changes in the level of short-term interest rates. Protection against interest rate risk was the primary motivation behind the creation of the T-bill futures contract.

The amount of price change caused by a given movement in interest rates is in turn a function of the maturity of the investment. Simply put, the shorter the maturity, the smaller the price change, up or down, that a particular rate fluctuation will induce. Institutions with large amounts of cash to invest for several days to several weeks are able to reduce their exposure to interest rate risk by "parking" the funds in Treasury bills that are close to maturity. The tradeoff they accept in buying such short-term securities is a lower rate of return than is probably available from a longer maturity. The use of futures as an alternate and, in some cases, the preferred method of reducing the exposure to interest rate risk will be explored in later chapters.

The availability of bills with maturities ranging from several days to a year gives companies holding large cash balances numerous alternatives in matching maturities to desired holding periods and selecting acceptable rates of interest return relative to price risk. In weighing these alternatives, institutional investors will consider not only the relative attractiveness of various bill maturities, but also the comparable yields of such other money market instruments as commercial paper and certificates of deposit.

Computing Yields

Investors who are accustomed to regarding interest in terms of compounded payments in thrift accounts or semi-annual bond coupons often have some initial difficulty grasping the discount method of yield

computation upon which the prices of Treasury bills
and commercial paper and their futures contracts are
based. Anyone contemplating participation in the interest rate futures market must feel equally comfortable with both methods of calculating interest return,
and be able to convert yields from one to the other at
will. Although yield tables are available to ameliorate
the mental strain, it is essential to have the basic concepts firmly in mind before getting into the market.

As a simple illustration, assume that the Last
National Bank buys on the day of issue a one-year bill
that will be redeemed by the Treasury at its face value
of $1 million 360 days later. Yields on Treasury bills
and other discounted securities are computed on the
basis of a 360-day year; that's one reason why the discount rate must be converted to its bond equivalent,
which is calculated on the basis of 365 days and thus
is always somewhat higher. Supposing the bank pays
$940,000 for the bill, the $60,000 *discount* is what the
bank will earn on its investment for 360 days.

$$1) \quad \frac{\text{Dollar}}{\text{Discount}} = \frac{\text{Face}}{\text{Value}} - \frac{\text{Purchase}}{\text{Price}}$$
$$(\$60,000 = \$1,000,000 - \$940,000)$$

The same discount can be expressed in percentage
terms, which is in fact the way Treasury bills are
quoted in the government securities market. The percentage discount is calculated by dividing the dollar
discount by the face value of the bill, which in our Last
National Bank example works out to be 6%.

$$2) \quad \frac{\text{Percentage}}{\text{Discount}} = \frac{\text{Dollar}}{\text{Discount}} \div \frac{\text{Face}}{\text{Value}}$$
$$(6\% = \$60,000 \div \$1,000,000)$$

The exercise would be simple enough if all bills
ran for 360 days and were held until maturity. But in

the real bill market maturities range from several days to one year so that a time adjustment must be added to the equation. Taking our elementary illustration another step, assume that the Reliable Insurance Company wished to invest $1 million in the bill market, but for only 90 days instead of 360. At what price must it buy three-month bills in order to earn 6%? Remember, yields are on an *annualized* basis, so earning 1½% on your money in three months is the equivalent of 6% in 12 months. For Reliable Insurance to earn the same 6% annualized return as the Last National Bank but on a 90-day investment, the dollar discount would need to be only one-quarter of $60,000, or $15,000. The purchase price for the three-month bill (the terms three months and 90 days are used interchangeably in the money market)[1] would therefore be $985,000. Apart from multiplying the earlier figure by the fraction of the year to be invested to express the rate of return on an annualized basis, the equation remains the same:

$$3) \quad \frac{\text{Percentage}}{\text{Discount}} = \frac{\text{Dollar Discount}}{\text{Face Value}} \times \frac{360}{\text{Maturity of Bill}}$$

$$\left[6\% \quad = \quad \frac{\$15,000}{\$1,000,000} \times \frac{360}{90} \right]$$

Although Treasury bills are quoted in the daily press on a discount basis, bids are submitted at the weekly auctions conducted by the Federal Reserve Banks as a percentage of par (100). The only change from the procedure described above is that the decimal is moved four places to the left. To secure a yield of 6%

---

[1] We have again departed from reality for simplicity of illustration. Three- and six-month bills actually run for 91 and 182 days respectively, following the calendar year rather than the 360 day convention. Hence, three- and six-month maturities also are referred to as 13- and 26-week bills.

on any face amount of three-month bills, the bidder would submit a tender of 98.500. If he believed that there were other investors like Last National Bank and Reliable Insurance so eager to buy bills that they would submit higher bids, he might feel compelled to raise his bid to 98.550—which, as the alert reader will by this point recognize, means he is willing to accept a lower yield of 5.8%. To reinforce this overriding concept by repetition, the higher the price is bid toward par (face value), the smaller the dollar and percentage discounts become. Yet a third time, price up, yield down; price down, yield up. Figure 2-1 presents the same principle graphically.

Once again, the example just cited does not conform to actual market conditions because the increments of yield changes are far less than 2/10 of 1% (6.0% − 5.8%). A Treasury bill's minimum unit of change is one basis point, or 1/100 of 1%. If the dis-

FIGURE: 2-1

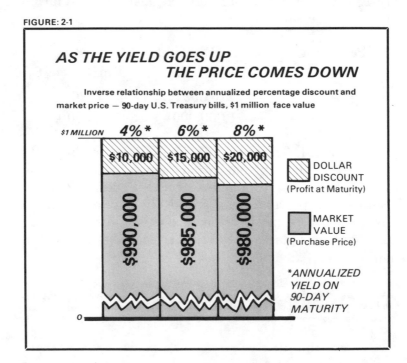

count yield on 90-day bills rises from 6.00% to 6.50%, meaning that their market price drops from $985,000 to $983,750 per $1 million face value, it is referred to as an interest rate increase of 50 basis points.

The dollar value of a basis point varies with the face amount of the bill and its maturity. Returning to our original example of Last National Bank's one-year bill, 1/100 of 1% of $1 million is $100, which is the value of one basis point for that face amount and maturity. For each basis point that the discount on Last National's Treasury bill rises (falls), its market value drops (increases) by $100. Because the dollar value of a given interest rate movement is proportionately smaller on bills of shorter maturity, a basis point change on a 90-day $1 million bill amounts to $25.

$$4) \frac{\text{Value of One}}{\text{Basis Point}} = \text{}^1\!/_{100} \text{ of } 1\% \times \frac{\text{Face}}{\text{Value}} \times \frac{\text{Days to Maturity}}{360}$$

$$(\$100 \quad = \quad .0001 \quad \times \$1,000,000 \times \frac{360)}{360)}$$

$$(\$\ 25 \quad = \quad .0001 \quad \times 1,000,000 \times \frac{90)}{360)}$$

The general formula for determining the value of one basis point for any size and maturity of bill is to multiply the number of days to maturity times the face amount by $ .27778, which is the value of one basis point per day (.01% ÷ 360) on $1 million. Since the two Treasury bill futures contracts currently traded specify the delivery of $1 million face value of 90-day bills and $250,000 of one-year bills respectively, the basis point value is $25 in both cases.

The Auction Process

Treasury bills are offered to investors through successive competitive auctions. The procedure is fast, simple and allows the Treasury to raise $5 billion to $6 billion in new borrowings weekly (a large portion of which is used to pay off maturing bills) without placing undue pressure upon other segments of the government securities market, which are notes, bonds and agency issues. On their part, banks, non-financial corporations, pension funds, state, local and foreign governments and other institutions with substantial amounts of short-term funds to invest on a recurring basis are assured of a predictable supply of new securities suited to their size and maturity requirements.

Approximately $2.5 billion of new three-month bills and $3.5 billion of six-month bills are offered weekly by the Treasury through the facilities of the twelve Federal Reserve Banks and their branches. The amounts to be sold are determined by the Treasury on the Thursday preceding the auction, and bids are accepted until 1:30 p.m. Eastern Standard Time on the Monday it is held.

Bids, also referred to as tenders, are submitted on either a competitive or non-competitive basis. The competitive bidders are generally the larger banks and other dealers with sizable amounts to invest each week, and for whom fine gradations in yield significantly affect the profitability of their trading operations. They are constantly active in the secondary bill market, and invariably wait until just before the deadline to enter bids closely in line with prevailing prices. Although there is no stated regulation to the effect that the 30 or so banks and dealers who comprise the core of the government securities market must submit bids at every weekly auction, their obligation as primary dealers to maintain an orderly market in securities offered by the Treasury implies their regular participation. To assure them of some share in any week's auction, competitive bidders are permitted to enter bids for different quantities of bills at different prices.

Non-competitive bidders are usually smaller investors, often individuals, who wish to buy a certain amount of bills and are not inclined to wield so fine a pencil. Non-competitive tenders are awarded in full up to $500,000, although the minimum bid accepted is for $10,000 since that is the smallest denomination in which bills are issued. The number of non-competitive bids submitted is invariably large, but their aggregate dollar value is normally only about 10% of the much more substantial amounts bid for by the dealer firms and other institutional investors.

The Treasury makes the non-competitive awards after the subscription books are closed at 1:30 p.m., and then allocates the remaining bills according to the order of competitive bids down to the stopout price, the lowest bid at which it will make awards. Settlement day, when payment for the bills is due and they are available for delivery, is on the Thursday following the auction.

The weekly auction system allows market forces to determine the rates at which new bills are offered, which affect and are in turn affected by the tone of the secondary market. If investors are more eager to buy bills, their higher bids serve to narrow the discount, thereby reducing the Treasury's borrowing cost. When demand falls off, bids are lowered, increasing the discount and borrowing expense to the government. On the supply side, the amount of bills offered at auction has an effect on their rates.

The results of each Monday auction are announced by the Treasury late in the afternoon and reported in the financial press the following day. On Sept. 25, 1978, for example, $2.6 billion face value 13-week bills maturing Dec. 28, and $3.6 billion 26-week bills maturing March 29, 1979, were sold. It is worth noting that when the 13-week (or 90-day) bill matured on Dec. 28, the March 29, 1979, bill was trading as a 90-day bill since it was midway through its original

180-day life. At the Sept. 25 auction, bids totaling $5.2 billion were submitted for the 90-day bill, of which $2.3 billion was accepted as competitive bids and $339 million accepted non-competitively. The competitive tenders that were accepted ranged from a high bid of 97.953 (expressed as a percentage of par taken to three decimal places) to a low of 97.949. The average price of 97.951, at which the non-competitive bids were awarded, represented a discount on the 90-day bill of 8.10 (as you may verify by applying equation 3 on page 37). This yield represented an increase from the prior week's rate of 7.88%. In dollar terms, this meant that institutions which paid $980,300 for an investment which returned $1,000,000 in 90 days were able to buy a similar 90-day instrument a week later for $550 less, the value of 22 basis points (8.10 − 7.88) for 90 days.

To compare these discount rates to the equivalent yield of a coupon security of the same maturity, it is necessary to convert from a 360-to a 365-day year calculation by means of the equation:

5) $$\frac{\text{Discount}}{\text{Issue Price}} \div \frac{\text{Maturity}}{\text{of Bill}} = \frac{\text{Coupon Yield}}{365}$$

$$\left(\frac{2.049}{97.951} \div 90 = \frac{8.48}{365} \right)$$

The 8.10 discount on the 90-day bill issued Sept. 25, 1978, is the equivalent, then, of an 8.48 coupon yield on a short-term bond or note bearing the same maturity. This computation is significant for futures traders when comparing prices of the Treasury bill and commercial paper contracts with those of Treasury bond and GNMA futures.

One-year, or 52-week bills, are auctioned separately, usually on every fourth Wednesday. The Treasury also occasionally offers special cash management and federal funds bills, as well as tax anticipation bills and "strips," a series of consecutive bills.

The Secondary Market

After bills of various maturities are issued, they are traded in an over-the-counter market comprised of the same dealer firms and major banks that are the principal competitive bidders at the auctions. About 30 of these organizations are recognized by the Federal Reserve Bank of New York as primary dealers. As such, they are accorded the distinction of dealing directly with the "Fed" when it is conducting its open market operations and of being included in the bank's weekly report of dealer activity. These primary dealers trade among themselves over direct telephone lines and do business with the non-dealer banks, insurance companies and non-financial corporations that are the other active participants in the Treasury bill market. Government bond brokers are sometimes used as intermediaries to give transactions a greater degree of confidentiality, but they are not dealers in the sense that they assume market positions for their own account and risk.

The dealer's function, unlike that of a commission broker, is to buy securities from sellers and sell them to buyers. He is expected to make a market, which entails the risk of carrying securities in inventory. His compensation for this risk-bearing comes from the spread between bid (to buy) and asked (to sell) prices of the bills he turns over plus whatever trading profits he may accumulate during the course of his market-making activities. Dealers typically operate with narrow spreads (or "markups," if you will), low profit margins, and high inventory turnover. Because government securities are risk-free in the credit sense, dealers are able to obtain bank loans to finance inventories many times their net worth, allowing them to carry out a highly leveraged operation.

The most recently issued Treasury bills are the most actively traded in the secondary market. The available supply and daily turnover are the heaviest for these new issues, and their price spreads are the most narrow. The normal spread on the latest 13-week bill is two to four basis points, or $50 to $100 per $1 million face value. Assuming no change in the discount, this close range between the bid and offered price allows a sizable investor to liquidate his position without a loss after a two-day holding period. As new issues are placed on the market, the level of trading subsides in the older bills, and their spreads grow wider. After bills have been on the market for more than a month, their spreads open to as wide as 10 basis points, imposing a significant transaction cost for dealing in them.

Like the three- and six-month maturities, one-year bills are actively traded immediately following the auction, but soon become inactive. Bills which bear year-end maturities are regularly in demand by corporations that wish to show in their annual balance sheets interest-bearing investments instead of idle cash. Corporate demand also lends a certain scarcity value to bills which mature on or near tax or dividend payment dates since they provide a convenient place to "park" cash until it is needed at those times.

Composite closing quotations for Treasury bills and other government securities are published daily by the Federal Reserve Bank of New York, along with a weekly consolidated report of primary dealer volume, positions and types of accounts which traded during the latest period. Several dealer firms also issue daily quote sheets, with the published yields based on the asked side of the market. Treasury bills are listed along with government notes and bonds in the financial section of many daily newspapers. Unlike the coupon issues, however, they are quoted on the basis of their annualized discount yield rather than as a percentage of par. Since a higher discount signifies a lower price, the bid figure which is quoted in the newspaper is higher than the offered discount. This is logical since the dealer furnishing the quote stays in business by selling securities at a higher price (asked) than what he pays for them (bid).

The Risk Factor

If bills are purchased at any discount and held until they mature at their face value, they are riskless investments in the sense that no loss of principal can be incurred. Should an investor for whatever reason need to raise cash by selling bills before their maturity, however, he will earn less than the original discount and possibly suffer a loss if interest rates rise sharply between the times that the bills are bought and sold.

Another simplified example will illustrate the point. Suppose that the Rockbound Savings Bank submitted a noncompetitive bid at the Sept. 25, 1978, auction described earlier. But instead of buying the 90-day bill maturing on Dec. 28 at what turned out to be the average discount of 8.10, Rockbound Savings' investment officer purchased $1 million of 26-week bills dated to mature March 29, 1979, to earn the higher yield customarily available on longer maturities. In this instance, the 26-week bill was offered noncompetitively at 8.28, a yield advantage of 18 basis points.

But suppose that the bank had to raise cash at year-end to meet seasonal withdrawals, and that by late December, new 90-day bills were being offered at an 8.60 discount, a very high rate historically for short-term government securities. If on Dec. 28, the bank sold in the dealer market what was by that time a 90-day bill, what would have been the dollar and percentage return on the bill for the 90 days that it was held? A variation of equation 3 determines that the bank paid a principal amount of $958,600 for the 26-week bill at the auction.

6) $$\text{Principal Amount} = \text{Face Value} - \text{Percentage Discount} \times \text{Face Value} \times \frac{\text{Days to Maturity}}{360}$$

$$\left(\$958,600 = \$1 \text{ million} - 8.28\% \times \$1 \text{ million} \times \frac{180}{360}\right)$$

Using the same formula for a 90-day bill at an 8.60 discount, we discover that the bank sold the bill for $978,500, a gain of $19,900 or a discount of 7.96 (equation 3). Instead of receiving a higher yield, because short-term interest rates rose from September to December, Rockbound Savings earned 14 basis points less on its three-month investment than it would have by buying the Dec. 28 bill and holding it until it matured. A difference of 14/100 of 1%, or $350 on roughly $1 million, does not seem a great deal, but the same percentage applied to millions traded daily by the primary dealers could cover the salaries of an entire trading department. A typical profit on a $1 million dealer transaction would be two basis points, or $50.

Because of the active market, narrow spread and minimal price reaction to interest rate changes (remember that one basis point is the equivalent of $25 for a $1 million 90-day bill and $100 for a year bill), bills close to maturity are nearly ideal short-term investments for many institutional investors. The U. S. government, including the Federal Reserve Banks, is itself the largest buyer of Treasury bills. Commercial banks purchase bills as secondary reserves which can be quickly converted to cash as the need arises. State and local governments and non-financial corporations are the other major investor categories.

In terms of total purchases, private investors are not a significant factor in the bill market. The Treasury eliminated the then smallest denominations of $1,000 and $5,000 in 1970 in an attempt to make the market more institutionally oriented and to discourage disintermediation, which is the withdrawal of funds from savings accounts for investment in such higher yielding money market instruments as Treasury bills.

From the government's perspective, Treasury bills have become central instruments for the implementation of debt management and monetary policy, two areas that will be considered at some length in Part Two of this book.

Treasury Bill Futures Contracts

Trading in the original Treasury bill futures contract commenced at the International Monetary Market in January 1976, some three months following the introduction of the Board of Trade's GNMA mortgage interest rate contract. The contract specifies the delivery of 90-day U.S. Treasury bills with a face value at maturity of $1 million. The success of the 90-day T-bill contract over its first 2½ years prompted the IMM to initiate a companion contract in September 1978, this one for $250,000 one-year bills. Apart from their contract size and maturity specifications, and therefore their discount yields and prices, the two contracts are essentially alike. Moreover, since the dollar value of one basis point on $1 million 90-day bills is the same ($25) as a basis point on $250,000 one-year bills, they are priced on a comparable basis.

Both contracts have quarterly delivery dates, meaning that on the third Thursday of each March, June, September and December the remaining "shorts" (sellers) must deliver to the remaining "longs" (buyers) Treasury bills of the designated amount and maturity. The delivery date of the futures contract should not be confused with the maturity of the actual bill. The deliverable instrument is a bill which will mature 90 or 360 days from the delivery date of whichever of the two contracts is involved.

Because of the discount yield method of quoting cash (actual) Treasury bills, price quotations for bills differ from those for other futures contracts. In fact, the published quotations are not strictly prices, but index figures which represent the difference between the discount on the deliverable bill and 100. For example, on Sept. 28, 1978, the 90-day T-bill contract for delivery in March 1979 closed at an index figure (hereinafter referred to as a price for simplicity's sake) of 91.65, signifying a discount of 8.35 on bills to be issued the third Thursday of the following March.

$$7) \quad \frac{\text{Index}}{\text{Quotation}} = 100 - \frac{\text{90-day}}{\text{Discount}}$$

$$(91.65 \quad = 100 - \quad 8.35)$$

That day's high and low prices for the March 1979 contract were 91.68 and 91.59 respectively, indicating a range in the discount from 8.32 to 8.41. The actual dollar price that the contract buyer, or long, would pay for the 90-day bills if they were delivered to him at an 8.35 discount in March 1979 could be determined by equation 6 (page 46):

$$\$979,125 = \$1 \text{ million} - \left(8.35\% \times \$1 \text{ million} \times \frac{90}{360}\right)$$

Since March 1979 T-bills rose nine basis points over the previous day's close, the prior closing discount of 8.44 (for the fourth and, the last time: price up, yield down, and vice versa) would by the same calculation have specified a principal amount of $978,900. Note that anyone who was long one March 1979 contract on Sept. 28, 1978, enjoyed the same price appreciation (nine basis points or $225) as if he actually owned $1 million face value 90-day bills. By the same token, anyone short that contract on the same day would have suffered an equal paper loss.[2]

The minimum price fluctuation, or futures equivalent of a ⅛ "tick" in the stock market, is one basis point (or $25) for both the 90-day and one-year contracts. Unlike the stock exchanges where there is no stipulated limit on the amount any stock may rise or fall during a trading session, the IMM in keeping with normal futures exchange practice imposes a limit of 50 basis points from the previous day's closing price, above or below which no contract may be traded. It is possible for a contract, or usually all delivery months, to be up or down "the limit" on two successive days, meaning that the anticipated discount on bills yet to be issued falls or rises by a full percentage point; that's a rare event in the cash bill market. After two days of limit moves, the regular limit is expanded to 75 basis points to give traders who are locked into losing positions a better opportunity to get out of the market.

The 90-day Treasury bill was selected by the IMM as a vehicle to represent short-term interest rate movements not only due to its importance as a money market instrument in its own right, but because of the close relationship between bill rates and the yields on such other short-term securities as commercial paper, which is described in some detail in the following section, certificates of deposit and bankers acceptances. Correlation, the statistical measure of these yield relationships, is taken up in conjunction with the discussion of cross-hedging later in the book.

The characteristics which make cash Treasury bills popular institutional investments also make them suitable for futures trading. These "commodity" features include:

---

[2]On the same day, March 1979 one-year T-bill futures closed at 91.69, +4 basis points. The reader is encouraged to perform the same calculation, keeping in mind the longer maturity and smaller contract size, to ensure a firm grasp of the concept.

1) Familiarity—All institutional and most individual investors are aware of Treasury bills, and many have dealt in the cash market.
2) Safety—As obligations of the U. S. government, there is no credit risk. Price movement is therefore entirely a function of maturity and the prevailing level of interest rates.
3) Liquidity—The weekly auction of 13- and 26-week bills, and a vast secondary market assure an ample supply of the "cash commodity."
4) Fungibility—There is no variation in the credit-worthiness of the sole issuer, making all Treasury bills identical apart from their maturity and yield.
5) Ease of Delivery—The Federal Reserve wire system facilitates prompt settlement of all transactions.

Table 2-1   90-day T-bill contract prices Sept. 28, 1978. Source: *The Wall Street Journal.*

U.S. TREASURY BILLS (IMM)	–$1 mil.;			pts. of 100%		
Dec	91.75	91.88	91.75	91.86	+ .14	8.14	− .14
Mar79	91.59	91.68	91.59	91.65	+ .09	8.35	− .09
June	91.45	91.56	91.44	91.54	+ .12	8.46	− .12
Sept	91.34	91.42	91.34	91.40	+ .09	8.60	− .09
Dec	91.26	91.31	91.23	91.29	+ .08	8.71	− .08
Mar80	91.17	91.22	91.14	91.21	+ .05	8.79	− .05
June	91.13	91.14	91.07	91.13	+ .04	8.87	− .04
Sept	91.04	91.07	91.02	91.05	+ .03	8.95	− .03

Est. sales 2,936; sales Wed.: 4,343 contracts.

Commercial Paper

Following through from the previous section, commercial paper may be thought of as a type of bill issued by private companies instead of by the U. S. Treasury Department. It is defined more precisely as short-term, unsecured promissory notes sold by large corporate borrowers either directly or through dealers to banks, corporations and other institutional investors. Used by well-known, financially strong companies when it is less costly to them than bank credit, the market is restricted to firms with the highest credit standing. Equally substantial investors consider the debt instruments of such high grade companies an attractive short-term, low risk investment that offers a higher return than Treasury bills or other money market instruments. Maturities vary between 30 and 270 days, the majority running for 60 days or less. The smallest denomination generally available is $25,000, increasing in multiples of $1,000 to amounts as large as $5 million or more. Due to the relatively high minimum denomination for commercial paper and the absence of a secondary market where it can be traded after the original sale, private investors are not normally attracted to this instrument.

The market has evolved through several major phases since its inception in the late 1800s, as different classes of borrowers and investors emerged and then receded as the predominant forces. Investor confidence was shaken by the bankruptcy of the Penn Central Transportation Co., a large issuer of commercial paper, in 1970. But the volume of outstanding paper has nevertheless increased more than fourfold during the past ten years. As of Dec. 31, 1978, approximately 720 issuing firms had commercial paper outstanding totaling over $85 billion.

Commercial paper was first issued on a modest scale during the late 19th Century, followed by the establishment around 1900 of a rudimentary dealer market. By 1920, over 4,000 companies were issuing paper through more than 30 dealer firms. General Motors Acceptance Corp., the first major issuer to place paper directly in the early 1920's, was joined within ten years by CIT Financial and Commercial Credit Corp. The principal investors during this period were commercial banks that purchased commercial paper as secondary reserves.

Following a hiatus during World War Two, the market resumed its growth in pace with the post-war expansion in business activity and consumer borrowing. It was at this stage that non-bank investors became the chief buyers as commercial banks turned to Treasury bills for reserve purposes. The expansion accelerated as the rising cost of borrowing prompted a growing number of companies to rely more heavily on short-term financing. At the same time, the Federal Reserve's Regulation Q restricted commercial banks in selling large denomination CDs at competitive market rates, and instead induced them to sell commercial paper through their parent holding companies.

The liberalization of the interest ceiling provisions of Regulation Q plus the placing of holding company commercial paper under the reserve requirements led to a sharp reduction in the volume of bank-related paper in the second half of 1970. On the other hand, non-financial issuers remained active in the market even after bank credit again became readily available. Outstanding dealer paper did in fact contract, however, as interest rates rose in early 1971, and the cost advantage shifted back to the side of bank credit.

The market's greatest disruption in recent history occurred when the bankruptcy of the Penn Central left $82 million in defaulted commercial paper in its wake, arousing investors' concerns regarding the ability of other well-known issuers to redeem their paper at maturity. The immediate crisis passed as confidence revived, but quality considerations have remained paramount since 1970 as investors, no longer mistaking size for financial strength, scrutinized potential borrowers far more carefully. New borrowers found access to the market to be more difficult, and the rate spread between the highest and lowest rated paper grew wider. The extreme selectivity of investors has relaxed somewhat since the credit shortage of 1974, but spreads of up to 0.375% (37 basis points) remain between high- and medium-quality paper.

The Issuers.

Over 60% of the commercial paper currently issued is sold directly to investors by the borrowing firms, which are predominantly large finance and bank holding companies with an on-going need for short-term credit to conduct their own lending operations. Such organizations as CIT Financial and Chrysler Credit Corp. possess the necessary banking and money market relationships that enable them to market large amounts of commercial paper without dealer assistance.

Approximately 70 companies currently place sufficient quantities of commercial paper to justify the substantial fixed costs of maintaining an independent sales force and administrative staff. Average monthly sales in excess of $100 million is considered the minimum volume for economic direct distribution. The average of total paper outstanding per direct issuer at the end of 1978 was approximately $700 million. Bank loans are a less significant source of funds for such firms than their commercial paper sales, which typically account for about 65% of their short-term debt.

Direct issuers have the flexibility to adjust the rates and maturities of their paper to suit the needs and preferences of prospective buyers. They also observe the practice of accepting all purchase orders at the quoted rate, which sometimes results in their selling more paper on a given day than they intend. In the absence of a secondary market, an issuer will usually accommodate a good customer with a pressing need for cash by repurchasing his paper before the stated maturity even though he is under no contractual obligation to do so.

Direct commercial paper is normally sold at a higher price (lower yield) than paper offered through dealers in recognition of the strong financial condition of the finance and bank holding companies which account for over 90% of the total amount outstanding. Avoidance of the dealer commission (0.125%) further serves to offset the costs of direct sales.

Despite their high credit rating, all issuers are expected to maintain back-up lines of bank credit to insure prompt repayment at maturity. A standby letter of credit guarantees that if necessary the bank will redeem the paper. In addition to their regular fee, the banks providing the back-up lines generally require compensating balances of 10% of the total line plus an additional 10% of the amounts that are actually drawn down.

Other companies may elect to place their paper through a dealer because they are not sufficiently well-known to issue directly, their borrowing requirements are temporary, or the amount is not sufficiently large to warrant an in-house sales organization. Over 650 corporations issued nearly $35 billion of commercial paper through dealers in 1978. The major dealer issuers are industrial corporations and public utilities with net worth of $100 million or more that turn to the commercial paper market to meet seasonal cash needs when the cost is below that of bank borrowing. About a fourth of the firms which sell dealer paper are the smaller, often regional finance and bank holding companies that lack the stature considered necessary to go to the market directly. Their average net worth is between $40 million and $50 million, or less than half that of the non-financial borrowers; also, their ratings are generally lower, requiring them to pay higher interest rates. A number of smaller borrowers, the oil pipeline company in particular, rely on the guarantees of their parent corporations to gain access to the market.

The Ratings

All of the approximately 700 issuers are rated by at least one of the three rating services. Moody's Investors Service evaluates the largest group, followed by Standard & Poor's and Fitch Investors Service. Each company pays a fee to have its commercial paper rated. Of the four basic classifications used by each of the services as indicated in Table 2-2, paper rated below A_3 or P_3 is difficult to sell and unrated paper is almost automatically excluded from the market. Following the Penn Central collapse, many investors adopted a policy of purchasing paper with a rating no lower than A_2 or P_2.

A borrowing company's bond rating also affects the interest rate it must pay to sell its commercial paper. As a rule, the better the bond rating, the lower the rate on its commercial paper.

Table 2-2. Commercial Paper Ratings.

Fitch Investors Service		Standard & Poor's		Moody's Investors Service
F-1:	Highest grade	A-1:	Highest investment grade	Prime-1
F-2:	Investment grade	A-2:	High Investment grade	Prime-2
F-3:	Good grade	A-3:	Medium investment grade	Prime-3
F-4:	Not recommended	B:	Medium grade	Not rated
		C:	Speculative	
		D:	Expected to default	

The Dealers

About 10 investment firms act as commercial paper dealers. In the aggregate they purchase the paper of over 600 issuers for either immediate resale to investors or to carry in their inventories for up to 10 days. Dealers are compensated by a price mark-up of 0.125%, or $1,250 per $1 million, on the paper they resell. Their inventories are financed by overnight repurchase agreements or secured call loans, for which the lending bank will normally charge ⅛ to ¼ percentage point above the repurchase rate on Treasury securities.

Dealers lack the flexibility of direct issuers in tailoring the terms of the paper they offer to suit the requirements of their customers. The paper they hold in inventory extends out to 60 days, with an average maturity of 30 to 40 days. Commercial paper issued by firms with comparatively low ratings tends to have a shorter average maturity than that of prime issuers. Dealers and investors require standby credit lines which cover 100% of the face value of paper rated less than A_1 or P_1. They are generally satisfied with less than total coverage for paper offered by the highest-rated companies.

Terms of Issue

The absence of a secondary market for commercial paper is not considered a serious liability in view of the short maturities. Dealers do not observe the direct issuers' "gentleman's agreement" to repurchase paper, but institutional investors do have some latitude in selecting offerings with maturities which coincide with their scheduled cash needs.

Commercial paper normally is sold in denominations of $100,000, $500,000 and $1 million, although a dealer will accommodate a good customer if he should request a smaller amount. The average sale to a single investor in one day is about $2 million. On occasion dealers do not have in their inventory sufficient paper of a particular issuer to satisfy the demand.

Separate quotations for direct and dealer paper, with maturities ranging from 30 to 270 days, are published daily in the Money Rates column of the financial press. Commercial paper rates are quoted on the same 360-day annualized discount yield basis as are interest rates on Treasury bills. The numbered equations and the accompanying discussion in the previous section are therefore applicable in computing commercial paper discounts, yields and principal amounts.

Paper is most frequently issued in bearer form by

money center banks acting as agents for the borrowing corporations. The issuing agents also pay holders the final principal and earned discount on maturity. All income from commercial paper is fully subject to Federal, state and local income tax.

The Investors

The principal change in the investor side of the market over the past 30 years has been the replacement of commercial banks by non-financial corporations as the principal suppliers of funds. The declining participation by the banks is due in large part to their increased use of Treasury bills as secondary reserves against deposits, a role formerly filled by commercial paper. The industrial corporations and public utilities which have more than taken up the slack are attracted by the liquidity (in the sense of short maturities), safety and return which commercial paper provides.

Other important investors have been insurance companies, pension and endowment funds, and state and local governments. Individuals have not played a significant role in the market even though direct issuers reduced to $25,000 the minimum denomination for paper with maturities of 30 days or longer.

The Rates

Commercial paper rates are affected directly by the ratings, reputation of the issuers, maturities and yields on alternative investments such as Treasury bills and certificates of deposit. Since companies that resort to dealers to place their paper are perceived to be not quite as sound financially as the direct issuers, dealer rates are generally 0.125% or more above rates on direct paper of the same maturity.

Rates move as a group with those of other money market instruments. They may at any given time be somewhat higher or lower than rates on bank CDs, depending upon the particular circumstances in either market. Yields on the highest-rated commercial paper move in close harmony with those on Treasury bills of the same maturity, but normally range ⅛ to ¼ percentage point, or 12 to 25 basis points, higher, reflecting the presence of investment risk and the lack of a secondary market. During periods of tight money and investor concern over the ability of private borrowers to redeem their obligations, the yield spread between commercial paper and Treasury bills grows wider. At the peak of the 1974 "credit crunch," the spread grew to an unprecedented five full percentage points, or 500 basis points, as investors demanded a larger premium than usual to compensate for what they perceived to be greater risk.

The primary inducement of commercial paper to borrowers is its normally lower cost as compared with bank loans. The relative advantage changes over successive stages of the business cycle because the administered prime lending rate is slower to respond to economic developments than are money market rates. Consequently, borrowers tend to rely more heavily on bank loans during the expansion phase as commercial paper rates are likely to rise more rapidly than the prime rate. The reverse holds true during the contraction phase as market rates fall faster than bank rates, giving the volume of commercial paper sales a contracyclical bias.

This tendency is reinforced by the banks' greater willingness to finance dealer inventories when their loan demand contracts, and their inclination to curtail dealer credit in favor of customer loans during a business upswing.

The supply of commercial paper is also a function of the aggregate demand for short-term funds as compared with long-term funds. Corporations may sell commercial paper as a temporary expedient when conditions for long-term borrowing appear unattractive.

Commercial Paper Futures Contracts

Although commercial paper and Treasury bills are priced on the same discount basis in their respective cash markets, the futures contracts were until recently quoted differently. Unlike the IMM's T-bill futures index, the Board of Trade's 90-day commercial paper contract initially was quoted as the discount rate itself. In mid-1979 the method of contract pricing and delivery of commercial paper were redefined to conform with the other interest rate contracts.[3]

The 90-day commercial paper contract stipulates the delivery of the same $1 million face value of securities as does the 90-day T-bill contract. The dollar value of one basis point, therefore, is also $25. The 30-day commercial paper contract, introduced in May 1979, has a specified size of $3 million, placing the value of its minimum fluctuation at $25 as well.[4]

The number of approved issuers of deliverable commercial paper differs between the two contracts. Whereas delivery of any one of 41 approved names may be made under the 90-day contract, the approved list was sharply reduced to four issuers under the terms of the 30-day contract.

All Treasury bills are identical in their investment quality due to the absence of credit risk, but the quality of commercial paper varies according to the financial condition of its issuer. The Board of Trade designates as deliverable grade commercial paper rated A_1 by Standard & Poor's and P_1 by Moody's

---

[3]Because this book was going to press at the time the change was made, the commercial paper examples and case histories cited throughout are based upon the original system. The differences between the two are largely a matter of mechanics, however, and do not materially affect the outcome of the illustrations.

[4]Readers can refer to the discussion on page 36 concerning the relationship between maturity and discount yield. The method of calculating the dollar amount per basis point for various maturities applies to commercial paper as well as to Treasury bills.

Investor Service and issued by one of 41 issuers approved by the exchange. The commercial paper itself is held in an approved depository for safekeeping, and delivery is made in the form of a Financial Receipt that in turn may be surrendered in exchange for the commercial paper. Under the contract's terms there is no price adjustment for delivery of paper with less than 40 days outstanding.

In other respects the commercial paper futures are similar to T-bill futures. The contract trading unit is commercial paper with $1 million face value at maturity. The minimum price fluctuation of one basis point is the equivalent of $25 per contract.

U.S. Treasury Bonds and Notes

Debt obligations of the U. S. government are classified according to their maturity and method of paying interest. As was discussed in the first section of this chapter, Treasury bills are discounted securities with original maturities of up to one year. The Treasury also has issued three types of marketable coupon securities bearing stated rates of interest: certificates, notes and bonds. Treasury notes are offered with maturities between one and ten years, and bonds for terms longer than ten years. Since their original maturity is the single feature which distinguishes notes from bonds, these two types of government securities and their respective futures contracts will be considered together. Like 52-week bills, Treasury certificates have a maturity of one year, but none have been issued since 1967. They have no immediate relevance so far as futures trading is concerned.

Treasury notes and bonds are among the most widely held and actively traded fixed-income securities. As obligations of the U. S. government and therefore free of credit (but not interest rate) risk, their yields are generally below those of other debt instruments of comparable maturity. The actual yield spreads between Treasury bonds vary with the premiums investors choose to pay for the greatest possible safety at different points in time.

Prices and Yields

Notes and bonds can be purchased either at the Treasury's refunding auctions or following their issue through a government-securities dealer in the secondary market. They are deliverable in registered or bearer form in denominations ranging from the minimum $1,000 to $1 million. Semi-annual interest payments are mailed directly to registered holders or, in the case of bearer securities, made upon presentation of the designated coupon at a Federal Reserve or commercial bank. Interest is subject to Federal income tax, but is exempt from state and local taxes.

Accrued interest is added to the purchase price of securities. Regular settlement is made on the business day following the transaction, or up to five business days for amounts less than $100,000. Because of their inherent safety, Treasury securities may be bought on margin as low as 10% which isn't to be confused with the margin required to trade a futures contract. Such margin transactions remain speculative, however, since rising interest rates can cause bond prices to drop beyond the point at which the entire margin is eradicated.

Prices of coupon securities are quoted as percentages of their par value plus fractional 32nds of a point. Dealer quotes and newspaper listings abbreviate fractions so that a price of 102 4/32, or $1,021.25 per $1,000 face amount would read 102.4. The indicated interest rates are yields to maturity calculated on the offered side of the quotation. Daily price fluctuations are reported as changes in the bid.

For example, the following quotation appeared in

the newspaper listing of Treasury issues for Sept. 15, 1978:

7¼s, 1992 Aug . . . . 91.4   91.12   +4   8.30

The issue listed is a Treasury bond which bears a stated interest rate of 7¼% meaning that interest of $36.25 per $1,000 face amount ($1,000 × .0725 ÷ 2) is paid each February and August until maturity in 1992. Because interest rates on Sept. 15 were above the 7¼ (or 7.25) rate at which the bond was issued, the market price on that day was below par. Dealers were bidding 91 4/32, indicating their willingness to buy bonds from customers at $911.25 per $1,000 face value, and were offering them for sale at 91 12/32, or $913.75. The dealer furnishing the quotation had increased his bid by 4/32, meaning that he was prepared to pay $1.25 more per $1,000 bond than he was bidding the previous day. The yield to maturity of 8.30%, the value of the 7.25 coupon at the offer price of 91 12/32, what investors would pay for the bond at the time it was so quoted, is derived by the formula included in Appendix C.

The Auctions

The method used by the Treasury to auction coupon issues resembles its sale of bills except that the bidding is done on a yield rather than price basis. The reader should by this time be clear that the dollar amount the bidder is willing to pay can be expressed either way. Prospective investors may either submit their bids themselves or pay a commercial bank to enter subscriptions on their behalf. Bids entered directly by private parties must be accompanied by a deposit of about 10%, which is applied to the purchase.

The Treasury usually announces a new offering one to three weeks before the intended issue date and accepts subscriptions until the books are closed. As in bill auctions, tenders may be entered on a competitive or noncompetitive basis. If subscribers elect to submit their bids through a bank or dealer, the fee charged for the service will reduce their effective yield on the bonds if their bids are successful.

Auctions are frequently oversubscribed by the closing day. The Treasury reserves the right to reject any or all bids. After selecting the competitive bids it will accept, it will award a small portion, generally $200,000, of each winning subscription in full, and allot the balance on a prorated basis. Certain official classes of subscribers, notably Federal Reserve Banks and domestic and foreign government entities, may be accorded preferential treatment in the form of full allotments. The noncompetitive awards are made at the weighted average price of the accepted competitive bids, which may be below, equal to or over par. The coupon rate placed on the security is also set at the average of accepted bids.

A large portion of the funds raised at Treasury auctions is earmarked for the repayment of maturing debt. Any one of several refunding techniques may be employed. In an exchange refunding, new securities are offered in return for ones that are about to mature. Holders of maturing bonds have the option of accepting a new bond or taking cash. The Treasury may offer those seeking a shorter-term alternative a choice between a long-term bond and an intermediate-term note. Advance refundings are held to exchange new bonds for outstanding issues that are not immediately due to mature, giving the Treasury greater flexibility in arranging its financing calendar. A third method is the cash refunding, whereby securities are sold for new cash which may later be used to retire a maturing issue.

Since the Treasury's refunding operations create a continual supply of government bonds, the timing of new offerings as well as the amounts, maturities and coupon rates affect the level of interest rates in that segment of the fixed-income market. As will be discussed in Part Two, these refinancings accordingly influence activity in long-term and in some instances short-term interest rate futures. To avoid disrupting the market by making surprise moves, the Treasury has tended to give advance indications of its estimated cash needs in the upcoming quarter and the types of financing it has under consideration.

The major quarterly refundings customarily are conducted in February, May, August and November, coincident with the expiration of a major amount of outstanding debt. Since bonds which bear coupons above 4¼% are subject to the statutory ceiling on government debt, a greater number of notes have been offered in recent years. Three-year notes dated and maturing on or near the 15th of the month of issue are currently included in the quarterly refunding package, with seven- or ten-year notes sometimes used as alternative options. Every recent quarterly refunding has included a 25-year bond issue callable five years before final maturity.

Two-, four- and five-year notes also have been offered at various intervals throughout the year, payable in a staggered schedule of maturities. Banks in particular find such spaced maturities suitable in providing for possible demands for funds. Non-financial corporations frequently purchase short notes as higher yielding alternatives to Treasury bills.

The Secondary Market

After they are initially offered at auction, notes and bonds are traded by the same government security dealers who make a secondary market in Treasury bills. Because their price behavior and marketability vary with their maturity, "coupons" are further divided into short, intermediate and long issues, each assigned to a trader who specializes in that segment.

Though there are no clear-cut divisions, short coupons are considered to be those which mature within two years. Since their maturities to a certain extent coincide, their interest rates tend to move in concert with Treasury bills, commercial paper and certificates of deposit. This linkage is reinforced by the sensitivity of short-coupon yields to the same forces that affect the money market: the federal funds rate, open market operations of the Federal Reserve, and the general tone of the Treasury bill market.

Their safety and yield make short-coupon issues attractive to corporate investors. Because their short maturity limits their price volatility, they are not preferred vehicles for speculative traders, who find greater profit opportunities in the intermediate sector. Trading does become quite active during Treasury refundings, however, as investors adjust portfolios to improve their yield and capital position.

Trading activity is also heaviest in the two- to five-year intermediate coupon range during refunding periods. The potentially depressing effect of the new supply about to reach the market and the volatility of the extended maturities give traders an opportunity to sell bonds short prior to the refunding and then to reverse position in anticipation of a subsequent rally. The appeal of intermediates for investment purposes is restricted by their limited maturities. The market is relatively inactive between refundings, as evidenced by the growing spreads between bid and asked prices.

The market for long coupons beyond five years is extremely thin and volatile. Trades amounting to $500,000, a relatively small order in the government securities market, can have an exaggerated effect on the market price, while bid-asked spreads can range from one-half (16/32) to one full point (32/32). By contrast, the spread on short coupons is generally 1/32 to 2/32, while intermediate spreads usually fall between 1/32 and 4/32.

In the face of a contracting average maturity on its outstanding debt, the Treasury seizes every opportunity to sell long-term bonds, but is hampered by limited demand. Banks and savings and loan associations, which are large buyers of the intermediate coupons, are reluctant to extend beyond three-year maturities, leaving the bulk of trading activity in the longer issues to dealer speculation.

As the short coupons are closely tied to the money market by virtue of similar maturities, long-maturity issues are heavily influenced by developments in the corporate bond market. The largest volume of trading in this maturity sector is the result of swaps with long-term corporate bonds when yield spreads between the two groups appear to be historically narrow or wide.

Government securities dealers derive their profits from the spreads between bids and offers, speculative gains from owning securities when interest rates fall or being short as they rise, and the interest earned on their inventories. Offsetting the latter is the interest cost of carrying securities in inventory.

The willingness of dealers to bid aggressively and to maintain narrow spreads has a determining effect on their trading performance as well as on the overall condition of the secondary market. Their attitudes are in turn conditioned by the prevailing market climate. When customer orders and speculative dealer activity slacken during periods of rising interest rates, the market risks of carrying positions increase, prompting many dealers to take defensive action by increasing their spreads and accepting orders only on a best-efforts basis, contingent on their obtaining a matching order on the other side. To the extent that dealers are deterred from exercising their primary function of bearing risk, the viability of the market is itself diminished.

In both favorable (falling interest rates) and unfavorable (rising rates) market environments, the propensity to assume risk varies from dealer to dealer. An individual dealer might himself shift his posture from aggressive to defensive and back in response to changing conditions. By increasing his spreads to allow himself a greater cushion to absorb risk, he reduces his utility to his customers and his contribution to a liquid market. If he regards a 101-¼ spread as insufficient to allow him to buy and sell a particular issue without incurring a loss, the trader may open it up to 101-102, meaning that his customer must see a full percentage point move merely to cover his transaction cost.

In reaching these decisions, the trader's attitudes are as much influenced by market psychology and mood as they are by hard economic data and the flow of orders to his desk. As often occurs in the futures market, sudden changes in mood can trigger price moves which have no rational justification. Although these attitudes and decisions are arrived at individually, the herd instinct is as prevalent, if not more so, among professionals as it is among private investors. In the aggregate, they determine the market's capacity to absorb large transactions without precipitating sharp price changes. Not surprisingly, it was the dealers who first recognized the value of futures as instruments that could mitigate the risk of carrying inventories and quoting narrow spreads, without impairing the liquidity of the market.

Treasury Bond Futures Contract

The four variables which determine the price of a U. S. Treasury bond are: (1) coupon rate—the amount, expressed as a percentage of par, paid each year to the holder; (2) call feature—the year prior to maturity that the government may elect to retire the bond by repaying its principal; (3) maturity—the year in which the bond must be redeemed; (4) yield—the annual coupon payment expressed as a percentage of market price rather than par.

To reiterate with another issue the earlier illustration, the Treasury 8½s of 94-99 pay $85 annually for each $1,000 face value, can be called at the option of the government at any time after May 1994, and must be redeemed for cash or exchanged for a new bond by May 1999. During 1978 the market price of this bond fluctuated between 106 and 95, reflecting a range in yield of 7.8% to 9%.

By designating standardized terms for the coupon rate, call date and maturity, the Chicago Board of Trade's Treasury bond contract reflects the remaining variable—interest rate change—by fluctuations in price. Deliverable grade under the specifications of the contract is a U. S. Treasury bond which, if callable, may not be called for at least 15 years from date of delivery or, if not callable, does not mature for at least 15 years from date of delivery.

The specified unit of trading is bonds of the same issue with a face value at maturity of $100,000 and a coupon rate of 8%. Bonds with coupon rates other than 8% constitute good delivery at equivalent price discounts for bonds with coupons less than 8% and premiums for bonds with coupons greater than 8%.

The newspaper price quotations for Aug. 4, 1978, list 11 successive quarterly delivery months for the Treasury bond contract, from September 1978 through March 1981. In addition to the daily high, low and closing quotations for each delivery month, the two columns to the left indicate the high and low prices during the life of each option. The December 1978 contract had a range 10 11/32 (102-00– 91-21) or a change of $10,343.75 per $100,000 bond, while the March 1981 contract, the most distant, traded within a much narrower range of 3 5/16 (93-14 – 90-09). This difference does not necessarily mean that the distant option is less volatile, but having been traded for a briefer period it had not reflected the year-long rise in bond rates as did the nearby contracts.

Since the contract amount of $100,000 face value is the same for Treasury bond and GNMA contracts, the 1/32nd point minimum price fluctuation represents $31.25 for both contracts ($100,000 $\times$ .01 $\times$ 1/32).

Table 2-3. Long Term Treasury Bond Contract Prices (Price Quotations for Friday, Aug. 4, 1978)

8% — $100,000 principal; points and 32d's of 100%							
Season							Open
High	Low		High	Low	Close	Change	Interest
102-14	92-04	Sep	96-00	94-31	95-10	+02	3168
102-00	91-21	Dec	95-17	94-10	94-25	——	2626
101-26	91-11	Mar	95-00	94-03	94-14	−02	1221
98-11	91-03	Jun	94-30	93-31	94-05	−01	928
96-10	90-30	Sep	94-20	93-23	93-27	−04	1050
96-06	90-24	Dec	94-19	93-20	93-24	−03	752
96-02	90-18	Mar	94-14	93-10	93-18	−04	315
95-31	90-17	Jun	94-10	93-10	93-15	−05	289
95-23	90-15	Sep	93-25	93-10	93-12	−06	437
95-04	90-12	Dec	93-20	93-08	93-08	−07	463
93-14	90-09	Mar	93-14	93-05	93-05	−10	145

Sales Thursday: 2,736 contracts.
Total open interest Thursday: 11,394, up 248 from Wednesday.

Bonds and mortgage-backed securities, like Treasury bills and commercial paper, have certain common characteristics, but are different kinds of obligations, possess different kinds of security and have different methods of yield computation.

Delivery under the terms of the government bond contract is made by book-entry through commercial banks which are members of the Federal Reserve System in accordance with Department of the Treasury Circular 300.

GNMA Pass-Through Securities

GNMA mortgage-backed pass-throughs, a new type of security with some of the characteristics of a bond, have become one of the fastest-growing fixed-income investments since their introduction in 1970. The program from which they originate represents a successful coalition of the public and private sectors in pursuing social goals within the framework of the capital market.

As part of its policy of improving housing conditions throughout the country, the federal government has encouraged the flow of private capital into residential financing since the Housing Act of 1934. FHA, the Federal Housing Administration, was established under the Act to insure residential mortgage loans. The functions of purchasing and re-selling these FHA-insured mortgages were originally delegated to the Federal National Mortgage Association. Under the terms of the Housing Act of 1968, FNMA was turned into a private corporation and made primarily responsible for providing supplementary assistance to the secondary market for federally guaranteed or insured mortgages.

FNMA's other activities were assumed by the Government National Mortgage Association, or GNMA, which was created under the 1968 act as a wholly-owned government corporation within the Department of Housing and Urban Development (HUD).

GNMA's primary program in accomplishing its mandate of supporting new home construction has been its guarantees of three types of obligations, participation certificates, mortgage-backed bonds, and pass-through securities. Participation certificates, of which approximately $5.5 billion were outstanding as of Dec. 31, 1978, are issued as beneficial interests in principal and interest payable on a pool of mortgages held by several federal trusts. The sale of mortgage-backed bonds was discontinued in 1973, after GNMA had guaranteed some $3.4 billion of bonds with maturities varying from one to 25 years.

The greatest success has occurred in the pass-through security program, which from a modest beginning in 1970 has mushroomed into a $67 billion market. GNMA pass-through securities are debt obligations collateralized in most instances by 30-year, single-family FHA and VA (Veterans Administration) mortgages. They are created when an issuer, normally a thrift institution or a mortgage banking company which specializes in such originations, assembles and deposits at a custodian bank a minimum pool of $1 million FHA-insured or VA-guaranteed single-family residential mortgages bearing the same coupon and maturity. Certificates which represent a prorated share in these pools are then sold through dealers to investors to whom principal and interest payments collected on the underlying mortgages are "passed through" under a GNMA guarantee backed by the full faith and credit of the United States.

Pass-through securities, properly referred to as certificates and not bonds, are unique in the sense that holders receive monthly rather than semi-annual payments of principal and interest. These payments are made on a *modified* pass-through basis, meaning that payment is guaranteed to certificate holders regardless of whether it is collected on the mortgages in the pool. A *straight* pass-through security would pay investors only as payment is received on the individual mortgages.

For the sake of clarity, the nickname "Ginnie Mae" will henceforth be used in connection with the pass-through securities, and the acronym GNMA reserved for references to the association itself. The Ginnie Mae modified pass-through is the security upon which the Board of Trade futures contract is based.

Originating Mortgages

"Origination" is the term used to describe the process of creating mortgages secured by real property. Developers, builders, real estate brokers and home buyers make up the demand side of the financing equation. They look to mortgage investors—savings and loan associations, insurance companies, pension funds, commercial and savings banks and, in some instances, individuals—to supply the capital needed to buy, build or otherwise develop a particular property.

The supply and demand sides establish contact through a financial intermediary, usually a mortgage banker but sometimes a savings bank or savings and loan association, which in this situation serve as middlemen rather than as permanent investors.

The mortgage banker or other intermediary observes the following sequence in originating a pool of residential mortgages:[5]

1. Agrees to finance house purchases.
2. Executes documents and closes mortgage loans with payment of his own funds.
3. Packages group of mortgages into a pool.
4. Secures commitments from dealers or investors to purchase mortgage-backed securities at specified yields and prices.
5. Requests and receives a commitment to guarantee from GNMA.
6. Transfers mortgage documents to custodian bank and submits pool documents to GNMA.
7. Receives mortgage-backed certificates from GNMA.
8. Delivers certificates to dealers or investors for payment.
9. Services mortgages in the pool, collecting mortgage payments from homeowners.
10. Remits monthly principal and interest payments to certificate holders along with monthly accounting statement.

The minimum dollar value of a pool of single-family mortgages must be $1 million, or $500,000 for project and mobile home mortgages. The final maturity of Ginnie Mae certificates is equal to the nominal 30-year term of their underlying mortgages. The buyer, however, is never certain of the actual maturity of his investment. Due to prepayments of principal, which may

---

[5]*The Ginnie Mae Manual*, GNMA Mortgage-Backed Securities Dealers Association, Homewood, Illinois: Dow Jones—Irwin 1978 p. 26.

be made without penalty, and possible foreclosures, the actual average life of a single-family mortgage pool is less than half its stated maturity. To conform more closely with actual experience, Ginnie Mae pass-through yields are predicated upon the assumption that all mortgages in the pool are amortized according to a 30-year schedule, then totally prepaid in their 12th year.

The issuer becomes an approved mortgagee when GNMA approves the securities collateralized by a specified pool of FHA or VA mortgages. If the issuer and all security holders agree to termination of a pool prior to its stated maturity, formal notification of termination is made to GNMA, which cancels its guarantee when all outstanding pool certificates are returned to it. Currently, there are about 500 active issuers of Ginnie Mae certificates.

The securities are always issued in registered form. The minimum original face amount is $25,000, rising in increments of $5,000 up to $30,000, and in $10,000 increments for greater amounts. The minimum certificate denomination should not be confused with the $1 million minimum pool size.

Prices and Yields

Ginnie Mae prices and yields, like those of conventional bonds, are quoted as percentages of par. Stated interest rates, which are the amounts paid annually per face value, are expressed as 7½%, 8%, 8¼%, etc., while current yields are computed to a thousandth of a percent, such as 8.436%. Market prices are quoted as percentage points and 32nds of a point.

Yield is the percentage value of the fixed annual interest payments to the principal amount. If the security is purchased at par (100), the yield is equal to its stated rate. To illustrate, when purchased at par, a $100,000 face value Ginnie Mae bearing a stated rate of 8% would cost the buyer $100,000 and pay him

$8,000 in annual interest plus scheduled return of principal for a yield also of 8%. Since the $8,000 interest payment is a fixed figure, the same Ginnie Mae bought at less than par (that is, at a discount) would yield more than 8%, while an investor who pays a price higher than 100 (a premium) would receive a lower yield. If the stated rate is known, it is possible to derive the market price from the yield, or vice versa, through use of yield tables or application of the formula:

9) $$\frac{\text{Percentage}}{\text{Annual Yield}} = \frac{\text{Net Annual Interest}}{\text{Invested Principal}}$$

Again assuming an 8% stated rate, a Ginnie Mae purchased at a discount price of 96 would yield 8.333%, while its yield would fall to 7.843% if the investor pays a premium of 102.

$$\left(8.333\% = \frac{\$8,000}{\$96,000}\right)$$

or

$$\left(7.843\% = \frac{\$8,000}{\$102,000}\right)$$

In practice, the actual yield cannot be computed with such precision due to the uncertainty regarding slow payments, defaults, prepayments and early payoffs of principal. As was stated earlier, Ginnie Mae yield calculations are based upon the premise that regular monthly payments will be made for 12 years and then the mortgages in the pool will be paid off in full. To the extent that experience departs from this assumption the actual yield will vary from the presumed rate. The payoff of mortgages sooner than the estimated 12-year prepayment period increases the yield of a Ginnie Mae purchased at a discount. If the pass-through was bought at a premium, the yield is decreased by fast payoffs. If, for example, an investor buys an 8% Ginnie Mae at 104½ to yield 7.656%, and the underlying mortgages are prepaid within eight years rather than the assumed 12-year period, the true yield to him will be 60 to 70 basis points lower.

The continued validity of the 12-year prepayment assumption is currently a matter of discussion within the mortgage industry. Ginnie Mae pass-throughs have not existed for a sufficient period to provide an empirical record from which an average maturity of a mortgage pool can be derived.

Another feature unique to pass-through securities which alters their actual annual yield is the 45-day delay from the time payments are due on the mortgages to when they are remitted to the Ginnie Mae holder. The resulting interest-free lag of 15 days to the first payment produces a yield of 15 to 30 basis points less than the result of the formula cited above.

Conversion to Bond Equivalents

Because of the monthly payments of principal and interest, Ginnie Mae yields, like Treasury bill discounts, must be converted to their bond equivalents to provide a valid comparison with conventional fixed-income securities. Inasmuch as the holder has an opportunity to reinvest payments received prior to the regular semi-annual coupon dates, pass-through yields are 15 to 20 basis points higher when restated on a semi-annual basis. The higher the annual yield as stated on a monthly basis, the greater the "add on" to obtain the bond equivalent semi-annual yield.

Like coupon securities, the market price of pass-throughs fluctuate in inverse relation to their current yield. The value of a 32nd of a point on the principal amount of $1 million, the normal transaction size in the dealer market, is $312.50 ($1,000,000 × .01 × 1/32). A price advance from, say, 96 9/32 to 99 1/32 would therefore comprise a gain of $29,375 on a Ginnie Mae 8% rate. The alternate method of expressing this price move is as a drop in yield from 8.474% to 8.062%.

Pass-through securities have been issued at face

rates ranging from 5¼% to 9½%, depending upon the prevailing yield on FHA-VA single-family residential mortgages at the time of their origination. The mortgages placed in a particular pool must all bear the same face rate and maturity date. The stated rate of the Ginnie Mae, entered on the face of the certificate (hence, face rate), is always ½% below that of the mortgages in the pool. Of this 50 basis-point difference, 44 basis points are deducted by the issuer as his annual service fee, and the remaining six basis points go to GNMA as its guarantee fee.

Ginnie Mae equivalent yields have ranged from 50 to 200 basis points above those on Treasury bonds of comparable maturity. They have even been as much as 150 basis points above the yield on AAA corporate bonds, which is something of an anomaly since GNMA's guarantee of timely payment of all amounts due to investors is backed by the full faith and credit of the U. S. government. The ability of GNMA to borrow from the Treasury to meet its guarantee obligations imparts to pass-throughs the safety of a general obligation of the United States. The unusual spreads between Ginnie Maes and Treasury and corporate bonds can most likely be attributed to investors' initial unfamiliarity with this new type of security and a faster rise in mortgage interest rates than in corporate bond yields in late 1973.

Figure 2-2 depicts the several levels of tangible and institutional backing contained in the GNMA guarantee process. In the ten years since the program's inception, there have been no instances of an investor not receiving the monthly payment.

Buyers of Ginnie Maes

During the early years of the GNMA program, traditional mortgage investors were the principal buyers of pass-through securities. When the unusually high yields of 1973-74 caught the attention of such

FIGURE 2-2

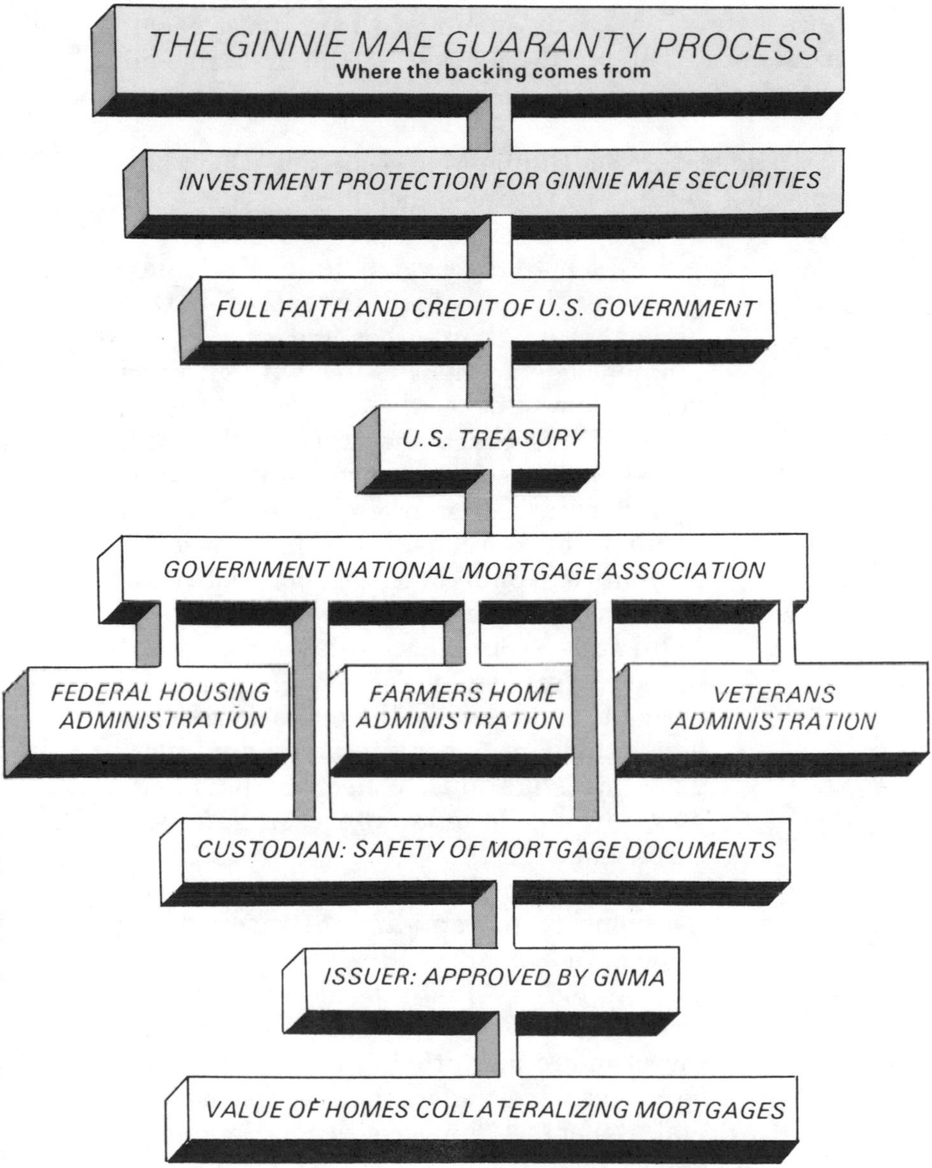

THE GINNIE MAE GUARANTY PROCESS
Where the backing comes from

INVESTMENT PROTECTION FOR GINNIE MAE SECURITIES

FULL FAITH AND CREDIT OF U.S. GOVERNMENT

U.S. TREASURY

GOVERNMENT NATIONAL MORTGAGE ASSOCIATION

FEDERAL HOUSING ADMINISTRATION

FARMERS HOME ADMINISTRATION

VETERANS ADMINISTRATION

CUSTODIAN: SAFETY OF MORTGAGE DOCUMENTS

ISSUER: APPROVED BY GNMA

VALUE OF HOMES COLLATERALIZING MORTGAGES

Source: The Ginnie Mae Manual

other institutional investors as pension funds, insurance companies, credit unions and bank trust departments, they entered the market for the first time and remained after the spreads returned to more normal levels.

The features of Ginnie Mae securities which have appealed to these institutions include:

1. Yield—As noted above, Ginnie Maes have consistently provided investors with a higher return than either Treasury or government agency debt issues without sacrificing their safety.

2. Marketability—Since the start of the mortgage-backed securities program, an active secondary dealer market has evolved, absorbing the purchase or sale of sizeable amounts of Ginnie Maes on short notice and without excessive price concessions.

3. Administrative Simplicity—Pass-throughs allow participation in the mortgage market without encountering the operational problems attendant to making individual mortgage investigations, collecting payments, maintaining records, processing foreclosures and so forth.

4. Continuous Cash Flow—Many investors prefer monthly to semi-annual interest and principal payments.

5. Legal Eligibility—Institutions which are restricted in the types of securities they may invest in are permitted to buy Ginnie Maes because they are government-backed.

6. Social Benefits—The pass-through program allows institutions to support medium-and low-cost housing in the areas where they are situated without compromising the interests of their depositors, beneficiaries or other vested parties.

Their attractive yield and the federal guarantee which qualify them as legal investments for many regulated institutions are the primary features of mortgage-backed securities that have attracted the major buyers of Ginnie Maes.

Savings and loan associations, active in the market as both originators and investors, may buy pass-throughs as eligible securities, but are not permitted to treat them as liquid assets to satisfy Federal Home Loan Bank Board requirements. Ginnie Maes are not subject to area or percentage-of-assets limitations which normally apply to the conventional mortgage loans that associations make.

Many of the considerations favoring the purchase of pass-throughs by savings and loans apply to mutual savings banks as well, except that the latter have a wider choice of eligible investments. The regulations in most of the 17 states in which mutual savings banks are chartered stipulate that up to 65% of total assets may be invested in mortgages and real estate, with other acceptable investments including U. S. Treasury and federal agency obligations and municipal and prime-rated corporate bonds.

Pension funds are a general classification which includes retirement funds, health and welfare trusts, union trust funds, endowments and bank trust departments. The government guarantee makes Ginnie Maes eligible investments for public employee pension and welfare funds. Federal backing also makes it easier for trustees to comply with the fiduciary provisions of the Employment Retirement Income Security Act of 1974 (ERISA). On an administrative level, Ginnie Mae's monthly principal and interest payments are often suited to the disbursement schedule of pension funds.

Relatively less committed to the mortgage market than the savings banks, commercial banks have not been as important buyers of Ginnie Maes. However, many of them did not hesitate to take advantage of

the extraordinary yield spreads over Treasury and corporate issues in 1973. The Comptroller of the Currency
has ruled that national banks may purchase mortgage-backed securities without limitation as to
amount for their own portfolios and as trust investments. Most state banking commissions also have authorized the purchase of Ginnie Maes by banks which
come under their supervision.

Individual investors, unless subject to certain
trust provisions, have the broadest latitude in making
investments to fit their particular circumstances and
objectives. Conservative investors are drawn to the
safety, yield and administrative simplicity of mortgage-backed securities, but many potential buyers
have until recently been deterred by the $25,000 min-
imum denomination. The introduction within the past
two years of Ginnie Mae funds, or investment trusts,
offering units of $1,000 has opened public access to the
market and made more individuals familiar with this
type of investment.

Ginnie Mae transactions have different methods
of settlement. The most frequently employed is the
purchase or sale for immediate delivery, what is in
effect a cash market transaction. The realized profit or
loss on this type of transaction must be booked at the
time of the sale.

A dealer and his customer also may enter into a
trade for delayed delivery, usually six months from the
time of the transaction. A mortgage banker may sell
for delayed delivery to assure the disposition of a mortgage pool he is in the process of assembling, or an
institution may buy to fix the price of an issue prior
to putting it on their books. The sale for deferred delivery, or forward commitment, was a precursor of the
organized futures market for Ginnie Mae securities.

A third type of transaction is the standby commitment. Here, the potential buyer is paid an advance
fee to accept delivery on a stated date at a specified
yield (and price) if the seller, who pays the fee, elects

to deliver. This technique is basically an option to sell Ginnie Mae securities that affords mortgage bankers and other originators an alternate means of price protection against adverse yield movements. Having paid for assurance that there will be a buyer for his mortgages at a definite price, a prospective seller may walk away from his commitment if market conditions during the interim allow him to sell for immediate delivery at a higher price. The standby fee is invariably higher than the cost of a comparable firm delayed-delivery commitment or immediate sale. But in return the seller stands to gain from the price appreciation resulting from any interest rate decline that may occur while the standby commitment remains in force.

Direct and Secondary Markets

Pass-throughs are offered to investors either directly by the issuer or through a Ginnie Mae dealer for immediate or delayed delivery. The annual dollar volume of new issues has tripled in recent years, from $5 billion in 1975 to $15 billion in 1978. From the initial $2 million Ginnie Mae offering in February 1970, total face value of outstanding securities has grown to $67 billion by Dec. 31, 1978.

Outstanding securities are traded in an active secondary market maintained by 70 or so dealer firms, including many of the primary dealers in U. S. government securities. Like Treasury bills and coupon issues, Ginnie Maes are bought and sold on a net basis, the dealers' profit derived from a spread of about 4/32nd point between their bids and offers. The principal balance of a Ginnie Mae traded in the secondary market is its face value less the amount by which it has been amortized and prepaid since the time it was issued. For example, a certificate with a $100,000 face value representing mortgages on which principal of $1,200 has been repaid within five years of its issue would be priced to reflect this drawdown. As in the original-issue market, transactions are made on an immediate- or deferred-delivery basis.

The novelty of the Ginnie Mae instrument when first introduced prompted traders to draw upon skills and techniques peculiar at that time to the government and corporate bond, mortgage, money and commodity futures markets. In conjunction with their market-making activities, the GNMA Mortgage-Backed Securities Dealers Association was formed in 1972 to educate the investment community in the nature of the security and its market, and to adopt rules for self-regulation of their industry. The practice of entering into transactions for deferred delivery (not to be confused with futures contracts traded on the Chicago Board of Trade) without any margin deposits required of institutional customers led to several cases of alleged improper sales practices by dealers or excessive speculation by customers which prompted the association to intensify its program for self-policing. Rules were promulgated requiring verification of the suitability of a client's trading practices and restricting the sale of forward commitments to situations where they are consistent with his operational or investment requirements.

Tax Treatment

Monthly payments of principal to individuals are normally treated for tax purposes as a return of capital, while interest is considered as ordinary income. Proceeds from the sale of Ginnie Maes by individuals are subject to short- or long-term capital gains, depending upon the length of time the securities were held. According to IRS Ruling 70-545, the purchase of Ginnie Maes does not impair the tax-exempt status of a pension fund. The same ruling accords favorable tax treatment to savings banks which hold Ginnie Maes. There are no comparable advantages which accrue to commercial banks. They are taxed on the same basis as individuals, with interest received considered ordinary income and principal payments a return of capital.

Pass-through investments are described in Section 7701 (a)(19)(c) of the Internal Revenue Code as "loans secured by interest in real property." Since they are regarded as undivided interests in a pool of collateralizing mortgages, the securities are qualifying assets as if the investments were made in the underlying mortgages.

Mortgage-backed securities have not been accorded any specific tax exemptions by state or local authorities.

The Ginnie Mae Futures Contracts

The foregoing was devoted to an overview of the Ginnie Mae cash market, where dealers and their customers buy and sell the actual securities in various amounts and interest rates, either for immediate or delayed delivery. Many of the same participants also are active in the Ginnie Mae futures market, where a standard contract is traded.

To summarize the difference between the two markets (which also apply to Treasury bills and coupon issues but not to commercial paper where there is no effective secondary market) the cash market is an over-the-counter market where dealers negotiate transactions on a net basis for their own accounts. The futures market is a two-way auction in which brokers buy and sell competitively on an exchange floor for commission compensation. Purchases and sales of Ginnie Mae securities for deferred delivery have until recently been made on credit, with no margin deposit or any other type of payment required until actual delivery is made. Margin must be deposited for all futures trades and adjusted daily to reflect the changed value of the contract.

While the sale for delayed delivery in the cash

market resembles a futures transaction in some respects, it is still an individually negotiated agreement between dealer and customer based upon the good faith of both parties, rather than a standard contract traded on a regulated exchange and guaranteed by its clearing house. Though asserting that each serves a useful function in the appropriate situation, a commentator experienced in both markets cites two attributes of the futures market that the Ginnie Mae cash deferred delivery market lacks: 1) there are currently traded Chicago Board of Trade futures contracts for at least ten successive quarterly delivery months, offering price protection up to 2½ years compared to the maximum six months' coverage normally obtainable through deferred delivery commitments in the cash market; 2) forward cash commitments do not easily lend themselves to the type of aggressive hedging and related arbitrage strategies involving futures described in Part Three of this book.[6]

Of the various face interest rates at which Ginnie Mae securities have been issued from time to time, the Chicago Board of Trade contract stipulates the delivery of certificates which bear a stated rate of 8%—"Ginnie Mae 8s," meaning that the FHA or VA mortgages in the collateralized pool are 8½% loans to allow for the issuer's annual service fee and GNMA's guarantee fee. In the event that the seller of a contract elects to deliver actual Ginnie Maes rather than liquidating his short position through an offsetting purchase transaction, he may substitute certificates carrying rates other than 8%, provided they are adjusted in amount to equal the value of 8% certificates at par. According to the following table of equivalent amounts for Ginnie Maes with the most common face rates, a short trader could deliver $103,806.20 principal amount of Ginnie Mae 7½s.

---

[6]David R. Ganis, Cash Market or Futures Market? Which One is Best for Mortgage Bankers? *Mortgage Banker,* November 1978, pp. 7-11.

Table 2-4   Ginnie Mae 8s Equivalents.

Stated Interest Rate	Equivalent Principal Balance of $100,000 Ginnie Mae 8s
6.50	$112,123.30
7.00	107,816.70
7.25	105,820.10
7.50	103,806.20
7.75	101,867.50
8.00	100,000.00
8.25	98,219.80
8.50	96,501.80
9.00	93,167.70

The contract size is $100,000 principal balance of Ginnie Mae 8s, when calculated at par under the assumption of a 30-year maturity prepaid in the 12th year, which is the same average or "half-life" basis upon which pass-throughs are priced in the cash market.

Like the actual Ginnie Mae securities, contract prices are quoted as a percentage of par plus 1/32nd point. In the daily newspaper price tables, the fraction is abbreviated, so that 96 19/32 ($96,593.74 principal balance or paid down equivalent) is shown as 96-19.

Since the $100,000 contract amount is one-tenth the size of a regular cash market trade, the dollar value of a 1/32nd price fluctuation is comparably less, $31.25 ($100,000 × .01 × 1/32). The value of the 8/32 gain in the June 1980 contract on Oct. 3, 1978, for example, is $250, or the increase in principal from $90,125 (90-04) to $90,374 (90-12). This gain in price was the equivalent of a .039% decline in yield from 9.395% to 9.356%.

Whereas the spread between the successive T-bill and commercial paper contracts is expressed in terms of basis points, for the Treasury bond and Ginnie Mae futures the spreads are measured on a price basis in 32nds or as yields to .001%. In the Oct. 3, 1978, listing, the spread between the nearby and most distant delivery months was 30/32 (December 1978 91-01 vs. June 1981 90-03) or .146% (9.400% – 9.254%).

Table 2-5.   Chicago Board of Trade Ginnie Mae contract prices Oct. 3, 1978.

GNMA 8% (CBT)—$100,000 prncpl; pts.; 32nds of 100%

	Open	High	Low	Close	Net Chg.	Yield Close	Yield Chg.
Oct	.....	.....	.....	91-05s	+ 7-32ds	9.234	− .034
Nov	.....	.....	.....	91-03s	+ 8-32ds	9.244	− .049
Dec	90-27	91-04	90-27	91-01s	+ 8-32ds	9.254	− .034
Mar79	90-21	90-31	90-21	90-28s	+ 8-32ds	9.278	− .029
June	90-20	90-27	90-20	90-25s	+ 6-32ds	9.292	− .030
Sept	90-18	90-23	90-18	90-21s	+ 4-32ds	9.312	− .019
Dec	90-16	90-21	90-16	90-20s	+ 8-32ds	9.317	− .039
Mar80	90-08	90-17	90-08	90-14s	+ 7-32ds	9.346	− .034
June	90-08	90-14	90-08	90-12s	+ 8-32ds	9.356	− .039
Sept	90-05	90-12	90-05	90-12s	+ 9-32ds	9.356	− .044
Dec	90-06	90-08	90-05	90-08s	+10-32ds	9.375	− .049
Mar81	90-04	90-06	90-01	90-06s	+ 9-32ds	9.385	− .044
June	90-01	90-04	90-01	90-03s	+ 8-32ds	9.400	− .039

Sales Mor..: 2,493 contracts.

U.S. TREASURY BILLS (IMM)—$1 mil.; pts. of 100%

Dec	91.70	91.77	91.70	91.72	+ .04	8.28	− .04

Source: *The Wall Street Journal*

The original Ginnie Mae contract established in 1975 did not provide for the delivery of actual securities. In their place, good delivery consisted of the transfer of a Collateralized Depository Receipt (CDR) which certified that $100,000 principal amount Ginnie Mae 8s or their equivalent had been placed in safekeeping at a commercial bank designated by the Chicago Board of Trade as an approved depository. For delivery purposes, these receipts are accepted as validated evidence of ownership of the Ginnie Maes held in deposit.

A second Ginnie Mae contract, introduced in September 1978, dispenses with the CDR and stipulates the direct delivery of the securities themselves. This direct-delivery contract was deemed to be more suited to the needs of mortgage bankers and other originators who, unlike most futures market participants, have occasion to deliver actual pass-through certificates in the normal course of their business.

A second distinguishing feature of the certificate delivery contract is its modified par cap provision, which restricts the securities which may be delivered to those bearing coupons at or below the stated rate on Ginnie Maes currently being originated. This limitation prevents delivery of premium certificates with stated rates higher than their current yield, which due

to the likelihood of their early prepayment and resulting lower equivalent yield, make them less desirable to the recipient than securities bearing lower current coupons.[7]

The Board of Trade's action in creating this modification of the original contract was in large part a
response to the creation by the American Stock Exchange of its own interest rate futures market, the
American Commodity Exchange, and the trading of a
similar Ginnie Mae direct-delivery instrument as its
first futures contract.

---

[7]See Chapter 5, Pages 148-151 for a discussion of the principal methods
of calculating yield and their consequent effect on market price.

Chapter Three
The Membership

In contrast to the dispersed dealer markets for government securities, Ginnie Mae pass-throughs and commercial paper, trading in the futures contracts for these financial instruments is the exclusive prerogative of the members of the exchanges where they are listed. Members of the Board of Trade or IMM perform one of two basic functions in the trading pit. They either execute customer orders, collecting commissions for the service, or trade for their own or their firms' account and risk. In either role, they "make the market" for a particular contract. To understand more fully the composition and operation of that market, it is useful to examine the objectives and techniques of each of the several categories of floor members.

Members who act as agents for outside customers are designated "commission brokers," while those who trade for themselves are known as the "locals." The latter are in turn subgrouped into "scalpers," day traders and position traders. A fourth type of local, the spreader, will be discussed in a later chapter devoted to that particular trading technique. These labels are neither hard and fast nor mutually exclusive, but they are helpful in identifying the different attitudes with which professional traders approach the market.

The Scalpers

Scalpers are so named because they seek to clip the minimum fluctuations, or "ticks," from the second-by-second price changes that occur with the flow of buy and sell orders into the pit. The rationale of such tactics is that a price tends to return to its previous level after a purchase order momentarily has raised it or a sale depressed it. The scalper is prepared to accommodate a seller, for instance, by taking the buy side one or two ticks—1/32nd or 2/32nds in Ginnie Mae or Treasury bond futures—below the last sale with the intent of taking his $31.25-$62.50 profit per contract when the next incoming buy order lifts the price back to the prior point. Scalpers in the T-bill and commercial paper pits will sell on a one basis-point "uptick" in anticipation of the price dropping after the momentary boost from a buy order abates. Such round turns are normally made within moments of the time the positions are initiated. By endeavoring to profit by the smallest price fluctuations, scalpers are constantly in the market as both buyers and sellers. In so doing, they contribute to the liquidity of the market, allowing other brokers to fill their orders quickly at small price concessions from the previous sale. In that respect, the role of the scalper resembles that of a stock exchange specialist, with the distinction that his trading decisions are prompted solely by the pursuit of personal profit rather than from any obligation to maintain an orderly market.

A scalper's trading cards typically record numerous transactions by the end of the day's session, many closed out at a loss. Since his basic trading technique is to take the opposite side of orders that originate off the floor with the expectation that the market will return to its previous equilibrium after they are executed, he cannot hesitate to liquidate his position as soon as the market shows signs of moving against him (down when he is long, up when he is short) to a new equilibrium position. The scalper adds market liquidity regardless of whether he closes his contracts out at a profit or loss. He will not be in any condition to provide much liquidity, however, if he should sustain too many losses.

Although the scalper's trading tactics are geared more to technical floor activity than to the direction of the market, his buy and sell decisions do take the prevailing trend into account. In a somewhat stable market environment, such as when T-bill futures move within a narrow range of, say, 92.32 to 92.34 during the course of the day's session, he will tend to be indifferent as to whether he buys at 92.32 or sells at 92.34. But if the market starts to probe upward toward 92.38, say, there begins to be a greater degree of risk implicit in a short than in a long position, prompting him to make more trades on the buy side. Conversely, should the market turn lower to test the 92.30 level, his sales would outnumber his purchases. To the extent that a scalper trades on balance with the market's prevailing trend, he tends to accentuate price movement. On the other hand, his frequent intervention on both sides of the market smooth what otherwise would be erratic fluctuations caused by large orders depressing or forcing the market inordinately higher to attract a member willing to assume the other side of the trade.

As will be discussed in a later chapter, a certain type of scalper known as a spreader seeks to exploit minute changes in the price differences between various delivery months of the same contract. During periods of extreme activity, an alert trader may observe the same delivery month being bid and offered at different prices on opposite sides of the pit, and capture an immediate profit by accepting both simultaneously.

Whatever his individual technique, the scalper's profits are derived from his net gain on as many as 1,000 transactions during the trading session. The fact that he is able to complete these rapid turns without paying floor brokerage makes it worthwhile for him to trade for minimum increments, whereas an outside customer who must pay commissions would not find such a strategy profitable.

The Day Traders

The day trader differs from the scalper in a matter of degree. He is likely to carry a larger position for a longer period with the expectation of capturing a wider price swing. Whereas the scalper is likely to close out a position within a matter of minutes, the day trader focuses on intra-day price changes, in most instances offsetting his contracts before the session's close. In the case of Ginnie Mae and Treasury bond futures, a daily fluctuation may range between 3/32nds and a maximum move of 24/32nds per contract, or $93.75 to $750. In the absence of pronounced Federal Reserve open market operations, daily movements of the short term interest rate contracts—Treasury bills and commercial paper—are usually less volatile, normally from three to 12 basis points, or $75 to $300 per contract.

Like the scalpers, day traders have their favored techniques. Some trade with the trend of the market, while others go against the tide. Much of their activity is predicated on their anticipation of the orders that commission brokers supposedly are about to execute. If they foresee an influx into the pit of outside orders to sell from customers of the commission firms, they may buy into this selling on a "scale down" (i.e. at predetermined intervals) as prices decline, with the intention of reversing their actions to sell on a "scale up" after the selling pressures subside and the market recovers. In carrying out such contramarket tactics, the day traders are not so much striving to reach specific price objectives as they are reacting to orders which they observe coming into the pit.

Some day traders who sense that an intermediate price move is in the making will position themselves to go with that particular trend. Their decision to buy or sell may be predicated upon what they see and hear in the pit—their assessment of other brokers' intentions—outside news affecting the cash market, or most likely a combination of the two. Others believe that the market habitually overreacts to such forces, and try to move with the inevitable readjustment. Traders themselves have difficulty in articulating their precise reasons for a particular market decision because much of what they do is an instinctive reaction to a combination of circumstances suggestive of past experience. Whether they tend to trade with or against the prevailing trend, successful day traders, like scalpers, are quick to acknowledge that the market is moving contrary to their expectations and close out losing positions without any hesitation. What was taken to be a technical rally or retraction might have been in retrospect the first leg of a major trend. Or an anticipated intra-day move of, say, 9/32nds of a point might fade after a flurry of 3/32nds. In either case, the day trader's strongest asset is the discipline to recognize that he is on the wrong side of the market and take his losses before they grow to damaging proportions. Such self-control and objectivity are prerequisites for all who aspire to success in futures trading, not only those who operate in the pit. Since the day trader works within a briefer time span and closer price tolerances than most outside customers, he must be more sensitive to price changes which exceed his acceptable limits and be quicker in taking the appropriate measures to protect himself.

If, from observing prior bids and offers, a day trader thinks that a commission house broker is holding an order to buy, say, 100 June Treasury bond contracts at 93-16, he will feel fairly confident about buying several contracts at 93-17 or 93-18. His reasoning is that the commission order, if it becomes effective, will not only provide a temporary floor just below his purchase price, but may also stimulate additional buy orders which could drive the price up to 93-24, for example, where he could sell his position for a profit of six points or $187.50 per contract. The reverse procedure would be indicated when a large order to sell is overhanging the market. If 100 December T-bill contracts were offered at 92.60 while the market was trading at 91.56, an order to sell at 91.58 would be well situated since the presence of the 100-contract order would most likely serve to depress the market long enough for a day trader to cover his short contracts at a reasonable profit.

Outside traders often complain that the locals buy or sell for the sole purpose of triggering protective stop orders, enabling them to establish positions of their own at momentarily depressed or inflated prices for a fast profit when the market returns to its earlier level.[1] The locals stoutly maintain that this sort of financial tug of war is a positive by-product of a free market place, and that no one is compelled to play the game.

Whatever their preferred tactics, day traders seldom carry positions overnight. Their customary practice is to walk onto the floor in the morning with no position and to clear their books by the close of the session. Unlike the scalpers, who generally remain in one pit trading the same or related contracts, such as 90-day and one-year T-bill futures, day traders tend to gravitate to the market where they can find their particular type of action. As one local puts it, "We could be trading hubcaps in there. It's all a matter of price."

The Position Traders

The position trader is the third category of floor member who usually works on his own behalf. Whereas the scalper's and day trader's operations are

---

[1] See Chapter Four for a discussion of the nature and uses of stop orders.

timed in seconds and hours, his holding period typically runs into days or even weeks. While the former
two are essentially technicians who seek to capture
the one or several "ticks" resulting from the continuous interplay between buy and sell orders, the position
trader sets his sights on more extended price moves
that reflect basic shifts of supply or demand in the cash
securities markets. These may range from 40 to 200
basis points for T-bill and commercial paper futures,
or between 24/32nds and four percentage points in the
case of the Ginnie Mae and Treasury bond contracts.

Like the other locals, position traders do not lock
themselves into one plan or technique. They may on
occasion behave like day traders, moving in and out
of the market during one session, and at times let their
positions remain undisturbed for prolonged periods.
They may trade with the trend of the market or
against it. They may elect to add to a position or cut
it back, adjusting to developments which alter their
initial assumptions.

Position traders have been known to accumulate
holdings totaling hundreds of contracts. They are as
a rule indifferent regarding the side of the market they
take, guided in their decision to buy or sell by their
assessment of the numerous factors which influence
the trend of interest rates. A discussion of these yield
determinants is reserved for Part Two, since this type
of trading more closely resembles the longer-range activity of outside speculators than the minute-by-min-
ute maneuvering of the other locals.

It should be noted that floor traders pay a substantial fee in terms of their membership cost for
whatever advantages they may derive from their physical presence in the pits. Outside traders who begrudge
the locals their ability to capitalize on small price
changes would find the market substantially less liquid and efficient without the activity of the floor members.

Exchange Memberships

The introduction of interest rate contracts led to the creation of new classes of memberships on both Chicago futures exchanges. Insofar as the successful launching of any new contract depends in large part on the number of floor brokers who will actively trade it, the exchange decided that the best way to get the interest rate contracts off to a running start was to offer prospective traders an inducement to participate in the incipient market.

The membership committee of the Chicago Board of Trade reasoned that individuals with backgrounds in fixed-income securities or other financial areas were the logical prospects to form a "new breed" of members who would trade what was at that time an unprecedented and untested Ginnie Mae contract. It was hoped that by offering special memberships with trading privileges limited to that one contract at a price substantially below the going cost of a full Board of Trade membership, a sufficient member of venturesome souls would be attracted to form a nucleus around which the new market could be built. After an initial period of uncertainty, the experiment proved successful. Ginnie Mae futures demonstrated the fastest growth in terms of volume of any newly introduced contract, and the value of the original Financial Instrument Membership increased three-fold within three years.

A similar method was employed to promote trading interest in the Treasury bond and commercial paper contracts when they were introduced in 1977. The exchange offered 50 special permits for each of the two new contracts, with which the holder was entitled to trade for himself or for customers that one contract, and to apply the initial fee against the cost of a Financial Instrument Membership by making additional payments over several years. Through this arrangement, the Board of Trade offered aspiring floor members an opportunity to establish a business and develop their trading skills, gaining in return the fresh blood it sought to help build volume and liquidity in the new markets. The existing membership also was encouraged to try their hands at trading the new contracts.

The Chicago Mercantile Exchange had its International Monetary Market division already in place for several years when the 90-day T-bill contract was introduced in January 1976. As was occurring at the Board of Trade, the IMM attracted a fresh crop of traders who had no prior involvement with the CME's traditional contracts. Here also, the new entrants were permitted to participate in the interest rate futures market through an IMM membership at a cost considerably less than the going price for a full seat on the CME.

The Brokers

Full memberships on either exchange, an IMM seat or a Board of Trade Financial Instrument Membership all entitle their holders to deal in the interest rate contracts traded in that particular market for their individual accounts and risk, and as agents for non-member customers. Since the simultaneous performance of these separate functions is liable to give rise to conflicts of interest (no pun intended), members tend to specialize either in trading for personal gain or executing customer orders for commissions. Although the terms "trader" and "broker" are used interchangeably in referring to floor members, the former is usually applied to the locals discussed on preceding pages of this chapter, while "floor broker" or "commission broker" generally denotes a member acting on behalf of another party. It occasionally happens that a floor trader will hand orders to a floor broker for execution even though he is fully capable of making the trades for himself in an effort to mask his intentions from the other traders in the pit.

Floor brokers themselves fit into one of several categories. They may be officers or employees of a national commission house, executing customer orders transmitted to the trading floor by telephone or a private wire network. Their employer may be a large commercial user such as a bank or government securities dealer whose operations in the futures market are of a sufficient scale to warrant its own membership. Or they may be independent contractors, known as $2 brokers, who execute orders for other members to hide their origin or who act for commission firms that do not have a full-time broker on the floor or whose people are unable to handle a particularly heavy order inflow. Some of the larger commission firms may employ several floor members on the more active exchanges, but may still find it expeditious to pass some orders on to $2 brokers for swift execution during busy trading sessions. The label is a carry-over from the time such members received a commission of $2 per contract for this service.

While the scalper or day trader is concerned with choosing the best moment to buy or sell to secure a profit for himself on the long or short side, the floor broker is obliged to carry out someone else's instructions. The customer and his account representative, perhaps after consultation with the floor broker regarding the current situation in the pit, usually make the decision to buy or sell and either give their floor man an order to execute at a specific price or allow him a certain leeway within which he will try to fill the order most advantageously for the customer.

From the standpoint of the mechanics of trading, the floor broker's task resembles that of the scalper. The two have analogous perspectives which often put them on opposite sides of a transaction. Both are concerned with the immediate action in the pit rather than with an assessment of the long-term outlook for interest rates or the formulation of a complex strategy. These determinations already have been made elsewhere. The floor broker's responsibility is to advise the decision makers of the feasibility of their plan in light of current market conditions, and then to implement the agreed-upon strategy by the skillful execution of their instructions.

Like the behavior of the locals, the floor broker's conduct in the pit is conditioned by his experience in handling similar orders under comparable market conditions. If the order desk at his firm's head office calls an order in to sell 40 September T-bill contracts at 92.85 with five basis points discretion, he has the leeway to offer the contracts as low as 92.80 should he deem it necessary to make the sale promptly. If the current bid for the September contract is 92.82, the broker must promptly decide whether to offer all 40 contracts to the pit at that price, or perhaps "hit the bid" with five contracts and hold back on the remaining 35 if he sees the possibility of incoming buy orders bidding September to 92.85 or higher. If the new buying does not materialize, he runs the risk of selling the balance of his order at 92.80 or, worse yet, having the price fall below his cut-off level if another large sell order should reach the pit at that moment.

In deciding whether to execute an order at the last price, bid up to complete a buy order, or offer down for a sell order, a floor broker must make some educated guesses about the intentions of the other traders in the pit while at the same time attempting to veil his own purpose. As a consequence, the action tends to become hotly competitive, with each member attempting to outguess and outmaneuver the others in the crowd within the limits of the accepted rules. To compete successfully, each floor member must plan the arrangement of his "deck" of orders with his estimate of the orders held by other brokers in mind, and exercise great agility in executing them when various trigger prices are reached. While a local's trading profits are determined by his ability to make timely purchases and sales, a floor broker's commission income varies with the volume of orders he is able to execute. Over the long run, however, the volume will hinge upon his skill in filling orders at prices advantageous to his customers' interests.

This continuous vying for price advantage redounds to the benefit of everyone who participates in the market, whether as a hedger or speculator. Contrary to uninformed criticism of the floor trader's role, the seemingly unreasoned tumult in the pit is the source of the accessibility, liquidity and supply-demand sensitivity necessary to any viable market. This view is not a paean to the heroic floor trader, who is well-paid for what he does, but simply an acknowledgement that the alternative is the erratic and arbitrary price changes from trade to trade which are characteristic of defective markets.

The Commission Merchants

The links between the members on the exchange floor and the public customers are the so-called commission merchants, the futures counterparts of securities broker-dealers. Many firms are active in both markets. Futures commission merchants (FCMs) are not necessarily exchange members, though most of the larger ones do hold memberships on the major commodity exchanges so they can keep the full brokerage commission. The national firms usually employ one or more floor brokers on each exchange to handle their customers' orders exclusively. Some smaller firms establish correspondent relationships with independent members or have their orders executed by a $2 broker. Non-member FCMs must place their orders through an exchange member, most likely the firm with which it has a clearing arrangement.

All firms that solicit and transact futures business with the public must register with the Commodity Futures Trading Commission, the federal regulatory agency. The CFTC defines futures commission merchants as ". . . individuals, associations, partnerships, corporations and trusts engaged in soliciting or in accepting orders for the purchase or sale of any commodity for future delivery on or subject to the rules of any contract market (exchange) and that, in or in connection with such solicitation or acceptance of such orders, accepts any money, securities, or property (or extends credit in lieu thereof) to margin, guarantee, or secure any trades or contracts that result or may result therefrom."

As the individual exchange members are themselves a varied lot, the 330 or so firms registered with the CFTC as FCMs differ in size, composition and thrust of their business. They range from the commodity divisions of the largest international investment firms such as Merrill Lynch or Paine Webber which employ thousands of account representatives situated in hundreds of branch offices, to one-person proprietorships. The big firms do the most futures business. Until recent years, the commodity departments of the big, diversified firms were relegated to "stepchild" status behind the basic securities business. But mushrooming futures volume, in contrast with the lackluster performance of the equity market, coupled with fully negotiable stock exchange commissions, have won the commodity operations new stature as strong profit centers in their own right.

Such other commission houses as Hennessy & Associates and Stotler & Co. are exclusively futures-oriented, but do some cash commodity business in conjunction with their futures market activity. Cargill Investor Services, the brokerage subsidiary of the giant grain trading firm, utilizes for public customer business the exchange memberships purchased in the first instance to service the hedging needs of the parent company. Though the bulk of these commission

firms' business is still derived from the staple commodities, such as grains and livestock, several of them
have developed expertise in the financial instruments
sector which rivals that of the better-known securities
firms.

In addition, there are a number of FCM firms that
do relatively little outside customer business. They
exist primarily to handle and clear the transactions of
their member partners, who either trade on their own
behalf or act as $2 brokers for other FCMs.

The minimum financial requirements to become
registered as a FCM are less than the cost of a full
membership on the Board of Trade or IMM. As such,
they permit relative ease of entry into the business. A
non-member FCM must deal through an exchange
member to gain access to the trading floor, however,
and in so doing must adhere to the rules of conduct set
forth by the exchanges as well as CFTC regulations.

Like the brokers who execute customer orders on
the exchange floor, the commission firm's revenues are
a function of its trading volume. That is determined
in turn by the number of customer accounts the firm
carries, and ultimately its success in helping its clients
achieve profits in the futures market. To solicit customer accounts and to service them after they are
opened, the larger commission houses employ sizeable
sales forces of account representatives[2] who must
themselves possess an adequate knowledge of the futures markets and be registered with the CFTC. At
some firms account representatives handle security
and commodity accounts, while at other houses the two
functions are divided between separate departments,
each with its own personnel. As a general rule, a pro-

---

[2]The CFTC designates these representatives as associated persons.
Their titles at their respective firms are, variously: account executive, registered commodity representative, investment executive, customers' man
or commodity solicitor. Whatever their title, they work and are compensated as salesmen.

spective trader is better off dealing with a representative who specializes in the market in which he proposes to become involved.

Inasmuch as account representatives are themselves compensated in relation to the commissions
which their customers generate, they have a direct
monetary incentive to expand their client base and
assist their customers to trade profitably. Salesmen
who place their customers' interest second to commission activity in the account—known as "churning"—
are not likely to remain with a reputable firm for any
length of time. They invariably drift to the fringe operations which manage to dupe unknowledgeable individuals until they are caught overstepping the rules
drafted to protect customers and are closed down by
the CFTC. Legal action is usually too late to help vic-
timized customers retrieve losses, however. It is the
prospective customer's responsibility to investigate
thoroughly any individual or firm with which he may
consider dealing before signing any papers or handing
over any money.

The Client-Account Executive Relationship

The most conscientious of the responsible customer representatives employed by the majority of
firms must consider the capability of prospective
clients to bear the high degree of risk which speculative futures trading invariably entails. The best account executives probably turn away more new accounts than they accept, either due to the would-be
trader's lack of sufficient risk capital, or because the
representative feels the prospect might have difficulty
dealing with the fast and often erratic pace of the market and the numerous losses he will most likely be
required to absorb.

On his part, the client not only must be certain of
his account executive's integrity and competence, but

it is essential that a working rapport be developed that allows them to reach objective decisions together in what is often a stress situation. This relationship is likely to evolve over time, fortified by trading profits and tested by losses, but an individual about to enter the market for the first time should interview a number of account persons at several firms before selecting the one with whom he or she can easily communicate and feel comfortable about entrusting with his or her money.

The commission houses not only support the efforts of their representatives to screen prospective accounts, but may, to avoid future problems and comply with CFTC or exchange regulations, require elaborate documentation to ensure that they do so. The most exacting firms ask new customers to demonstrate a substantial net worth and to attest that a certain percentage of that total is true risk capital, meaning that they are reconciled to its complete loss should the worst possible result occur.

Even so, federal regulations require that new customers read and return a signed caution letter confirming their recognition of the risks of futures trading and agreeing to submit any disputes concerning the handling of their accounts to the arbitration procedures of the exchange where the contested transactions took place. Most misunderstandings of this nature arise from an imperfect understanding between representative and client of what they are attempting to accomplish (objective) and what their reaction will be in the event the market should turn against them by a predetermined amount (loss limit).

Financial institutions and other corporations that open commodity accounts to trade interest rate futures are presumably doing so not to speculate but to reduce certain kinds of financial risk, which is hedging. Moreover, the investment and financial officers who make the trading decisions on the customer side are supposedly every bit as knowledgeable and experienced in the ways of the market as are the brokers. Nevertheless, since the use of futures is a new departure for many of these companies, they too are apprised of the high risk factor.

As a deterrent to improper trading, the CFTC requires FCMs to obtain documentation from a corporate officer, in most instances the secretary or treasurer, that the corporation is empowered by its directors or stockholders, or by its charter, to engage in futures trading, and that employees authorized to buy and sell futures for the corporation's accounts are supervised at a higher level. A resolution to this effect passed by the board of directors may be required. Another document attests that all purchases and sales ordered in the corporation's name are in fact hedging transactions and not made for speculative purposes. Certain regulated institutions, notably national banks and federally chartered savings and loan associations, are subject to more comprehensive rules and controls to prevent speculative trading.

Brokerage firms perform three basic services for their individual and commercial accounts in return for commission compensation: research, executions and record-keeping. The account representative, as the firm's point of contact with the customer, is supported by specialists (and computers) in these areas.

Phil Plunger and Dan Decimal

A transaction normally begins with a discussion between the customer, whom we shall irreverently christen Phil Plunger, and his account executive, Dan Decimal. Plunger has watched the steady rise of short-term interest rates and believes they are approaching their peak for the year. He phones Decimal to inquire whether he and his firm, Stable & Co., have any current recommendations in the interest rate futures market. Decimal notes that 90-day Treasury bills were sold with an 8.25 discount at that week's auction, and that he shares Plunger's opinion that the yield on 90-day T-bills will not exceed the record high of 9% reached during the "credit crunch" of 1974. He allows as how this might be the time to buy T-bill futures, but reserves a definite recommendation until checking with his firm's research department.

Decimal calls his customer back a short time later and gives him the following report: Stable & Co.'s interest rate futures analyst also thinks that short-term interest rates are about to turn down. He bases his opinion on the probability of an economic slowdown during the first quarter of the coming year, easing of the country's 8% inflation rate and an anticipated recovery of the U.S. dollar in world foreign exchange markets. He cautions Decimal to advise his client, however, that the major New York City banks are expected to increase their prime rate to 10% and the Federal Reserve Bank likely will lift federal funds to 9% within the week in a further attempt to contain inflation. Both these measures could force money market rates, including those of 90-day Treasury bills, somewhat higher during the next several days, so the analyst says he would not be in a hurry to buy futures.

Decimal also has spoken with the firm's chartist regarding the technical outlook for T-bills. He too feels that there is further room for downward action on the 90-day bill contracts. His opinion is that the September contract, then priced at about 91.30, will shortly test a major support level at 91.15. The chartist would be a buyer if the contract drops to that price, and would then hold it for a near-term rally to 91.55.

Decimal points out to Plunger that an index price of 91.15 for the September contract would mean a discount of 8.85 for 90-day bills issued on the delivery date. If they are correct in believing that the discount for cash bills will not go above 8.75, 91.15 is in fact an attractive buying point. Plunger asks if he has sufficient margin in his account to buy two contracts. Decimal checks his daily computer print-out and replies that there are enough funds to cover the $1,000 requirement for each contract. Plunger instructs him to make the trade if he can buy two September contracts at 91.15, with the understanding that his potential loss, exclusive of commissions, is limited to $1,000. Decimal agrees to do so by placing a stop-loss order 20 basis points under their entry price if the contracts can be bought at 91.15.

These conversations took place on Monday. The following day September T-bills rose five basis points on the strength of reports that the Federal Reserve was buying government securities for foreign central banks. Plunger calls to say that they should not have waited for a lower price and that he does not want the market to get away from them. What does Decimal advise? The broker counsels patience, urging Plunger to stick to their original plan. Sure enough, by Wednesday there was clear evidence that the Fed had tightened the funds rate another notch, waiting until it hit 9⅛% before moving to provide member banks with reserves. Along with the other delivery months, September futures sell off sharply at the close, ending the day at a settlement price of 91.20. Decimal tells Plunger he is confident that they will see their price on the market opening the following morning. Plunger tells him to go ahead and enter an order before the opening bell. Decimal writes the following order up for transmission to the IMM over Stable & Co.'s leased teletype wire the next morning:

Buy 2 Sept. T-bills   92.15
P. Plunger 852-95072   5469

The 852-series is Plunger's account number, and 5469 Decimal's broker designation.

At the same time that Plunger's order is being wired to Chicago, the Department of Commerce announces that the Consumer Price Index rose by .8% in the previous month, indicating another increase in the inflation rate rather than the hoped-for reduction. Fu-

tures are offered down across the board on the supposition that interest rates will not decline as long as
inflation threatens to run into double digits. As his
runner hands the order to Stable's floor broker, September T-bills are being offered in the pit at 91.12,
down eight basis points from the previous day's close
and three below Plunger's bid. Without any hesitation,
the floor broker bids 91.12 for two September contracts
and the trade is made. The report is wired back to
Decimal's office. When he phones Plunger to tell him
that they were able to buy the contracts for three
points less than their agreed price, his client begins to
have second thoughts. Did they do the right thing? In
view of the CPI report should they have waited for a
still lower price before buying? Now that the 91.15
support level mentioned by the chartist has been violated, will the locals in Chicago drive the price down
to trigger his stop-loss order? Should he tell Decimal
to lower the stop? But where will the price stop falling?

While Plunger agonizes over these questions that
night, the IMM clearinghouse processes his trade with
all others made in the T-bill futures market that day.
Stable & Co.'s operations department computer prints
the details of the transactions onto a trade confirmation notice for mailing that night. Decimal knows that
Plunger will be on the phone at 9:05 the next morning.
What will he tell him? The game goes on.

Chapter Four

The Mechanics and Arithmetic of Trading

Having introduced the characters at Stable and Co., the cast will be retained to illustrate the operational aspects of maintaining a commodity account and trading futures.

Inasmuch as the average investor is more familiar with securities than with futures contracts, a brief review of the principal differences between them is a useful point of departure. The most obvious contrast stems from the limited life of a contract. A buyer of 100 shares of stock makes an investment that is theoretically open-ended, or at least continues until the issuing corporation is dissolved or is absorbed by another company whose shares are offered in exchange. If a government or corporate bond bears a 30-year maturity and is not callable sooner, it is possible to retain the same instrument for that length of time if the holder so chooses.

The life of a futures contract extends from the day it is first traded to its delivery date, a period initially spanning 24 to 36 months in the interest rate group. Since an expiring contract is normally replaced by a new one at the distant end of the delivery series, a trader usually may choose among eight to ten contracts with remaining lives ranging from several weeks to several years. The delivery date of any contract marks its absolute termination. To retain a long or short position in any contract beyond its expiration date, it is necessary to "roll it over" by liquidating the position and re-establishing it in a later delivery month. The longer a trader remains long or short a particular contract, the closer he comes to the "spot" or "cash" month and the obligation to make or accept delivery of the specified securities. He may elect either to close his position with a liquidating transaction or to go through with the delivery procedure; he does not have his stock market counterpart's alternative of "putting it away and forgetting about it." A futures trader cannot behave like an ostrich even when he fervently wishes he might.

Carrying on with the Phil Plunger saga, our protagonist has precisely until the third week of September to make a profit or realize a loss on his two T-bill contracts. His hope is that at some point between the time he established his long position and the contract's delivery day, the market's projection of the 90-day T-bill rate as of the latter date will fall sufficiently below a 8.88 discount to allow him to take a substantial gain on the contracts he bought at a 91.12 index price. Since he has no intention, or the capital for that matter, of putting up approximately $2 million in the event the bills are delivered to him, his remaining alternative would be to sell his contracts at a loss before delivery day. In either event, it is more than likely that he will close his position out long before September and may even trade in and out of that contract or others several more times by then.

Margins and Commissions

Another major difference between securities and futures trading lies in the nature and extent of the required margin deposit. An investor can buy 100 shares of General Motors at a price, say, of 60 and pay the entire $6,000 plus commissions. Or he may buy the 100 GM on margin, putting up perhaps $4,500 of his own money and having his broker advance him the $1,500 balance, on which he will pay a monthly interest charge.

All futures market transactions are made on margin. Neither Phil Plunger nor anyone else is expected to put up the $2 million or so full value of two T-bill contracts or $500,000 for five Ginnie Mae contracts. Unlike the $4,500 margin[1] on the purchase of 100 GM or any other shares, futures margin is not a partial payment against the full contract value. Rather, it is required by the exchanges and their members as a good faith deposit or performance bond to ensure that both parties to a contract make good any losses which result from their long or short positions. The system of daily margin settlement is the exchanges' principal means of guaranteeing the integrity of the contract, since each price change represents an equivalent profit and loss to the buyer and seller whether the price rises or falls.

The margin established by the IMM for 90-day bill futures at the time Plunger took a long position was $1,000 per contract. When he asked his account executive whether there were sufficient funds in his account to buy two contracts, he was referring to an excess credit of $2,000. If the excess was not in his account at the time he traded, he would have received a $2,000 margin call the following day. There is no debit balance as such in a commodity account, and therefore no interest charges.

Commissions on futures transactions are charged on a "round turn" basis—that is, both purchase and sale of a contract, or sale first and purchase later in the case of "going short." They are fixed-dollar amounts charged to the account when a position is

---

[1]The 75% margin is selected arbitrarily for illustrative purposes. The actual rate is set by the Federal Reserve Board through its authority under Regulation T of the Securities Act.

closed out. Positions that are taken and closed out the same day, and spreads in which a trader buys and sells different delivery months of the same contract have reduced margin and commission rates. Minimum commission rates, until recently set by the exchanges, have given way to the same type of negotiated discounts that have become the practice in the securities market.

Short Sales and Fluctuation Limits

Short sales of futures contracts are more common and easier to make than of securities. A vestige of 1930s New Deal legislation to rid the stock market of such manipulatory practices as pools and bear raids is the requirement that a short sale of stock be made on an "uptick," or a price at least ⅛ point higher than the prior different price. There is no such restriction in the futures market. Sales to establish short positions and liquidate long ones are treated alike. The bias in the stock market is overwhelmingly on the long side. Short interest—the number of shares of stock that speculators have sold short—is usually a small percentage of the total outstanding shares. The short interest figures corroborate the fact that comparatively few investors, or speculators to term them more accurately, feel comfortable selling stock short, and fewer still do so with consistent success. It is essential that futures traders develop the facility of going long (buying) or short (selling) with equal ease.

In futures, there are an equal number of long and short positions since each contract must by definition have a buyer and seller. The relevant measure in the futures market is the open interest, which is the number of contracts in existence for each delivery month. Open interest increases when new contracts are created, and decreases as they are liquidated.

There are no specialists on a futures exchange. Floor members trading directly with one another provide the market liquidity that is one of the functions of a stock market specialist.

There are limits to the extent futures prices are allowed to rise or fall during the course of each trading session. They may not exceed a set amount above or below the prior day's final settlement price. If there are no offers when a contract is bid "up the limit," or no bidders when it is offered "down the limit," no transactions will take place until at least one buyer and seller can agree to a price within that range.

Other Details

When a company announcement or some other development causes an imbalance of buying and selling orders for a particular security, stock exchange officials will suspend trading long enough to give traders an opportunity to evaluate the price implications of the news. The market will then re-open at whatever price their reassessment determines.

Futures traders must deal with more information and contract details than most stock investors seem to concern themselves with. Whether or not it is sufficient in any given instance, stock selection is often limited to a cursory appraisal of the financial condition and earnings prospects of a particular company, and a quick comparison of the market price of its shares with the high and low points over the recent past. In addition to the mass of fundamental market data they need to absorb and weigh, futures traders should know on which exchange a particular contract is traded, hours of trading, unit size, minimum and maximum price fluctuations and commission rates, among other contract specifications.

Securities purchased at one brokerage firm can be sold without any difficulty through another house. If an investor's stocks and bonds are held by a broker in "street name," he can instruct the broker to deliver any or all of them for sale elsewhere. Or if a security is listed on more than one exchange, it need not be sold on the one where it was bought. A futures contract in most cases must be closed out at the commission house where it was initiated, and always on the same exchange. One cannot, for example, sell a Ginnie Mae contract on the Chicago Board of Trade and expect to cover it by buying a contract at the American Commodity Exchange (ACE).

Initiating the Order

Once the decision to buy or sell has been made, the immediate task is to execute it. (Lest any readers feel the decision-making process should not be passed over so readily, they may be reassured that 100 or so pages of excruciating detail on the subject await them in Part Two.) The first step in the execution phase, then, is for the customer and his account executive to agree on the type of order they will employ, and then write it in a form that can be transmitted to the exchange and which will tell the floor broker precisely what they seek to accomplish. Traders sometimes become so preoccupied with the cerebral aspects of the game such as fathoming the intentions of the Federal Reserve that they neglect the "nuts and bolts" of order writing and execution. But they soon learn that vague instructions and the resulting uncertainty between broker and client negate the best analysis. Professional—meaning careful—execution is as vital to trading success as good decision-making and is, in fact, an integral part of it.

The first two elements of a trade—whether one is buying or selling and the number of contracts—are straightforward enough. Most of the potential problems lie in the determination of price. The critical part of an order is the price the trader is bidding or offering and the conditions under which he is attempting to attain that price.

The basic order is the *market order*. It tells the

floor broker to buy or sell so many contracts of a given delivery month at the prevailing price when the order reaches the pit. It gives him no time or latitude to wait for a better price. It says, in effect, "Do it, and do it *now!*"

The use of a market order is a proper method of buying or selling 100 shares of AT&T when its price fluctuates between, say, 61⅜ and 61¾, as it might during a normal trading session. The average investor is not likely to get very excited over making $25 more or less on a transaction that involves over $6,000. When trading futures, however, it is not always the best idea to enter orders "at the market." Futures prices can move with astonishing speed during active trading. Even with instant communication with the pit and the help of a very adept floor broker, a customer who instructs his account representative to place a market order is often dismayed to learn, perhaps only two minutes later, that the order was executed at a price drastically different from what appeared on the quotation screen when it was sent. These abrupt price changes invariably seem to go counter to a trader's purpose rather than moving in his favor. Neither the trader nor his representative has any way of knowing whether a large order to buy or sell the same contract will reach the pit moments before their order arrives. By that time, it is too late for the floor man to wire back and ask, "Are you really sure you want to do this?" He already has his marching orders, and march he must, even if it is directly into an ambuscade.

Returning to our scenario, the order to buy two September T-bill contracts specified a price of 91.15. If Plunger and Decimal had instead simply entered a market order, and with incredibly bad luck (to them) the floor broker for a government securities dealer had just received an order to buy 100 September contracts or it was announced that the price of beef had declined by 4% in the prior month prompting an unexpected revision of inflation forecasts, Decimal might have had to call Plunger and tell him they paid 91.21, or an additional $150 for each contract. In percentage terms, such an execution would be comparable to placing a market order to buy 100 AT&T thinking you would pay 61½, give or take ⅛, and then discovering the shares cost you 70⅝![2] That is not a plausible situation with AT&T or most other listed stocks. But it can and often does occur in the futures market, which is the reason professional traders avoid market orders whenever possible.

Such nasty surprises are usually avoided by employing a *limit order* of the type used to buy Plunger's T-bill contracts. There, the floor broker was instructed to bid up to 91.15 and no higher. It was understood that if he could execute the order at a lower price he would do so, which is what happened in that instance since September T-bills were being offered at 91.12 at the time the order reached the pit. A limit order directs the floor broker to buy the designated contracts at or below the stipulated price or to sell them at the limit price or higher. Limit buy orders are normally entered below the prevailing market price and sell limits above it. An exception is when a trader is willing to pay the market price but wishes to protect himself against the type of runaway movement described above. He might in that instance place the limit order one or two basis points, or 32nds depending upon the contract, above the last price to assure a buy in a rising market or slightly below to get a sale off in a falling market. If the market remains unchanged during the time that the order is en route, the floor broker may be able to fill it at a better price, but he is given a certain amount of leeway in which to maneuver in the event the market suddenly begins to move.

The risk of using a limit order rather than a market order is that should the price move through it be-

---

[2]If this analogy is unclear remember that the initial margin on T-bill futures was $1,000 per contract at the time of the Plunger-Decimal example.

fore the order can be executed, the trader must sit emptyhanded and watch the market go in the direction he anticipated. If, for example, September T-bills were at 91.18 and rising by the time Plunger's order to buy contracts at 91.15 reached the pit, he would have faced the alternatives of chasing after the price by raising his limit or doing nothing and hoping it would dip back to 91.15 where the order could be executed. On the other hand, had he been a prospective seller at the 91.15 level, 91.18 would represent a better price and the order would have been executed immediately. If that had been the case, however, Plunger as a short would be losing money if the market continued to rise.

Traders who enter market orders, therefore, have the assurance that their orders will be executed, but they have little control over the price. Those who employ limit orders retain control, but run the risk of "missing the market." Given the shortcomings and relative risks of each approach, traders usually are better off using limit orders, which always can be revised if they and their account representatives decide such a move is warranted.

Time Restrictions in Orders

Orders are also limited as to the time they remain valid. Again, assume that Plunger missed the market at 91.15 and that September T-bills are trading above his price limit. How long does he wait for their price to come back down? Whatever decision he and his representative reach, it must be indicated on the order so that the floor broker is aware of the length of time it is to stay in force. They may consider the current rally a temporary flurry which is likely to subside by the end of the trading session, and choose to enter a *day order* to be executed the first time the contract trades at 91.15. If the order is not filled by the close, the order is cancelled automatically, and they must enter a new one the following morning if they still wish to buy.

But there may be a good reason to change the order while the market is still open. Suppose it has been announced that the President will hold a special press conference at 4 p.m. and there is speculation in Washington and in the market that he will announce a sharp cutback in government spending as an anti-inflation measure. Plunger strongly feels that if he is to buy, he must do it before the press conference. He therefore instructs Decimal to enter the order with a specific *time limit*, say 1 p.m., when he is prepared to raise his bid to ensure his buying the two contracts before the close of the market. He also has the option of canceling his existing order at any time and replacing it with another at a price closer to the one at which the contract is then trading.

If there is no compelling reason from a tactical standpoint to execute the order that day, it may be left in the floor broker's book as a *good through week*, or perhaps an *open order* which stays in force until the client and his account executive decide to cancel it.

Stop Orders

A type of order which is particularly important in futures trading is the *stop order*. Since it is most commonly used to limit potential loss, it also is referred to as a stop loss order, although it does have other applications. When they made the decision to buy September T-bills at 91.15, Plunger told Decimal he wished to limit his potential loss to $1,000. He meant that if and when his long position incurred a loss in that amount, the broker should liquidate the two contracts. By determining at the outset the amount of loss he was prepared to absorb, and seeing to it that the position would be closed out if that point were reached, Plunger was following the cardinal rule for survival in the futures market.

Knowing that the dollar value of a "tick," or minimum fluctuation, of a T-bill contract is $25, Plunger calculated that he would be losing $1,000, not including commissions, when the September contracts fell 20 basis points from his purchase price. (Two contracts × $25 × 20 basis points = $1,000.) If Plunger determined to hold his loss before transaction costs to $1,000, he would have to sell at 90.95, or 20 basis points below his purchase limit if the price subsequently fell to that point. At the time he entered the original buy order, then, he would also place a contingent open order to sell two September T-bill contracts at 90.95 "stop." The second order would remain inactive until a transaction took place or a contract was offered for sale at that price, at which time the open stop order would become a market order to sell, and Plunger's position immediately would be closed out. As with any regular market order, there is no assurance that it would be executed at precisely the stop price, so the $1,000 figure is not in fact a guaranteed limit. If Plunger were so unfortunate as to see the price offered "down the limit" through his stop level, he would be locked into his losing position until trading resumed at whatever price bids and offers could be matched. Though such a situation occurs only infrequently it nevertheless constitutes a major risk of futures trading.

Since Plunger actually bought his two contracts at 91.12, he could lower his stop order by three basis points and retain the 20-point spread between his purchase and stop prices. By allowing it to remain at 90.95 he would give himself the leeway of those additional three points to be taken out within his $1,000 limit, and possibly include commissions as well. On the other hand, that would bring him three points closer to being knocked out of the market on a temporary price decline. The art of setting a stop price lies in deciding how much of an adverse price move is a temporary correction, and when it becomes a reversal of a major trend.

Plunger's remaining choice would be to use a *stop limit order*. If he is not willing to accept a price lower

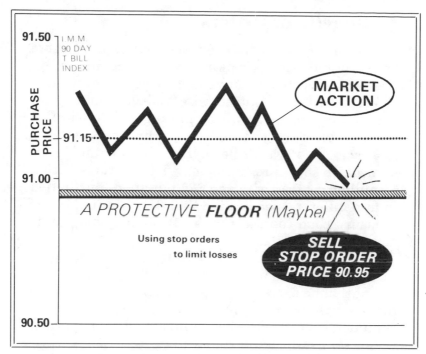

Figure 4-1. Use of Stop Order to Limit Loss.

than 90.95, he can have Decimal make the order read "Sell 2 September T-bills 90.95 stop limit open," meaning that if the stop price is reached, the floor broker will hold a regular limit order instead of a market order and may not sell the contracts for less. The disadvantage of a stop limit is again that if the market falls through the limit price before the order can be executed, there is no assurance that the price will return to the level where it can be filled. To avoid an even greater loss, it may prove necessary to cancel the existing order and enter one closer to the market.

If Plunger instead had sold two contracts at 91.15, the stop would have been placed above rather than below his entry price since a rising price means a growing loss on a short position. In that event, the stop order would become a market order to buy if and when the stop price was touched.

Arithmetic of Orders

We have stated that few speculators or hedgers have any intention of making or receiving delivery of the securities underlying the contracts they trade.[3] Nevertheless, the contract size and minimum price fluctuation are factors determining the amount of profit or loss a trader is liable to incur, and are therefore facts about which he ought to be thoroughly informed. He should regard 90-day T-bill futures with a $1 million contract size and $25 minimum fluctuation from a different perspective than the Ginnie Mae or Treasury bond contracts with $100,000 trading units and "ticks" of $31.25.

Continuing with our illustration, the trader's decision to risk $1,000 in buying two T-bill contracts meant that he fixed his stop price 20 basis points below the purchase price. If Plunger had instead bought two Ginnie Mae contracts, the arithmetic of that contract would set a stop 16/32nds away (2 × $31.25 × 16 = $1,000). On the other hand, his account executive might advise him that 16/32nds was too narrow a spread to avoid being stopped out on a normal daily price swing in the Ginnie Mae market, and that Plunger would be better off risking $1,500 by pegging his stop 24/32nds under his buy point, or else confine his purchase to one contract.

The allowable daily price limits established for each contract also have a bearing on the potential profit or loss to which a trader is subject. The purpose of the daily limit is to prevent some news item from causing a greater disruption to the market than would be the case if traders had time to consider its implications, or at least to diffuse the effects over several trading sessions. If no trades take place within the permissible range on one day, the limit is extended by

---

[3]The exception that proves the rule is the mortgage banker who settles his short positions by delivering the Ginnie Mae pass-throughs he originates.

the same amount for the following session and so on until bids and offers can be matched at a new equilibriun level.

In our model, Plunger wanted to establish his long position by the close of that day's trading in anticipation of a Presidential press conference. Suppose that his conjecture happened to be right: The President, in addition to confirming the rumors of budget reductions, surprised reporters and the television audience by announcing that in the previous month the increase in the Consumer Price Index was substantially less than had been projected, suggesting that the inflationary tide was turning. Moreover, the administration's official forecasts were being revised in line with an expectation of further improvements through the balance of the year and the one following. The interest rate futures market, along with the rest of the financial community, was taken completely by surprise. Traders who had predicated their market decisions on an assumption of an 8% inflation rate were forced to modify their thinking overnight. American securities and the dollar surged on European exchanges before the markets opened in New York and Chicago. Traders at the IMM and Board of Trade watched the cash government securities market open sharply higher, and braced themselves for an explosion of futures prices upward when their markets opened.

No such thing happened. Nothing could happen. Realizing that a reduced inflation rate would mean lower interest rates across the board, traders with long positions and those who were uncommitted at the time withdrew their offers as shorts kept increasing their bids in an effort to close out their positions, but to no avail. No one was willing to sell.

Having succeeded in buying his two T-bill contracts at 91.12 the previous day, Phil Plunger was naturally ecstatic when his account executive called shortly after the opening to inform him that "Septembers" were bid "up the limit" to 91.62. What should they do, he demanded. Dan Decimal replied that though the market could go still higher on the strength of the favorable economic news, an overnight profit of 50 basis points was in his opinion too great a windfall to pass by. Decimal pointed out that Plunger had more than doubled his margin deposit (two contracts × $25 × 50 = $2,500) and common sense dictated that at least partial profits should be taken. Other traders were reaching the same conclusion as this conversation was taking place, for after the delayed opening September T-bills had begun trading between 91.60 and 91.62. Plunger directed Decimal to enter a limit order to sell one of his long contracts at 91.60. They were too late. The market had already begun to drop. By the time Decimal and Plunger agreed to take what they could and entered a new order (not forgetting to cancel the existing one at 91.60), they managed to obtain an execution at 91.52. Even so, that represented a gain, not counting commissions, of 40 basis points or $1,000 for the one contract, exactly the margin Plunger had committed the day before.

It is easy to contrive a happy outcome when writing fiction. It must in fairness be pointed out, however, that the limit move could just as easily have gone against the trader, inflicting a severe loss. Suppose that instead of buying, Plunger had sold T-bill futures short at 91.12. Remember that he had intended to limit his loss to $1,000, which in this instance would have meant entering a buy stop order 20 basis points *above* his selling price, or 91.32. But even though the price went through his stop as it was bid up the limit, there were no sellers there who would allow him to cover his short position. When trading resumed at or below the 91.62 limit, Plunger would have been "stopped out" with a loss of approximately $2,500, or considerably more than the $1,000 he was prepared to lose. This is the type of situation which makes futures trading a speculative pursuit under the best of conditions.

To place the matter in proper perspective, however, a limit move has yet to occur in the T-bill futures market. Daily price swings of 15 to 20 basis points do occur with some regularity, and are still substantial moves in relation to the margin commitment. While infrequent, such limit moves have on occasion taken place in Treasury bond and Ginnie Mae futures trading. The daily limits of 24/32, or $750, for Ginnie Maes and one point, or $1,000, for bonds are major percentage moves, though not as extensive as the T-bill limit.

Volume and Open Interest

Next to price movement, the two most relevant measures of market activity are the daily volume and open interest. The conventional wisdom of the futures market states that increasing volume and open interest corroborate the continuation of a particular price trend.

Volume is the number of contracts traded on a given day. It is reported by delivery month and as a total of all months of a particular contract. The figure is the same for the number of purchases and sales, since each transaction has a buy side and a sell side. A trade is made either to initiate a new position or to close out an existing one. Both types are included in the volume figures irrespective of which it is. Volume generally increases as a market matures and more speculators and trade customers participate. Daily volume for the T-bill and Ginnie Mae contracts averaged about 300 contracts during their start-up months in 1975 and early 1976. Volume for each was 1,000 contracts a day by the end of their first year, and continued to increase to an average of 4,000 contracts by the beginning of 1979. Based upon their unit size, these contracts represented a daily turnover of $4 billion in

90-day T-bills and $400 million face value of Ginnie Mae 8s.

Open interest is the futures equivalent of the number of outstanding shares of a company's common stock. The difference is that open interest constantly expands and shrinks as new contracts are opened and then liquidated. When both parties to a trade are initiating new positions—that is, a new long making a contract with a new short—the open interest increases by one. If they are both liquidating, open interest diminishes by the number of contracts they trade. A transaction between a liquidating trader and one opening a new position results in no net change.

Traders who follow these statistics reason that when volume and open interest increase as prices rise, buyers are the preponderant force in the market and further strength can be expected. If volume and open interest grow larger as prices decline, the shorts are presumed to be in control and the market is considered to be technically weak. When volume and open interest shrink as prices rise or decline, the interpretation is that longs or shorts are liquidating their positions and at least a temporary change in market direction is likely.

Two Kinds of Margin

Futures traders must contend with two types of margin. *Initial margin* is the price of entry, the funds a customer must have in his account to assume a long or short position. *Maintenance margin* is the additional deposit he must make to hold a position when it goes against him. On the other hand, a trader is entitled to withdraw funds from his account if the market moves in his favor.

As stated at the outset of this chapter, initial margin is a performance bond which ensures that the trader makes his potential losses good in advance. It is not a purchase price or partial payment of the total contract value, but a means of preserving the integrity of the contract by depositing with the clearing corporation sufficient funds to pay out the profits that are due to the party on the winning side.

Initial margin is the dollar amount required to buy or sell any contract. It is determined by the exchange on which the contract is traded, and is subject to revision as the level and volatility of the contract price change. If $1,000 is adequate margin for contract X at price level P when the average daily price change is C, it will probably not be sufficient if the price level moves to 2P and daily fluctuations are on the order of 3C.

Table 4-1 lists the speculative margins in effect for the various interest rate contracts at the end of 1978. Since they are subject to frequent change, traders should consult the exchange or a member firm to verify the current figures before taking any action in the market.

In the Plunger-Decimal example, $2,000 was the initial margin required to buy two T-bill contracts. As mentioned in the previous chapter, most commission firms require that new customers make a minimum deposit of perhaps $10,000 upon opening a commodity account. If, in this case, there were no other positions carried in Plunger's account, the minimum deposit would have more than covered the transaction. If Plunger already was long or short 10 contracts of the same or some other commodity, committing the entire amount of the deposit, Decimal would call for an ad-

Table 4-1. **Speculative Hedge and Spread Margins in Effect Dec. 31, 1978.**

Exchange Minimum	Speculative	Hedge	Spread
90-Day T-bills	$ 800	$ 800	$300
One-year T-bills	600	600	400
90-Day Commercial Paper	750	600	500
Ginnie Mae	1,000	750	500
Treasury bonds	1,250	1,000	500

ditional $2,000 to cover the purchase of the two T-bill contracts.

Following through with the two contracts bought at 91.12, there would be no further problem with margin if the price immediately rose. For every basis point increase in price, the account would be credited with $50. If the account were instead long Ginnie Mae or Treasury bond futures, each contract would accrue $31.25 per 1/32nd increase.

When the position starts to go against the trader, however, his margin is eroding with every basis point or 1/32nd change. As pointed out in Chapter One, exchange clearing members must make daily deposits with the clearing corporation to cover any net deficit in their customers' positions. The customers must in turn replenish their accounts by an equivalent amount. If Plunger's two contracts were (to illustrate the point) the only September T-bill position his firm carried with the IMM clearing house, each day that the contract fell, say, five basis points, Stable & Co. as a clearing member would deposit $250 to cover that session's loss on the position. If the price went up five points, or if the customer were holding a short position, the firm would withdraw an equal amount and credit it to the customer's account.

To maintain its own standing with the other firms with which it does business and to uphold the integrity of the clearing procedure, the clearing broker must deposit the full amount of the customer's losses, whether or not they are covered in his account. The firm sees to it, therefore, that its customers do have sufficient funds on deposit by calling for additional cash when their initial margin is expended by a designated amount.

At the time of Plunger's transaction, the maintenance margin on 90-day T-bill contracts was $750; so if Plunger's long position declined in price by more than 10 basis points, he would be called for funds to bring his margin back to the $1,000 level. If September

T-bills dropped to 90.95, Decimal would call Plunger to send $850 to bring the margin on two contracts back to the required level. If the price fell further to 90.85, Plunger would have to deposit an additional $500. But since he instructed Decimal to place a stop order to sell at 90.92, the position presumably would have been liquidated before a margin call was incurred. One piece of trading wisdom says that a maintenance call should be met through liquidation rather than by fresh cash since the loss that has accrued by that time ought to be realized and the remaining capital conserved for another attempt to get on the profitable side of the market.

Not all member firms adhere to the minimum margin requirements established by the exchanges. Some may request higher margins, but for competitive reasons the majority of firms stay at or close to the exchange minimum.

A reduced schedule of margins normally is applied to the transactions of commercial customers who use futures contracts to offset market risks encountered in the course of their regular business operations. The reason is that the inherent nature of a hedging operation exposes the customer to less rather than greater market risk. In the case of the interest rate contracts, however, speculative and hedge margins have tended to remain the same.

Lower margins also are required for spread or straddle positions where an account is simultaneously long and short two or more related contracts. Again, the reduced requirements are justified on the grounds that a position of this type has less intrinsic risk than an outright long or short position.

Account Arithmetic

The foregoing examples were held to the most basic level in illustrating the principles and procedures involved in placing orders, computing profits and losses and determining margin requirements. Since futures traders often carry more than one position at any given time, it is necessary to complicate the problem somewhat by considering a typical account in its entirety.

One should first understand the distinction between *paper* profits and losses and *realized* profits and losses. The value of a futures contract changes from moment to moment as its market price moves up or down. As long as the contract(s) is carried in the trader's account these price changes result in paper profits or losses to him. The moment a particular position is closed out, however, the profit or loss becomes permanent for that particular transaction, and is said to be realized.

The aggregate paper profit in an account at a given time is the total number of contracts carried times the dollar value of a minimum fluctuation times the number of basis points or 32nds the current market is removed from the various prices—above for long positions and below for short contracts—at which the contracts originally were bought or sold. The same calculation applies to losses when the market is moving against the trader.

The paper profit on one long March Ginnie Mae contract purchased at 90-07, for example, is $2,187.50 when the market is trading at 92-13 ($1 \times 70 \times \$31.25$). Profit is incurred on a short position as the market drops below the sale price. When the market in June T-bills is 91.70, the gain on one contract sold at 92.35 is $1,625 ($1 \times 65 \times \$25$). Obviously, a loss develops on a long position when the market declines below the purchase price. If two December bond contracts were bought at 95-15, there would be a paper loss on that position of $4,437.50 when the market was at 93-08 ($2 \times 71 \times \$31.25$).

If all of those position changes occurred simultaneously in the same account, the net paper loss would

FIGURE: 4-2

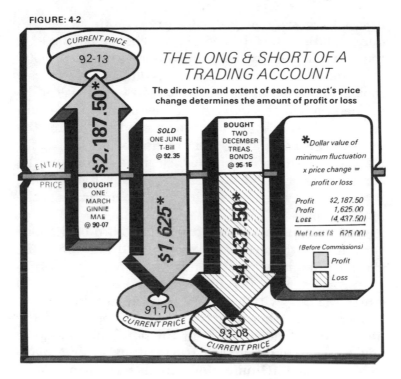

CURRENT PRICE
92-13

THE LONG & SHORT OF A TRADING ACCOUNT

The direction and extent of each contract's price change determines the amount of profit or loss

$2,187.50*

ENTRY PRICE

BOUGHT
ONE
MARCH
GINNIE
MAE
@ 90-07

SOLD
ONE JUNE
T-Bill
@ 92.35

BOUGHT
TWO
DECEMBER
TREAS.
BONDS
@ 95-16

$1,625*

$4,437.50*

*Dollar value of
minimum fluctuation
x price change =
profit or loss

Profit	$2,187.50
Profit	1,625.00
Loss	(4,437.50)
Net Loss	($ 625.00)

(Before Commissions)

☐ Profit

▨ Loss

91.70
CURRENT PRICE

93-08
CURRENT PRICE

be $625. If the short T-bill contract were covered at 91.70, the $1,625 paper profit on that position would be transformed into a realized profit, leaving a paper loss of $2,250 on the remaining Ginnie Mae and bond contracts. The obvious objective, more easily stated than accomplished, is to time purchases and sales so that realized profits are maximized and realized losses are held to a minimum.

The *equity* in an account is its total of free cash and net paper profits. It represents the dollar value of the account if all positions were closed out and commissions were deducted. Assuming a cash balance of $8,000 in the hypothetical account just described, its equity of $7,175 is arrived at by deducting the $625 net paper loss and $200 round-turn commissions on the four contracts. If, on the following day, futures prices were stronger, with March Ginnie Maes +8, June T-bills +4 and December Treasury bonds +10, the account's equity would have increased to $7,950.[4]

Equity minus the margin requirements for all contracts carried in the account is its *excess*. It can be applied toward the margin on new positions that are assumed. Excess is also a measure of the amount the market can go against the account before a call for maintenance margin is issued. Or, if he so chooses, the customer may withdraw the excess from his account, though he may have to restore it if the direction of the market turns.

Continuing with the illustration, each of the four contracts in the account—one long Ginnie Mae, one short T-bill and two long bonds—has an initial margin requirement of $1,000, creating an excess of $3,950 which could be withdrawn from the account or used to buy or sell another four contracts without requiring an additional deposit. If no further positions were added, the account could withstand an adverse move totaling $4,950 (Ginnie Maes and bonds down, T-bills up) before incurring a $1,000 maintenance call to bring equity back up to the $4,000 requirements. If equity fell by $4,500, say, and then began to increase once again, no margin call would be issued because equity remained greater than 75% of requirements.

By keeping a close watch on the condition of his account, a trader knows when he has sufficient excess to assume additional positions, or when he should liquidate some contracts to avert an impending maintenance call. By closing out a position, total requirements are reduced, either putting the account into an excess position or at least eliminating the need to meet a margin call.

---

[4]$7,175 + March Ginnie Mae $250 + Dec. T-bonds $625 − June T-bills $100 = $7,950

The extremely low initial margin requirements relative to the contract size give futures trading a large degree of risk as well as its substantial profit potential. Both are a function of high leverage, or the ability to participate in sizable price swings for a moderate cash outlay. A $1,000 initial margin is .1% of the $1 million 90-day T-bill contract size and 1% of the specified $100,000 face value for Treasury bond and Ginnie Mae futures. Consequently, a 10 basis-point move in the T-bill contract or 8/32nds for bonds and Ginnie Maes, by no means unusual fluctuations in the futures market, amount to a 25% gain or loss in relation to the initial margin. In the foregoing example, if March Ginnie Maes and December bonds were both off 6/32nds and June T-bills up five basis points—which are moderate moves in those markets—that day's net loss of $687.50 would consume nearly 10% of the account's total equity.

Account Statements

Customer account statements spare traders the effort of making such computations manually. These statements should be read carefully by the client upon receipt, and any inconsistencies immediately reported to the representative handling the account for reconciliation.

The basic notification is the *trade confirmation* mailed to the customer immediately following each transaction itemizing the number of contracts bought or sold, the particular delivery month and the price at which it was made. If an order involving several contracts is executed at different prices, the number of contracts done at each price is listed. The trade confirmation only reports price information. It does not indicate the money involved. That is reported in the *purchase and sale statement* sent out when a position is liquidated. The P&S lists the initial and closeout prices of each transaction, and subtracts (adds) the commission charge from the gross profit (loss) to arrive at a net profit or loss figure.

Open order confirmations advise the customer of the open limit and stop orders in force in his name, and give notice when they expire or are canceled on his instructions. It is the client's and his broker's joint responsibility to keep track of their open orders so that the same order is not executed twice because a previous order was not canceled. Such errors are expensive to rectify during a fast-moving market, and can easily be avoided with a modicum of care.

All transactions and money transfers into and out of the account are included in the *monthly statement.* It is headed by the ledger balance, the cash in the account carried over from the previous accounting period. The statement then itemizes all money entries such as cash deposited to or withdrawn from the account and positions liquidated at a profit (credits) or loss (debits). The net total of these entries is the current ledger balance which will be carried forward to the next statement.

The second part of the monthly statement lists all open contracts by long and short positions and the closing settlement price of each contract. The customer easily can derive the equity, margin requirements and excess from the data provided. For example, the sample statement reproduced in Figure 4-4 reflects an equity of $9,052.50 and excess of $8,052.50[5] which could be withdrawn from the account or used to buy or sell additional contracts.

More current than the statements mailed to clients are the daily computer printouts many firms provide their account representatives giving account data based upon the previous trading session's settlement prices. These time-saving aids notwithstanding, a periodic manual computation of the figures will assist the trader in monitoring and controlling his account.

---

[5]The position shown in Figure 4-4 is a Treasury bond futures spread, which entails a lower margin requirement than an outright long or short position. See Chapter 11 for a discussion of spread trading.

FIGURE 4-3

IN ACCOUNT WITH

A. M. LOOSIGIAN & CO.

Five Landmark Square
Stamford, Conn.06901

MEMORANDUM OF TRADES MADE THIS DAY FOR YOUR ACCOUNT AND RISK.

SAMPLE STATEMENT

Arthur Collins
52 Holly Lane
Westport, CT. 06880

ACCOUNT NO.

1 - 00000

| DATE | | | BOUGHT | SOLD | COMMODITY | PRICE | EXCHANGE |
MO.	DAY	YR.					
5	22	78		5	DEC T-BILLS	92.35	IMM
				5*			
					CURRENT ACCOUNT BALANCE - - SEGREGATED FUNDS		19,650.00
					SAMPLE STATEMENT		

GRAIN IN THOUSANDS OF BUSHELS; OTHER COMMODITIES IN CONTRACTS OR OTHER UNITS CUSTOMARY ON EXCHANGE WHERE EXECUTED

▼

FORM # 0210

FIGURE 4-4

NOTE	PLEASE REPORT ANY DIFFERENCES IMMEDIATELY	IN ACCOUNT WITH

A. M. LOOSIGIAN & CO.

Five Landmark Square
Stamford, Conn. 06901

	SAMPLE STATEMENT	DATE	ACCOUNT NO.
Arthur Collins	MONTHLY COMMODITY STATEMENT	July 31, 1978	1 - 00000
52 Holly Lane			
Westport, CT. 06880	ACTIVITY AND OPEN POSITIONS		

	Position				Amount	
Date	Long	Short	Commodity Description	Price	Debit	Credit
6-30-78	BALANCE FORWARD					19,650.00
7-31-78	ACCOUNT BALANCE - - SEGREGATED FUNDS - -					19,650.00
X X X X	X X X	X X X	OPEN POSITIONS X X X X X X X X X X	X OPEN POSITIONS X X	X X X X X X	
7-18-78		5 * 5*	MAR T-BONDS OPEN TRADE EQUITY	92 4/32 92 27/32	3,593.75 3,593.75	
7-18-78	5 5*	*	1MAR T-BONDS OPEN TRADE EQUITY	90 31/32		.00 .00
6-09-78	*	5 5*	DEC T-BILLS OPEN TRADE EQUITY	92.35 92.41	750.00 750.00	
			TOTAL OPEN TRADE EQUITY		4,343.75	
			TOTAL EQUITY			15,306.25
			SAMPLE STATEMENT			

FORM 0220 REV 9-73

Delivery Procedures

Every piece of literature dealing with futures trading emphasizes that the great majority of open contracts are closed out through offsetting purchases or sales before their delivery dates. Only 2% to 3% of all contracts are settled by shorts delivering securities to holders of long positions. Speculators, including the traders on the exchange floor, never have any intention of owning government bonds, Ginnie Maes or whatever security the contract stipulates. Even most of the commercial users turn to the cash markets described in Chapter Two when they need to buy or sell the actual securities. Hedgers use futures to reduce their exposure to adverse price changes in the cash market as interest rates rise or fall, but close their long or short contracts out in the same way as speculators at the time that they make their cash market transactions. That is why futures markets are referred to as price-determining rather than delivery markets. The price-determining process will be covered in some detail in Chapter Ten.

Nevertheless, all futures traders, be they speculators or hedgers, should have more than a passing acquaintance with the procedures whereby delivery is made, however infrequently. It is the delivery mechanism that ties futures prices to cash prices. The terms under which delivery of securities can be made in themselves affect a futures price. And as the delivery date approaches, cash and futures prices normally converge until they reach parity as contracts and securities are interchangeable on delivery day.

The delivery process is supervised by the clearing corporation of the exchange where the contracts are traded. It is integrated into the system of daily margin deposits and withdrawals and settlement of closing transactions, so that the money transfers are made by the same method of offsetting entries in the brokerage accounts of the parties making and receiving delivery.

The complete delivery sequence takes place over a three-day period. Traders normally have until the final week of the delivery month to liquidate their long or short positions through an offsetting transaction. On what is known as first notice day or position day, every short who has elected not to buy his contracts in must notify his commission firm of his intention to fulfill his contractual obligation by delivering securities. The firm in turn files a formal Notice of Intention to Deliver with the clearing corporation, which has by that time compiled a list of all accounts that still carry long contracts for the expiring month. On the following day, the clearing house assigns delivery notices to the longs on the list according to the length of their holding periods. In his notification, the long holder of a contract is advised of the coupon rate and maturity of the specific security that will be delivered to him. These details in turn determine the exact dollar value of the securities and the invoice amount his account will be charged.

The actual delivery of securities and payment for them are made on the third day. Government securities are transferred by book entry within the Federal Reserve System. The contract amount of T-bills or bonds are credited to the long's account at a member commercial bank; the long makes payment by the wire transfer of federal funds to the commercial bank account of the short's clearing member.

The brokerage accounts of the parties making and receiving delivery are adjusted to reflect the dollar difference between the last contract settlement price and the value of the securities delivered. That brings both accounts into balance since each had been debited or credited by the amount of daily price changes during the time each was long or short the contract. Though speculators need not be concerned with the details of computing these adjustments, they are on occasion applicable to those institutions that for whatever reason do find themselves in a delivery situation. As such, they warrant a brief illustration.

Suppose that a government securities dealer is short 10 December Treasury bond contracts and decides to deliver bonds instead of buying the contract in. His obligation is to deliver $1 million principal amount (covering 10 contracts) of bonds at a price which yields 8% at its current term to maturity. Since the Chicago Board of Trade contract specifies bonds with a call date or final maturity at least 15 years from the day of delivery, the dealer must select from his inventory an issue with a maturity exceeding the 15-year minimum. He chooses the 7⅝s of 2002-07, which are eligible since they are not callable until Feb. 15, 2002, and fall due five years later.

The first step is to obtain from a set of bond tables the price at which annual interest of $76.25 per $1,000 face value represents an 8% yield to maturity. If the bonds are to be delivered on June 17, 1977, say, the tables indicate that a 7⅝ coupon would yield 8% in the 24 years, 8½ months to their call date at a price of 96-00. That figure, multiplied by the settlement price of the December contract on position day and the $100,000 contract size furnishes the principal invoice amount which the account receiving the bonds will be billed. Assuming a settlement price of 99-15, the calculation for this illustration is as follows:[6]

1) Invoice   Price to yield 8% on   Position day settle-   Contract
   Principal = call or maturity × ment price (decimal × size
   Amount   date   equivalent)

   ($95,490 =   .960000   ×   .9946875   × $100,000)

The invoice calculation is not complete until allowance is made for the accrued interest on the bonds to which the delivering party is entitled. In this instance, the

---

[6]Chicago Board of Trade, "Making and Taking Delivery on Interest Rate Futures Contracts," p. 8.

semi-annual interest payment of $3,812.50 on the $100,000 contract amount would be multiplied by the fraction of the half-year between the last payment date and the day the bonds are delivered, 122/181, for accrued interest of $2,569.75 per $100,000.

The receiving institution, perhaps an insurance company that chooses to carry the bonds in its investment portfolio, will therefore be billed for a total invoice amount of $980,597.50, which it will pay into its account with the clearing broker, who in turn transfers the funds to the seller's commercial bank account.

The seller's and buyer's brokerage accounts are credited or debited, whichever the case, with the differences between their opening transaction prices and the settlement price on position day. If the government securities dealer sold the 10 December bond contracts at 101-08, for example, and delivered the 7⅝s of 2002-07 at a settlement price of 99-15, its account would be credited with $17,812.50, less commissions and other charges. In adding this credit to the settlement price, the dealer sold the bonds at the rough equivalent of 101¼, which was the purpose of selling futures to hedge the long bond position. The insurance company that took delivery of the bonds might have purchased its contracts at 97-11, causing its account to be credited with $21,250, less commissions. Subtracting its profit on the 10 December contracts from the settlement price determines that the insurance company was able to invest at an 8.680% yield to maturity instead of the 8.457% rate it would have received by simply buying bonds in December.

The fact that the securities dealer and the insurance company established their futures positions at different prices indicates that they were not opposite parties to the same 10 contracts. Moreover, since both showed profits on their respective transactions, there were another pair of traders who at some point closed their positions out at equivalent losses. Rather than going through the delivery procedure, the dealer and insurance company could each have accomplished the same result by liquidating its contracts at the settlement price and buying or selling the appropriate securities in the cash market, which is the usual method of terminating a futures hedge.

The delivery procedures for the other interest rate contracts correspond to the characteristics of their underlying securities. The delivery date for the 90-day T-bill contract falls on the Thursday following the third weekly bill auction of the delivery month, allowing shorts to deliver bills awarded at the most recent auction. Like the system of government bond deliveries, Treasury bills are transferred between member banks of the Federal Reserve against payment in federal funds, and their invoice price is adjusted to permit delivery of 91- and 92-day bills in settlement of the contract.

As was mentioned in Chapter Two, the Chicago Board of Trade currently lists two Ginnie Mae contracts whose principal difference lies in their delivery provisions. The original contract stipulates the delivery of a Collateralized Depository Receipt (CDR) representing ownership of Ginnie Maes held in a bank vault; the modified contract calls for the direct delivery of the actual certificates. The newer contract was designed to accommodate mortgage bankers and other originators of pass-through securities who are the exception to the general rule that hedgers prefer to cover their short contracts and deliver the actual securities in the cash market. The calculation to adjust the settlement price in the event Ginnie Maes with stated rates other than the specified 8% are delivered is similar to the one just described for government bonds. Again, while they are not of great significance to speculative traders, savings and loan associations and mortgage bankers that contemplate making or taking delivery of either CDRs or Ginnie Maes should make themselves thoroughly familiar with the delivery provisions of the appropriate contract. One reason is that the stated rate and remaining life of the securities selected for delivery determine the current yield of the investment.

The commercial paper contract is unique in that the commercial paper of any of 41 approved issuers may be delivered as contract grade. Although all must have Moody's and Standard & Poor's highest rating, their quality is not in all cases uniform, which creates a problem regarding delivery not encountered in the case of Treasury obligations or Ginnie Maes.

Similar to a Ginnie Mae CDR, delivery under the terms of the commercial paper contract is accomplished through the medium of a Financial Receipt created by a Board of Trade clearing member certifying the deposit of sufficient contract grade commercial paper in an approved commercial bank depository. Deliverable grade is limited to commercial paper maturing on a business day not more than 90 days from the date on which delivery of the Financial Receipt is made. As is recommended in the case of the other contracts, a clearing member and the regulations of the Board of Trade should be consulted if delivery or acceptance of a Financial Receipt is contemplated.

The Board of Trade and IMM both distribute through their member firms an abundance of literature which describes the various contract specifications and delivery procedures in some detail. Prospective hedgers and speculators should digest this material before making their first commitments.

Research and Reporting

Some brokerage firms issue internally generated research reports and statistical information. Although the futures market usually moves too quickly from day to day for these reports to be of much value for current trading ideas, the economic and technical analyses provide a helpful background for formulating longer-range strategy. Several houses put daily news summaries and trading recommendations on their private branch office newswires, enabling their account executives to relay more timely information to clients. News that is likely to have an immediate effect on prices during the trading session is broadcast to representatives and customers in the branches over a speaker-phone hookup.

Daily price quotations are reported in the financial press. The opening, high, low and closing settlement prices for each contract are listed by delivery month, from the nearby to the most distant expiration. Closing settlements and daily changes are quoted on a yield as well as a price basis. The T-bill yield is the projected discount of the deliverable bill on delivery day. If the market foresees rising interest rates, each delivery month carries a lower price and higher discount than the one preceding. Treasury bond and Ginnie Mae yields are computed on the basis of the contract's specified face rate of 8% at par, so that the lower the contract price falls below 100-00, the higher the yield rises above 8%. Conversely, a price greater than 100-00 has an equivalent yield of less than 8%.

A trading day normally ends with a number of trades occurring at slightly varied prices at different locations within the pit, so there is no specific closing price as such. One of the major responsibilities of the clearing corporations is to select among the range of final prices a daily settlement price which they deem to be the most representative. This official settlement price is important because it is the basis upon which daily maintenance margins, delivery prices and the following day's price-fluctuation limits are computed.

Volume and open interest for each contract are reported with the price information. Because all trades are processed overnight by the clearing corporations, there is a day's delay in reporting the official volume. Estimated volume is reported the following morning on the basis of transactions registered by exchange reporters who oversee trading from a "pulpit" above the pit, but the estimate invariably understates actual volume by a wide margin.

Futures traders should become accustomed to following interest rates in the cash market as well as futures prices. A summary of the weekly bill auction is published the following morning. The government securities section reports bill and coupon security yields for the prior day's secondary market trading. Prices and yields for the various Ginnie Mae issues are listed among the agency issues. A money market summary includes commercial paper rates for various maturities as well as the federal funds rate, an indicator futures traders watch closely.

Part Two

The Prices

Chapter Five
Prices, Yields and Curves

It is time to return to school. NFL linebackers are required to devote so many hours between games to studying playbooks and game films. Futures traders are advised to emulate them in that regard for the same reason: It will help them to win. Some discerning readers who might otherwise object to the change of analogy from chess to football within 100 pages have gathered from the foregoing chapters, I hope, that futures trading involves elements of both games.

Those who have watched the action from the visitors' gallery probably failed to notice anything that connects the controlled bedlam in the pit with the elegant curves economics instructors love to draw on blackboards. Nevertheless, there is a relationship between theory and practice, however tenuous or obscure it often seems, and the would-be trader who neglects the "chalk talk" aspect of his training will find himself at a serious disadvantage soon after setting foot on the field.

This chapter and the one following do not purport to be a comprehensive analysis of the accepted theories of interest rate behavior. To that end, the academically inclined reader is referred to any of the specialized studies listed in the bibliography.[1] Rather, these chapters summarize the various ideas of recognized scholars concerning the manner in which interest rates *should* behave, and then review what rates actually did over the past decade. The immediate conclusion is that interest rates seldom accommodate us, at least in the short run, by acting in the way the theories would lead us to believe. Yet even though the irrational nature of the market all too often makes a mockery of the best analysis, as traders who put complete reliance on logic soon learn, a theoretical framework is a necessary precondition to formulating an effective trading strategy. If for no other reason, there are monetary benefits to be gained from knowing when the market is not behaving as it "should."

Statistics, charts and their accompanying commentary are unavoidably tedious to all but those professionals for whom they are stock in trade and amateur enthusiasts who thrive on numbers. Interest rates are expressed in terms of numbers. So is money. Anyone who is enthusiastic about money and plans to trade interest rate futures had best become equally enthusiastic about the mass of numbers that measure these things, and believe that the credit crunch of 1974 is as fraught with historical drama as the Normandy Invasion. Otherwise, he is advised to find a different game. For my part, I have endeavored to make the reader's lot more bearable by avoiding obscure jargon when plain English will do the job.

Advanced students and practitioners of economics and finance may be excused for skimming most of the present chapter as it contains little that is likely to be new to them. Lest they be tempted to skip over it entirely, however, they should be advised that the con-

---

[1]Particularly Burton Malkiel, *The Term Structure of Interest Rates,* Princeton University Press 1966; book by the same title by David Meiselman, Prentice Hall, Englewood Cliffs, N.J., 1962; Sidney Homer and Martin Leibowitz, *Inside the Yield Book:* New Tools for Bond Market Strategy, Prentice Hall, Englewood Cliffs, N.J., 1972.

cluding pages of the chapter begin to tie the theory of interest rate behavior to futures market activity, and as such deserve more than a passing glance.

Three Perspectives

The immediate task is to go beyond the common but for our purposes inadequate expression, "the general level of interest rates." We are here concerned with specific rates on specific securities, and must therefore not only identify them but understand why they differ. We can then look at the ever changing numerical relationships between the various rates and determine how these shifts can present profit opportunities in the futures market. Why did September Treasury bond futures advance 18/32nds yesterday, while September Ginnie Maes went up only 6/32nds? Or why did the June 1979 90-day T-bill contract decline nine basis points when March 1981 T-bills fell 15 basis points? Was there some trading strategy which might have exploited these differences?

Before being able to make such an evaluation, it is necessary to examine each specific interest rate from at least three perspectives. The first consideration is the *level and direction* of interest rates. Are three-month Treasury bills yielding 6% or 8%? Is the discount moving up or down? Second, what is the *yield spread* or *differential* between unlike securities? How do three-month T-bills compare with commercial paper of the same maturity? If the spread is 50 basis points in favor of commercial paper (that is, above the T-bill rate), does that mean commercial paper is cheap or expensive relative to T-bills? What is the historical range of spreads between them? Finally, how do yields on like securities with different maturities relate to each other? We are interested in the relationship, for example, between Treasury bills of various maturities and notes and bonds of two to 10 years and beyond. Are three-month bills yielding less than six-month bills or more? If so, why? These latter questions raise the issue of what is known as the *term structure of interest rates*, a favorite topic for research by academic economists and practicing financial analysts.

Despite the abundance of theoretical literature on the subject, a great deal remains unknown about the behavior of interest rates. The reader will recall that it was the uncertainty associated with rate movements that was the primary impetus behind the establishment of a futures market in interest rates. He should not be misled into believing, therefore, that the neat charts and complex formulas that follow hold the key to whether Ginnie Mae futures will go up or down tomorrow, or even next month. Such tools may be effective in gauging the *probable* trend of interest rates over the course of a business cycle, and even that is not certain. Nevertheless, it is important for speculator and hedger alike to have a firm grasp of the theoretical principles, and some feeling for their application. There are many forces at work in the market. Like the NFL linebackers, success comes to those who are well-prepared at all levels.

Computing Interest and Yields

It would be useful by way of introduction to review the various ways of computing interest. There was a time when every schoolchild was taught the formula for *simple interest*:

$$i = p \times r \times t$$

where i is the interest payment in dollars, p is the principal amount, r is the rate and t the time frame. Transposed to express the annual percentage rate, the same formula would read:

$$r = \frac{i}{p \times t}$$

If, for example, you loan someone $100 with the understanding that he will repay the principal plus $10 at the end of a year, your agreement calls for you to receive interest at an annual rate of 10%.

In the case of *compound interest*, each interest payment is added to the existing principal and the next payment is calculated at the same rate on the total. A $1,000 savings deposit compounded by 8% annually will earn $80 in interest the first year, $86.40 the second ($1,080.00 × .08), $93.31 the third ($1,166.40 × .08), and so forth. If interest were compounded semi-annually, as is the case with most bond coupon payments, principal would accumulate faster because compounding would take place every six months instead of once a year. The $1,000 compounded at a 4% semi-annual rate, for instance, would accumulate principal of $1,265.30 by the end of the third year rather than the $1,259.71 from 8% compounded annually.

As was noted in Chapter Two, the semi-annual coupon payment remains constant over the life of a bond (hence, "fixed-income" securities) while the current dollar price varies inversely with the prevailing interest rate on comparable bonds. The coupon rate is the yield produced by two semi-annual interest payments when the bond is priced at par (100). If the coupon rate is 8.50%, the holder of a bond with a face value of $1,000 receives two $42.50 interest payments a year. If on any later date similar bonds of comparable safety and maturity paying $90 a year—9% at par— are offered to investors, bond traders will continue to sell the 8.50% coupon issue until its price falls to the level where it also yields 9%, which it will do at a price of about 94½:

$$i = p \times r \times t$$
$$(\$85 = \$944.44 \times .09 \times 1)$$

On the other hand, when bond yields are falling and new issues of the same type are being sold with

7.50% coupons, the 8.50% bond will be bid up to 113⅜ at which price it too will yield about 7.50%.

$$(\$85 = \$1,133.33 \times .075 \times 1)$$

The *current yield* on a coupon issue, therefore, is computed by dividing the annual interest payment in dollars by the prevailing market price. When general market yields rise above its coupon rate, the price of a fixed-income security will fall to a *discount* below par. If yields decline instead, the price will rise to a *premium* above par where current yield is again in line with that of similar securities.

With the exception of issues with special call provisions, bonds are retired at par. That means that whatever happens to interest rates during the interim, the 8.50% coupon bond cited above must rise from 94½ or decline from 113⅜ to mature at par. Since current yield does not take this ultimate price appreciation or depreciation into account, it is not the best measure of an investor's annual rate of return when he buys a bond at either a discount or premium and holds it through its remaining life to maturity. A more accurate representation of a bond's true return is its *yield to maturity*, which reflects the ultimate gain or loss of principal at maturity in addition to the current yield at the time of purchase.

Yield to maturity is derived through a complex formula which the reader will be mercifully spared at this juncture, but which he may refer to in Appendix C. Fortunately for the non-mathematicians of this world, the relevant figures are available in bond value tables that list the correct yield to maturity for each coupon rate, price and maturity. Reference to these tables indicates that an 8.50% coupon bond with a remaining life, say, of 10 years has a yield to maturity at a price of 94½ of 9.21%, and at 113⅜ of 6.71%. The yield to maturity is higher than the 9% current yield in the case of the discount because of the certain appreciation of the bond's value to par, whereas it is less than 7.50% when the bond sells at a premium because of its ultimate depreciation by the maturity date.

Yield to maturity is the method of computation most often used to express the return on bonds with different coupons, prices and maturities. As such, it is the accepted measure of comparative yield and is the specified means of stating the return on securities deliverable under the GNMA and Treasury bond futures contracts.

Some analysts have argued that even yield to maturity is an inadequate gauge of an investment's true return since it does not take into consideration the immediate reinvestment of interest payments as they are made, thereby neglecting the incremental compounding effect of "interest on interest" on a bond's actual return.[2]

Finally, the reader is encouraged to refer back to Chapter Two for a discussion of the arithmetic differences between computing interest on a yield and a discount basis. By way of a reminder, the two money market instruments of principal concern to the futures market, Treasury bills and commercial paper, are traded and quoted on a discount basis, and must therefore be converted to the appropriate bond equivalent yield for an accurate comparison with coupon rates.

Risk and Rates of Return

Having reviewed the principal methods of expressing interest, it is possible to address the question of why different securities pay different rates of return. The operative word here is *risk*. Risk and reward are opposite faces of the investment coin. Investors whose primary objective is the preservation of capital will forego the risk premium to be gotten from making less secure investments. They endeavor to realize their

---

[2]Homer and Leibowitz, *Inside the Yield Book*, p. 21.

requirements by buying and thereby bidding up the price of securities they consider most desirable while remaining indifferent to those with relatively less appeal. The process is therefore self-fulfilling as the securities whose prices are bid higher yield less while those that are not in demand depreciate until their higher yields provide sufficient incentive for what investors perceive to be their added exposure to risk.

The primary types of risk to which fixed-income securities are subject can be described as: 1) credit risk, 2) interest rate risk, 3) maturity risk, and 4) marketability or liquidity risk. Of the various interest rate contracts currently traded in the futures market, all but two either represent direct obligations of the U. S. Treasury (bills, notes and bonds) or enjoy a government guarantee (Ginnie Maes). Consequently, credit risk, or the possibility of default, is of direct concern to futures traders only with regard to the 90-day and 30-day commercial paper contracts.

Since interest rate risk is essentially what this book is about, a central purpose of the present and later chapters is to isolate its effects insofar as possible and then to evaluate its impact on the prices of fixed-income securities. As it is impracticable to separate the various elements of risk and assign a relative weight to each, it is not a total digression to consider briefly the factors which influence investors' appraisal of credit risk in bonds and short-term instruments. When attention is given to the feasibility of using Treasury bond futures to hedge corporate obligations, the question of credit risk will assume further relevance.

Bonds that are not issued by the U. S. Treasury generally have one or more of the features that are indicative of a borrower's ability to make timely payments of interest and principal. The most visible of these is the quality ranking accorded them by one or more of the several rating agencies. As they do in rating the issuers of commercial paper, Standard &

Poor's, Moody's and Fitch Investors Service perform the various ratio tests that are intended to measure a company's financial strength, hence its capacity to meet its obligations. Many private and institutional investors have sufficient confidence in the judgement of the rating services to base their decisions solely on whether a particular bond carries a rating of, say, A or better. Even those professional bond portfolio managers who conduct their own balance sheet analyses pay careful attention to the ratings because of the heavy emphasis placed upon them by the investment community at large.

Important though such arithmetic tests as capitalization, earnings coverage and working capital ratios may be in assessing the safety of a particular bond, risk remains a subjective attribute of any security and is therefore not susceptible to precise measurement. That quality is a determining factor, however, can be demonstrated by comparing the relative yields of securities according to their ratings. Consistent with the principle that successively higher degrees of risk must be compensated for by a greater interest return, each step down the rating scale denotes a lower price and consequently a higher yield. Therefore, two bonds with similar features except for their rating usually sell at different prices, reflecting the extra return, or risk premium, investors require to purchase the lower quality issue. According to Table 5-1, as of the close of 1978, corporate bond buyers could have increased their yield by about 100 basis points if they were willing to lower their quality requirements from AAA to BBB.

Table 5-1.   **Corporate Bond Yields by Investment Rating.**

	AAA	AA	A	BBB
Week of Dec. 27, 1978	9.06	9.24	9.38	10.05

Source: Standard & Poor's *Fixed Income Investor*

Similar considerations apply in the short-term market where lower-rated commercial paper must be sold at a larger discount to provide investors with a greater return. Even the highest-rated paper usually yields more than Treasury bills of the same maturity since government securities are free of credit risk, though not of the other varieties of risk.

These yield spreads between securities of different perceived quality vary over time, reflecting changes in investor attitudes and confidence at successive stages in the business cycle. Although the past record does not always confirm the accepted theory, investors are supposedly not overly concerned with the possibility of default and loss of principal during periods of economic expansion and general prosperity, and the spreads between the various quality classifications tend to get narrower. That is tantamount to saying that a smaller risk premium is required during good times. In periods of adversity and spectacular business failures such as the bankruptcy of Penn Central, investor consciousness of credit risk is heightened, and the quality spreads, or risk premiums, grow appreciably wider. Traders in both the cash and futures markets continually encounter the question of whether a marked change in a particular spread relationship from, say, 30 to 60 basis points is a transitory market dislocation which holds out the prospect of a fast profit, or signals a broader shift in investor sentiment.

The frequency of their interest payments is another feature of fixed-income securities which creates yield disparities between them. It was noted in Chapter Two that Ginnie Mae pass-throughs make interest and principal payments monthly while regular bonds have semi-annual coupon dates. According to the "interest on interest" theory, holders of Ginnie Maes are able to reinvest their interest payments sooner than other bond investors, thereby obtaining the benefit of greater compounding which in turn is reflected in a higher yield on their investment. By the same token,

Eurobonds yield comparatively less because their interest is paid once a year.

Liquidity, or marketability of a particular issue, also can influence its yield. A security is said to be highly liquid when it can be bought or sold in large quantities quickly and without excessive price change. If a number of bonds cannot be sold except after a significant delay and a substantial price concession, that is another manner of risk for which the potential buyer will require compensation in the form of higher yield. The larger the size of an outstanding issue, the more trading and greater degree of liquidity it is likely to enjoy. U. S. government securities, with their immense volume and secondary market activity, are the most liquid of all fixed-income obligations. Yet even their liquidity is sometimes impaired when the market experiences temporary imbalances in supply and demand.

The "seasoning" of certain bonds, as well as any call protection, sinking fund and convertibility features they may have, affect their yields because each influences investors' estimates of the likelihood of regaining their capital intact. Moreover, if the bonds in question receive unusual tax treatment, or are denominated in a foreign currency, these factors also are taken into account when the market considers the potential risk. Market psychology, even more difficult to measure than quality and therefore harder to assess, can be consequential as certain classes of issuers or their securities for one reason or another fall into disfavor, and the shunned borrowers must offer higher rates of return to overcome investor disenchantment in obtaining the necessary funds.

All of the characteristics of fixed-income securities described above pertain to either credit or liquidity risk. Investors require assurance that interest and principal will be paid when they fall due and that, if it should prove necessary, they will be able to dispose of their securities in the secondary market without a

great sacrifice in price. The yields on various short-
and long-term securities reflect in large part their assessment of the extent to which that assurance is
forthcoming.

Interest Rate Risk

As was indicated earlier, although these considerations are of prime importance to every fixed-income
issuer, dealer and investor, they are something of a
diversion from the principal concern of this book, interest rate risk. Since it is not possible in practice to
compartmentalize the several types of risk as they affect short- and long-term yields, futures traders at
least should be aware of their significance. Having acknowledged their existence, we will put them aside for
the time being and devote the remainder of the chapter
to a more detailed examination of the closely integrated interest rate and maturity risks.

To isolate the effects of interest rate movements
and maturity on the price behavior of fixed-income securities, the following discussion is limited to a consideration of U. S. Treasury obligations where no
credit risk and only occasional liquidity risk (except
for the longer maturities) come into play. This restriction is appropriate because it will focus the analysis
on the three types of Treasury securities—bills, notes
and bonds—currently represented in the interest rate
futures complex. Having gained some understanding
of the variables which affect the short, intermediate
and long sectors of the government securities market,
we can then proceed in Chapter Six to expand our perspective to include the additional factors which bear
on Ginnie Mae and commercial paper rates.

The Effect of Changing Maturity

In considering the effect of changing maturity on
yield, we soon encounter the imposing expression, "the

term structure of interest rates." In this context, "term" is used in accordance with the dictionary definition of "a space of time granted to a debtor for discharging his obligation," in describing the remaining life of an investment. The concept of term structure refers to the relationship between short- and long-term interest rates on otherwise like securities. In the case of securities issued by the Treasury, the yield spreads between, say, three-month bills and 20-year bonds may be as wide as the variations between those of separate corporate issuers with different quality ratings. Although these short- and long-term rates generally move up and down together, the spreads between them may vary widely. Although short-term rates during this century have tended to be lower than long-term rates, this customary relationship has been on occasion reversed as short-term rates moved above concurrent long-term rates.

These movements and the forces which prompt them go to the crux of trading interest rate futures. Anyone who aspires to succeed in the market must become very comfortable with these concepts for they are where profits (and losses) originate. The discipline is called yield curve analysis, and it is critical. Trading futures without understanding the yield curve is as treacherous as navigating through strange waters without a chart.

Economists and bond market analysts have attempted to explain the term structure of interest rates by way of two distinct theories which are to a certain extent contradictory. Adherents of the *expectations* hypothesis maintain that relative yields on successive maturities of the same security are determined by investors' anticipation of future interest rates. They reason that through an ongoing process of adjustment, any long-term interest rate on a particular investment equals the average of consecutive short-term rates over the same period. Those who support the *segmented markets* theory hold that short- and long-term securities are imperfect substitutes for one another, and that there are in effect at least two separate fixed-income markets, each with its own group of buyers and sellers. According to this concept, the relative supply of, and demand for, securities in each maturity range is the determining factor in setting the rate structure.

The expectations hypothesis states that if, for example, one-year interest rates currently are 6%, but are expected to rise to 8% a year from now, today's two-year rate must approximate 7%, the average of the two one-year rates. In "economese," the present long-term rate is determined by the geometric mean of successive forward one-year rates. If this equality of return did not prevail, speculators would bring it about by buying the relatively cheaper maturity (higher yield) and selling the more expensive one.

The presumption upon which this line of reasoning is based is that securities with different terms to maturity are perfect substitutes for one another, and disregarding transaction costs, investors will be indifferent as to whether they should make, say, four one-year, two two-year or one four-year investment. If that be so, the obvious implication for the subject of this book is that it should be possible for traders to make an assessment of expected future short-term rates on the basis of existing long-term rates.

There is evidence to indicate, however, that investors are not perfectly indifferent to whether they hold short or long maturities. On the contrary, it is highly likely that, in view of the wider price swings to which longer-term securities are subject, they demand a bonus in the form of higher yield for exposing themselves to a greater risk of capital loss.

Another way of expressing the same concept is that investors are willing to pay a price premium, and accept a lower yield, for the liquidity of a short-term investment. Liquidity was defined earlier in this chapter as the ability of a market to provide or absorb sub-

stantial amounts of securities quickly and without in-
ordinate price change. The maturity of a fixed-income
security is a major determinant of its liquidity due to
the characteristic noted above that short-term issues
respond in price to a given change in interest rates by
a lesser magnitude than do longer maturities. The
value of one basis point on a $1 million face value one-
year Treasury bill is $100, but drops to $25 on a 90-
day bill of the same amount. If the bill had a remaining life of 30 days, a basis point change in discount
would be the equivalent of $8.33. The sharply reduced
price exposure to a change in the discount and the
proximity of the maturity date when the bill will be
redeemed by the Treasury at par, make dealers and
other investors more willing buyers of the near maturities than the more distant.

Statistical tests confirm that investors value the
"near money" quality of Treasury bills and short-term
coupon securities sufficiently to pay a premium to hold
them rather than longer maturities. The available evidence indicates that this preference extends out to two
and perhaps as long as three years. If such be the case,
it is necessary to modify the expectations hypothesis
to take the liquidity preference into account. In so
doing, long-term interest rates can no longer be regarded as simply the average of expected future rates,
but yields which pay investors an incremental return
for accepting the greater price risk of the longer maturities.[3]

Once the existence of liquidity preferences and
risk premiums is acknowledged, it is difficult to support the argument that short- and long-term securities
are perfect substitutes which investors exchange at
will. One must then place greater weight on the seg-

---

[3]To cloud the issue even more, some investors prefer the certainty of
a particular interest payment over an extended period despite the wider
price swings, and are willing to pay a negative risk premium, i.e., accept
relatively lower yields on longer maturities.

mented market theory. To quote two eminent bond market analysts:

> The short-term money-market credit instruments at one end of the curve are so drastically different from the long-term bonds at the other end, in purpose, in contract, in behavior, in mathematical content, and even in historic origin that it can be misleading to link them together in this way. The fact is that we are looking at two distinct types of investment, short loans and long bonds, that are as different from each other as stocks are from bonds, or more so. Medium maturity bonds, which partake of some of the quality of both shorts and longs, seem to serve as a link, but this should not be allowed to obscure the basic differences between the extremes.
>
> The purchase of a long-term bond is not so much a loan of money as it is a purchase of income. This is so because, to the debtor and creditor alike, the payment or receipt of the interest is more important than the ultimate repayment of the principal. On the other hand, in the case of a short-term loan, repayment of principal far outweighs the payment of interest as a concern of both debtor and creditor.[4]

Given these diverse qualities of short- and long-term debt securities, it stands to reason that individuals and institutions with different financial requirements and objectives will lean toward one end of the maturity range or the other. Insurance companies and pension funds, for example, customarily hold their investments to maturity. As a result, they are not overly concerned with price fluctuations over a security's life,

---

[4]Sidney Homer & Richard Johannesen, *The Price of Money 1946-1969: An Analytical Study of United States and Foreign Interest Rates,* Rutgers University Press, New Brunswick, N.J. 1969, p. 122.

nor do they have any particular incentive to keep rolling over short-term investments. Commercial banks, on the other hand, in endeavoring to match short-term assets with short-term liabilities are more concerned with maintaining liquidity and consequently stay near the short end of the maturity range when investing their reserves.

On the borrowing side, companies which turn their inventories over frequently usually look to the short end of the market for financing, while manufacturing firms planning to build plants and purchase capital equipment generally require long term funds. According to the segmented market hypothesis, a pronounced shift in the supply of securities (borrowing demand) from the long to the short side or vice versa will alter the term structure of, in this instance, corporate rates.

Since the theorists have found a way to make the expectations and segmented market theories compatible, the reader is fortunately not required to opt for the one or the other. The much maligned speculator, of all people, has been cast in the role of conciliator in bridging the two approaches to the term structure. The composite theory states that while the primary issuers and buyers of fixed-income securities cluster around that segment of the maturity range most suited to their requirements, speculators serve as a link between the short and long sectors by watching for and closing yield disparities as they materialize.

By way of summary, two assertions can be made without much fear of contradiction. First, there is, and probably always will be, uncertainty regarding the general behavior of interest rates. Second, the financial world has yet to be presented with one definitive theory to explain the term structure of rates. Imperfect though the current level of understanding may be, there are a number of conclusions that can assist the futures trader in his pursuit of profits.

The Maturity-Price Relationship

A major consideration is the relationship between maturity and price movement. We recalled earlier in this chapter that one basis point difference in yield on a one-year bill is worth in dollars four times the same change in the 90-day discount. That this must be so is demonstrated by the fact that the same percentage discount involves four times the dollar discount on a year bill, and consequently must recover in the same ratio in order to mature at par.

Inasmuch as a similar relationship holds for other securities and time frames, it may be stated as a general rule that as maturity is extended, a given change in yield will cause a greater fluctuation in price. That is the reason behind the bond market adage that when rising interest rates are forecast, the proper defensive maneuver is to switch out of long-term bonds into shorter maturities. It also explains why a higher yield is often a necessary inducement to draw investors into the long end of the market.

Price volatility increases with maturity on coupon securities as well as on the shorter-term discount issues. A five-year bond with a 7% coupon will drop from par to 96 when the current yield rises to 8% for example, incurring a capital loss of $40 per $1,000 bond. Yet a bond identical in all respects save a 10- instead of a five-year maturity will under the same conditions drop $67.50, a capital loss nearly 70% greater than the one realized on the shorter issue.

As a bond's current yield continues to rise above its coupon rate, the discount grows progressively larger. Since yield to maturity is expressed at an annual rate, the dollar discount, as is the case with Treasury bills, must become greater as maturity grows longer for the bond to generate the additional return per annum as the discount is amortized.

In the opposite situation, as interest rates decline the price appreciation on the longer-term bonds is proportionately greater, indicating that when falling interest rates are anticipated maturities should be extended to obtain the maximum price gain. Increases in volatility start to diminish after maturities reach a certain point, until there is almost no difference in price movement from a given rate change on bonds of, say, 35 years or longer.

The reverse phenomenon is that short-term securities exhibit wider variations in yield for each dollar price change than do long-term issues. These relationships have important implications for futures traders in assessing the relative effect of certain projected rate changes on bond and T-bill contract prices as well as on successive delivery months of the same contract.

Several other aspects of the relationship between yield and price bear mentioning. Because it represents a greater percentage movement, a specific change in yield signifies a wider price fluctuation on a low-coupon security than a high-coupon issue. Consequently, bonds with low coupons are the preferred investment as interest rates are declining; contrariwise, high-coupon bonds decline comparatively less in price when rates are rising. Prices are more volatile when rates move up or down from a high initial level than from a low level. Risks are therefore greater on both the long and short sides when traders enter the market at a high rate level.

The level of interest rates has an added effect on the relationship between short- and long-term yields when long-term rates are sufficiently high that investors are willing to suspend their normal liquidity preference to buy long bonds in the belief that their rates are likely to fall. Meanwhile, prospective borrowers hesitate to go into the long-term market at the high levels, preferring to meet their immediate needs through short-term financing. The net result of these supply and demand departures from the normal pattern is that short-term rates are pushed higher and long-term rates are pushed down.

The opposite sequence occurs when interest rates are historically low. As they expect rates to rise, investors' liquidity preference is revived. They place their funds in short-term instruments, depressing their yield even further. At the same time, borrowers are anxious to take advantage of favorable (from their viewpoint) long-term rates. The increased sale of long-term securities pushes rates higher at that end of the maturity range.

The Yield Curve

It is at last time to unveil, to the accompaniment of ruffles and flourishes, the Amazing Yield Curve. With apologies for letting those readers down who have awaited this awesome moment with dread in their hearts, the celebrated yield curve is merely a graphic representation of the term structure of interest rates. To dispel the aura of mystery which surrounds this imposing line, we shall proceed to draw not one, but three yield curves.

On the facing page are the closing quotations for U. S. government securities on Nov. 1, 1976, as published the following day in *The Wall Street Journal*. Our project is to plot the interest rates on three-, six- and 12-month Treasury bills and four-, six- and 10-year bonds for a pictorial view of the yield relationships between those issues. In constructing our chart, we follow the convention of plotting yield up the vertical axis and maturity along the horizontal axis.

The bills maturing nearest to 90, 180 and 360 days from Nov. 1, were those dated Jan. 27 (4.82), April 28 (5.01) and Oct. 18 (5.11). Since bill rates are quoted on a discount basis, it is necessary to convert them to their bond equivalents for an accurate comparison with the longer-term coupon issues. Using the conversion formula cited in Chapter Two, page 42, we arrive at the following bond equivalent yields:

90 days	4.94
180 days	5.21
360 days	5.40

The coupon issues which most closely matched the selected long-term maturities on Nov. 1, and their respective yields, were:

6⅞s	1980	6.45
7⅞s	1982	6.95
8s	1986	7.34

Laying out our vertical and horizontal axes and plotting Xs for each of the six issues in the designated locations, we are able to extend a line through, or reasonably near to all of the Xs and, voilà, we have actually drawn a yield curve, not a contrived replica with imaginary dates and interest rates, but the real thing!

But wait, the fun is just beginning. The Nov. 1, 1976, yield curve is an accurate representation of the relative rates on the government securities indicated for that day only, and strictly at the close of the market at that. If, as is almost certain, prices of any of the six bills or bonds fluctuated by so much as one basis point or 1/32nd during the trading day, the shape and position of the curve would have changed by a seemingly imperceptible but nonetheless real amount. Then, as days and weeks elapse, and changing market conditions cause more substantial price movements, shifts in the yield curve become more visible and represent meaningful profit opportunities for investors in fixed-income securities and even more so to interest rate futures traders.

To illustrate the point, leap ahead one year and redraw the curve as it was determined by market prices prevailing on Nov. 1, 1977, and again one year later. In each case, the bills plotted earlier had by then matured and the life of the original bonds had become one and two years shorter. For our purposes it is the interest rate and not the specific security that matters,

Table 5-2

Government, Agency and Miscellaneous Securities

Friday, October 29, 1976

Over-the-Counter Quotations: Source on request.
Decimals in bid-and-asked and bid changes represent 32nds 101.1 means 101 1-32. a-Plus 1-64. b-Yield to call date. d-Minus 1-64.

Treasury Bonds and Notes

Rate	Mat.	Date	Bid	Asked	Bid Chg.	Yld.
6¼s,	1976	Nov n	100	100.4	.....	2.35
7⅛s,	1976	Nov n	100.5	100.9	.....	3.21
7¼s,	1976	Dec n	100.10	100.14	− .1	4.34
8s,	1977	Feb n	100.26	100.30	.....	4.56
6s,	1977	Feb n	100.7	100.11	.....	4.87
6½s,	1977	Mar n	100.15	100.19	.....	4.98
7⅜s,	1977	Apr n	101	101.4	.....	5.03
6⅞s,	1977	May n	100.25	100.29	.....	5.13
9s,	1977	May n	101.30	102.2	+ .1	5.15
6¾s,	1977	May n	100.24	100.28	.....	5.18
6½s,	1977	Jun n	100.23	100.27	.....	5.18
7½s,	1977	Jul n	101.17	101.21	.....	5.20
7¾s,	1977	Aug n	101.25	101.29	.....	5.24
8¼s,	1977	Aug n	102.8	102.12	.....	5.27
8⅜s,	1977	Sep n	102.17	102.21	− .1	5.34
7½s,	1977	Oct n	101.28	102	.....	5.40
7¾s,	1977	Nov n	102.3	102.7	− .1	5.51
6⅝s,	1977	Nov n	101	101.4	− .1	5.53
7¼s,	1977	Dec n	101.23	101.27	− .1	5.59
6⅜s,	1978	Jan n	100.23	100.27	− .1	5.66
6¼s,	1978	Feb n	100.16	100.20	− .2	5.74
8s,	1978	Feb n	102.21	102.25	− .3	5.79
6¾s,	1978	Mar n	101.6	101.10	− .1	5.77
6½s,	1978	Apr n	100.27	100.31	.....	5.81
7⅛s,	1978	May n	101.23	101.27	− .1	5.85
7⅛s,	1978	May n	101.24	101.28	− .1	5.86
7⅞s,	1978	May n	102.24	102.28	− .1	5.86
6⅞s,	1978	Jun n	101.12	101.16	− .2	5.91
6⅞s,	1978	Jul n	101.13	101.15	− .2	5.98
6⅝s,	1978	Aug n	101	101.2	− .4	6.00
7⅝s,	1978	Aug n	102.20	102.24	− .2	5.98
8¾s,	1978	Aug n	104.14	104.18	− .2	6.00
6¼s,	1978	Sep n	100.12	100.14	− .4	6.00
5⅞s,	1978	Oct n	99.23	99.25	− .2	5.99
6s,	1978	Nov n	99.28	100	− .2	6.00
8⅛s,	1978	Dec n	103.31	104.3	− .3	6.07
7s,	1979	Feb n	101.26	101.30	− .2	6.08
7⅞s,	1979	May n	103.19	103.27	− .3	6.21
7¾s,	1979	Jun n	103.15	103.23	− .1	6.21
6¼s,	1979	Aug n	99.28	100.4	− .2	6.20
6⅞s,	1979	Aug n	101.16	101.18	− .1	6.26
8½s,	1979	Sep n	105.17	105.25	− .1	6.29
6⅝s,	1979	Nov n	100.26	101.2	− .2	6.24
7s,	1979	Nov n	101.28	102.4	− .2	6.22
7½s,	1979	Dec n	103.2	103.10	− .2	6.33
4s,	1980	Feb	93.10	93.26	.....	6.11
7½s,	1980	Mar n	102.31	103.7	− .3	6.43
6⅞s,	1980	May n	101.4	101.12	− .2	6.43
7⅝s,	1980	Jun n	103.14	103.18	.....	6.52
9s,	1980	Aug n	107.26	108.2	− .2	6.56
6⅞s,	1980	Sep n	101.8	101.10	.....	6.49
3½s,	1980	Nov	90	91	− .4	6.05
7s,	1981	Feb n	101.4	101.12	− .1	6.62
7⅜s,	1981	Feb n	102.14	102.22	− .1	6.64
7⅜s,	1981	May n	102.12	102.20	− .1	6.69
7⅝s,	1981	Aug n	103.12	104.12	− .3	6.76
7s,	1981	Aug	101.26	102.26	.....	6.31
7s,	1981	Nov n	101.4	101.6	− .3	6.72
7¾s,	1981	Nov n	103.28	104	− .3	6.80
6⅜s,	1982	Feb	98.20	99.4	.....	6.57
8s,	1982	May n	104.21	105.5	− .3	6.86
8⅛s,	1982	Aug n	105.2	105.10	− .8	6.99
7⅞s,	1982	Nov n	103.30	104.6	− .8	7.01
8s,	1983	Feb n	104.14	104.22	− .6	7.06
3¼s,	1978-83	Jun	84.12	84.28	− .2	6.06
6⅜s,	1984	Aug	96.12	97.12	− .2	6.82
3¼s,	1985	May	84.14	85.14	.....	5.40
4¼s,	1975-85	May	85.12	86.12	− .2	5.34
7⅞s,	1986	May n	103.6	103.10	− .2	7.38
8s,	1986	Aug n	104.4	104.8	− .4	7.38
6⅛s,	1986	Nov	93.16	94.16	.....	6.89
3½s,	1990	Feb	84.10	85.10	− .2	5.03
8¼s,	1990	May	105.18	106.2	.....	7.53
4¼s,	1987-92	Aug	85.8	86.8	.....	5.57
4s,	1988-93	Feb	85 2	86.2	− .8	5.27
6¾s,	1993	Feb	92	93	− .4	7.50
7½s,	1988-93	Aug	98.24	99.24	− .2	7.53
4⅛s,	1989-94	May	84.20	85.20	− .4	5.40
3s,	1995	Feb	84.6	85.6	− .4	4.17
7s,	1993-98	May	93.22	94.22	− .2	7.50
3½s,	1998	Nov	84.12	85.12	.....	4.56
8½s,	1994-99	May	106.18	107.2	− .4	7.76
7⅞s,	1995-00	Feb	101.6	101.14	− .4	7.74
8⅜s,	1995-00	Aug	105.20	106.4	− .4	7.73
8s,	1996-01	Aug	102.19	102.23	− .1	7.73
8¼s,	2000-05	May	104.22	105.6	− .2	7.76

n– Treasury notes.

U.S. Treas. Bills

Mat	Bid Discount	Ask Discount	Mat	Bid Discount	Ask Discount	Mat	Bid	Ask	Mat	Bid	Ask
						12-23	4.74	4.62	4-14	5.06	5.00
						12-30	4.74	4.64	4-21	5.07	5.01
11- 4	4.90	4.58	2-24	4.94	4.88	1- 6	4.82	4.74	4-28	5.06	5.04
11-11	4.87	4.55	3- 3	4.99	4.91	1-11	4.87	4.77	5- 3	5.10	5.02
11-15	4.83	4.53	3- 8	4.99	4.91	1-13	4.87	4.79	5-31	5.12	5.04
11-18	4.83	4.53	3-10	5.00	4.92	1-20	4.88	4.80	6-28	5.13	5.05
11-26	4.80	4.52	3-17	5.02	4.94	1-27	4.89	4.87	7-26	5.16	5.10
12- 2	4.74	4.62	3-24	5.03	4.95	2- 3	4.93	4.85	8-23	5.18	5.12
12- 9	4.74	4.62	3-31	5.03	4.95	2- 8	4.94	4.86	9-20	5.18	5.12
12-14	4.71	4.57	4- 5	5.04	4.96	2-10	4.94	4.86	10-18	5.18	5.16
12-16	4.74	4.62	4- 7	5.04	4.98	2-17	4.93	4.87			

so as with the 1976 curve, we consult the government securities quotation list to select the issues closest to the desired maturities. The results are shown in Figure 5-1. Ponder them for a few moments before we proceed to plumb their secrets.

The importance of yield-curve analysis to profitable futures trading cannot be overstated. The twists, turns and gyrations of such geometric arcs as those we have just drawn have very real significance in terms of past and prospective price change, and are therefore worthy of close study by novice as well as combat-hardened traders. It must be reiterated that this is far from an exact science. But that should not deter us from

understanding and using the knowledge and tools that
have proven useful to others.

Curves can be plotted for any group of fixed-income securities that are similar in every respect save
their maturity. It is possible to draw curves for corporate and municipal bonds, but if they differ in the
features discussed earlier in this chapter—quality, frequency of interest payments, tax treatment, etc.—the
relationship between yield and maturity is obscured
by these other factors. Treasury securities, apart from
the need to convert discounts to bond equivalent
yields, are the only group with the homogencity necessary to isolate the effect of maturity on yield.

As was just noted, yield curves are highly perishable items. Theoretically, they can change as quickly
as they are drawn. In practice, the important relationships hold fast for more extended periods, though not
generally so long as the one-year intervals used for
our example. Also, each time a curve is redrawn, new
issues which correspond to the desired maturities must
be priced and plotted as the prior ones elapse with
time.

For cash market investors, the yield curve is useful in identifying the individual securities that offer
a higher yield than others in their group. On the other
side, prospective borrowers can select the point along
the curve where a new issue can be offered at the lowest cost.

Bond investors who adopt a more dynamic approach to buying and selling will benefit by a careful
study of the yield relationships depicted by the curve,
since it is this graphic representation of available interest income, hence price, that pinpoints the greatest
relative value among similar investments and therefore the largest immediate profit potential. By the
same token, futures traders who take the trouble to
absorb this method of analysis will have made a long
stride toward understanding the connection between

prices of the successive contract delivery months and those of their underlying securities.

Yield curves generally assume one of three basic shapes. A *positive,* or upward-sloping, curve is the result when yields become successively higher as the maturity of a security grows longer. It represents the most common pattern of interest rates on U. S. government and other debt securities since the 1930s.

Our 1976 model is a good example of a positive curve. From the three-month bill through the 10-year bond, each succeeding maturity bears a higher yield than the one before it, although it can be observed that the rate of increase begins to taper off somewhere after the sixth year—that is, the slope of the curve becomes less positive. This type of curve usually develops during periods of both moderate economic growth and recession. According to the expectations hypothesis, a positive curve is a reflection of investors' belief that interest rates will continue to rise in the future. This conviction has been fortified during the past decade by a rising rate of inflation.

Though short- and long-term rates usually rise and fall together, the greater yield (though not price) volatility at the short end of the curve is what generally accounts for changes in its shape and direction. When short-term rates rise faster than long-term rates, the yield curve turns *negative*, or downward-sloping. This configuration normally appears at or near peaks of economic expansion when interest rates are high and investors expect them to decline.

When short- and long-term rates are approximately equal, the curve runs parallel to the horizontal axis and is therefore said to be *flat*. This position is something of a way station while the curve is in the process of shifting from a positive to negative slope or vice versa. On occasion, the curve becomes hump-backed where rising short-term yields reverse direction at some intermediate maturity. The explanation usually advanced for this pattern is that investors believe a decline in rates is imminent, but their liquidity preference prolongs the demand for short-term securities.

The three curves for 1976-78 display many of these tendencies. While both short- and long-term rates continued to rise during those years, each of the curves approximated one of the three fundamental patterns. The 1976 curve, as we have observed, had a typical positive slope. But between November of that year and the same month a year later, the discount on the three-month bill rose 124 basis points (4.94 to 6.18) while the yield on 10-year bonds increased by only 26 basis points (7.34 to 7.60). As a consequence, while the 1977 curve was still nominally positive, beyond the one-year maturity it became very nearly flat as the yield on the 10-year bond was scarcely 60 basis points above the equivalent rate on the one-year bill.

The 1978 curve demonstrates both a hump, which peaked at the one-year maturity, and a negative curve from that point on. Even three-month bills at a 9.11 bond equivalent yield were more than 50 basis points above the 10-year bond rate, and investors on the whole apparently believed that all rates had risen so far over the previous years that the likelihood was that they would start to decline in 1979.

How the Yield Curve Responds

Yield-curve analysis is not only pertinent to private investment and borrowing decisions, but assumes importance at the governmental level in the areas of monetary policy and debt management. When, for example, the Federal Reserve engages in open market operations in its efforts to regulate credit availability, its choice of securities to buy or sell has an immediate and marked effect on the interest rate structure.

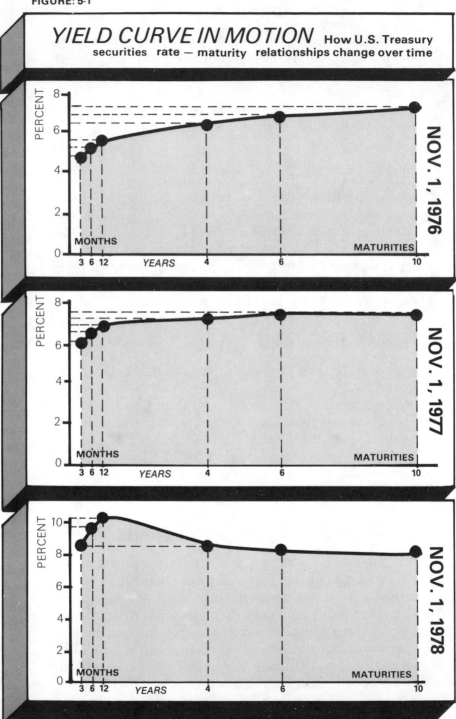

YIELD CURVE IN MOTION How U.S. Treasury
securities rate — maturity relationships change over time

170

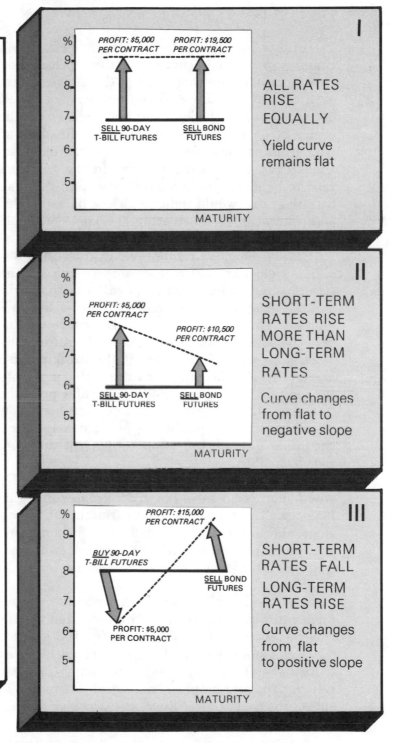

Figure 5-2 depicts the hypothetical effects of three changes in the yield curve on futures prices. For ease of comparison, the short end of the curve is taken in each case to coincide with the maturity of the 90-day bill contract and the long end to coincide with the maturity of government bond futures. Readers should bear in mind, however, and will be reminded several times over, that in the real world the relationships tend to be more subtle and elusive than these simplified diagrams would indicate. They do serve the purpose, however, of illustrating the basic principles involved.

Case I depicts a rising level of interest rates with a flat yield curve. The curve is in this instance a straight line which remains parallel to the horizontal axis as short and long maturities rise by an equal amount. The expectation of such a move would indicate the sale of both T-bill and bond futures contracts since both will fall in price if the anticipated move materializes. In keeping with the stated principle that the long maturities experience a greater price fluctuation from the same rate change, the bond contract would in this case produce a profit nearly four times the dollar gain on the T-bill contract if rates on both rose from 7% to 9%.

Case II illustrates the effect on the yield curve when short-term rates rise by a greater amount than long-term. As the curve moves from a flat to negative slope, short positions in both T-bill and bond contracts will prove profitable with the greater gain resulting from the latter even though the increase in yield is not as great.

In *Case III*, short-term rates decline while long-term rates continue to rise. The indicated positions in this instance are long T-bill futures and short bonds.

Remember, we are dealing here with price volatility in relation to interest rate change. It bears repeating that if the profit potential is greater at one side of the curve or the other, so is the risk if the actual behavior of interest rates fails to fit the expected pattern. That yield curves will move in one of these ways is likely. Which of the three cases will in fact be realized at any given time is the question that begs a ready or confident answer.

Riding the Yield Curve

What may not be so obvious from the foregoing discussion is that the yield curve, when it has a positive slope, has a built-in price appreciation factor even as it remains fixed in the same position. To grasp the concept, one need only visualize a Treasury bill, or discount bond for that matter, inexorably climbing in price toward par as each day passes.

The expression "riding the yield curve" refers to the purchase of a fixed-income security whose maturity coincides with the crest of an upward-sloping curve, and holding it for the amount of time necessary to move down the slope toward the origin of the horizontal and vertical axes. In effect, the investor is using the yield curve to his advantage by adding an element of capital appreciation to the indicated discount at the time the security is purchased.

By way of illustration, let us return to the Nov. 1, 1976, yield curve. As of that date, 90-day bills were offered at a 4.82 discount, and 180-day bills at a 5.01 discount. Assuming our intention was to make a three-month investment, we could simply have bought the 90-day bill and held it to maturity to earn 4.82% (4.94% on a bond-equivalent basis). But that would not have been our only alternative. We instead might have bought the 180-day bill at 5.01 with the intention of selling it back to a dealer the following Jan. 27, when it had another 90 days left to its maturity.

What would have been the result of such a transaction? Assuming that the yield curve remained stationary between Nov. 1 and Jan. 27—an essential but problematical assumption as we shall shortly see—and overlooking transaction costs for the purpose of our illustration, we would have bought a 180-day bill at 5.01 and sold it as a 90-day bill at 4.82. Employing the formulas provided in Chapter Two, we would have paid $974,500 for a bill with a face value of $1 million and sold it 90 days later for $987,950. The $13,450 capital gain would have represented a 5.52% return for the 90-day investment, or an increase in yield of 70 basis points over the 4.82 discount that would have been earned by buying and holding to maturity the bill dated Jan. 27.

Rather than remaining in position as this strategy requires, the yield curve in reality moves about with capricious and tantalizing undulations that would give a belly dancer cause for envy. The reader is invited to test his grasp of the process by calculating what the result would have been if the passage of time was accelerated and the Nov. 1, 1978, curve was in place on Jan. 27.[5] Because the level of the yield curve rose, the expected gain in yield turned out instead to be a surrender of 426 basis points, or most of the anticipated return.

All is not lost, however. This is, after all, a book on interest rate futures. One of the principal applications of these contracts is to protect investors against the consequences of such rate changes. We shall return to this strategy in Chapter 11, and demonstrate how, by using the T-bill contract to offset any increase in the level of interest rates, there is still an advantage to be gained from engaging in a "hedged yield curve ride."

---

[5]The solution:

Nov. 1:

Buy $1 million 180-day bills @ 5.01

    Cost = $974,950   Discount = $25,050

Jan. 27:

Sell $1 million 90-day bills @ 9.27

    Proceeds = $976,825 $\dfrac{\text{Discount}}{\text{Profit}} = \dfrac{23,175}{\$\ 1,875}$

Chapter Six

Comparative Yields, 1969-1978

This chapter strives to invest the abstract concepts discussed in Chapter Five with hard data, measuring and comparing the behavior over the past decade of those particular interest rates with which we are concerned in the futures market. The purpose is to gain an understanding of those recurring relationships which may be helpful in making profitable trading decisions.

To obtain the desired perspective over the course of one or more complete interest rate cycles, we have charted the pertinent rates from 1969 to the close of 1978. The analysis becomes more detailed for the last three years of the period, insofar as they span the history of interest rate futures to date.

Our attention is drawn once again to the three aspects of rate behavior: level, spread and term structure. The focus remains on 90-day Treasury bills and long-term bonds as they make up both ends of the government securities yield curve. Not to overlook the other instruments within the financial futures complex, we give due consideration to the relationship between commercial paper and Ginnie Mae securities and their Treasury counterparts on the maturity scale.

The data upon which the analysis is based are presented in chart and tabular form, in most cases ac-

cording to the peak and trough of each rate cycle.[1]
Average monthly interest rates are plotted on a semi-
logarithmic scale to depict the difference in proportion
between, say, a 200 basis-point rise from 4% to 6%
(50% change) and 6% to 8% (33⅓% change). The format is similar to the one adopted by Sidney Homer
and Richard I. Johannesen for their analytical study,
The Price of Money, 1946-1969,[2] to which readers of
the present volume are urged to refer for an excellent
account of short- and long-term rate behavior throughout that earlier period. To a limited degree, the present
chapter purports to be a continuation of their historical analysis. The keynote of the chapter is that what
appears at first glance to be statistical minutiae is in
fact the stuff of which trading profits are made.

How the Rates Moved

Although a detailed discussion of the economic
and political environment in which interest rate
changes occur, and which in some cases influences
such movements, is reserved for the two subsequent
chapters, those external events that were obviously
consequential will be noted as we proceed.

If the initial year of this survey had been selected
to coincide with a cyclical turn in interest rates rather
than simply to provide a round 10-year record, we
would begin our analysis in January 1970, when short-
term interest rates had completed a steady climb that
extended through the 1960s and embarked on what
proved to be a two-year decline. Ninety-day Treasury
bills, which had yielded less than 2.50% in 1960, completed the final leg of their 10-year advance by rising
from approximately 6% to 8% during 1969. The 1970s
experienced two complete cycles of decline and recovery. As the period under review drew to a close at the

---

[1]Average monthly rates were obtained from the *Federal Reserve Bulletin,* various issues. See page 248, footnote 1.

[2]Page 160, footnote 4.

end of 1978, yields on 90-day T-bills approached a record 9% for the second time in the decade.

Long-term Treasury bonds with maturities exceeding 20 years traded at prices which provided yields ranging from 4% to 4.25% during the first half of the 1960s, then declined in price through the remaining years of the decade, driving yields over 6% for the first time in 100 years by the end of 1969. Long-term rates continued to advance through mid-1970, briefly reaching 7% before commencing a two-year decline back to the 5½% level. Between 1973 and 1974 they returned to the 7% area, where they held until 1977 when a renewed advance brought them to 8.75%, the highest yield to that date in modern history for long-term government securities. The pair of related circumstances which helped fuel this escalation of interest rates during the decade were the 1973-74 Middle East oil embargo and the precipitous fall of the U.S. dollar in the international foreign exchange market during 1977-78. The former incited, and the latter lent further stimulus to, an accelerating inflation rate which, as it reached what was considered an intolerable double-digit pace, became a matter of overriding national concern.

Short-term rates continued to exhibit greater volatility than long-term yields, reversing trend more frequently and rising or falling by a greater number of basis points. While the return on long-term government coupons rose slightly more than 100 basis points (5.74% to 6.81%) during 1969, the movement in three-month T-bills (6.13% to 7.81%) was two-thirds greater. During the ensuing decline from June 1970 to November 1971 (6.99% to 5.44%) bond yields declined 155 basis points as the discount on 90-day bills fell 449 basis points (7.87% to 3.38%), recovered 201 basis points (3.38% to 5.39%) and then surrendered the gain (5.39% to 3.20%) in a saw-tooth pattern through the February 1972 low. During the long rise over the following 30 months, rates on 90-day bills nearly tripled

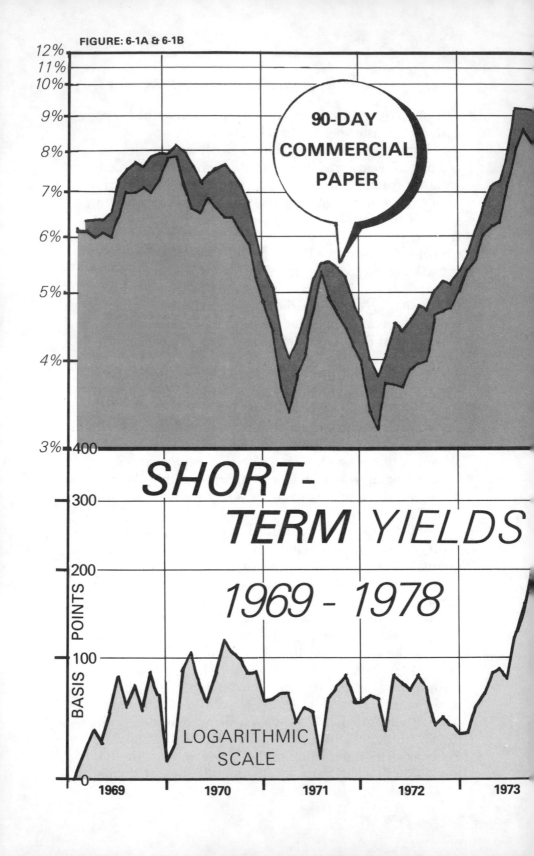

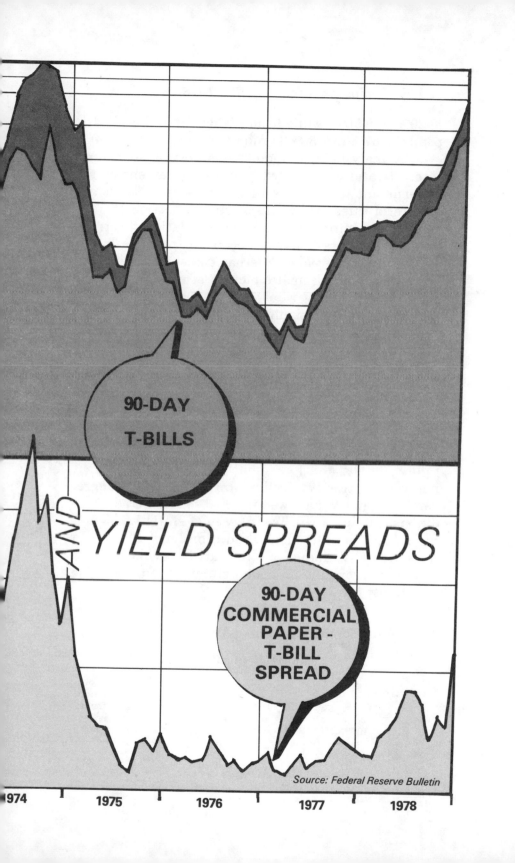

(3.20% to 8.96%) while bond yields climbed 166 basis points (5.67% to 7.33%), an increase of less than 30%.

As analysts have frequently observed, short-term interest rates are affected to a greater extent by the government's monetary-policy measures than are long-term rates, which are a truer reflection of independent commitments by a large population of borrowers and investors to pay or receive a stated cash flow over a period of years. Whereas the short-term chart presents a more dramatic picture of change than the gentle sweeps of long rates, it is the latter that portend a greater economic significance.

With the sole interruption of one contracyclical rally of 120 basis points, short-term rates receded some 470 basis points (8.96% to 4.26%) over 28 months from the cyclical peak of the 1973-74 credit "crunch," while long-term yields registered a comparatively moderate decline of 71 basis points (7.33% to 6.62%). Apart from a sharp increase in the nation's money supply during April 1976, which prompted the Federal Reserve to tighten credit and force short-term rates higher at mid-year, successive declines in the monetary aggregates (M_1 and M_2) allowed the Fed to relax credit conditions through 1976. The release of statistics signaling a slackening economy and a prolonged strike in the automotive industry stimulated speculation of a recession, providing an added stimulus to the decline in interest rates.

Table 6-1.   Summary of Short-Term Rate Changes, 1969-78.

(in basis points)

	Rates Early 1969	1/69 to 1/70	1/70 to 3/71	3/71 to 7/71	7/71 to 2/72	2/72 to 8/74	8/74 to 12/76	12/76 to 12/78	Net change from early 1969
Treas. Bills (3 mos.)	6.13	+174	−449	+201	−219	+576	−469	+450	+287
Prime C.P. (3 mos.)	6.14	+200	−409	+149	−173	+798	−714	+550	+411

From the December 1976 cyclical low, short- and long-term rates embarked on a two-year advance where the only distinguishing variable was the pace at which they increased. Nine uninterrupted months of steadily advancing rates brought the 90-day bill discount up 190 basis points (4.26% to 6.16%) by September 1977, followed by seven months of lateral movement within a 30-point range, and then a resumption of the upward movement from the 6.30% level in May 1978 through year-end and into 1979.

Bond yields also trended higher during 1977-78, though again in a more subdued manner. The high yields of the bear bond market of 1973-74 were matched by June 1977 and the 8% level was broached in January 1978. As occurred in the short-term sector, a late summer turnaround kindled investor hopes that the long price decline had run its course, but the premature optimism was soon dispelled when, after the brief rally, rates resumed their ascent to the 9% level.

Throughout 1978, the money supply continued to expand faster than the target growth rate set by the Federal Reserve, prompting it to force the federal funds rate repeatedly higher, which lifted other money market rates with it as was the Fed's intent. Successive increases in consumer and producer prices and unprecedented weakness in the foreign exchange value of the U. S. dollar nevertheless exacerbated the same inflationary pressures the Fed was attempting to dampen.

Table 6-2.   Summary of Long-term Yield Changes, 1969-78.

(in basis points)

	Yield Early 1969	1/69 to 6/70	6/70 to 11/71	11/71 to 8/74	8/74 to 12/76	12/76 to 12/78	Net Change From Early 1969
Long-term government bonds	5.74	+125	−155	+189	−71	+125	+300

Presuming that loans and deposits ultimately would be repaid in depreciated dollars, savers and lenders deemed it necessary to secure higher nominal interest rates to maintain a constant "real" return on their savings and investments.

Ninety-day prime commercial paper rates generally traced the same path that Treasury bills of the same maturity followed over the ten-year period. The greatest disparities appeared at the cyclical peaks when the rate on 90-day paper rose substantially higher than the T-bill discount. Commercial paper rates remain above T-bill rates at cyclical troughs as well, but the spread between them narrows considerably at these lower levels.

While bill rates rose by 576 basis points during the February 1972 to August 1974 advance, commercial paper rates increased 650 basis points (3.81% to 10.31%), fell 231 (10.31% to 8%), and then moved back up another 393 (8% to 11.93%) before beginning the two-year decline to December 1976.

When the next cyclical rise got underway, paper rates were a mere 25 basis points above bill rates. By the peak in late 1978, the former had doubled (5.18% to 10.24%) while the spread between them multiplied eight-fold to over 200 basis points.

Rates on Ginnie Mae 8s paralleled those on long-term government bonds, while maintaining the yield premium that has been characteristic of pass-through securities since their inception. From a cyclical low of 7.60% in February 1977, yields on the 8s had risen to 9.30% by November 1978, a move 20 basis points greater than on 20-year Treasury bonds during the two-year bear market.

The Cash-Futures Relationship

The futures market almost invariably followed the lead of the cash market from 1976 to 1978. Apart from, or perhaps on account of, the time difference, the most distinguishing characteristic between them was that futures price behavior was generally an exaggerated reflection of cash price movement. For example, while the cash 90-day bill rate remained within a 35-basis-point range (4.75% to 5.10%) between January and April of 1976, the December 1976 T-bill contract fell 200 basis points in price from a 5.70% discount (94.30 Index) to 7.70% (92.30 Index), then recovered 130 basis points to 6.40% (93.60).[3] During the seven months from June to December 1976 that cash rates declined 120 basis points (5.50% to 4.30%), the December 1976 contract rose 320 basis points in price from 7.40% (92.60) to 4.20% (95.80). This difference of 200 basis points between the changes in yield on cash bills and the December 1976 contract is explained by the fact that during the first five months of 1976, the traders active in the futures market had anticipated an increase in short-term rates by year-end, when they in fact declined. Since cash and futures prices must converge by the delivery date of the contract, the December 1976 contract ultimately had to retrace the amount by which the market had mistakenly projected a rise in rates.

The same type of exaggeration occurred during July-August 1978, when the two-year rise in short-term rates was broken by a four-week hiatus during which the cash 90-day bill discount dipped 35 basis points (7.15% to 6.80%) and the December 1978 T-bill contract concurrently rallied 70 basis points from 92.10 to 92.80.[4] As during the June–December 1976 period, the fact that cash rates turned down while the futures market was projecting a discount 100 basis points higher, or nearly 8 %, raised the possibility that

---

[3]This overly exaggerated movement was probably due to the fact that trading in T-bill futures had just commenced, and traders were still getting the "feel" of the new contract.

[4]To avoid any possible confusion between the two markets, futures contracts, with the exception of commercial paper, henceforth will be quoted on a price basis, cash rates will continue to be quoted on a discount or yield basis as the case may be.

the end of the cycle had come sooner than had generally been anticipated. Traders who had sold the December 1978 contract in the belief that bill rates would continue to rise hastened to cover their short positions while those who had remained on the sidelines went long so as not to miss the turnaround. This sort of anticipatory trading that is the *raison d'être* of the futures market drove the price of December 1978 T-bills twice as high as the movement in the cash rate might have justified.

Similar volatility is evident in the long-term sector. During the July–August 1978 bear market rally, yields on 20-year Treasury bonds fell back temporarily from 8.65% to 8.40%, the equivalent of a $2^9/_{32}$ price increase from $93^{28}/_{32}$ to $96^5/_{32}$. Yet in the same four-week period, June 1979 Treasury bond futures raced from 91 to 95, a rise 75% greater than the one that occurred in the cash market.

Such disparate rates of advance and decline in the cash and futures markets imply a variable price and yield relationship between the securities underlying the futures contract and each of its successive delivery months. These changing differentials, referred to in futures market usage as "alterations in the basis," will receive their due consideration in a later chapter devoted to hedging. It is the basis difference between cash and futures prices that is the critical element in the successful conduct of a hedging operation.

Yield Spreads

Other relationships that hold the attention of traders in both markets are the yield spreads that were discussed in general terms in Chapter Five. To reiterate, these differentials in yield arise from the degree of risk investors attribute to one type of security vis-a-vis another, or their expectations concerning changes in interest rates in the case of two like securities of different maturity. An example of the former instance would be the comparison between Treasury issues and securities of private issuers, be they bonds or commercial paper, where credit risk is a significant factor. When the comparison lies between, say, 90-day and one-year T-bills, the controlling factors are the interrelated ones of liquidity preference and expectations of rate change.

Their study of yield spreads between like and different instruments gives investors in the cash market a clue to those securities which, as of a given moment, are relatively undervalued and suitable for purchase or, on the contrary, relatively overvalued and thus candidates for sale. The same principle—spreads which deviate substantially from their historic norms ultimately return to their customary range—affords speculators trading opportunities in the futures market. The standard spread strategy is to sell the "expensive" contract and simultaneously buy the "cheap" one with the intention of "unwinding," or liquidating both the short and long positions, when the relationship between the two returns to its regular level. If the spread should move to the other extreme, that is to say become unusually narrow, the long and short positions would be reversed with the expectation of profit as the differential again grows wider.

There are as many possible spread comparisons which can be monitored as there are combinations of money market instruments and bonds of every rating and maturity. To be aware of each and every trading opportunity on a day-to-day basis would require the aid of a computer, which in fact is a service that several of the larger dealer firms provide. The following illustrations are limited to three specific spreads which are particularly relevant to futures trading: (1) 90-day T-bills vs. 90-day commercial paper, (2) 90-day vs. one-year T-bills, (3) Ginnie Mae 8s vs. long-term Treasury bonds.

The cash market spreads are tracked from 1969 through 1978. The T-bill–commercial paper and Ginnie Mae–bond futures spreads are traced for 1978 only, the first full year of trading in the commercial paper and bond contracts. The one-year T-bill contract has not been in existence sufficiently long to provide any meaningful comparisons. Differentials are expressed in terms of basis points since that form of presentation is compatible with the trading scale of the T-bill and commercial paper futures contracts. Inasmuch as they are quoted in 32nds of par, Ginnie Mae and Treasury bond futures prices must be converted to their decimal yield equivalents. Like the charts depicting absolute rate changes, the spreads are plotted on a semi-logarithmic scale, the method which more accurately portrays the relative magnitude of spread changes at low and high interest rate levels.

T-Bills and Commercial Paper

With the exception of the 1973-74 credit "crunch," when commercial paper rates surged to inordinately high levels and the spread above the 90-day T-bill discount ballooned to an unprecedented 438 basis points, the gross spread between the two short-term instruments has tended to range between +25 and +100 in favor of the commercial paper yield. This range has been exceeded several times on either side, but the spread has remained within those limits with sufficient consistency to justify their use as guides to framing trading decisions.

The conventional wisdom of the market says that the commercial paper–T-bill spread will open to its wider limit during periods of economic uncertainty, and approach the narrow end of its historic range when more serene times mitigate investors' concern over risk and preoccupation with safety. The record from 1969 to 1978 would indicate that the absolute level of interest rates was more of a determining factor than the condition of the economy, although there was plainly some sort of causative relationship at work be-

Table 6-3.   Peaks and Troughs of the Yield Spread Between 90-Day Prime Commercial Paper and T-Bills, 1969-1978
(in basis points)

	Trough	Peak
January 1969	+1	
October 1969		+87
December 1969	+12	
July 1970		+119
July 1971	+15	
July 1972		+85
December 1972	+33	
September 1973		+202
March 1974	+68	
July 1974		+438
August 1975	+15	
December 1978		+125
Average Trough & Peak	+24	+176
Average January 1969–July 1972		+53
Average December 1972–December 1978		+151

tween the two. During the recession of 1969-70, the spread did, to be sure, open to +120, a level that remained unmatched until January 1973. On the whole, however, the spread fluctuated between +60 and +100 through most of 1970, a range not appreciably different than during the prosperity year 1972. Subsequent to the 1974 explosion, the record did conform to the expected pattern, as the spread remained within 20 basis points of the narrow limit from mid-1975 to early 1978.

As Homer and Johannesen point out with regard to the 1946-1969 period, and as is borne out by the experience of the ensuing nine years, T-bill rates tend to rise faster than commercial paper rates during the early stages of economic expansion, but commercial paper rates take the lead during the later phase. By the same token, bill rates begin their decline earlier than commercial paper rates at the onset of recession, but are overtaken as the contraction continues. Consequently, the spread between the two rates in the cash market tends to be at the narrow side of the range at the start of an expansion phase, and at the wide end early in a recession. Though there was yet to be compiled through 1978 a futures price history covering a complete interest rate cycle, the experience that year, the first to provide comparable price data for T-bill and commercial paper contracts, conformed with the just-mentioned pattern in the cash market.

Table 6-4 lists monthly changes in both cash and futures yield spreads over the course of the year. While short-term rates remained steady or declined moderately during the first four months, yield spreads between the cash instruments opened somewhat wider, but the yield advantage of the December 1978 commercial paper contract over December 1978 T-bill futures became moderately narrower. By June, when the general increase in rates gained momentum, the spreads grew wider in both markets, but the differ-

Table 6-4.   90-Day Commercial Paper-Treasury Bill Spreads: Cash and Futures Markets, 1978.

	Cash 90-day Commercial Paper Rate[1]	Cash 90-day T-bill Rate[1]	Cash Spread	Dec. 1978 Commercial Paper Futures Yield	Dec. 1978 T-bill Futures Yield	Futures Spread
Jan. 16	6.80	6.50	+30	8.60	7.74	+86
Feb. 13	6.76	6.46	+30	8.48	7.63	+85
Mar. 13	6.75	6.27	+48	8.15	7.50	+65
Apr. 10	6.80	6.35	+45	8.36	7.62	+74
May 8	6.96	6.39	+57	8.51	7.74	+77
June 5	7.34	6.61	+73	8.62	7.72	+90
July 3	7.78	6.99	+79	9.33	7.91	+142
July 31	7.81	6.78	+103	8.85	7.60	+125
Aug. 28	7.93	7.35	+58	8.82	7.54	+128
Sept.25	8.52	8.04	+48	9.34	8.26	+108
Oct. 23	9.09	7.67	+142	9.95	8.35	+160
Nov. 20	10.21	8.36	+185	11.20	8.83	+237

[1]Weekly averages, Federal Reserve Report.

ences between the two futures contracts increased at a faster pace.

By the end of August, the futures spread (128 basis points) was more than double the cash market spread (58 basis points). As 1978 drew to a close, both cash and futures spreads had grown considerably wider than their levels at the outset of the year. The greatest relative change occurred in the cash spread, which expanded approximately six-fold while the futures spread nearly tripled, probably reflecting the fact that by December cash rates were surpassing the levels that futures prices had forecast early in the year.

90-Day and One-Year T-Bills

Changes in the spread between 90-day and one-year Treasury bills are a reflection of shifts in slope at the near end of the yield curve for government securities. An upward shift to a more positive slope means that yields on intermediate-term securities are rising more rapidly than those of short-term securities, causing the spread between them to grow wider. This behavior is indicative of heightened liquidity preference on the part of investors when rates are at a relatively low level in absolute terms as they assume the standard defensive posture against rising rates by shortening maturities in their fixed-income portfolios. It is also explained by the greater yield volatility of the shorter-term instruments. Conversely, this spread has the tendency to narrow and even reverse itself with the 90-day yield rising above the one-year yield as the Treasury curve turns flat and then negative.

The statistical record during the 1969-1978 period corroborates these assumptions. In the post-recession recovery year 1972, and again during 1975 and the first half of 1976, the discount on the one-year bill ranged from 50 to 90 basis points above the 90-day rate. Those were the years during our time frame in which rates on both maturities were at or near their

Table 6-5.   Peaks and Troughs of the Yield Spread Between One-Year and 90-Day T-Bills, 1969-1978.
(in basis points)

	Trough	Peak
June 1969		+43
January 1970	−37	
April 1972		+94
January 1974	−76	
July 1974		+49
December 1974	−36	
March 1976		+82
December 1976	+25	
December 1978		+40
Average	−31	+62

cyclical lows. When rates reached their cyclical peak in January 1970, the average discount for the month was 7.87% on three-month bills and 7.50% on the one-year issue, meaning that the spread had inverted to 37 basis points in favor of the 90-day bill. The reverse spread grew even wider during the 1974 peak, opening to −76 (7.77% on 90-day bills vs. 7.01% on one-year) in January, seven months before the August peak when the two discounts were within eight basis points of one another (8.96% on 90-day bills vs. 8.88% on one-year). While Treasury bill yields set new record highs at the close of 1978, the 90-day–one-year spread again had narrowed from the +90 level in favor of the longer maturity to +40 basis points.

Ginnie Maes and Treasury Bonds

The yield spreads between Ginnie Mae 8s and long-term government bonds have a peculiar bias in that it has taken the greater part of the decade under review for the investment fraternity at large to become familiar with pass-through securities. As the 1970s wore on, the spread tended to grow narrower simply because investors required less of a yield premium to attract them to the initially unfamiliar mortgage instrument. Another factor which has affected this spread is the disintermediation that takes place during high interest rate periods as investors withdraw funds held on deposit at thrift institutions to secure a higher return through the direct purchase of such money market instruments as Treasury bills and commercial paper. As the major buyers of Ginnie Mae securities during the 1970-1973 period, savings and loan associations that suffered heavy withdrawals perforce cut back on their Ginnie Mae purchases, a step which had notable effects on the spread against government and other bonds in the latter half of 1973.

In September 1973 and again a year later as the 1974 crunch entered its most extreme phase, the spread between Ginnie Mae 8s and long-term Treasury bonds opened from its customary 40 to 60 basis-points range to as wide as 125 basis points before settling back to its more limited span by December 1974. Between early 1976 and mid-1978, the spread held fairly consistently within the 35 to 45 basis-points range before an acceleration in the rate of increase in yield and again the prospect of disintermediation brought about a wider spread, although the 1974 extremes had not been reached by late 1978.

As was the case with the commercial paper contract, the introduction of the Treasury bond contract in late 1977 affords only a year's history of this relationship as it has developed in the futures market. The spread between the June 1979 Ginnie Mae and June 1979 Treasury bond contracts, for example, traded fairly consistently at a three-point price differential in favor of June 1979 bonds throughout 1978. A futures trader who followed this spread closely would have been moved to take action during the several occasions when the prices of the two contracts drew appreciably closer or apart from the three-point relationship. On Sept. 12, for example, at the apex of the late summer rally, June 1979 Treasury bonds traded at 96-00 at the

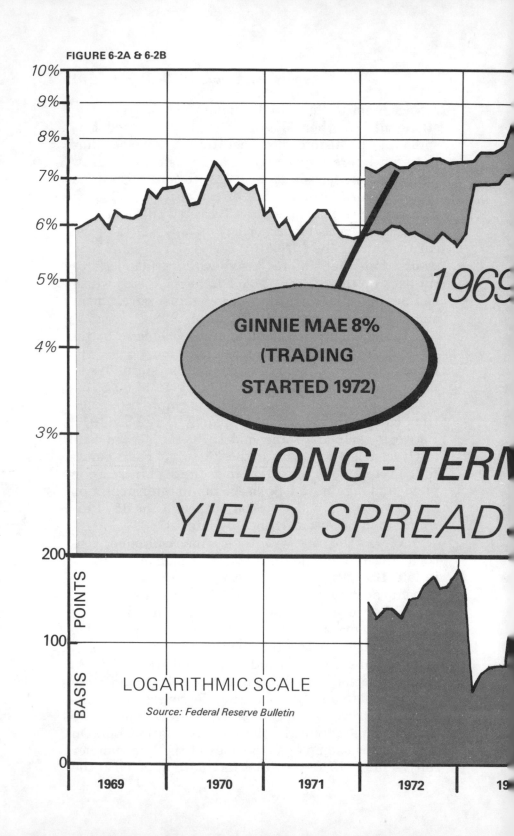

FIGURE 6-2A & 6-2B

10%
9%
8%
7%
6%
5%
4%
3%

1969

GINNIE MAE 8%
(TRADING
STARTED 1972)

LONG - TERM
YIELD SPREAD.

200

POINTS

100

BASIS

LOGARITHMIC SCALE
Source: Federal Reserve Bulletin

0

1969   1970   1971   1972   19

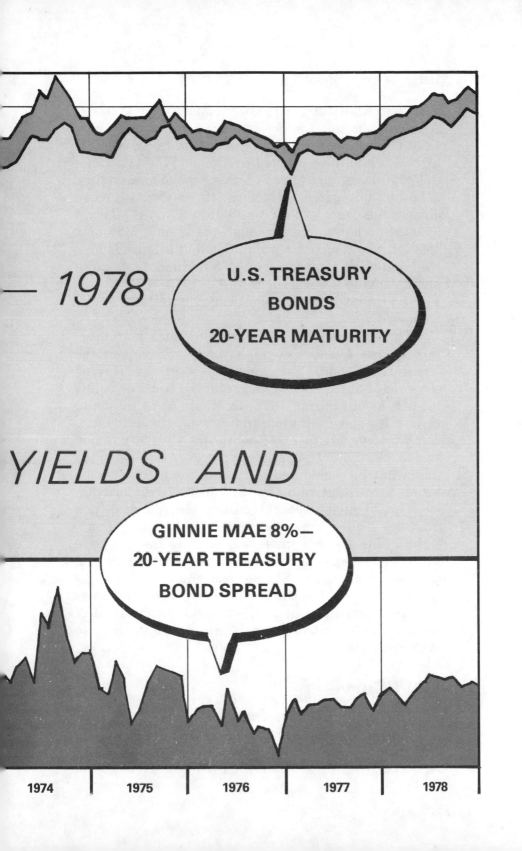

same time that June 1979 Ginnie Maes were at 92-16. A trader who sold the bond contract and bought June 1979 Ginnie Maes because the spread had increased by $^{16}/_{32}$ would have profited by $^{24}/_{32}$ or $750 (1½ times the $500 margin required on this type of transaction) if he had liquidated both contracts on Oct. 12, when June bonds were at 94-00 and June Ginnie Maes at 91-08. In other words, although the Ginnie Mae long position would have been liquidated at a $1^{8}/_{32}$nds loss, the bond short sale would have generated a two-point profit, leaving a net gain before commissions of $^{24}/_{32}$, or the amount by which the bond-Ginnie Mae spread narrowed.

The trader's risk in undertaking such a transaction is that the spread might grow wider than the $3^{16}/_{32}$nds differential at which it is initiated. Having observed that the spread had returned to three points in each month during 1978, he would have reason to believe his risk is limited. If, however, the July-October 1974 episode recurred while the spread position was in place, the trader would discover to his dismay that what he considered to be a minimal risk transaction turned out to be more than he bargained for.

The 90-day-one-year Treasury bill spread differs from the T-bill-commercial paper and Treasury bond-Ginnie Mae spreads inasmuch as it is the only one which involves a comparison between like instruments of different maturity. A closer examination of that relationship, as well as the one between short- and long-term government securities, entails a continuation of the type of yield curve analysis introduced at the close of Chapter Five.

Yield Curves

The continual movement of yield curves over time is illustrated by the three curves in the previous chapter which depict comparative yields on Treasury issues for successive Novembers from 1976 through 1978. As it happened, those three Novembers spanned three phases of an interest rate cycle, so that the progression through the three fundamental slopes—positive, flat and negative—is clearly shown in the yield curves. The remainder of this chapter is given over to a more systematic analysis of these shifts by plotting the Treasury yield curves at the cyclical peaks and troughs of short- and long-term rates during the 1969-1978 period. Since our primary purpose is to assess how these undulations influence the behavior of interest rate futures, we shall relate the movement of the "cash" yield curve to the yields on the pertinent futures contracts as of the same date.

In contemplating the following series of curves, Homer and Johannesen's contention that the short- and long-term segments are in fact separate albeit loosely related markets should be kept in mind. Moreover there is no assurance that the precise shape that the curve assumed in the summer of 1974, for example, will be duplicated during late 1978 or some other high interest rate period. There is always a tendency in any market situation for general patterns to recur, just as we observe the repeated appearance of the basic yield configurations. Beyond the assumption that the collective participants in the money and bond markets will perform their jobs in a rational manner, however, there is no law or formula which dictates the precise form of the curve under a given set of monetary and general economic conditions. It behooves the futures trader to know how and why yield curves behave as they do over time, but to rely completely on such considerations for guidance in decision-making would be tantamount to emulating those generals who purportedly are always fighting the last war.

Though there have been occasions when short- and long-term interest rates moved in opposite directions, the usual experience is that they rise and fall together. The more common disparity, of which the yield curve is but a graphic representation, lies in the extent and speed of their respective advances and declines, i.e., their relative volatility.

A comparison of the 90-day bill and long-term bond charts corroborates the assertion made in Chapter Five that short-term rates are subject to much wider swings. The arithmetic of extending maturities demonstrated, however, that the dollar consequences of the more moderate movement in long-term yields are considerably greater. We have also observed, and will return to address the issue in some detail in the following chapter, that short-term rates are highly susceptible to government monetary policy, which must rely on its immediate impact in the short-term money market to set into motion the chain of causative factors that ultimately make their influence felt in the long-term sector. The direct determinants of long-term interest rates, such as expectations regarding the future inflation rate, are more deeply rooted in the attitudes of professional and private investors, and not likely to vary from day to day or even week to week. Shifts in the yield curve, therefore, are more conspicuous at the short-term end, where the broader movement accounts in large part for the changes in slope and position. A rise or fall in bill rates is generally responsible for the change from a positive to negative slope or vice versa, and an adjustment in the relationship between three-, six- and 12-month maturities usually accounts for the hump formation that emerges near the cyclical peak in rates.

The data for the 1969-1978 decade verify the prevalent assumption that curves assume a positive slope at a cyclical trough or the early stages of a business expansion, gradually turning flat and ultimately humped and/or negative by a later and perhaps waning stage of prosperity. The logic usually advanced to account for this phenomenon is that when both short- and long-term rates reach cyclically high levels, as they did in 1970, 1974 and 1978, investors direct their buying interest toward the longer maturities, foregoing their usual liquidity preference to "lock in" high long-term rates and enjoy the benefit of capital appreciation as they ultimately decline. Meanwhile, corporations defer long-term borrowing if possible and raise whatever funds they may require in the short-term sector, thereby adding to the supply of near-term securities and raising their yield.

The supply and demand pressures are reversed when rates approach their cyclical lows. The general expectation then is that rates are about to turn upward, prompting investors to shorten maturities, thereby forcing down near-term rates by buying securities at the short-term end, while the corporations take advantage of the existing low level of rates by borrowing long-term and forcing up yields in that sector. That was the situation in March 1971, February 1972 and November 1976 when the curves on those respective dates assumed the conventional positive slope.

At the January 1970 peak, the curve was flat through the intermediate three- to five-year maturities, then turned negative through the long-term Treasury issues. In addition to moving up the vertical axis in reflection of a higher rate level, the August 1974 curve was positive at the near-term end, then assumed a more negative slope after the first year than occurred at the 1970 peak. The November 1978 curve originated at about the same level it had in 1974, but had a more obvious hump which was as negative as the 1974 curve between the first and fifth year, after which it became considerably flatter through the longest maturities.

The three positive sloping curves which took form at the cyclical lows also had their distinctive features. The March 1971 curve, very much like the hypothetical examples depicted on page 198, was practically a straight line. As usual under actual circumstances as it is common in textbook illustrations, this sort of "curve" has no crest in the short to intermediate area,

FIGURE 6-3

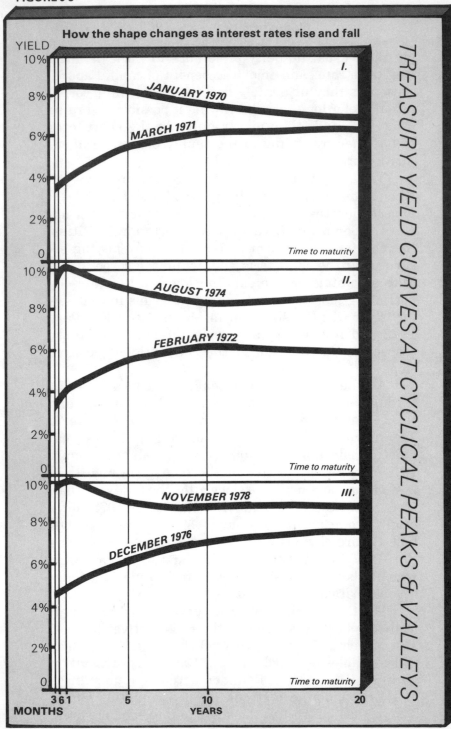

How the shape changes as interest rates rise and fall

TREASURY YIELD CURVES AT CYCLICAL PEAKS & VALLEYS

nor does it flatten out as the longer maturities are approached. The February 1972 and November 1976 curves are truly curved, although they too differ somewhat in shape. February 1972 is a more perfect parabola that does not begin to flatten until approximately the fifth year. November 1976, which originated about 150 basis points higher, crested in the three- to six-month range, after which the curve became progressively flatter as it approached the fifth year and beyond.

Once again, the reader is cautioned not to look for magic in these pictures. They invariably raise more questions than they supply answers. The yield curves do serve to demonstrate, however, that there is more to the business of trading financial futures (or fixed-income securities for that matter) than merely speculating whether interest rates per se are about to rise or fall. That accomplishment is not to be disparaged. Anyone who is blessed with the prescience to forecast rate movements accurately and consistently need not trouble himself with this book or any other for that matter, but simply buy or sell when his reason, instinct or whatever shapes his decisions so dictates. Those of us who are not so fortunate, however, need as much assistance as we are able to summon, and an understanding of the relationships that yield curves portray falls into that category. Given a particular economic environment, should the futures trader go long T-bills or bonds? Or in a different situation, should he be a seller of nearby- or deferred-delivery months of the same contract? While it offers no "magic," the yield curve can and does provide a conceptual framework for thinking through such questions.

By superimposing on the chart the hypothetical T-bill and bond futures yields that existed at the time the November 1976 and 1978 yield curves were drawn, we note that in each instance the projected futures market yields tended to extrapolate the expectations embodied in the cash curve.[5] When the slope of the curve was positive in November 1976, T-bill futures yields formed the steepest portion at the short-term end, rising approximately 20 basis points every quarterly delivery date or about seven basis points monthly. This positive futures slope was a manifestation of the market's belief that rates were likely to rise from the cyclical low at the 1976 year-end.

When the curve had turned negative a year later, futures prices mirrored the change. The nearby-delivery months of the T-bill contract closely followed the cash curves. By the September 1979 delivery, T-bill futures yields reversed their trend, moving downward for the next two delivery dates (six months) before exhibiting a flat trend for the remainder of the T-bill series. At the distant end of the November 1978 curve, the successive bond contract deliveries extended the flat to slightly negative slope prevailing in the long sector.

The price consequences of the changes in yield as the curves altered shape and position were comparable in the cash and futures markets. Though, as previously noted, T-bill rates displayed greater volatility at the short-term end, the price change was more substantial in the long-term sector. As 90-day bill rates rose approximately 425 basis points from November 1976 to November 1978, long-term bond rates increased 110. In line with those yield increases, $1 million invested in bills during the 24-month period would have incurred a capital loss of $10,625, as compared with a loss ten times greater on an equivalent amount invested in long-term bonds.

Futures prices followed the same trend. Between

---

[5]Some people who read my manuscript were unhappy with my use of the words "hypothetical" and "projected." A Board of Trade publication says, "Yield equivalents on futures prices are provided as interest rate reference points only for futures traders would not actually receive a bond yield unless they took delivery on the contract and then only from the date of delivery." That seems to me an important distinction.

November 1976 and November 1978 the nearby T-bill contract[6] declined approximately 400 basis points, a loss of about $10,000. There is no futures comparison for the long-term bonds for the same two-year period, but during 1978 bond futures generally traced the course of the cash market.

Yield Curves and Spreads

There are four basic shifts in the slope and position of the futures yield curve which are consequential in interest rate contracts. All involve differences in the relative movement of nearby and deferred-delivery months of the same contract, i.e., securities bearing the same maturity deliverable at successively later dates. These differences comprise the rationale to the trading technique known as spreading, wherein various expirations of a particular contract are simultaneously bought and sold for the purpose of profiting from perceived price discrepancies.[7]

When the curve assumes a more positive slope but while shifting upward does not intersect with its original contour, deferred-delivery prices will drop further than the nearby-delivery prices, making it more profitable to be short the distant contracts. When the shift is so acute that the new curve crosses the earlier one.

---

[6]There are, of course, no Treasury bills which have a maturity of two years. Nor do any bills held to maturity entail capital depreciation. The purpose of this contrived comparison is merely to demonstrate the relative dollar values of changes in bill and bond yields in cash and futures markets.

[7]Chapter Eleven is devoted to a discussion of spreading and related trading techniques. For our present purpose readers should take care to differentiate between the expressions short- and long-term, which refer to the maturities and applicable interest rates on the various financial instruments with which this book deals, and the expressions nearby- and deferred-delivery, which designate the months in which the securities underlying a futures contract are to be delivered. For example, in November of a given year that year's December delivery is considered the nearby contract. Contracts calling for delivery the following December and beyond are regarded as deferred- or distant-delivery months. In each instance securities conforming to the contract specifications must be delivered, be they 90-day Treasury bills or 15-year bonds.

Here a trader would derive maximum profits by being simultaneously long the nearby-delivery month as the rate drops below its previous level and short one of the deferred months as its rate rises.

If the futures curve turns negative, but does not cross its former configuration, the relative advantage lies with a long position in the deferred month. Should the curves intersect, the combination of a nearby short and deferred long position would generate profits on both legs of the spread.

Although the various types of spreading operations are treated in some detail in Part Three of this book, it is timely to introduce the subject at this point to underline its connection with the yield curve movement we have been discussing. The projected futures curve formed by quotations on T-bill and government bond contracts for successive delivery months is usually an extension of the actual Treasury yield curve as of any given date, a relationship which simply confirms that trading activity in both the cash and futures markets are governed by the same set of expectations concerning the developing trend in interest rates.

Even if futures prices have no life of their own, so to speak, it is worthwhile to consider them apart from the cash market for a moment by way of illustrating the concept under discussion. In Figure 6-5 are plotted five curves which represent the distribution of yields for eight successive T-bill delivery months totaling two years on five dates spread throughout 1978. It will be recalled that the year was one of moderate, and then sharply rising interest rates, as the discount on 90-day bills climbed steadily from the 6% level in January to around 7% by mid-year, and then accelerated their rise in the second half to close the year in the neighborhood of 9.30%.

The T-bill futures curve remained fairly constant from mid-January to mid-April 1978, projecting an increase in the discount over a 24-month period of approximately 175 basis points or a rate of about seven

FIGURE 6-4

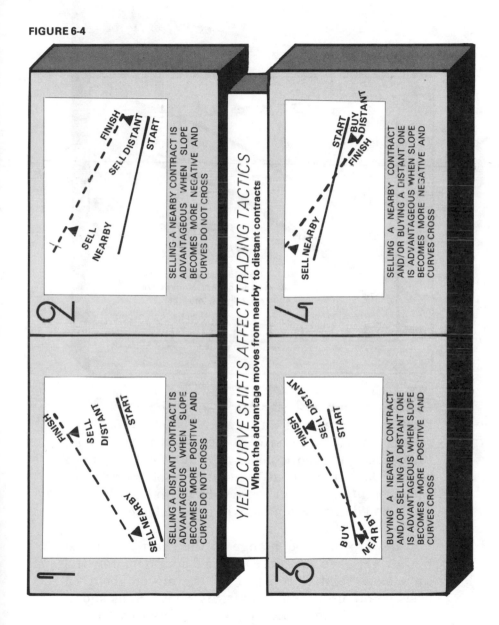

YIELD CURVE SHIFTS AFFECT TRADING TACTICS
When the advantage moves from nearby to distant contracts

1. SELLING A DISTANT CONTRACT IS ADVANTAGEOUS WHEN SLOPE BECOMES MORE POSITIVE AND CURVES DO NOT CROSS

2. SELLING A NEARBY CONTRACT IS ADVANTAGEOUS WHEN SLOPE BECOMES MORE NEGATIVE AND CURVES DO NOT CROSS

3. BUYING A NEARBY CONTRACT AND/OR SELLING A DISTANT ONE IS ADVANTAGEOUS WHEN SLOPE BECOMES MORE POSITIVE AND CURVES CROSS

4. SELLING A NEARBY CONTRACT AND/OR BUYING A DISTANT ONE IS ADVANTAGEOUS WHEN SLOPE BECOMES MORE NEGATIVE AND CURVES CROSS

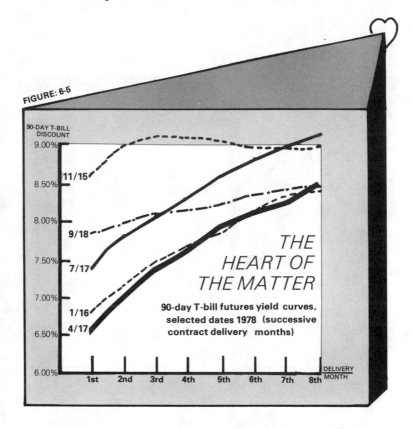

FIGURE: 6-5

90-DAY T-BILL DISCOUNT

THE
HEART OF
THE MATTER

90-day T-bill futures yield curves,
selected dates 1978 (successive
contract delivery months)

basis points a month. By April, when the nearby contract had expired and was replaced by a new deferred contract at the far end of the series, the curve had turned slightly more positive. The April 17 curve crossed Jan. 16 at about the mid-point of the delivery range signifying as in Figure 6-4 that the nearby contracts had declined in yield while the deferred months rose.

The first marked change on the chart took place by July 17, when the curve retained approximately the same slope relative to April 17, but moved about 75 basis points up the yield axis. By Sept. 18, as short-term rates began to soar in the cash market, the futures curve had shifted radically, with nearby-delivery months rising in yield relative to July and the distant deliveries falling. By returning to a less-positive slope, the market had lowered its estimated rate of increase to 3-4 basis points a month from the 8-10 basis points it forecast in July.

As cash rates continued to advance toward the 9% high established in 1974, the market arrived at the consensus that they would not rise much farther, and for the first time since the inception of futures trading in T-bills, the curve assumed a hump and turned negative in the deferred maturities. As of Nov. 15, 1978, the market was "saying" that 90-day T-bill rates would continue to rise sharply through March of the following year, maintain a more moderate advance through June and then start to decline by September 1979.

Phil Plunger Rides Again

But what do all of these twisting, turning, flattening and crossing lines have to do with an actual trading situation? Let us look at a typical spread transaction, and try to relate the theory to realized profits and/or losses in the futures market. Returning to our friends at Stable & Co., in mid-January 1978, Phil Plunger, by that time a seasoned futures trader, asked his account executive, Dan Decimal, what the firm's opinion was concerning the outlook for interest rates throughout the year. Decimal replied that Stable's economist had recently published a study forecasting rising short-term rates through most of 1978, nearing their cyclical peak late in the year. Plunger and Decimal know that they can profit from rising rates by selling interest rate futures short, but if rates start to decline before they are expected to, they stand to incur losses on a short position.

Plunger asks: Is there a strategy which will insulate him from the day-to-day rallies and declines to which a long or short position would be exposed but still allow him to profit from a turndown in rates if and when it comes? By way of response, Decimal proposes that Plunger consider spreading nearby and deferred T-bill contracts at an opportune time. He explains that by buying one delivery month and selling another, outright losses on the short position will be offset by profits on the long, and vice versa, since all delivery months of the same contract tend to move up and down together on a daily basis. But when a consensus forms that a top in rates is on the horizon, the deferred contracts—which are closer to that horizon—will rise faster, or at least fall more gradually, than the nearby-delivery months. The logical move, then, would be to sell a nearby contract and buy a deferred one. Having done that, their concern would be not whether contract prices rose or fell on a given day, but whether the basis-point difference between them grew wider or narrower.

Specifically, Decimal recommends that Plunger sell one December 1978 T-bill contract and buy one December 1979 contract. The question is, as always, at what price? In this case, the relevant "price" would be the spread between the two delivery dates. When this discussion took place on Jan. 16, December 1978 T-bills were being traded at 92.26 and December 1979 at 91.57 (reflecting discounts of 7.74% and 8.43%) the deferred contract priced 69 basis points below the nearby inasmuch as the futures yield curve was at that time positive. Since the transaction Decimal suggests involves the sale of the higher-priced contract (less yield) and purchase of the lower-priced contract, their objective is to have the spread become narrower. The closer the two prices come together, at whatever absolute level they happen to be, the greater the profit on the short-long position. As they move farther apart, from the point at which the spread was initiated, the paper loss grows larger. In fact, Decimal believes that 69 basis points is too narrow a spread and suggests that they wait for it to open wider before committing themselves. Plunger is inclined to rely on his broker's opinion in this instance, and asks Decimal to advise him when he thinks the timing is right.

Decimal holds off for three months, patiently waiting for the spread to grow wider to provide a more attractive trading opportunity. On April 17 he calls Plunger and tells him he believes the time has arrived to activate their plan. December 1978 T-bills have risen to 92.61, up 35 basis points since they first discussed the idea in January. But the December 1979 contract has gone only to 91.67, up 10 from its January level, meaning that the spread has widened to 94 basis points. Plunger gives his authorization to sell December 1978 and buy December 1979 at that difference.

Table 6-6 tells the rest of the story. By July 17 the spread had grown even wider, so that at a 99 basis-point difference the position had incurred a $125 loss [$25.00 × (99-94)] but on Sept. 18, after the yield curve started crossing and twisting, the spread had accrued a $1,500 profit [$25.00 × (94-34)]. Decimal and Plunger agreed to remain in position for further gains. But by Nov. 15 the spread had opened back to 40 basis points, as December 1979 started to fall in relation to December 1978. Broker and client decided not to risk any further erosion of their profit and closed out the two positions, buying in December 1978 at 91.38 (at a $3,075 profit before commissions) and selling December 1979 at 90.98 (loss of $1,725 before commissions). Both are satisfied with the results of their seven-month commitment inasmuch as the $1,350 gross profit (54 basis points) represented a handsome

Table 6-6.   T-Bill Futures Spreads
Dec. 1978-Dec. 1979 Contracts

1978	Dec. 1978 T-bills	Dec. 1979 T-bills	Difference
Jan. 16	92.26 (7.74)	91.57 (8.43)	+69
Apr. 17	92.61 (7.39)	91.67 (8.33)	+94
July 17	92.19 (7.81)	91.20 (8.80)	+99
Sept. 18	92.00 (8.00)	91.66 (8.34)	+34
Nov. 15	91.38 (8.62)	90.98 (9.02)	+40

return on the $500 margin required to initiate such a spread position.

Are Futures Really Forecasts?

After that brief flight into fiction (the prices used were, however, the actual ones at which the contracts were traded on the dates indicated), it is appropriate to conclude this chapter with some remarks concerning the question, frequently asked, "How well does the futures market predict interest rates?" If by that it is meant, how often during the life of any contract does its price approximate the interest rate on the underlying securities on delivery date, the answer must be, "Not very well."

The nature of the delivery process requires that cash and futures prices achieve parity by the delivery date because the two are at that time interchangeable. Under normal market conditions this convergence does not abruptly occur during the final days of a contract's life, but rather transpires gradually as it approaches its expiration. As the element of "futurity" elapses during the last month or two of a contract's existence, the price becomes more closely linked to its cash counterpart because the time in which expectations can play a determining role is running out.

In the case of the deferred-delivery contracts still 12 to 24 months removed from delivery, expectations as to where prices and yields will be one and two years hence are the controlling influence. To the extent that reports of changing supply-demand relationships affect today's (cash) prices, they play an even greater role in shaping expectations regarding tomorrow's (futures) prices.

If futures prices invariably and accurately forecast the interest rate of a particular financial instrument as of the delivery date, they would not vary for the 12, 18 or however many months remaining to the contract. That is tantamount to claiming that expectations do not change over so long a period or that the market enjoys perfect prescience concerning prices. Both assumptions are manifestly unrealistic. If they were not, there would be no need for a futures market since investors and borrowers would base their market decisions on complete foreknowledge. It was precisely because they have become so volatile, hence even more unpredictable than in the past, that a futures market for interest rates was established.

By way of illustrating what turns out after the fact to be a remote, almost haphazard connection between the futures market forecast on any given date, and the actual interest rate on delivery day, consider the case of the December 1977 T-bill contract. The cash 90-day bill rate at the close of 1977 was about 6%, and the "spot" (delivery month) contract accordingly went off the board on Dec. 21, its final trading day, at 94.04, reflecting a 5.96 discount. But throughout its 18-month life, or approximately 360 market sessions during which the December 1977 contract was traded, it changed hands at a price of 94.00 on no more than 25 separate trading days dispersed over the 1½ years as follows: October (twice) and November (once), 1976, and January (1), April (5), May (1), June (6), July (4), August (2), September (1) and December (1), 1977. Between the time trading in that contract began in June 1976 and its expiration, the price ranged between 248 basis points below (91.52) and 80 basis points above (94.84) the 94.00 Index/6.00% discount at which it was closed out in late December.

As was noted above, however, cash and futures prices tend to converge as delivery day approaches. The price trend of the December 1977 contract adhered to this pattern as the swings above and below the 94.00 level (or where cash rates happened to be at the time) became less pronounced from August 1977 on. During December, the "spot" month, the trading range grew still narrower as prices fluctuated some 25 basis points (93.80 to 94.05).

It was also observed that expectations can shift markedly during the term of a contract, a fact of economic life that provides considerable profit (and loss) opportunities for speculators and pricing headaches for hedgers. The wide price swing in the December 1977 contract was due in part to the broad adjustment that took place in the second half of 1976 as cash rates declined instead of rising as the futures market had anticipated earlier in the year. As late as May 1976, the futures market was projecting a 90-day discount of 7.40% by the following December when the then-present cash rate was about 5.40%. Not only did the actual 90-day discount fail to rise 200 basis points by December, it in fact declined over 100 basis points, which meant that between June and year-end, the December 1976 T-bill contract had to advance some 300 basis points for the futures market to correct its earlier forecast.

When the market's projection is not so far removed from the actual trend of rates, futures volatility is not as extreme. In January 1978, the starting point for the last Plunger-Decimal scenario, for example, the consensus was again on the side of higher rates by year-end. The December 1978 T-bill contract, the short "leg" of Plunger's spread, was priced to reflect a 7.75% discount while cash bills were yielding about 6.50%. Through the first half of 1978, futures prices had little reason to move very far in either direction since steadily rising cash rates generally matched the estimates made in the market at the beginning of the year. By the end of June, in fact, the December 1978 contract was precisely where it was the prior January. As our survey of the changes in the T-bill futures yield curve during 1978 demonstrated, however, the conviction grew during the third quarter that 90-day rates would not only reach 7.75% by December, but might go on to exceed the 1974 record high of 9%. As a consequence, futures prices broke sharply below the moderate downward trend they had displayed throughout the first half-year. During the course of only five consecutive trading sessions at the end of October, December T-bills collapsed 100 basis points, more than three times the contract's entire trading range over the first six months of 1978, as the market suddenly revised its earlier estimate of the extent of the climb in rates.

To reiterate an earlier statement, futures prices do not have a life of their own. They are of necessity tied to the prevailing interest rates on the securities the contracts represent and to one another. The decisive factor that concerns both speculators and hedgers is the linkage between cash and futures prices and between the successive delivery months of the various short- and long-term contracts. A close study of the cash and futures yield curves serves to shed much-needed light on these important relationships.

Chapter Seven

What Determines Interest Rates?

Nineteenth Century economists referred to their calling as "the dismal science." Unfortunately, much of the literature they and their successors have passed down to us has been fairly dismal as well. The layman who perseveres with a serious work on money and banking, for example, is continually confronted with such arcane terms as liquidity preference, monetary base, bank credit proxy, coincident indicators and $\frac{\Delta Md}{Md} \div \frac{\Delta i}{i}$.[1] Little wonder, then, that after a valiant effort, his attention is drawn to a more alluring volume on the order of *How I Made a Million in the Market Between Breakfast and Lunch.*

Inasmuch as this book purports to be a "serious" (even if somewhat brash) treatment of one phase of the money world, the author must regrettably forego the glamour and elan associated with the "smart money," and plod doggedly ahead with the everyday humdrum tools of ordinary working money. By enduring this far in spite of such formidable obstacles as modified passthroughs and yield curves, the reader has shown himself to be made of sterner stuff than the typical in-

---

[1]This is the formula expressing the elasticity, or degree of responsiveness, of total money demand to the level of interest rates.

vestment dilettante. He may not qualify for the ranks of the smart money after absorbing the necessarily "dismal" subject matter of this chapter and the one following, but he can console himself with the profits it will help him to secure in the interest rate futures market.

Money and Credit

Much of the confusion attending the subject of money arises from the ambiguity of the word itself. We all know what money is, but we aren't so certain how best to define it. Money has been variously described as the medium of exchange people use to pay for things, one of the assets which collectively comprise wealth, and the accumulation of funds within the banking system. An individual who is paid a wage or salary or who purchases a product or service, is either earning income or making an expenditure for which coins, currency and checks are a medium of exchange. Two people engaged in a credit transaction also exchange money, but the relationship between them obviously differs from the one between the employer and employee or customer and sales person. Total credit within the banking system not only includes actual borrowings throughout the country, but is concerned with the capacity to accommodate potential borrowing.

Interest is sometimes described as "the price of money." Strictly speaking, it is the price of *borrowed* money, or credit. The indiscriminate use of the expressions "availability of money" and "availability of credit" contributes to the confusion. Money in the aggregate sense is a stock or supply, a certain number of dollars in circulation or contained within the banking system, not all of which is available or intended to be loaned out at interest. Credit, as suggested by the term "extension of credit," is a flow concept signifying a certain use to which a part of the money stock is put. Funds are supplied to a borrower by a lender, usually a bank or some other financial institution, for a particular period at the end of which the flow is reversed, and the loan is repaid. Money and credit, therefore, are distinct though closely related economic variables that are subject to different determinants.

We shall skirt the problem of semantics by referring to that portion of the total money stock that has a direct effect on interest rates as "the supply of loanable funds." We can then proceed with the conventional supply-demand analysis familiar to onetime readers of economics texts. The interest rate is indeed the price of loanable funds, which is set by the inclination of prospective lenders to supply funds at various rate levels and the level of demand by prospective borrowers. In graphic terms, the demand curve (no immediate relation to the yield curve) sweeps down and to the right of the horizontal axis, depicting a growing desire to borrow at successively lower rates of interest. Meanwhile, the supply curve moves up and to the right, describing lenders' increasing willingness to make funds available as rates rise. The intersection of the two curves, as with any supply-demand chart, marks the interest rate at that particular time. Any change in the economic or financial situation that

FIGURE: 7-1

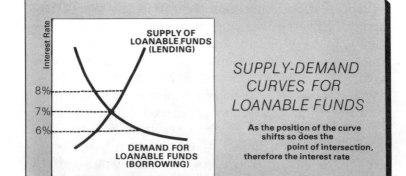

SUPPLY OF LOANABLE FUNDS (LENDING)

SUPPLY-DEMAND CURVES FOR LOANABLE FUNDS

As the position of the curve shifts so does the point of intersection, therefore the interest rate

DEMAND FOR LOANABLE FUNDS (BORROWING)

Interest Rate

8%

7%

6%

Loanable Funds in Dollars

causes an increase in the demand for loanable funds without any corresponding increase in the supply of those funds, is reflected in a movement in the demand curve to the right while the supply curve remains stationary. The two curves would then intersect at a higher point, or interest rate, perhaps 8%. If, for any reason, the supply of loanable funds should increase while demand stayed constant, the supply curve would shift to the right, bringing the interest rate down to possibly 6%.

Flow-of-Funds Analysis

The chart serves to demonstrate the theoretical effect on interest rates of changes in the supply of and demand for loanable funds. For a more practical quantitative evaluation of the probable results of such changes, analysts turn to what is known as a sources-and-uses, or flow-of-funds analysis. The first step in performing this type of analysis is to segregate the constituents of net supply and demand for loanable funds to appraise each element individually.

The preponderance of loanable funds is supplied to the credit market by banks and other financial intermediaries to whom individual savers entrust their funds. Table 7-1 indicates that over the past several years approximately half the total was provided by deposit institutions, which are commercial and savings banks and savings and loans, with the bulk of the remainder coming from the contractual institutions, such as pension funds and insurance companies. Nonfinancial corporations have on occasion also been important suppliers of funds, with the residual taken up by individuals and foreign sources.

The net demand or use side of the flow-of-funds table consists of private business and consumer borrowing and government debt issued at the federal, state and local levels. Mortgage financing is listed as a separate category within the private demand sector,

Table 7-1. Summary of Financing-Total Funds (In billions of dollars).

	1973	1974	1975	1976	1977	1978 (est.)	1979 (proj.)
FUNDS RAISED							
Investment funds		115.8	120.8	151.0	198.8	205.5	209.3
Short-term funds	61.3	57.2	4.6	55.8	86.3	102.3	87.3
U.S. Government and budget agency securities, privately held	−.4	10.2	78.1	59.4	51.5	46.8	47.7
Total uses	182.4	183.2	203.5	266.2	336.6	354.6	344.3
FUNDS SUPPLIED							
Insurance companies and pension funds							
Life insurance companies	15.9	15.2	19.0	26.7	29.4	33.7	36.4
Private noninsured pension funds	9.2	7.9	14.1	12.5	16.5	11.7	19.2
State and local retirement funds	6.7	8.0	10.5	11.7	13.3	15.3	17.7
Fire and casualty insurance companies	5.8	4.4	6.0	12.4	19.3	19.8	21.0
Total	37.6	35.5	49.6	63.4	78.5	80.5	94.3
Thrift institutions							
Savings and loan associations	26.5	19.6	36.4	51.9	65.0	59.5	56.8
Mutual savings banks	4.7	3.4	10.9	12.5	11.7	8.7	8.2
Credit unions	3.6	3.0	5.0	6.3	8.0	10.2	8.2
Total	34.8	26.0	52.3	70.8	84.7	78.4	73.2
Investment companies	1.4	2.0	3.1	1.4	2.9	5.8	3.5
Other financial intermediaries							
Finance companies	8.5	5.5	2.0	8.3	16.2	16.4	13.8
Real estate investment trusts	5.6	.2	−4.9	−3.7	−2.4	−1.3	−.6
Mortgage brokers	2.2	−1.4	1.2	2.7	4.0	−1.0	2.0
Total	16.3	4.3	−1.7	7.3	17.8	14.1	15.2
Commercial banks	78.3	59.3	30.0	64.8	85.4	100.7	85.4
Business							
Business corporations	−2.2	13.4	18.1	17.5	7.3	12.2	11.5
Noncorporate business	1.0	.7	1.0	1.2	1.6	1.7	1.5
Total	−1.2	14.1	19.1	18.7	8.9	13.9	13.0
Government							
U.S. Government	−.3	4.6	6.4	1.2	2.2	1.1	2.5
Nonbudget agencies	7.7	12.8	6.6	6.9	2.8	13.7	11.4
State and local general funds	4.1	3.1	9.2	9.7	14.3	14.9	8.0
Total	11.5	20.5	22.2	17.8	19.3	29.7	21.9
Foreign investors	4.0	12.2	10.4	17.9	42.2	40.2	38.3
Individuals and others	31.4	32.9	23.7	19.9	24.0	38.1	42.5
Total gross sources	214.1	206.8	208.7	282.0	363.7	401.4	387.3
Less: Funds raised by financial intermediaries							
Investment funds	5.7	5.5	4.4	8.2	10.9	8.5	8.6
Short-term funds	10.1	4.5	−.9	5.6	10.2	13.8	13.4
Nonbudget agency securities, privately held	15.9	13.6	1.8	2.0	6.0	24.5	21.0
Total	31.7	23.6	5.2	15.8	27.1	46.8	43.0
Total net sources	182.4	183.2	203.5	266.2	336.6	354.6	344.3

Source: Bankers Trust Co., New York

while direct and sponsored agencies of the federal government are treated apart from the Treasury itself.

Sources-and-Uses Analysis

Having identified and listed the individual items on both sides of the flow-of-funds table, the analyst proceeds to estimate the projected supply or demand for each during the period under consideration, usually the upcoming quarter or year, and then calculates the probable change in interest rates required to bring the new totals into balance.

When total projected supply fails to match the projected demand, interest rates will rise on those securities in which those institutions responsible for the shortfall traditionally invest (the demand for securities being a function of the supply of funds and vice versa). With regard to the funds they do have available, the institutions' expectations of future short- and long-term rates can influence their pattern of investment, which may in turn have a near-term technical effect on rate behavior. The method employed for a sources-and-uses analysis, therefore, is to project the likely flow of funds to each debt sector, and to estimate the rate change on each security necessary to bring the new balances into equality.

The extent to which each estimated rate must be raised or lowered to reconcile the projected supply and demand for funds depends upon the degree of sensitivity to rate change. If supply and demand in a particular credit sector are very responsive to moderate changes in rates, a small increase is sufficient to reduce demand or raise the supply if either is what is required to balance the projections. If supply and demand in that sector are less sensitive to interest rate change, a larger increase will be necessary to achieve the same result.

To assist in carrying out this reconciliation process, a matrix worksheet is often employed. A typical matrix lists the individual supply factors in a vertical column at the left and the demand elements horizontally along the top, allowing a direct comparison between the possible flow of funds from each of the former categories to each of the latter. If, for example, the demand for credit in the form of corporate bonds is projected to be $10 billion in the coming year and insurance companies and pension funds, the principal institutional investors in those securities, are expected to buy only $8 million of them, some other source of supply must be funneled into that sector or the yield on corporate bonds must rise sufficiently to induce the customary investors to increase their purchases above the original projection. The additional funds most likely would be diverted from another sector for which they were initially intended, but which no longer holds the same relative attraction for various classes of investors. After several rounds of adjustment, wherein estimated rates are raised to reconcile increased demand and/or reduced supply, or lowered in line with diminished demand and/or greater supply, total projected demand will be made to equal total projected supply in the lower right corner of the matrix.

Table 7-2.   Matrix Worksheet for Sources and Uses of Funds (Hypothetical)

Sources of Funds	Corporate Bonds	Government & Agency Bonds	State & Local Bonds	Business Loans	Mortgages	Consumer Credit	All Other	Total
Commercial Banks		−2	8	45	36	22	4	113
Savings Banks	1	.5	.5	8	.5	.5		11
Savings and Loans		1.5		.5	56	1	3	62
Insurance Cos.	20	3.5	11	3	9		5.5	52
Pension Funds	13	6		1	4			24
Finance Cos.				15		10		25
Credit Unions					2	7		9
Nonfin. Corps.		−1		14	16	5	−2	16
Government		10	.5		10		4.5	25
Indiv. & Others	−.5	49	5	16	15		−3.5	81
Total	32.5	68	25	95	140	45.5	12	418

Uses of Funds (in billions of dollars)

The matrix analysis demonstrates visually what is intuitively known, that it is not feasible under actual conditions to consider the yield on a particular security in isolation from other yields. Our earlier discussion of yield spreads established that when these differentials widen appreciably beyond their customary range, swap trades help to bring them back to the norm. An abrupt change in supply or demand cannot force a specific yield too far out of line vis-a-vis other credit instruments, therefore, before trading activity starts to diffuse its effect among securities that are regarded as suitable substitutes.

Business Cycle Analysis

The private demand for loanable funds—business and consumer borrowing—as well as the supply of credit from that sector are heavily influenced by the current (and anticipated) level of general economic activity. The state of the overall economy not only affects the amount of credit demanded from the various financial intermediaries, but has a great deal to do with the volume of individual savings that flows into those institutions. The government's budget, therefore its level of borrowing, is also to a significant extent determined by the growth or decline in economic activity. Any attempt to forecast the future level of interest rates must as a consequence take the broad economic picture into account. This wider perspective entails a progression from flow-of-funds to business-cycle analysis for the purpose of determining what connection, if any, exists between the cyclical movement of the economy from stages of contraction to expansion and the recurring advance and decline in interest rates.

Basic economic theory states that well into an extended period of rising economic activity the demand for funds starts to increase faster than the supply, exerting upward pressure on interest rates. But after the economy has faltered and gone into a decline, demand falls more rapidly than supply, causing rates to slide. Our task is to test this view with the available evidence, and if it can be confirmed, to look for signs within the broad economic panorama that might offer some early warning of the direction and extent of related interest rate movements.

The record does show in fact a correlation between bond yields and the level of economic activity at least during the latter stages of a growth or contractionary trend. Periods of prosperity have in the past witnessed rising yields, hence falling prices. Owners of bonds are said to be sanguine about recessions, therefore, because they have generally been accompanied after a certain time lag by lower yields and higher prices. One should take such lags into account when anticipating cyclical turns in the direction of interest rates. But in their eagerness not to miss the turn, many futures traders hasten to buy interest rate contracts at the first sign of an economic slowdown and sell at the first hint of recovery, only to find they have acted precipitously and prematurely.

There occurred two clear-cut recessions during the 1969-78 decade covered by the analysis in Chapter Six. Industrial production as measured by the Federal Reserve Board Index declined from December 1969 through November 1970, and again from November 1973 through March 1975. The latter slump, lasting over 16 months, was the most protracted and severe the U.S. has suffered since the Great Depression of the 1930s. Both periods of economic decline were accompanied by falling interest rates, although in both cases bond yields did not begin their descent until the downturn was fairly well along.

In the first instance, yields on long-term Treasury bonds continued to climb seven months longer, rising another 48 basis points (6.51% to 6.99%) after the FRB Index had turned down from its cyclical peak. By way of contrast, short-term rates responded far more quickly to the change in economic conditions, with the

90-day T-bill discount heading down by January 1970. Despite a strong recovery commencing December 1970, which carried into a two and one-half year climb in industrial production, the attendant reversal in yields was short-lived as rates returned to their cyclical lows, where they remained until late 1972. Again, short-term bills were more attuned to the turnaround, as 90-day rates started rising in March 1971 (only to reverse trend once again the following July).

Though as stated above, the 1973-75 contraction was of greater magnitude and duration, the sequence of interest rate movement was similar to that of the previous cycle. Economic activity began to flatten out as early as July 1973, essentially remaining on a plateau through September 1974 before plunging some 15% in terms of the FRB Index over the next six months. While industrial production moved along its horizontal course during the first three quarters of 1974, long-term Treasury yields advanced another 74 basis points (6.56% to 7.30%). Short-term rates turned down from their peak in August 1974, not resuming their upward trend until January 1977, 22 months following the trough of the recession. Having risen to unprecedented levels at their 1974 peak, they were not as sensitive to the economic recovery as they were after the milder 1969-70 contraction.

In summary, the experience of recent business cycles confirms that interest rate behavior is indeed linked to economic trends; but, at least in the case of long-term rates, the high and low points are attained after the economic peak and trough. That is to say, bond yields continued to rise for several months after the general economy turned weaker. But after they finally started down, they kept dropping well beyond the time the recession had run its course.

As the charts in Chapter Six demonstrated, yield curves also change their shape and position over the course of a business cycle. When rates are at a low point at or following the cyclical trough, the wide-

FIGURE: 7-2

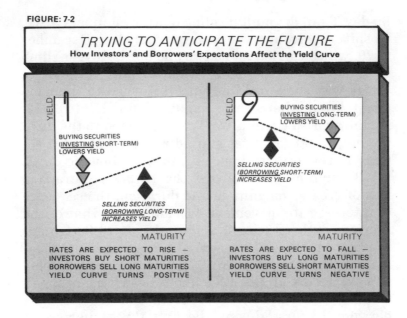

TRYING TO ANTICIPATE THE FUTURE
How Investors' and Borrowers' Expectations Affect the Yield Curve

spread expectation that they are more likely to rise than to drop much farther prompts investors to buy short-maturity securities (supply of funds) and borrowers to sell long-term securities (demand for funds), thereby giving a positive slope to the curve. At or near presumed peaks, the yield curve turns negative as investors seek to lock up high rates for a longer term and borrowers try to stay in the short-term sector, hoping for an opportunity to do their long-term financing at a lower rate in the future.

Measuring Economic Trends

If interest rates can reach their tops and bottoms six or seven months after the FRB Index has reversed its trend, the latter is not a particularly reliable signal for taking action in the futures market. Economists are constantly developing statistical indicators that will provide timely warning of turns in the business cycle, not only for the purpose of forecasting interest rate trends, but as planning aids in many situations where economic conditions are an important determinant. In a long-standing study to identify the peaks and troughs of business cycles in the U.S. extending back over 100 years, the National Bureau of Economic Research, a private nonprofit institute, has compiled and analyzed extensive data relating to the direction and rate of economic change. From this wealth of data, it has developed three statistical series respectively labeled leading, coincident and lagging indicators. Updated figures for each of the three series are published monthly in the U. S. Department of Commerce *Business Conditions Digest*. Of the three, the series most closely watched for clues to cyclical changes in economic activity is the leading indicators, which are listed in Table 7-3.

Of the many gauges of economic activity the NBER has monitored over the years, the 12 leaders were selected because they consistently provided an early warning of cyclical turns in the economy. The following summary explains the reasons why they are usually among the first to register a changing business climate.

1. Average Hours in Workweek of Manufacturing Production Workers.

   Manufacturing is the most cyclical of all business categories, therefore most sensitive to economic improvement or slowdown. The average workweek is an earlier sign of hesitation than layoffs because it can be reduced without disrupting the workforce.

2. Layoffs of Manufacturing Workers.

   Again, the figure is included because manufacturing concerns are among the first to feel the effects of business contraction, and employers begin to order layoffs if conditions continue to deteriorate beyond the point at which the workweek was curtailed.

3. New Orders for Consumer Products.

   A slowdown here is the forerunner of declines in production, employment and income in the industries involved. It also signals a deterioration of consumer confidence.

4. Vendor Delivery Time.

Delays by suppliers in meeting delivery schedules are an indication of the condition of their businesses. As their order backlog is worked down without being replenished at the same rate by incoming orders, delivery time speeds up, signaling a slackening of demand for their services.

5. Net New Business Formations.

The establishment of new business enterprises is encouraged by increasing profits and profit margins, which historically have begun tapering off during the final stages of a business upswing. At the bottom end of the cycle, profits and margins begin to improve, providing a fresh impetus for new business ventures.

6. Permits to Build New Private Housing Units.

This statistic represents an earlier stage in the residential construction process than building material production, furniture and household appliance sales and mortgage commitments. It is a more consistent series than the closely watched housing starts figures and, relevant to our purpose, is particularly sensitive to short-term and mortgage interest rates.

7. Contracts and Orders for New Plant and Equipment (in constant dollars).

This is another indicator of expectations for continued profitability of corporate investment. It is a more suitable gauge of business sentiment since the cyclical peak has often been passed by the time the actual expenditures for plant and equipment are made.

8. Change in Business Inventories on Hand and on Order (in constant dollars).

Inventories do not start to shrink before the economy reaches its peak, but their rate of growth tends to fall off. As the low of a recession approaches, the rate of decrease likewise diminishes.

9. Common Stock Prices (S&P 500).

This index is especially germane inasmuch as bonds and stock are in many instances alternate investments, whose relative yields are decisive in determining investor preferences. In their own right, stock prices are closely attuned to changes in corporate profits and interest rates.

10. Changes in Wholesale Prices of Industrial Crude Materials.

The index is a composite of 13 raw material prices that have a history of anticipating cyclical turns. As with several of the other indicators, changes in profitability during the late stages of expansion and slump influence inventory decisions which in turn affect prices in the index.

11. Money Supply (in constant dollars).

This key monetary indicator will be considered at some length later in this chapter. The "real" money supply consists of total checking and time deposits within the banking system plus currency in circulation, all adjusted for price inflation. The monetarist school of economists contends that the money supply is not merely a passive measure of business activity but is in fact the decisive force behind economic change, a view which has far-reaching implications for government policy and the behavior of interest rates.

12. Change in Total Liquid Assets.

   Liquid assets consist of cash and those assets
   which can be converted into cash rapidly
   and with little depreciation. During periods
   of economic slowdown or stagnation, business managers prefer to build up their holdings of liquid assets to avoid being forced to
   realize them at a capital loss.

   Though the leading indicators are the most widely
heeded with respect to anticipating major turning
points in the economy, the coincident and lagging indicators, also listed in Table 7-3, bear watching for
confirmation that a turn is in the making or has already taken place. Some analysts have maintained
that the "laggards" deserve as much if not more attention than the leaders because they include developments which can in themselves affect the level of economic activity. Two components of the lagging series
which are directly related to the subject of interest
rates (one is in fact a rate, though not one of the market yields discussed throughout this book), are the
prime rate banks charge on loans to their best customers and the volume of commercial and industrial
loans outstanding at large banks. Both will receive
further attention later in this chapter.

   In addition to the individual indicators, the NBER
compiles composite indexes for each of the three series.
Apart from the convenience of monitoring three statistics as opposed to 26, the benefit to be derived from
using the composite figures is that they filter out ab-
errations in the separate components that can give a
misleading impression of the general trend. Another
means of gaining a broader perspective is to employ a
ratio of coincident to lagging indicators which has on
occasion signaled a cyclical turn before it was reflected
in the leaders.

   The coincident indicators are so named because
they historically have reached their highs and lows at
roughly the same time that the general economy

Table 7-3. The Economic Scoreboard: List of Leading, Coincident and Lagging Indicators

LEADING INDICATORS

Average workweek, production workers, manufacturing (hours)
Layoff rate, manufacturing (per 100 employees)
New orders for consumer goods and materials in 1972 dollars (billion dollars)
Vendor performance, companies reporting slower deliveries (percent)
Net business formation (index: 1967=100)
Contracts and orders for plant and equipment in 1972 dollars (billion dollars)
New building permits, private housing units (index: 1967=100)
Change in inventories on hand and on order in 1972 dol., smoothed (ann. rate, bil. dol.)
Change in sensitive prices, smoothed (percent)
Stock prices, 500 common stocks (index: 1941−43=10)
Change in total liquid assets, smoothed (percent)
Money supply (M1) in 1972 dollars (billion dollars)
Composite index of 12 leading indicators (index: 1967=100)

ROUGHLY COINCIDENT INDICATORS

Employees on nonagricultural payrolls (thousands)
Personal income less transfers in 1972 dollars (annual rate, billion dollars)
Industrial production, total (index: 1967=100)
Manufacturing and trade sales in 1972 dollars (million dollars)
Composite index of 4 roughly coincident indicators (index: 1967=100)

LAGGING INDICATORS

Average duration of unemployment (weeks)
Manufacturing and trade inventories, total, in 1972 dollars (billion dollars)
Labor cost per unit of output, manufacturing (index: 1967−100)
Average prime rate charged by banks (percent)
Commercial and industrial loans outstanding (million dollars)
Ratio, consumer installment debt to personal income (percent)
Composite index of 6 lagging indicators (index: 1967=100)

Source: U.S. Department of Commerce, Bureau of Economic Analysis.

changed its direction. One that deserves to be singled out as the measure most often used by economists when referring to the overall performance of the economy is the Gross National Product, or simply GNP. GNP is simultaneously the total value of goods and services produced in this country and total national income. It is computed by adding consumer expenditures, business investment, government outlays and net exports. The algebraic equation is familiar to economics students as:

$$GNP = C + I + G$$

Since expenditures whatever their source represent income to someone, rising GNP is a reflection of economic expansion. When GNP declines for several consecutive quarters it can be assumed that the economy has entered a period of contraction.

Calling the Turns

The problem with economic (as with interest-rate) forecasting is that it is most difficult at the times when it is most needed, i.e., at the major turning points. Otherwise, it would be sufficient, as is often done, merely to extrapolate the present trend into the future. Given the implications and importance of a reliable GNP forecast, "econometricians," or practitioners of quantitative economics, have created elaborate mathematical models intended to serve up a plausible GNP projection after a number of assumptions are fed into the model. The technique resembles that of a flow-of-funds analysis. One of the by-products of such models is in fact estimated interest rates at various projected levels of GNP.

Since such quantitative analysis presupposes a high level of mathematical ability as well as access to a computer, it is normally beyond the resources of most laymen. The larger investment firms either have the in-house capability to produce and interpret such models or else subscribe to the output of firms that specialize in such research. Clients of such houses should inquire about these studies if their account executives have not already made them available.

Definition of Money

Returning to the more immediate issue of the relationship between the supply and demand for loanable funds, the determinants of interest rates, it is necessary before proceeding any farther to confront head-on the question which was so adeptly side-stepped earlier, namely the real definition of money. Unfortunately, there is no hard and fast answer, a vexing state of affairs that gives economists an opportunity to exercise their debating as well as their analytical skills and provides students of money and banking (in whose ranks the reader has temporarily been pressed) with interminable headaches.

So what is money? We know that it has value and is used to buy things, but what form does it take? Clearly, the currency (including coins) we carry in pockets and purses, leave on dressers and stuff into safety deposit boxes is money. No one refuses to accept it in payment, and it is designated as legal tender, which means it must be accepted. But in today's world of trade and finance currency is, so to speak, small change. When the average consumer buys a car or takes out a mortgage on his home, neither he nor his banker stand at the counter peeling off $100 bills.

It is even less likely that the Chase Manhattan Bank would loan U. S. Steel Corp. $10 million in the form of currency. Since financial transactions of any size, at either a personal or corporate level, are in most instances conducted by check, funds held in a checking account are not only "as good as" money, they *are* money. When economists and money market analysts speak of the nation's money supply, or M_1 in their peculiar code, they are referring to currency in circulation plus total demand deposits (checking accounts) within the commercial banking system. To give some idea of the relative magnitude of the two segments, as of Dec. 6, 1978, M_1 consisted of approximately $248 billion demand deposits and $112 billion currency, or a ratio of roughly two to one.

But what, you may ask, of time deposits? If the dollars held in checking accounts are considered real money, surely those kept in savings accounts are no less so. Well, yes and no. The dollars are just as real, but they cannot be used until they are converted into cash or checks. As a consequence, time deposits are regarded as something on the order of "quasi-money," to be kept distinct from the other definitions. Economists have resolved the issue, at least to their satisfaction, by labeling M_1 (currency and demand deposits) the narrow definition of money, and alluding to M_2, which adds time deposits, as the broad definition. Together, M_1 and M_2 are referred to as the monetary aggregates.

There is a key relationship, then, between the checking account balances kept in commercial banks and the money supply in this country, however it is defined. Since currency in circulation comprises a minor portion of the money stock, and is in any case a relatively constant figure apart from seasonal changes, we must look to the demand-deposit component to gain an understanding of the forces which cause the monetary aggregates, hence the potential supply of loanable funds and the level of interest rates, to increase or contract over time.

The money supply is an elastic rather than a static quantity for the fundamental reason that banks are literally capable of creating money, and then of destroying it. We refer here to commercial banks, not savings banks, savings and loan associations or other thrift institutions, since it is only the former that are authorized to accept demand deposits.[2]

Economists who hold the government responsible for inflation by "printing" too much money are referring not to presses running overtime in the basement

---

[2] The distinction between demand and time deposits, therefore between M_1 and M_2, has become somewhat blurred since the introduction of NOW—negotiated order of withdrawal—accounts by thrift institutions and commercial bank automatic transfers from checking to savings accounts which allow the payment of interest on idle balances, a practice the U.S. Court of Appeals recently ruled is contrary to existing law. This overlapping and switching of deposits has led to the introduction of another money index, M_1 plus, which adds to standard M_1 savings accounts at commercial banks, NOW accounts at savings banks and credit union draft shares.

of the Treasury, but to the buildup of excessive (in their opinion) demand deposits within the commercial banking system.

Returning to the illustrations of the consumer taking out an auto loan or a major corporation borrowing millions of dollars, in neither case is the bank officer approving the loan likely to hand a check immediately over to the car buyer or corporate treasurer. Checking accounts in the amount of the approved loans are in most instances opened in the names of the private or corporate borrowers, and the funds withdrawn as they are needed. Where compensating balances are required under the terms of the loan, some funds may never be drawn from the account.

Where do the banks making these loans obtain the funds to place into these newly created checking accounts? Are they taken out of the vault or transferred from another customer's savings account? The answer is no. They are produced through the stroke of a pen, or in today's modern age, by a computer keypunch. Taken as a whole, the banking system "creates" billions of new dollars in this fashion, and just as effortlessly "destroys" them by erasing the credits when the loans are repaid. These debits and credits in the ledgers (or computer memories) of the nation's commercial banks are the real dollars on which our economy turns, not the "greenbacks" that people eternally complain do not go as far as they used to.

Under this system of instant checking-account money, banks theoretically could create unlimited amounts of fresh dollars, save the fact that government deems it desirable to restrict this privilege. Banks accordingly are required to maintain a certain level of reserves against their demand deposits or, looking at it the other way, can increase total demand deposits only by an amount permitted by existing reserves. Once an individual bank's (or the entire system's) checking-account dollars reach the reserve limit, no new demand deposits can be created for the purpose of making loans until additional reserves are in some way obtained.

Thus far, our search for the determinants of interest rates has brought us from the supply of loanable funds via the money supply and demand deposits to commercial bank reserves. What are bank reserves? They consist of (1) vault cash, which is self-explanatory, and (2) deposits at Federal Reserve Banks, which deserve a bit more attention inasmuch as they are where this discussion has been leading. Just as demand deposits at commercial banks constitute money for individuals and businesses, the banks have their counterpart in the form of deposits at their "bankers' bank," the Federal Reserve System. Since a great deal has to be said concerning "the Fed" in the remainder of this chapter and the one following, it is worthwhile at this point to outline its role in the banking system. The Federal Reserve occupies center stage in this production, because through its exercise of monetary policy it exerts a decisive influence on the level and direction of interest rates.

The Fed and Its Role

The Federal Reserve System is this country's central bank, comparable to the Bank of England or Germany's Bundesbank with the distinction that it consists not of one institution but twelve. These regional Federal Reserve banks are federally chartered, non-profit-seeking corporations privately owned by the member commercial banks in each region. The commercial banks do not exercise all the customary rights of ownership, however, since the system as a whole is an autonomous government agency responsible for regulating the more than 6,000 member banks, managing the money and credit of the country, and advancing its principal economic objectives of economic growth, full employment, price stability and balance of payments equilibrium. As will be recalled from our earlier description of Treasury bill auctions, the Federal Reserve also serves as agent of the Treasury for the collection and payment of government funds.

Though each of the 12 regional banks and their branches operate with a large degree of autonomy, they are subject on the policy level to the central control of the Board of Governors, an independent agency within the federal government whose seven members are appointed by the President and which reports directly to the Congress. Because of its authority in shaping and executing monetary policy, the board and especially its chairman exert a great deal of influence in the economic sphere.

It is the Board of Governors, for example, that determines the level of reserves member commercial banks are required to maintain against their demand deposits. This is a powerful instrument of policy with which the board is able to affect the money supply and, as a consequence, interest rates.

By way of illustration, suppose that the Last National Bank mentioned in Chapter Two has as of a given date $10 million in legal reserves, comprised of $8 million in deposits at its district Federal Reserve bank and $2 million in vault cash. If the Board of Governors has determined that commercial banks should hold reserves amounting to 20% of their demand deposits, Last National's limit on the basis of its existing reserves is $50 million:

Required Reserves	=	Demand Deposits	×	Reserve Requirements
($10 million	=	$50 million	×	1/5)

or

| ($50 million | = | $10 million | × | 5) |

since the level of allowable deposits is the reciprocal of the percentage reserve requirement.

Through its power to raise or lower *reserve requirements*, the Board of Governors has the means to control the amount of checking deposits Last National and all member banks as a group can create.

If the board considers that the economy would best be served by a larger money supply, it may elect to lower the reserve requirements from 20% to, say, 15%. In that event, Last National's $10 million in reserves would support not $50 million but $66.67 million in checking deposits. The bank would therefore have the capacity to make $16.67 million in additional loans without having to increase its reserves, as would all other banks in the Federal Reserve System enjoy an enhancement of like proportion. There is nothing which says that Last National or any other bank must make use of its extra resources, however. If no new borrowers turn up to apply for loans, or the bank chooses not to make further investments in securities, it might merely sit on its additional capacity. In Last National's case, the reduced requirements would mean that it could maintain its $50 million in checking deposits with reserves of only $7.5 million.

$$\$7.5 \text{ million} = \$50 \text{ million} \times .15$$

The difference of $2.5 million between the old and new required reserves has become *excess reserves* which the bank might utilize to make loans or buy securities in the future.

On the other hand, had the Board of Governors determined that a reduction in the money supply was to be desired, it might take the opposite course of raising member bank reserve requirements to 22%, the maximum level allowed by law. Last National suddenly finds that it needs $11 million in reserves to maintain its checking deposits at the $50 million level, making it deficient $1 million. What is to be done?

One option would be to call in sufficient loans to bring the bank's demand deposits down to the level permitted by the new requirements. That can be com-

puted by multiplying the existing reserves by the reciprocal of the increased percentage requirement:

$$\$10 \text{ million} \times 1/.22 = \$45.45 \text{ million}$$

Consequently, Last National would need to retire
about $4½ million in outstanding loans to satisfy the
new requirements if it had no means of securing additional reserves.

The remaining alternative open to banks with reserve deficiencies is somehow to raise their reserves
up to the required level. They might accomplish that
by selling securities from their investment portfolio or
by borrowing the needed reserves from other commercial banks or the Federal Reserve itself. Treasury bills
are regarded by banks as secondary reserves for precisely that reason. While they in themselves do not
qualify as legal reserves, the market liquidity of T-
bills allows banks to convert them into fresh reserves
without delay. Should Last National Bank elect to
raise additional reserves by this means, it would sell
about $4.5 million in the secondary market through a
government securities dealer, who would the following
day credit the proceeds of the sale to Last National's

**Table 7-4. Member Bank Percentage Reserve
Requirements.**

	Requirement for Demand Deposits	Requirement for Time Deposits
	(Percentages in Effect Dec. 31, 1978)	
Percentages in effect Dec. 31, 1978		
$10-100 million net deposits	11¾	6
100-400 million net deposits	12¾	
Over 400 million net deposits	16¼	
Minimum percentages allowable by law	10	3
Maximum percentages allowable by law	22	10

Source: *Federal Reserve Bulletin,* Volume 65 Number 3, March 1979.

account at its regional Federal Reserve bank, bringing its reserves up to the required level.

If for any reason it is not considered feasible or desirable to make a reserve deficit up by selling Treasury bills or other securities, banks are permitted to borrow the necessary funds. They are required to compute their reserve position on the basis of average daily deposits from Thursday of each week to the following Wednesday. If on the day of reckoning Last National tallies its position and discovers it is still deficient to the amount of $4.5 million, it can go to the "discount window," meaning that it has the privilege of borrowing from the Fed itself. When the Federal Reserve extends a loan to a member bank, it does the same thing that the bank does in lending to its customers. But when the Fed makes an accounting entry crediting the funds to the borrowing bank's account, it is in effect creating "high powered money" since each dollar so credited allows the commercial bank to expand its demand deposits by the amount permitted by the reserve requirement.

This type of lending is called "discounting" because the Federal Reserve like any ordinary bank requires that its loans be secured by collateral which usually consists of government securities, commercial paper or bankers acceptances with maturities of up to 90 days. The collateral is discounted, meaning that the borrowing bank's account at the Fed is credited by the face amount of the securities less the interest on the loan. The interest charged is accordingly called the *discount rate*, another important tool wielded by the Fed in its execution of monetary policy.

The Federal Reserve perceives itself as the banking system's "lender of the last resort," and tends to discourage would-be borrowers from coming to the discount window too frequently. Another option open to banks with shortfalls in reserves is to borrow them from other banks that have temporary surpluses. If

Last National Bank has a $4.5 million deficiency it must make up, there are presumably other banks throughout the country with excess reserves, that is to say deposits at the Federal Reserve over and above what is required of them to maintain their existing level of demand deposits.

Banks do not like to keep more than the required minimum on deposit with the Fed for the simple reason that such deposits earn no interest. In other words, they must pay (the discount rate) to borrow there, but receive nothing on the funds they keep on deposit. There is, therefore, an economic incentive to loan that portion of their total deposits at the Federal Reserve that are not required as reserves against their own demand deposits to banks such as Last National which have an immediate need for them. These loanable deposits are referred to, appropriately enough, as federal funds and the interest charged for their overnight use is known as the *federal funds rate*. Though the resulting market in federal funds is virtually the exclusive domain of member commercial banks, since they are the only private institutions that keep deposits with the Federal Reserve, the implications of the availability of such funds or the lack thereof are such that the Fed funds rate has come to be the most sensitive barometer of current money market conditions and the Federal Reserve's prevailing monetary policy. As a consequence, it is, along with the 90-day T-bill discount, the money market rate most closely watched by futures traders.

To reiterate, the discount rate and the federal funds rate are both the cost to commercial banks for the temporary use of reserves to make good deficiencies in their reserve positions. The former is paid to the Fed itself for the loan of funds which may be included as legal reserves. The latter is paid to other banks for the short-term transfer of what are for them excess reserves. The discount rate is normally changed at infrequent intervals by administrative decision with the publicly announced changes receiving wide media coverage. The market tends to regard such changes as anticlimactic, however, in the sense that any increase or decrease is usually taken to be confirmation of a policy the Fed has pursued without fanfare up to the time of the change. The federal funds rate, on the other hand, fluctuates from hour to hour, reflecting the shifting equilibrium between some banks' reserve deficiencies and other banks' surpluses. It is also subject to Federal Reserve control, but in a more indirect and subtle fashion.

The subtle policy measures, known as *open market operations*, are carried out by the Fed on a day-to-day basis without press announcements and consequently with little public attention. They seem to be cloaked in secrecy so far as outsiders are concerned, but as early indications of changes in Federal Reserve policy, they are the object of close scrutiny and much conjecture by money market and interest rate futures analysts. These obscure but nonetheless important policy moves arise from the simple fact that when the Federal Reserve buys Treasury bills and other government securities through dealers, the checks it writes on itself as payment are ultimately credited to a commercial bank's account at the Fed (a number of the reporting government securities dealers are themselves commercial banks), increasing that bank's legal reserves. When the Fed sells securities in the open market, dealers pay for them with checks drawn on their commercial bank accounts. These checks are cleared by debiting the member banks' reserve accounts at the Fed, resulting in a diminution in legal reserves.

When the Federal Reserve is a buyer of Treasury bills and other securities in the secondary market described in Chapter Two, it is said to be injecting reserves into the banking system, thereby easing credit conditions by making it possible for member banks to create more demand deposits.[4] The Fed is said to be intent on "draining" reserves out of the system when it is a seller of government securities, tightening available credit by forcing a reduction in demand deposits and therefore the money supply, or at least restricting its growth. When analysts speculate about what the Fed is really doing in the money market, they are usually guessing whether it is buying or selling securities and why.

The first people to know for certain are the members of the Federal Open Market Committee, which is comprised of the Board of Governors plus five of the twelve regional bank presidents who serve on a rotating basis. The one exception is the President of the Federal Reserve Bank of New York, who is a permanent member of the FOMC since it is the New York Fed that is charged with executing its directives.

The committee meets in Washington every three weeks to make policy decisions and issue the appropriate directives to the trading desk of the New York Fed for execution on behalf of the system open market account. The trading desk carries out its directive by buying or selling through the approved dealers government securities, principally three-month Treasury bills, in the amounts deemed necessary to attain the FOMC's policy objectives. To the confusion of even the most expert "Fed watchers," open market operations are not always conducted to achieve policy ends, but are sometimes used for technical or so-called "defensive" reasons related to changes in the time required to clear checks between different district banks (the

---

[4]Due to the system of fractional reserves described above, the capacity of the commercial banking system as a whole to create new deposits is enhanced by an amount greater than the initial injection of federal funds. This multiplier effect is the result of a diffusion of the original deposit among a succession of banks, giving each the potential to increase its outstanding loans by an amount permitted by the reserve requirements then in force. Conversely, open market sales by the Fed have the effect of reducing aggregate reserves by a similar multiple.

"float"), seasonal demands for currency, and gold movements.

In addition to its outright purchases of government securities, the trading desk will seek to achieve its ends through the execution of repurchase agreements, or "repos." These are self-liquidating transactions wherein the Fed buys securities for up to 15 days from dealers who commit to repurchase the securities at the same price plus interest at the end of the agreed period. The immediate result of executing repurchase agreements is the same as outright purchases inasmuch as the banking system enjoys a temporary increase in reserves.

Whatever the method used, when the Fed boosts the system's reserves by acquiring securities, the results are two-fold. The increase in reserves adds to the supply of federal funds banks with surpluses have available to lend, while at the same time it reduces the demand from banks with reserve deficiencies. The greater supply and diminished demand are reflected in a decline in the federal funds rate, which is in turn a signal to market analysts that the Fed is pursuing a policy of easing credit conditions. When the Fed drains reserves from the system, reduced supply and increased demand for federal funds combine to push the funds rate higher, a sign that the Fed is in the process of tightening credit and wants to see all interest rates move up.

The Happy Medium

What the policy makers (the Board of Governors and the FOMC) are striving to accomplish through all of this "fine tuning" of reserve requirements, discount rate and federal funds rate is to hit that happy combination of money growth and interest rates most beneficial to the economy at any given time. The monetary Scylla and Charybdis between which they have constantly tried to steer in recent years without mishap to the economy are inflationary "overheating," caused by too-rapid money growth, and the slump it is feared would result from insufficient growth. A major policy question, then, is what is the optimum rate of increase in the money supply, however measured, to sustain the desired level of economic growth.

The task of the FOMC in this regard is to agree upon and then periodically review a target range of acceptable growth in both M_1 and M_2 which it believes to be consistent with its overall monetary and economic objectives. A possible range might be something on the order of 4% to 7½% annual growth for M_1 and 6% to 9% for the broader M_2 measure. When the actual increase in the monetary aggregates exceeds the official targets, as they did throughout much of 1978, the committee normally would instruct the account manager to pursue a more restrictive policy, which usually amounts to open market sales to drain reserves and a higher fed funds rate. The reverse tactic of open market purchases to increase reserves would be in order if growth in M_1 and M_2 repeatedly fell short of their targeted rates, but it should again be noted that monetary policy makers have no way of compelling banks to make use of their additional reserves if fresh demand for funds is not forthcoming.

In terms of the day-to-day execution of its directives from the FOMC, the New York trading desk uses the fed funds rate to gauge the amount of ease or tightening it seeks to accomplish at any given time. Without any public announcement of its intentions, the desk simply goes into the dealer market as a buyer or seller and leaves it to the dealers themselves and other interested parties (such as interest rate futures traders) to surmise what its objective is. Sometimes it signals a change in policy by refraining from any action. If, for example, the fed funds rate has been at 8¾% for some weeks and the trading desk is observed to be a buyer of T-bills every time the rate inches up to 8⅞% or 9% (the injection of fresh reserves exerts downward pressure on the rate), on the occasion that the rate rises to 9% and the Fed does not enter the market to force it back down, the market takes its inaction as an indication that a more restrictive policy has been established calling for a fed funds rate of 9%.

The days on which the market realizes that such a change has taken place are likely to see the sharpest moves by both short- and long-term interest rate futures. There sometimes may be a period of uncertainty regarding the Fed's true intent. At one point during the winter of early 1978, the market generally assumed the Fed was pursuing a policy of credit easing only to learn a week later that it was actually undertaking defensive measures to offset an aberration in the check "float" caused by a storm-induced shutdown of the Cleveland airport. But in the example just cited, if the trading desk began selling bills when fed funds fell back to 8¾%, it would be taken by the market as confirmation that 9% was indeed the new target rate.

The fed funds rate is quoted in the money market section of the daily financial press. In addition to the previous day's high and low rates, the closing bid and offer are quoted, indicating the rates at which banks seeking to make up deficient reserves were "buying" (borrowing) federal funds and banks with excess reserves were "selling" (lending) them.

Other key statistics are released weekly (Thursday afternoon) by the Federal Reserve. They are required reading for interest rate futures traders. A sample report for Dec. 6, 1978, is reproduced on the adjacent page. On line six of Member Bank Reserve Changes are listed member bank borrowings, which are the total reserves banks had borrowed at the discount window. As of Dec. 6, total borrowings were $548 million, a reduction of $63 million from the prior week. At the end of the column is the breakdown of total reserves between deposits at the Federal Reserve ($31.4 billion) and vault cash ($10 billion). The report also indicates that member banks as a whole have only

Table 7-5

Federal Reserve Data

KEY ASSETS AND LIABILITIES OF 10 WEEKLY REPORTING MEMBER BANKS IN NEW YORK CITY
(in millions of dollars)

		– – Change from – –	
ASSETS:	Dec. 6 1978	Nov. 1978	Dec. 7 1977
Total assets	159,290	– 372	+14,279
Total loans and investments	98,979	– 621	+ 2,578
Included:			
Loan loss reserve	1,962	+1,158	+ 5,783
Fed funds sold and like assets	4,449	–1,902	– 236
Commercial and indust loans	38,506	+ 392	+ 3,143
U.S. Treasury securities	8,332	+ 49	– 3,058
Municipal securities:			
Short-term	1,533	– 97	– 723
Long-term	7,031	+ 33	+ 403
Other key assets:			
Cash items in proc of collection	15,350	– 561	+ 3,354
Reserves with F.R. bank	5,804	+ 271	+ 838
Currency and coin	1,091	– 46	+ 144
LIABILITIES:			
Total demand deposits	54,613	+1,215	+ 4,572
Demand deposits adjusted (a)	22,965	+ 764	– 2,008
Time & savings deposits	50,491	+ 330	+ 6,224
Includes negotiable CDs of $100,000 or more	29,180	+ 264	+ 5,777
Federal funds purchased and similar liabilities	20,097	–1,284	+ 3,942
Other key liabilities:			
From own foreign branches	5,580	+ 233	+ 1,889
Borrowings from F.R.	0	– 189	– 256
Total capital plus certain debt	13,507	+ 59	+ 759

(a) All demand deposits except U.S. Government and domestic commercial banks, less cash items in process of collection.

MEMBER BANK RESERVE CHANGES

Changes in weekly averages of member bank reserves and related items during the week and year ended December 6, 1978. were as follows (in millions of dollars)

		Chg fm wk end	
	Dec. 6 1978	Nov. 29 1978	Dec. 7 1977
Reserve bank credit:			
U.S. Gov't securities:			
Bought outright	110,600	736	+13,526
Held under repurch agreemt	842	+ 336	– 60

Federal agency issues:			
Bought outright	7,899	– 19	+ 570
Held under repurch agreemt	265	+ 123	+ 230
Acceptances – bought outright	....	....	....
Held under repurch agreemt	258	+ 117	+ 87
Member bank borrowings	548	– 63	+ 30
Seasonal bank borrowings	150	– 30	+ 85
Float	6,532	–1,070	+ 1,662
Other Federal Reserve Assets	2,413	+ 148	+ 310
Total Reserve Bank credit	129,507	–1,194	+16,440
Gold stock	11,642	....	+ 20
SDR certificates	1,300	....	+ 100
Treasury currency outstanding	11,807	+ 4	+ 463
Total	154,255	–1,191	+17,021
Currency in circulation	112,025	+ 143	+10,288
Treasury cash holdings	310	+ 5	– 132
Treasury dpts with F.R. Bnks	5,299	–1,169	+ 1,143
Foreign deposits with F.R. Bnks	308	+ 10	+ 8
Other deposits with F.R. Banks	618	+ 62	– 43
Other F.R. liabilities & capital	4,303	– 172	+ 751
Total	122,863	–1,121	+11,998
Member bank reserves			
With F.R. Banks	31,392	– 71	+ 5,024
Cash allowed as res.	10,027	+ 172	+ 773
Total reserves held	41,492	+ 100	+ 5,805
Required reserves	41,377	+ 25	+ 5,705
Excess reserves	115	+ 75	+ 100
Free reserves	–433	+ 138	....

MONETARY AND RESERVE AGGREGATES
(daily average in billions)

		One week ended:	
		Nov. 29	Nov. 22
Money supply (M1) sa		358.6	359.3
Money supply (M2) sa		869.1	870.1
Money supply (M1) nsa		359.2	360.1
Money supply (M2) nsa		864.3	865.6
		Dec. 6	Nov. 29
Monetary base		142.0	142.4
		Four weeks ended:	
		Nov. 29	Nov. 1
Money supply (M1) sa		360.4	362.2
Money supply (M2) sa		870.3	868.0
Bank time deposits sa		605.4	594.4

sa-Seasonally adjusted. nsa-Not seasonally adjusted.

KEY INTEREST RATES
(weekly average)

	Dec. 6	Nov. 29
Federal funds	9.87	9.85
Treasury bill (90 day)	8.93	8.98
Commercial paper (dealer, 90 day)	10.25	10.15
Certfs of Deposit (resale, 90 day	10.64	10.66
Eurodollars (90 days)	11.56	11.66

$115 million in excess reserves over requirements of $41.4 billion. Taking member bank borrowings into account, the system had net borrowed reserves of $433 million, indicating that there was little room for demand-deposit expansion without some easing action by the Fed. If free reserves were a positive figure, it would represent a degree of liquidity which the system did not have on Dec. 6.

The same report includes changes in the monetary aggregates as compared with the earlier week on an actual and seasonally adjusted basis. The Dec. 6 report showed a seasonally adjusted decline in M_1 of $700 million and M_2 of $1 billion. It bears repeating that the monetary statistics should be followed over a period of time to obtain a sense of their trend. For instance, the fact that the aggregates showed a decline as of Dec. 6 is interesting but not in itself very meaningful. But the fact, not reported here, that it represented the third consecutive weekly decline gives the figures added significance.

The Government's Influence

Beyond the influence of its monetary policy, the government affects the behavior of interest rates in its role as a major borrower of funds. As a consequence, its tax and spending plans and the state of the budget bear careful scrutiny. In a direct sense, when the budget is in deficit and borrowing is the government's only recourse to fund its numerous programs, its heavy demands in both the short- and long-term credit markets will, other factors remaining constant, very likely force interest rates higher.

In a broader context, a high level of government spending during periods of strong economic activity can stimulate further borrowing and spending in the private sector, prompting greater demand for credit and rising interest rates.

While they are not as likely to exert as marked day-to-day influence on futures prices as the Federal Reserve's open market operations, traders should be aware of the budget implications of new government programs and major changes in existing ones that may materially affect its borrowing plans. To the same purpose, any projected increases or reductions in tax receipts should be weighed. The current mood of the Congress may be significant in determining the likelihood of social, military and other programs proposed by the executive branch being legislated in their entirety or being cut back.

Apart from the federal budget itself, a number of government agencies are responsible for their own funding. Competition between them and the Treasury for access to the capital market during the same period may lead to intensified demand and higher interest rates. Futures traders should keep a close watch on the calendar of upcoming financing by the Treasury and the major agencies for some indication of demand pressures that could affect interest rates. The progress of major financings should be monitored for a suggestion of the prevailing mood on the supply (investment) side. A successful quarterly offering by the Treasury can signal an abrupt change in sentiment that could spark a sizable market rally, as occurred immediately following the August 1978 refunding.

Also of consequence are the financing plans of the numerous state and local government borrowers that have accounted for roughly one-fourth of all new bond offerings over the past five years. The smaller municipalities tend to disregard the level of interest rates when formulating their borrowing plans, whereas during periods of high rates many of the larger state and local entities postpone their financing plans and thereby exert a moderating influence.

Chapter Eight

How to Monitor Money Market News

In its earlier versions this chapter was tentatively entitled "How to Forecast Interest Rates." While that might have helped to sell more books it also would have been what is today popularly referred to as a "ripoff." Anyone can make a forecast. The difficulty lies in doing so with consistent accuracy. Otherwise, we are talking about mere guesswork. The most highly regarded professionals in the money market are the first to concede that forecasting interest rates ranks with bullfighting and bomb disposal on the list of hazardous occupations. Moreover, we are in the first instance attempting to anticipate immediate price movements of interest rate futures, which, as was demonstrated in Chapter Six, is not necessarily the same thing as predicting a particular rate six months removed.

The good news is that the Ph.D. economist who constructs elaborate mathematical models with the aid of a computer has no insurmountable edge over the amateur analyst who is willing to keep abreast of the relevant information and do his homework. The advantage that people who work "on the Street" enjoy, be it Wall or South LaSalle, is that they are attuned to what the market is expecting (since they help to form the consensus) and usually know enough to take immediate action when actual developments fail to bear out those expectations. The outside trader therefore must make it his business to know what news the market is anticipating and carefully check the accomplished facts against the expectations. This usually can be accomplished by reading the daily financial press. Sometimes a bit more digging is required.

While this chapter does deal with forecasting, it does so with the same skepticism with which we listen to the weather forecast for the upcoming week on the six o'clock news. Everyone (the weatherman most of all) is pleased when the forecast proves correct, but there is no great surprise when it falls far from the mark. Forecasting is not only a risky job, it does little to enhance one's popularity.

Nearly every investment manual ever written has stressed that the key to successful trading is not so much to be right (though that is by no means a drawback), but to recognize early on when you are wrong and to waste no time in doing something about it, i.e., get out of the losing position. This attitude is probably more critical in futures trading than in any other speculative or investment activity, and constitutes the aforementioned edge the "pros" enjoy over the amateurs. What this chapter is really about, therefore, is assembling the wherewithal—mostly statistics to form an intelligent opinion on the outlook for interest rates, and to keep sufficiently well-informed to know when and how that opinion should be changed.

We have chosen in this instance to confine our analysis to the sequence of economic events and resultant market action throughout 1978. Our purpose in adopting this case method is three-fold, namely to determine: (1) where to obtain the relevant information; (2) how to interpret it; and (3) how the futures market is likely to react to the news. The techniques used are those which were described in the preceding chapter—flow-of-funds, business-cycle, monetary and budget-policy analysis.

Readers are cautioned not to become immersed in the succession of figures that appear throughout this chapter. They are intended to serve an illustrative rather than substantive purpose and are in any case soon dated. The analytic process rather than the statistics themselves is what is here important.

Though the emphasis is on a do-it-yourself approach, that is not meant to imply that a trader should ignore any advice, research or statistical data his broker is able to provide. It is, however, very definitely meant to convey the conviction that every trader should develop the capability to seek out and critically assess the available information and to form his own opinion on the basis of that and any other material supplied to him.

Flow of Information

The initial step is to ensure the flow of timely information. Most of the pertinent data is reported in the daily financial press. *The Wall Street Journal* and the business sections of the major general-circulation dailies print official statistics the morning following their release by the Federal Reserve, and the Commerce and Labor departments. It is up to the reader to determine how timely and complete the coverage by a particular newspaper is, and to obtain a second source if all of the important statistical releases are not promptly reported.

Subscriptions to the *Federal Reserve Bulletin* and the *Business Conditions Digest* of the Department of Commerce are available at what must be considered bargain rates by anyone who intends to trade futures.[1]

---

[1] *Federal Reserve Bulletin,* Division of Administrative Services, Board of Governors of the Federal Reserve System, Washington, DC 20551. Monthly, $2 single copy, $20 per year.

Business Conditions Digest, U.S. Department of Commerce, Bureau of Economic Analysis. Monthly, $3 single copy, $40 per year.

Economic Indicators, Council of Economic Advisors. Monthly, $1.30 single copy, $15 per year.

The last two publications are available from the Superintendent of Documents, U.S. Government Printing Office, Washington, D.C. 20402.

For an additional charge, subscribers may have their names added to the mailing list for regularly scheduled reports of the latest monthly and quarterly statistics as they are released.

Much of the same statistical data with accompanying charts are presented in a somewhat clearer and more concise form in *Economic Indicators,* prepared by the President's Council of Economic Advisors for the Joint Congressional Economic Committee. A year's subscription to all three monthly publications can be had for the equivalent of three basis points on one T-bill contract. If used properly, they should pay for themselves many times over.

Though they contain data essential in making longer range flow-of-funds and business-cycle analyses, these publications are not available until several weeks after the market already has evaluated and adjusted to the most recent statistics. For more timely information futures traders must rely on newspaper reports the day following the release of the latest figures, or ask their brokers to alert them as soon as they are carried over the Dow Jones News Service or Reuter Financial Report. A calendar should be kept of scheduled release dates for important monthly and quarterly statistics. Reference to such a calendar enables traders to anticipate upcoming reports and to make their plans accordingly. The market's action prior to such reports is often as significant if not more so—as its response to the actual news. It is once again a matter of the final results confirming or refuting the prevailing expectations.

Flow-of-Funds Analysis

The *Federal Reserve Bulletin* includes in its monthly statistical supplement the latest figures for the flow-of-funds accounts. Although the sources and uses are broken down into more detailed components than were listed in Chapter Seven's simplified table, a little realignment will bring them into focus.

Among the considerations to which credit and capital market analysts paid heed, the projected flow of funds for 1978 led the majority to conclude that interest rates would rise moderately over the course of the year, a consensus shared by the futures market. Total credit demand was expected to rise somewhat above the $337 billion of 1977 owing to a higher level of business activity and a rising inflation rate while the mix between business and consumer borrowing changed as consumers curtailed their use of installment credit and corporations stepped up their short-term financing. Sizable increases in U.S. Treasury and federal agency borrowing also were anticipated.

The principal change foreseen on the supply side of the credit equation would be the result of sizable withdrawals from savings banks and savings and loan associations as depositors took advantage of the higher return available on such money market instruments as Treasury bills and commercial paper. Despite the planned introduction of a new six-month money market certificate of deposit to avert or at least minimize these expected outflows, the thrift institutions alone were believed to have about $12 billion less available for commitment in the credit markets at a time when business and government borrowing was increasing.

In the mortgage sector, demand was expected to increase in line with a high level of residential construction, rising home prices and the use of mortgage financing by homeowners as a source of funds for non-housing purposes. Including farm mortgages, total mortgage debt was projected to increase somewhat from the amount raised in 1977 to an estimated $136 billion.

Analysts tend to look for an adjustment in the catchall "other" category to balance any discrepancies in their supply and demand projections. In the case of the 1978 forecast of increased demand and diminished supply, a further increase in interest rates would be necessary to attract additional funds into the market from individuals and other residual sources.

By mid-year, actual credit conditions had outrun the January forecasts. Short-term interest rates already had climbed the 100 basis points or so many analysts had projected for the entire year, compelling them to raise their earlier estimates. One factor which contributed to the greater-than-anticipated demand was the increase in applications for business loans, beginning at the regional banks and moving on to the major money centers, first Chicago and then New York. By June, commercial and industrial loans at large New York commercial banks reporting to the Federal Reserve[2] were growing at greater than a 20% annual rate at the same time that corporations were increasing their offerings of commercial paper. Though the level of corporate borrowing was running ahead of earlier estimates, the biggest surprises came from the consumer sector where the level of consumer credit not only failed to decline as expected, but in fact rose to record highs, spurred by strong automobile purchases.

As had been foreseen, residential and commercial mortgage demand continued to grow at the same time that disintermediation was causing a 30% decline in deposit flows into savings and loan associations and as much as a 50% falloff at mutual savings banks. The resulting divergence in supply and demand prompted the two government housing agencies, the Federal Home Loan Banks and the Federal National Mortgage Association (Ginnie Mae's sister, Fannie Mae) to step up the level of their own borrowings to accommodate the heightened mortgage activity. A partial offset to this development was a level of borrowing by the Treasury, which, though higher than what it was in the first half of 1977, still was less than what official budget estimates had led analysts to project.

A greater increase in credit demand than what the analysts had anticipated at the beginning of the year prompted them to raise their forecast of total demand by about 3.5% to the $350 billion area, a figure which included an estimated $58 billion in U.S. Treas-

---

[2]See Figure 8-1 on page 254.

ury and budget agency financing. At mid-year, disintermediation at the thrift institutions caused estimates of their contribution to the supply of credit to be cut to $72 billion, or $12 billion below the 1977 figure. Part of this anticipated shortfall was expected to be taken up by increased insurance company commitments for commercial and multi-family properties as a result of their higher yields. Total projected supply from the contractual institutions—insurance companies and pension funds—was raised to $66 billion, approximately $4 billion above the 1977 level. Commercial banks, which also were confronted with a slowdown in time deposit growth, endeavored to meet the increased borrowing demand from business by issuing large denomination certificates of deposit. Their supply of funds to the credit market accordingly was projected at $96 billion, with the larger portion coming in the second half of 1978.

Another question unresolved at mid-year was how long state and local governments and foreign central banks would continue to be heavy purchasers of Treasury securities. The former were hastening to complete the sale of bonds, the proceeds of which were to be "parked" in T-bills pending their use to repay maturing debt, before the effective date of new regulations restricting such advance refundings. The central banks likewise were investing on a temporary basis dollars acquired in the course of their foreign exchange stabilization operations. The extent of their T-bill purchases ultimately would depend upon the condition of the U.S. dollar in world currency markets. Any reduction in the level of buying that might take place in either sector would have to be taken up by larger purchases on the part of individual investors. The full-year estimates for these three components called for state and local funds to commit $10 billion, foreign investors $25 billion and "individuals and others" $50 billion. The remaining $18 billion was slated to come from non-financial corporations investing liquid funds and Federal Reserve purchases of Treasury securities.

These flow-of-funds forecasts are at best "guessti-mates" based upon credit conditions as analysts per-ceive them at the time the forecasts are made. The fact that they must be revised continually, and still are likely to be far removed from the actual results, points up their provisional nature. Moreover, by the time the latest quarterly figures are reported in the *Federal Reserve Bulletin,* they are very nearly ancient history so far as the interest rate futures market is concerned. But while the day-to-day behavior of futures prices seems to be affected to a greater degree by more tran-sient events, perhaps undeservedly so, the flow of funds is the scoreboard for decisions numbering in the tens of thousands which determine the condition of the credit markets and in turn exert a decisive influence on the level and direction of interest rates. As such it deserves more than a passing glance by futures traders in their more reflective moments.

Business-Cycle Analysis

A simpler and more current sampling of the total business demand for credit is the level of commercial and industrial loans held by 10 large New York City banks as listed in the weekly Federal Reserve report of member bank reserve changes and money supply figures. As with the other statistical indicators, a sin-gle week-to-week change does not in and of itself sig-nify a great deal. The trend that emerges over the course of several months merits attention, however, as the accompanying chart indicates. There was a clear correlation between the trend of business loans by large New York banks and that of 90-day Treasury bill yields during most of 1978. As noted earlier, the New York money center banks were among the last to feel the effect of the increase in loan demand as the year progressed. Even so, the figures in the weekly Federal Reserve report began to show pronounced

FIGURE: 8-1

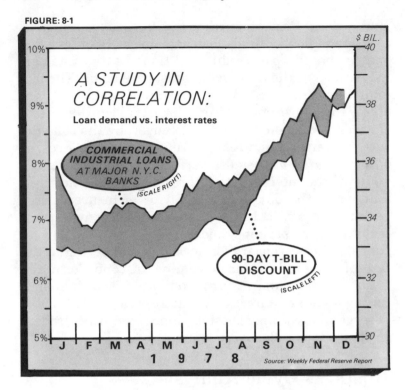

A STUDY IN CORRELATION:

Loan demand vs. interest rates

COMMERCIAL INDUSTRIAL LOANS AT MAJOR N.Y.C. BANKS *(SCALE RIGHT)*

90-DAY T-BILL DISCOUNT *(SCALE LEFT)*

$ BIL.

Source: Weekly Federal Reserve Report

gains in their level of business loans in May and June, two to three months before money market rates, already rising, started to soar. These figures in themselves by no means comprise an infallible indicator (there is no such thing) of the future direction of interest rates, but as a representative sampling of aggregate credit demand, they should be given due consideration in the shaping of market decisions.

To repeat, one or two weeks' figures do not constitute a trend. But traders should be alert to any sharp deviation from previous reports as a possible precursor to a more protracted change that may have a material effect on short-term rates. In the 1978 experience, the sustained increase in the level of loans at the 10 reporting New York banks above the $35 billion area correctly would have been taken as being representative of an intensification of corporate loan demand. The response of more rapidly increasing money market rates (and falling futures prices) was not long in coming.

Tracking GNP Growth

Among the other important statistics, gross national product (GNP) is significant for two reasons. As one of the seven coincident indicators, it is a measure of the rate of economic growth or contraction. But more than a mere indicator, GNP represents the nation's total output of goods and services, and promoting its growth at a sustainable rate is an explicit national policy. Since the generally accepted definition of recession is two successive quarterly declines in GNP, the figure has broad implications for the behavior of interest rates.

The problem with GNP is that it sends contradictory signals concerning interest rates. When it is increasing at what is considered an acceptable rate, the economy is expanding, demand for credit is increasing and interest rates are presumably moving higher. According to this line of reasoning, interest rates, at least in the short-maturity ranges, and GNP should move up and down together. On the other hand, GNP adjusted by a price deflator to wring out the effect of inflation, measures the rate of "real" economic growth. The counterpart of rising, real growth is a declining inflation rate, which should in turn induce a reduction in that portion of long-term rates investors regard as an inflation premium. As long as rising real GNP is the result of a lower inflation rate, long-term interest rates should hold steady or decline.

As with the other indicators, it is the rate of change in GNP rather than its absolute level that affects the market. Quarterly figures are released by the Bureau of Economic Analysis of the Department of Commerce and are widely reported. Statistics covering the past ten years are published in *Business Condi-*

tions Digest and *Economic Indicators*. Table 8-1 lists the percentage changes in GNP from 1969 to 1978 in current and constant (1972) dollars, along with the implicit price deflator used to translate one to the other. The reader should note that during 1974 and 1975, real GNP declined 2.7%, while in current terms it continued to rise some 16.3%. The difference is accounted for by an average annual inflation rate (deflator) during those two recession years of about 9½%.

Owing to severe weather and a coal strike, real GNP was virtually "flat" (no change) in the first quarter of 1978, followed by a strong but unsustainable recovery of 8.7% in the second quarter and a more moderate 2.6% gain in the third. The presumed topping out of the automobile and housing cycles, an anticipated drop in corporate profits and narrower productivity gains in the face of increased labor costs were expected to limit real GNP growth to an estimated 2% in the fourth quarter and lead to a decline of 1% to 2% in the first and second quarters of 1979, making the contraction, if it came to pass, an official recession.[3]

Table 8-1. Percentage Changes in GNP and GNP Price Measures.

	1969	1970	1971	1972	1973	1974	1975	1976	1977	1978	1978 1Q78	2Q78	3Q78	4Q78
Current Dollars	7.7	5.0	8.2	10.1	11.6	8.1	8.2	11.2	11.0	11.6	7.1	20.6	9.6	15.0
Constant (1972) Dollars	2.6	−.3	3.0	5.7	5.5	−1.4	−1.3	5.7	4.9	4.0	−.1	8.7	2.6	6.4
Implicit Price Deflator	5.0	5.4	5.1	4.1	5.8	9.7	9.6	5.2	5.9	7.4	7.2	11.0	6.9	8.1

Note: Annual changes from previous year and quarterly changes from previous quarter.

Source: Department of Commerce, Bureau of Economic Analysis

---

[3]It didn't. Confirming the earlier point about the hazards of forecasting, real GNP actually rebounded in the fourth quarter of 1978 at a strong 6.4% growth rate, and 1979 also opened on a firmer note than previously had been expected.

Like the flow-of-funds estimates, GNP figures are released too infrequently and too late to affect the futures market on a day-to-day basis. Latest results are not reported until well into the following quarter, although the Department of Commerce does make periodic forecasts prior to its release of the official statistics. If the actual figures are close to the earlier estimates, the market will more than likely have taken them into account and their impact upon release is likely to be minimal. The reported results are themselves frequently revised at some later date as additional data are processed.

By way of illustration, real GNP in the first quarter of 1978 initially was reported on April 20 to have declined at an annual rate of −.6%.[4] T-bill futures were unchanged to three basis points lower that day, and bond contracts were off about $^2/_{32}$nds. The first quarter figure was subsequently adjusted to −.4%, and later to −.1%. On Aug. 21, the department's Bureau of Economic Analysis announced that GNP had risen in the second quarter at an estimated annual rate of 8%. T-bills closed one to three basis points higher and bond futures went up $^{18}/_{32}$nds. The actual figure came in at +8.7% on Sept. 21. T-bill futures were unchanged to two basis points lower and bonds were down about $^8/_{32}$nds. When a third quarter gain of 3.4% was reported on Oct. 23, T-bills were considerably stronger, with gains ranging from 14 basis points in the nearby delivery month to three basis points on the deferred contracts. On the same day, bond futures also were stronger, with most months up about $^{18}/_{32}$nds.

With the exception of the third quarter results, which the market may have interpreted as signaling an impending economic slowdown (hence a general

---

[4]Official statistics and their revisions cited throughout this chapter are as reported by *The Wall Street Journal* the day following their release by the appropriate government agency.

decline in interest rates) the reaction to the quarterly GNP figures the days of their general publication was minimal. As with the flow of funds, however, the recent and anticipated trend in GNP is weighed heavily in government and corporate economic policy decisions and for that reason should be monitored by futures traders as well. A record ought to be kept of the figures for the last four quarters, as well as an estimate for the current quarter with the apparent reasons for any projected change from past results.

Monitoring Inflation

Inasmuch as an accelerating inflation rate became the overriding economic problem for the U.S. in 1978, creating international problems (a sharply declining dollar) as well as domestic troubles, the implicit price deflator used to convert current to real GNP deserves particular attention along with the other important price indexes. Simplified explanations have the effect of understating the complexity of a problem, but they do serve the purpose of making it more comprehensible. The definition of inflation as "too much money chasing too few goods" falls within that category. When it costs $1.50 to buy the same product or service (a copy of *Time,* a round-trip subway fare, anyone can provide his own examples) that $1 bought last year, the purchasing power of the dollar with respect to those items has declined by a third. That is what inflation is all about. Whatever its causes, the end result is higher prices. But there are many prices. Is the newsstand price of *Time* magazine an accurate measure of the inflation rate over the past ten years? Probably not. Even if you threw in *Newsweek* and *U.S. News and World Report,* you would only have a price index of three weekly news magazines. To measure changes in the cost of living, it is necessary to assemble far more price data.

The GNP deflator is an important price index be-

cause it is the most broadly based. It is a weighted
average of unit labor costs in the private sector, government wage costs, raw material and other product
costs and corporate profit margins. Two other widely
followed inflation indicators are the consumer and producer (wholesale) price indexes compiled by the U.S.
Department of Labor's Bureau of Labor Statistics. The
consumer price index (CPI) is comprised of sub-cate-
gories measuring price changes in food, other commodities and services on both an unadjusted and seasonally adjusted basis. The producer price index (PPI)
is broken down among consumer foods, other finished
goods, capital equipment and intermediate and crude
materials. The advantage of following these indexes is
that they are released monthly rather than quarterly
as the GNP deflator is.

Economists write about cost push, demand pull,
government induced and random and uncontrollable
types of inflation. Whatever the technical designation,
prices continued to move sharply higher in the U.S.
during 1978 largely as a result of: realized union wage
and benefit demands, legislated increases in the minimum wage and Social Security tax, rising domestic
meat prices, disruption of food supplies due to floods
in California, crop shortages in Russia, China, Brazil
and elsewhere, a large federal deficit, high rate of
money supply growth, and a normal cyclical decline in
the productivity growth rate. Relating these events
and circumstances to our simplistic definition of inflation, they all contributed to the phenomenon of more
dollars being spent on less productivity ("the dollar
doesn't go as far as it used to"), a broad textbook concept that consumers recognized as rising prices and
what many analysts warned was an escalating even
if understated economic crisis.

The annualized monthly changes in the consumer
and producer price indexes during 1978 as reported by
the Bureau of Labor Statistics are listed in Table 8-2,
along with quarterly changes in the GNP deflator. The

Table 8-2   Monthly Price Changes—1978[5]

	CPI[6]	PPI[7]	GNP Price Deflator[8]
January	8.4	7.2	
February	7.2	13.2	
March	9.6	7.2	7.2 IQ78
April	10.8	15.6	
May	10.8	8.4	
June	10.8	8.4	11.0 IIQ78
July	6.0	6.0	
August	7.2	−1.2	
September	9.6	10.8	7.0 IIIQ78
October	9.6	10.8	
November	7.2	9.6	
December	7.2	9.6	8.1 IVQ78
Annual Change	9.0	9.1	7.4

[5]Percentage change from preceding period, annualized rate (unadjusted).
[6]Source: Department of Labor, Bureau of Labor Statistics.
[7]*Ibid.*
[8]Source: Department of Commerce, Bureau of Economic Analysis.

largest disparities between the two Labor Department indexes occurred in February and April, when the PPI rate of increase surged ahead of the comparable consumer index figures. The accelerating price increases during the second quarter, however measured, were reflected in a sharp jump in the GNP deflator from an annual 7.2% rate of increase to 11%, its largest quarterly rise since 1974.

Price increases abated somewhat during the summer, as the PPI actually declined by 1.2% in August, a brief respite from the upward trend which prevailed through most of the year. It is probably not a coincidence that the money market and interest rate futures staged the year's strongest price rally during this period as the summer slack stirred talk of an impending recession, or at least an economic slowdown. By the middle of the fourth quarter, with CPI and PPI both coming in for three successive months around 10%, the politically sensitive double-digit level, it became apparent that the summer respite was over. Editorial writers resumed their dire warnings that "something" needed to be done to control inflation. Each had his own opinion of what that something should be, but they all invariably pointed their collective finger in the direction of Washington.

It was conceded with a hint of apology in an earlier chapter that statistical tables do not make for very exciting reading. But drab, lifeless and downright boring though they might be, these price indexes go to the heart of some basic bread and butter issues (such as how far did your paycheck stretch last month?), trigger intense debate in the high councils of government (spurred by the aforementioned editorial writers) and not incidentally have a significant effect on the behavior of interest rates which, to remind anyone who may have forgotten, is why we are dealing with such distasteful subjects as inflation in this book.

The distinction drawn earlier between nominal (current dollars) and real (constant dollars) GNP applies to interest rates as well. Throughout the second half of 1978 there was a great deal of hand-wringing in the money market and elsewhere over the high level of interest rates, how much more they were likely to rise, and what the Federal Reserve and other arms of the government should do about it. "But wait just one minute," opined a few irritating contrarians such as you will find in any crowd, "if people can borrow money at 8%, which they end up repaying a year later in dollars that have depreciated by some 9% (CPI and PPI 1978 annual increase) just what exactly are they paying for the use of that money? Hell, man, they aren't paying a red cent, they're actually making money on the deal!"[9]

In more subdued and reasoned language, but in effect saying the same thing, the president of the Fed-

---

[9]Source analysts contend that this is a specious argument. Unless the borrower is able to employ the proceeds of the loan in a more remunerative manner than the interest cost, they maintain, the real as well as the nominal cost of the loan increases as the interest rate climbs.

eral Reserve Bank of Minneapolis observed that if the
discount on our old friends, three-month Treasury
bills, were adjusted for the rate of inflation, i.e. the
GNP deflator, the real interest rate would not only be
far from high, it would be close to zero. At the end of
the third quarter of 1978 the equation would have
looked something like this:

$$\begin{array}{ccc} \text{90-day T-bill} \\ \text{discount} \end{array} - \text{GNP deflator} = \begin{array}{c} \text{Real} \\ \text{Short-term} \\ \text{Interest rate} \end{array}$$

$$(7.25 \qquad - \qquad 7.0 \qquad = \text{¼ percent})$$

One of the accusatory editorial writers, this at *The
Wall Street Journal,* stated the issue succinctly when
he asked and then answered his rhetorical question:
"Tight money? Not on your life. It's free!"[10]

The *Journal's* sarcasm was in this instance directed at the Federal Reserve's handling of the inflation problem, a matter we shall get to in due course.
The point to be made here is that present and anticipated inflation rates and interest rates are inextrica-
bly tied together, and futures traders are advised to
pay as careful heed to the drab CPI, PPI and GNP
deflator statistics as do the vigilant editorial writers.
Essentially, the higher the inflation rate, the greater
the premium potential lenders feel they must have as
compensation for their presumed loss of purchasing
power by the time the loan is repaid. Moreover, the
Federal Reserve is likely to come under increasing
pressure to do "something" about the problem. That
something usually takes the form of restrictive monetary policy, the inevitable consequence of which is
once again higher interest rates.

As in its reaction to the quarterly GNP figures,
the futures market, as demonstrated by the behavior
of the nearby T-bill contract the day the most recent
statistics were reported in the financial press, was not

---

[10]*The Wall Street Journal,* October 17, 1978.

particularly affected by the consumer and producer price indexes upon their release. T-bill futures did drop 10 basis points the day the sharp rise in the PPI was reported for April and again 35 basis points on the release of the September CPI figure. The latter price break was more a part of the general convulsion in the money market in late October, however, than a specific reaction to the CPI report. When the August decline in PPI was announced in mid-September, the futures market shrugged off the good news and fell five basis points when it logically might have been expected to rally.

In summary, one would have to conclude that there was no particular advantage to be gained from basing a trading strategy on the monthly release of consumer and producer price statistics. On the other

Table 8-3. Futures Market Response to Release of Price Data—1978[11]

Publication Date	Statistical	Release	Price Movement Nearby T-bill Futures Contract (in basis points)
1/23	January PPI	+7.2	+4
2/28	January CPI	+8.4	unchanged
3/10	February PPI	+13.2	−1
3/29	February CPI	+7.2	unchanged
4/7	March PPI	+7.2	+9
5/1	March CPI	+9.6	+2
5/5	April PPI	+15.6	−10
6/1	April CPI	+10.8	+5
6/5	May PPI	+8.4	unchanged
7/3	May CPI	+10.8	+6
7/10	June PPI	+8.4	−3
7/31	June CPI	+10.8	−10
8/5	July PPI	+6.0	+4
8/30	July CPI	+6.0	−4
9/11	August PPI	−1.2	−5
9/27	August CPI	+7.2	+2
10/6	September PPI	+10.8	−2
10/30	September CPI	+9.6	−35
11/3	October PPI	+10.8	−1
11/29	October CPI	+9.6	+14
12/8	November PPI	+9.6	−2

[11]Percentage change from preceding period, annualized rate.
Source: Department of Labor, Bureau of Labor Statistics.

hand, it was doubtlessly these increasingly disturbing figures which led in part to the Federal Reserve policy of credit tightening that *The Wall Street Journal* derided in its editorial columns but which was nevertheless the immediate cause for the sharp rise in interest rates and resultant break in futures prices in the fourth quarter of the year. If Fed-watching was "the name of the game" in the futures market in 1978, as we shall soon see it was, the monthly price figures were clearly an important part of the rules by which the Federal Reserve was then playing.

The Leading Indicators

The trend of the leading economic indicators is likely to have the same effect on the futures market as that of real GNP. Month-by-month increases confirm a continuing business expansion with an attendant increase in credit demand and interest rates. Any sign of faltering or decline—"the steam is going out of the economy," as the press might put it—is taken as a warning of an impending slowdown in economic activity, and the subsequent likelihood of declining interest rates.

In theory, at least, strong gains in the leading indicators should exert a bearish influence on interest rate futures because they presage an increase in the demand for credit. By the same line of reasoning, any hesitation in the upward path of the indicators is a possible signal of the slackening of such demand and should therefore be taken as a bullish development. Traders who go long futures share the bond buyers' perverse pleasure in beholding the onset of a recession.

The NBER's composite index of 12 leading indicators[12] uses 1967 figures as its base of 100, and expresses subsequent results as a percentage of that base. Following a rapid recovery from the cyclical

---

[12]See Chapter Seven, p. 223.

trough of the 1973-75 recession, the index plotted a steady upward trend from mid-1975 to late 1978. The gain throughout 1978 was on the order of 3.7%, moving from 135 in January to the 140 level by year end. Like the other statistical series, the figures for any month are subject to revision as the year progresses. The market, of course, reacts to the results that are initially reported. By the time any revisions are announced, the market usually is preoccupied with a new set of conditions, and is unlikely to look back on what is by that time "old news." With the benefit of hindsight, the two declines of any consequence in the monthly figures as revised were during the winter storm-affected January (initially reported as -1.9, later revised to 1.0) and the July slack (initially $-.7$, later -1.3) which happened, not surprisingly, to be the same month in which the price indexes experienced their mid year dip. The month-to-month gains from August on gave analysts reason to believe, as the year drew to a close, that there was still some "steam" left in the 3½-year advance. Even so, a few cracks were beginning to appear in the form of faltering individual indicators within the composite index, lending credence to a growing body of opinion that a recession, or whatever people chose to call it, loomed on the 1979 horizon. While contracts and orders for plant and equipment, average workweek, companies reporting slower deliveries and changes in liquid assets continued to show improvement, the layoff rate, change in sensitive prices of crude materials, stock prices, building permits and real money supply were not maintaining their earlier pace. Though the composite index continued to show strength on balance, those analysts who were predicting a decline in GNP during the first half of 1979 were anticipating an imminent downturn in the leading indicators.

The futures market showed no great propensity to respond to the reports of the leading indicators one way or the other. If the news seemed to confirm an

Table 8-4.   Futures Market Response to the Release of Leading Economic Indicators, 1978[13]

Publication Date	Monthly Gain or Decline	Price Movement Nearby T-bill Futures Contract (in basis points)
3/1	January −1.9 (revised to −1.0)	−2
3/31	February unchanged (revised to +.6)	−5
5/2	March −.1	+1
6/2	April +.5 (revised to +.7)	+8
7/5	May −.1 (revised to +.2)	−3
8/1	June +.4 (revised to +.5)	+1
9/1	July −.7 (revised to −1.3)	−15
10/2	August +.8 (revised to +.5)	−9
10/31	September +.9	−14
11/30	October +.5	unchanged
12/29	November −.6	+1

[13]Percentage change from preceding period.
Source: Department of Commerce, Bureau of Economic Analysis.

existing market trend, it was given a passing nod. If, on the other hand, it did not bear out the market's present inclination, it was largely ignored. On the day that the July decline in the leading index was announced, admittedly in early September, the market already had paid heed to the summer slump, and was responding to the renewed head of steam that was building in the economy, but which would not be reflected in the indicators until a month later. Again, the problem of delay in the release of the latest figures makes their use as a guide to current trading decisions a problematical matter.

Monetary Analysis

Among the 12 leading indicators, however, the money supply, specifically M_1 in 1972 dollars, was undoubtedly the single factor which most influenced the interest rate futures market throughout 1978. More precisely, it was the Federal Reserve's repeated attempts to limit the growth of the money supply through open market operations and raising the discount rate that propelled interest rates to historic high levels.

In terms of the simple metaphor of too much money chasing too few goods, the Fed perceived its role in the fight against inflation to be one of keeping the monetary aggregates in check. It has been stated that the arbiters of monetary policy are faced with a dilemma during the later stages of a business expansion. They wish to permit the money supply to increase at a rate sufficient to keep the economy growing, hold down the level of unemployment, keep corporate profits rising and attain other generally desirable policy goals. But if they allow M_1 and M_2 (Yes, folks, your broker is right. We've been holding back. There really is an M_3 as well. We can't do all his work for him.[14]) to rise at too rapid a rate, accelerating inflation, an "unhealthy" (because it cannot endure) boom, and the inevitable "bust" are the unwanted consequences. If the Open Market Committee is too zealous in restricting credit to ward off these economic evils, it may err in the other direction by choking off "healthy"—sustainable, non-inflationary—growth. As a result, the committee continually is engaged in something of a balancing act, walking a fine line between encouraging adequate money supply growth and preventing excessive growth. The trick lies in deciding what is at any given time adequate and what is excessive. In true democratic fashion, the committee resolves the issue by taking a vote.

As was mentioned in the previous chapter, the policy makers endeavor to make the best of a thank-

---

[14]If you insist, M_3 consists of M_2 plus time deposits at non-bank thrift institutions, notably savings and loan associations and credit unions. As such, it is a still broader definition of money.

less job by establishing separate target growth ranges for M_1 and M_2 that they consider to be consistent with a desirable rate of economic expansion. If over an extended period the aggregates continue to grow at a rate in excess of the Fed's tolerance ranges, the standard remedy is to drain reserves from the banking system by selling securities through the open market procedure described in Chapter Seven. If M_1 and M_2 growth falls short of the announced ranges for any length of time (the Fed is not inclined to take action on the basis of a mere one or two weeks' figures) the accepted course is to inject reserves into the system by buying T-bills and other government securities in the dealer market.

Since the target ranges are a matter of public record, futures traders and other interested parties watch the reported changes in the money supply from week to week and attempt to anticipate the Fed's moves. They know that when the New York trading desk moves into the market to drain reserves, the immediate result will be a higher federal funds rate which in turn pulls other money market rates up with it, making it a good time to be short interest rate futures. That, in brief, was the story of the interest rate futures market through much of 1978. Looking at the same weekly statistics, analysts and traders played the role of shadow FOMC members, attempting to predict when and to what extent the real committee would act to halt the growth in the money supply. The barometer in what essentially amounted to a high stakes guessing game was the federal funds rate, which the committee uses to measure the degree of tightening it wishes to accomplish.

Moving into 1978, M_1 and M_2 were growing at rates of about 8% and 9%, respectively. At its first monthly meeting of the year, the Federal Open Market Committee determined that acceptable ranges for the two measures should be 4% to 6½% for M_1, and 6½% to 9% for M_2. The adjacent chart illustrates the degree of success the Fed achieved in containing money growth within its tolerance ranges throughout the year. While M_2 generally remained below the assigned 9% ceiling, M_1 proved far more difficult to bring down to the 6½% growth limit. On a quarter-to-quarter basis, M_1 growth averaged about 8%, and for several sustained periods during the second and third quarters ballooned to an alarming 10% to 15% growth rate. It was at these junctures that *The Wall Street Journal* and other critics decried the Federal Reserve's seeming reluctance or inability to contain M_1 within its own established limits.

There was a political sidelight to this so-called "interest rate war." By early October, the President and concerned members of his administration were voicing their unhappiness over the high level of interest rates and earnestly expressing the hope that the callous recession-mongers at the Federal Reserve would not find it necessary to force them yet higher. There were bills introduced in Congress proposing that the Fed be stripped of its power to establish and enforce money supply targets. The savvy talk "on the Street" was that the Fed was afraid to assume the tougher posture the "interest rate hawks" advocated lest the chances of these proposals being passed into law be enhanced.

When the Fed did indeed start to get tough on inflation and the exploding money supply, the impetus came from a different though related quarter. The justification advanced by the "hawks" on the Open Market Committee for greater monetary restraint than up to that time had been exercised was that it was the only immediately realizable means of halting the collapse of the dollar in the foreign exchange markets. Only in the second instance was the inflationary threat advanced as grounds for curbing money growth. The culmination of the Fed's stricter stance came on Nov. 1, when in conjunction with other extreme measures, the discount rate was raised an unprecedented

FIGURE 8-2

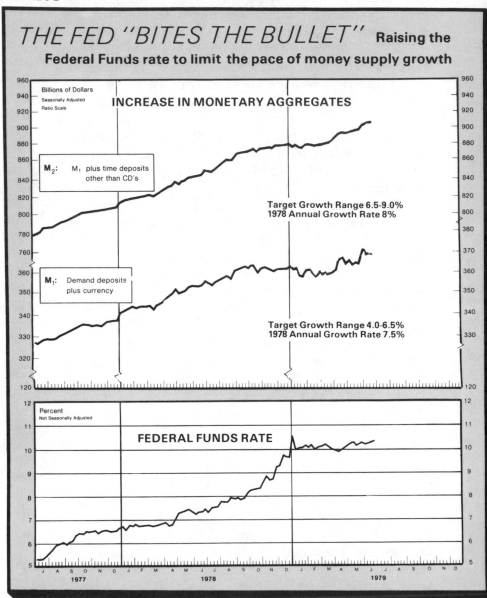

Source: The Conference Board

one percentage point to a record level of 9½%. Futures traders witnessed the spectacle of bond futures trading *up* the limit in reaction to short-term rates being forced sharply higher. It was the market's recognition that this tight policy was the best hope of containing inflation in the long run, and it signaled its endorsement of this decisive step by staging a strong, even if somewhat short-lived rally.

The reverse situation occurred exactly six weeks later following the decision of the OPEC oil ministers to raise the price of Mideast oil by nearly 15% in 1979. The unfavorable repercussions this move would have on the inflation rate in the U.S. were obvious, and the interest rate futures market reacted to the news by opening sharply lower the day following the announcement.

These episodes, both of which underscore the market's sensitivity to the inflation issue, also illustrate the futility of attempting to trade solely on the basis of published statistics. The greater part of the OPEC price increase would not go into force until the latter half of 1979 but for the futures market in mid-December 1978, it was the most important news item of the month.

The difficulty with assiduously following the weekly money supply figures is that they offer no clue as to precisely when or even if the Fed will decide to act when the target rates are exceeded in either direction. Moreover, as was just noted, in following a policy of "practical monetarism" the Fed moved increasingly away from reacting mechanically to the aggregates throughout 1978 and was compelled to give greater consideration to such other factors as the condition of the dollar in world currency markets and the general level of prices, as measured by the CPI and PPI, in arriving at policy decisions.

When the FOMC did decide on a change in policy, the thrust of its directive to the New York trading desk was sometimes evident as soon as the afternoon of the meeting date. On other occasions, the new policy did not become apparent for several days. In either case, it was useless to wait until the text of its directive was published in the *Bulletin* 60 days later. Like the OPEC price increase, the consequences of the new policy had long since been reflected in both the government securities and futures markets.

Whatever the difficulty of anticipating the timing of the Fed's actions, there can be no doubt about the impact of its open market operations. Inasmuch as the fastest trading profits were to be made by being short futures at the time the Fed had targeted a higher funds rate, the question most often asked by traders in 1978 was: Is the Fed tightening again?

In all, the Federal Reserve raised its funds target 17 times during the year from 6½% to 9⅞% in increments of ⅛% and ¼%. The discount rate was increased less often, seven times in all, but in steps of ¼% or ½% with the exception of the November percentage point boost made in conjunction with the administration's dollar support operations. According to Table 8-5, T-bill futures fell in price an average of 15 basis points the day of each Fed funds increase or the one following.[15] In most instances, the market broke sharply when traders came to the realization that the Fed had set a higher funds target, and then recovered somewhat after the initial reaction. It would appear with the benefit of hindsight that if the speculative trader was not able to make a short sale the moment a tighter Fed policy became apparent, the best alternative would have been to buy futures for a quick recovery after the market had overreacted to the news. That tactic would have been profitable eight times out of the 17 the funds target was raised in 1978, but as the

---

[15]For a graphic representation of this price history, readers can refer to the chart of the December 1978 90-day T-bill contract in Chapter Nine, page 287.

Table 8-5.   **Futures Market Reaction to Federal Reserve Credit Tightening.**

1978	New Federal Funds Rate	% Increase	Price Movement of Nearby 90-day T-bill Contract (in basis points)
1/9	6¾	¼	−29
4/20	7	¼	−15
4/28	7¼	¼	− 8
5/18	7½	¼	− 5
6/21	7¾	¼	− 6
7/20	7⅞	⅛	− 4
8/16	8	⅛	−21
8/18	8⅛	⅛	− 7
8/28	8¼	⅛	−12
9/8	8⅜	⅛	− 7
9/20	8½	⅛	−14
9/22	8⅝	⅛	−17
9/29	8¾	⅛	− 9
10/18	8⅞	⅛	− 3
10/30	9⅜	½	−35
11/1	9¾	⅜	−30
11/27	9⅞	⅛	−37

market entered into its precipitous decline from August on, during which the Fed went through 11 rounds of tightening, it increasingly became a losing proposition to take a long position in the market.

The seven increases in the discount rate throughout the year also served to reinforce the downward trend in futures prices, though the immediate market impact of each increase was not as marked as when the Fed funds rate was hiked up through open market operations. As was observed earlier, discount raises usually occur after money market rates have moved up, partially as confirmation of existing Federal Reserve policy and to reduce the disparity between them. The discount rate is therefore usually "catching-up" with other interest rates, and its changes are not as much of a surprise to the market.

Fiscal Policy Analysis

Turning in conclusion to federal budget and debt policy, early estimates of Treasury borrowing in calendar 1978 were in the area of $55 billion, not including the $13 billion expected to be raised by the non-budget agencies, particularly to satisfy the needs of the residential mortgage market. As was the case with private credit demand, these estimates were raised as the year progressed, to about $60 billion by the Treasury and some $30 billion by the agencies, the lion's share again going to assist in the financing of housing.

The preliminary projections for 1979 looked for a $10 billion reduction in the federal deficit to about $40 billion. The purported agreement between the Federal Reserve and the administration that monetary policy would be used more sparingly, i.e., less upward pressure on interest rates, as a quid pro quo for reductions in federal spending seemed to have reached an impasse as the likelihood of major spending cutbacks in the face of a possible recession became problematical. Total borrowing at the federal level, including that by the non-budget agencies again was expected to exceed $70 billion in 1979.

Keeping Abreast

Most individuals who undertake to trade interest rate futures, at least on a personal basis, are not trained economists or statisticians, and consequently cannot be expected to carry out the elaborate calculations a flow-of-funds or GNP analysis involves. As was pointed out at the outset and demonstrated throughout the chapter, even the most expert forecasts frequently prove to be far from the mark when the final figures come in. Anyone prepared to devote the time and effort (plus the cash outlay for a daily newspaper) has access to all of the statistics cited in this chapter and is capable of compiling his own data bank.

It would not be practical, and in any event probably superfluous, for futures traders to attempt to keep abreast of all of the monetary and general economic data that continually flows from government agencies and other sources. There are, however, certain basic statistics—usually easy to obtain—which should be sought and noted as part of any research and decision-making process.

Most of the requisite information is contained in the weekly Federal Reserve report released each Thursday and published the following morning in *The Wall Street Journal* (See Table 7-5, page 243), *New York Times* and other major newspapers. These weekly figures may be tallied in a worksheet like the one reproduced in Appendix F. The statistics which are not included in the Fed report, such as quarterly GNP figures and monthly consumer and producer price indexes, are usually featured in news stories in the same papers and can be noted in the worksheet as they appear.

The monetary aggregates, M_1 and M_2, should be tracked on a weekly basis and converted to four- and twelve-week averages, which can then be compared to the Fed's announced growth targets. A log of recent changes in the Fed funds rate also should be kept as a guide to the prevailing monetary policy of the Federal Open Market Committee. Trends in other money market interest rates also may be plotted from the weekly averages of key interest rates included in the weekly Fed report.

On the broader economic front, the latest figures as well as six- and 12-month averages can be derived for changes in the rate of increase (or decline) in GNP, leading economic indicators, industrial production, unemployment and monthly retail sales as guides to the apparent trend in overall economic activity and the likely effect on interest rates and related futures contracts. The same procedure can be followed in assessing inflationary trends as measured by the consumer and producer price indexes.

The demand for credit in both the private and public sectors can be monitored by following the trend of commercial and industrial loans at ten large New York City banks (See Figure 8-1, page 254) contained in the weekly Fed report and from reading the bond market and new financing columns in the *Journal* and other papers. Calendars of upcoming corporate, Treasury and municipal bond offerings can also be found in the paper or obtained through a broker.

Interest rate futures traders anticipate certain economic developments by assuming long or short positions before the actual statistics are released. As stated at the outset of this chapter, expectations have as great an impact on the market as do the accomplished facts. In this regard, it behooves a trader to be aware of consensus projections and to know when the statistics cited above are scheduled for release. Brokers also make available to clients monthly calendars of regular release dates, on which traders can note the key estimates. When the actual figures are released, one can tell at a glance whether the latest report is on target, and at the same time update the data bank. By taking the added trouble to note the price action of the particular contracts in which he may be interested in trading, he will soon have assembled a valuable aid in planning and executing trading strategy and tactics.

Part Three

The Users

Chapter Nine
The Speculators

Part Three of this book is the how-to-do-it section. It integrates the operating procedures and theoretical analyses presented thus far and applies them to actual trading situations. The following chapters examine in turn the objectives and techniques of the principal categories of futures market activity, namely speculation, hedging, spreading and arbitrage. The two latter terms are loosely used synonymously in many commentaries, though in the strictest sense they refer to quite different kinds of trading operations.

The concluding chapter, in summing up the current state of the art, provides an overview of the types of corporate users who have entered the interest rate futures market at this early stage, the services offered by the brokerage, banking and consulting firms active in the field and pertinent legal and regulatory issues which are likely to influence the market's long-range development.

Successful, which is to say consistently profitable, futures trading is no mean accomplishment. Most individuals who have attempted to do so will attest that it is downright difficult. The meager statistics that are publicly available suggest most traders come away from the market as losers. Yet, the opportunity to "win big" is there. Successful traders, like expert mountaineers, take care to plan for all contingencies before attempting to scale the heights of fortune. They may not reach the peak every time, but their preparations usually assure their return to base camp without being buried by an avalanche.

Some observers, probably a part of the disappointed majority, maintain that successful traders are born, not made, and that you either have the knack for it or you don't. That resigned view sounds suspiciously like sour grapes. As stated in the introduction, this book contains no enriching secrets, nor does it attempt to transform ordinary mortals such as ourselves into latter day Bernard Baruchs or Jesse Livermores. Its goal is the more modest, therefore attainable, one of outlining a set of guidelines which, *if followed,* will give would-be speculators a better-than-even chance of making money in the futures market.

That discipline in making and adhering to trading decisions is the key to a speculator's success has been stated and restated so often as to be reduced to a cliche. It is nonetheless true that the exercise of self-discipline is a trader's best shield against calamity, just as the lack of it will surely lead to his undoing. If there is a secret to trading success, it is to arrive at calculated decisions *before* getting caught in a market avalanche. A trading plan is the indispensable tool in arriving at these calculated decisions. Discipline is the quality which is required to stick to the plan when the crashing boulders of adverse price action might drive a trader to panic moves or freeze him into stunned inactivity.

The suitability of futures trading for any investor and the likelihood of his success at it are determined by his financial capacity to bear risk. If the money committed to the futures market is a relatively minor part of his investment capital, the less likely he is to lose sleep over it. Traders who lose sleep on account of the market are traders who are in over their heads and prone to make mistakes. Ironically, the investor who is able to contemplate the total loss of his futures

trading equity with relative equanimity (no one is saying he must relish the prospect) is the one who is most
likely to be successful. To paraphrase President Tru-
man's famous caveat: If you can't stand the losses, stay
out of the pit.

How much of one's total investment capital should
be allocated to a futures trading account also should
be determined with a healthy dose of caution. Consider
the contrasting connotations of the terms trading and
investment. Certain investments have customarily
been regarded as being more "solid" than others. The
ownership of such financial necessities as bank accounts, insurance and residential real estate is taken
for granted. Securities are generally considered to be
sounder holdings than commodity futures. On the
other hand, the accelerated rate of inflation during the
past decade and the resulting deterioration of security
values due to rising interest rates has cast doubt on
many traditional precepts and raised to quasi-invest-
ment status such tangible items as paintings, gems,
precious metals, antiques and other collectible goods.
Trading in the conventional agricultural commodity
futures, as well as those for gold, silver and platinum,
also has mushroomed as part of the stampede toward
supposedly inflation-resistant "investments." As a consequence, the expression "diversified portfolio" has
come to have a far broader application than its earlier
sense as investors turn in many directions in their
efforts to preserve their purchasing power.

Limiting the Dollar Risk

There is no hard and fast figure or rule of thumb
to determine the appropriate percentage of total net
worth that prudently may be set aside to trade futures.
A good deal depends upon the individual's circumstances and his attitude toward risk. In some cases,
20% may not be an excessive figure. Where preservation of capital is the paramount investment objective,

futures may have no place in the portfolio as a speculative medium. On the other hand, the type of hedging operations discussed in the following chapter not
only may be acceptable, but also desirable.

Having elected to allot a certain dollar amount to
a futures account, the prospective trader should take
further risk-limiting steps before making his initial
commitments. In light of the volatile and unpredictable nature of the futures markets, it is advisable to so
structure the account as to avoid placing more than a
fraction of the available funds in any single position.
A stated percentage or dollar amount always should
be held back as a reserve against unforeseeable shocks
and a prolonged string of trading losses.

Take the situation of a corporate executive who
earns $60,000 a year, has $100,000 invested in common stock and bonds and owns an equal amount of
equity in his home. Having determined that, under the
worst of circumstances, a loss of 5% of his net worth
or one-sixth of his annual income would not subject
him to undue financial strain, he opens a futures trading account and deposits $10,000 into it. But, he and
his broker go beyond that. They agree to divide the
account mentally into five trading units of $2,000
each, of which two are to be held in reserve for unforeseeable contingencies (including opportunities),
and commit the remaining units to three separate
promising positions as they materialize.

Moreover, they agree to hold the realized loss on
each individual long or short position to $1,000 or less,
and to enforce the loss limit through the proper placement of stop orders. In the case of the interest rate
complex, their plan entails locating stops 40 basis
points above or below the entry price of any short or
long positions taken in 90-day T-bill and commercial
paper contracts, and one point away with Treasury
bond and Ginnie Mae futures.

The plan, therefore, observes the cardinal rule of
futures trading: *limit losses, let profits run*. This rule

gives practical expression to the earlier enjoiner concerning the exercise of discipline in making trading decisions. It also is recited with the same near-religious fervor, and violated as often as the more spiritual commandments. Traders who observed the rule as faithfully in practice as they pay it lip service would show far better results than they do. Unfortunately, there always seem to be "valid" reasons to make an exception "just this one time."

An effective plan should also stipulate that a profit objective be set for each transaction. A good rule of thumb is to identify and take action in those situations where there is the possibility of making a profit three times greater than the acceptable loss. If the trader sets a risk limit of $1,000 as indicated earlier, he should wait for an opportunity which he believes holds a $3,000 profit potential. The actual ratio selected must be consistent with the market situation at hand. It would not have been possible to glean 120 basis points ($3,000) from T-bill futures on either the long or short side during the first eight months of 1978, for example, simply because the market never traded in that broad a range. But, if the profit objective was reduced to 60 basis points, a trader would have to use a 20-point stop to maintain the 3:1 profit-loss ratio, which would render him subject to being stopped out by a minor price fluctuation. The parameters are not chiseled in granite, therefore; but once having been set, they should be observed until market behavior offers a compelling reason to change them.

The element of time is another important consideration of each prospective transaction. The only rational justification for assuming the risks inherent in futures trading is to secure a higher rate of return than is obtainable on more conservative investments. Therefore, time limits as well as price limits should be placed on each position, since the holding period determines the annualized rate of return of a particular dollar profit.

Once the trading plan has been defined (and put in writing),[1] watching the market anxiously from hour to hour and agonizing over each adverse "tick" is not only unnecessary but counter-productive, when positions are taken consistent with its decision rules. By the time each trade is initiated, it already has been determined where a profit will be taken or, if necessary, a loss will be realized. Should neither of these price targets be attained within the projected holding period, the plan would call for the position to be liquidated, or in any case to be carefully reassessed.

Using Price Charts

Price charts are the tools futures traders use to "read" the market and execute their plans. Charting, or technical analysis, has won a large following of those who profess to see in the visual representation of price movement not only a record of past and present market conditions, but important clues to events which have yet to unfold. There are two principal types of charts: line and point and figure. The choice between them is largely a matter of preference by the analysts who use them. Whatever its form, a price chart is an essential aid to trading.

Though there are weekly chart subscription services available at reasonable rates and up-to-the-minute "real time" electronic displays in brokers' offices, many analysts (the author included) believe it is worth the time and effort to keep one's own charts. The daily exercise of updating the charts gives the trader a "feel"

---

[1]Unless these details are committed to paper they tend to become blurred and are all too often forgotten during the heat of trading, especially if the price action is adverse. To recapitulate, prospective traders should set down the dollar amount and percentage of total net worth to be deposited in a trading account, the number of trading units into which that amount will be divided, the number of positions to be assumed at any time, size of the trading reserve, designated loss limits and profit targets and other pertinent decision rules.

for market action that reference to someone else's work does not provide.

Charting tools are inexpensive and easy enough to obtain: One or more sharp No. 2 lead pencils with erasers, a straight edge and the appropriate chart paper. For contracts traded in basis points, 53 weeks of five-day segments by 10 divisions is suitable. Paper ruled in eight-unit divisions is satisfactory for the contracts which are priced in 32nds. The vertical lines for each day of the business week are standard. The price scale marked by the horizontal lines is set at the discretion of the chartist. On the aforementioned paper, two basis points per division for T-bills and commercial paper contracts and $2/_{32}$nds per division for bonds and Ginnie Maes make a clear chart. With these implements and the daily price listing from the newspaper, you are ready to become a chartist.

The first step is to decide which contracts to chart. Those with at least six months left before their expiration date should be selected to obtain a sufficient price history upon which to base trading decisions. Some analysts begin a chart on a particular contract when it is first traded, and maintain it over the life of the contract. Others will chart two or more delivery months of the same contract to track the price relationships, or spreads, between nearby and distant contract months. The major chart subscription services turn out special charts on these spreads, as well as spreads between different contracts such as 90-day T-bills to commercial paper. The beginning chartist probably is better off limiting his activity at the outset to one delivery month for each of the principal interest rate contracts. Within a short time, he will find himself posting the daily price changes in a matter of minutes, and can devote the remainder of his available time to conducting the sort of trend analysis described later in this chapter.

A line chart plots three prices for each contract:

the daily high, low and settlement price. On the vertical line representing the appropriate day, the chartist marks and connects the high and low prices for that trading session and notes the settlement price with a cross hatch.

A line chart of the last eight trading sessions of the December 1978 T-bill contract is shown in Figure 9-1, along with the daily volume for all contracts. Along the lower border are noted the eight trading dates, Monday, Dec. 11 through Wednesday, Dec. 20, the final trading day of the December contract. Only the first day of the trading week is normally marked on a chart. Prices run up the left-hand margin. The Dec. 11-20 segment, enlarged for clarity of illustration, spans a 60 basis-point range from 90.60 to 91.20. A standard scale might run from, say, 90.00 to 94.00, or can be enlarged to cover a narrower range if the chartist desires a magnified picture of daily price volatility. Since it is not known how far up or down the contract price ultimately will go when the price scale is laid out (if it were, traders would be too busy adding up their profits to bother keeping charts), the best method is to place the current price midway up the margin, so that subsequent advances and declines can be charted without cutting and pasting appendages as the weeks go past.

Many chartists also make a notation of the volume on the same vertical line as the daily price range. Daily volume is reported by the exchange as the aggregate contracts of all delivery months traded. That is the figure marked in the form of a bar at the foot of the chart in Figure 9-1.[2]

Many analysts believe that point and figure charts provide a more instructive picture of price behavior than the more frequently seen line charts. They might

---

[2]Open interest, or the total contracts in force for the delivery month being charted, also is considered an important enough indicator to warrant inclusion in some charts.

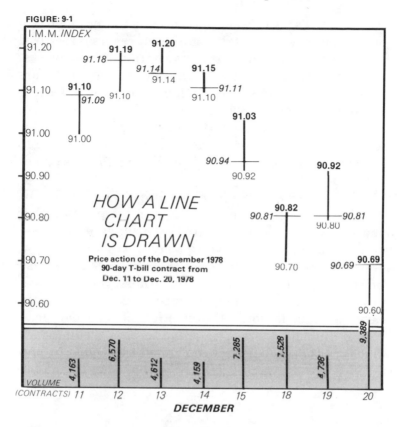

FIGURE: 9-1

HOW A LINE
CHART
IS DRAWN

Price action of the December 1978
90-day T-bill contract from
Dec. 11 to Dec. 20, 1978

more aptly be called cross and circle charts, as those
are the symbols used to identify price advances and
declines. Though somewhat mystifying at first glance,
point and figure charts are not difficult to read or
maintain, once the principle of the method is grasped.
The element that is initially confusing is the lack of
a distinct notation for each day's price action. Price
movement, irrespective of time, is what is being
charted. So long as the contract price continues to rise,
whether for three consecutive trading days or 15, the
chartist keeps on marking Xs atop one another in the
same column of boxes. When the price turns down, he
moves one column to the right and draws descending
Os as long as the price drops. The only factors within

the chartist's discretion are the price increment assigned to each box and the minimum reversal required to move from an up to a down column or vice versa. The purpose of awaiting a minimum reversal before indicating a change of direction is to filter out those minute fluctuations which have little significance in terms of the broader price movements the analyst is attempting to anticipate, yet retain sufficient scale to pinpoint activity that might hold clues to subsequent behavior.

Irrespective of whether they are drawn by the line or point and figure method, there is no question that charts are a convenient means of displaying price history. What moves a growing body of traders to draw, study and restudy them is not their historical interest, however, but the conviction that these visual records of past performance contain important clues to imminent price behavior. The question of whether price charts are sufficiently predictive to base trading decisions on their purported messages continues to provoke debate in the investment and academic commu-

FIGURE: 9-2

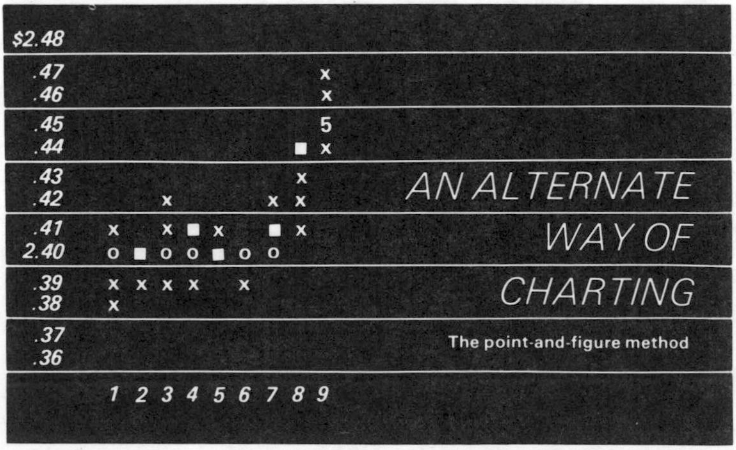

AN ALTERNATE WAY OF CHARTING

The point-and-figure method

Source: Commodity Trading Manual

nities. The issue was stated by one writer in the following terms:

> ... it is hard to find a practitioner, no matter how sophisticated, who does not believe that by looking at the past history of prices one can learn something about their prospective behavior, while it is almost as difficult to find an academician who believes that such a backward look is of any substantial value.[3]

Those skeptical academicians are the chief exponents of the so-called theory of random walk, which maintains that each successive price change is determined wholly independently of those that precede it.[4] The most extreme (and disheartening) expression of this view is that a chimpanzee tossing darts at the daily price listings is just as likely to make profitable buy and sell "decisions" as all the trained analysts with their elaborate charts and computer printouts.

Also arrayed against the chartists are those analysts who believe that the only legitimate areas of research are the detailed supply-and-demand studies (flow of funds, business cycles, etc.) discussed in the last chapter. To these pure "fundamentalists," any attempts to predict securities or futures prices from a series of lines or crosses and circles are tantamount to reading the future in tea leaves or tarot cards.

Whether technical analysis is a science, art, matter of faith or a combination of the three, no one who trades futures can afford to ignore it, if only because the believers have the power to move the market when they respond to the same chart signals in unison.

---

[3] Paul H. Cootner (Ed.) *The Random Character of Stock Market Prices,* The MIT Press, Cambridge, Mass., 1967. p. 116.

[4] See also Burton G. Malkiel, *A Random Walk Down Wall Street,* W. W. Norton & Co., New York, 1973. Eugene Fama, "The Behavior of Stock Market Prices," Journal of Business, Jan. 6, 1965. George Pinches, "The Random Walk Hypothesis and Technical Analysis," *Financial Analysts Journal,* March 1970.

Whether or not they are the next best thing to every investor's fantasy of receiving tomorrow's *Wall Street Journal* today, price charts are indispensible tools to be used in conjunction with the trading plan in making market decisions in a disciplined and objective manner.

The chartist attempts to read buy and sell messages in the price formations before him. Referring to the closing eight-day segment of the chart for December 1978 T-bills, we see a moderate rise from Monday to Tuesday, a gentle cresting Wednesday and Thursday, leading into a sharp break Friday and the following Monday, an unsuccessful attempt to stage a recovery on Tuesday and, finally, a resumption of the fall on Wednesday. Eight trading sessions do not generally provide sufficient data to draw any firm conclusions. But by continuing the daily process of posting prices over several weeks, familiar patterns begin to emerge. The chartist is attempting to spot these patterns in their early stages and is poised to take whatever trading action as would have been profitable in the wake of similar patterns in the past.

Reading the Charts

An exhaustive treatment of chart analysis and the numerous formations its practitioners claim have predictive significance would comprise a volume in itself.[5] Several of the important formations bear mentioning here by way of illustration.

The chartist's greatest challenge (and opportunity) is to recognize a trend reversal in its early stages. Theoretically, the best time to establish a short position is at the onset of a major downtrend, just as the

------

[5] Readers interested in pursuing this line of analysis are referred to what is generally recognized to be the definitive work by R. D. Edwards and J. Magee: *Technical Analysis of Stock Trends,* John Magee, Springfield, Mass., 1961. Most of the principles and chart formations discussed have the same significance for commodity futures as for common stock.

ideal moment to buy is when the trend is turning up. Anyone who has attempted to pinpoint such a reversal knows that it is far more obvious after the fact than while it is occurring. As a consequence, any chart pattern which signals such a reversal is of great value. One formation of this sort which has had an above-average degree of reliability is the head and shoulders top. Its anatomical designation stems from the outline that is traced as rising prices begin to lose their momentum, fail in three attempts to advance to new highs and, finally, retreat in what is the start of a new downtrend. The second of the three peaks rises higher than the two which flank it, giving the formation its head and shoulders designation. Each of the three rally attempts begins and returns to what is termed the neckline. If, after failing to sustain any of the three rallies which form the head and shoulders, the price fails to hold at the neckline on the third retreat, the expectation is for a continuing decline of some magnitude, said by some chartists to approximate the width of the overall formation from the left shoulder to the right one. Having identified and traced the development of a head and shoulders formation, the logical point at which to establish a short position to profit from the anticipated drop is when the price penetrates the neckline after the third rally attempt.

An approximation of a head and shoulders formation appears in Figure 9-3. Other patterns manifest themselves during the course of an established trend. In some cases you will see a "congestion area" of price ambivalence as traders await some indication, usually from the cash market, of whether the trend will continue in the same direction or develop into a trend reversal. Figure 9-4 contains such a congestion pattern, called a triangle, in which successive daily advances and declines steadily contract until they reach the apex of a triangular formation from which prices are likely to move in the direction they had followed earlier.

In addition to these patterns and such other geometric formations as rectangles, flags, pennants, V's and saucers which they scrutinize for signs of impending price activity, chartists lay great store by "gaps," or voids in which no trading takes place. These gaps are themselves open to varying interpretations, depending upon the stage of the trend and the circumstances under which they occur. A common gap is usually the result of some unexpected news item or the execution of a cluster of stop orders which drive a session's opening price sharply above or below the previous day's range. It is "closed" a day or so later when the price returns to its earlier level. A breakaway gap is more meaningful to the chartist, since it purportedly marks the breakout from a congestion area and is believed to signal a prolonged move in the direction in which it occurred. Runaway gaps appear near the midpoint of a trend and are taken as confirmation that a particular price move still has some momentum left to it. The exhaustion gap, as its name implies, is something of a last gasp. It is believed to mark the culminating upward thrust in a rising market, or the final downstroke of a decline, in either instance presaging a trend reversal.

The trouble with these interesting patterns, gaps and reversals is that they are far easier to identify and label after they have run their course, by which time their predictive value is sharply reduced. Moreover, like beauty, these formations often reside in the eye of the beholder, which makes the whole business of chart analysis more a matter of subjective judgment than of precise measurement.

All futures traders try at one time or another to identify buy and sell signals within chart patterns. Some have a greater flair for interpretation than others. Unfortunately, too many neophyte traders get the mistaken notion that chart analysis will enable them to "call the turns," that is, to buy before the market turns up and to sell before it heads down. Some cling

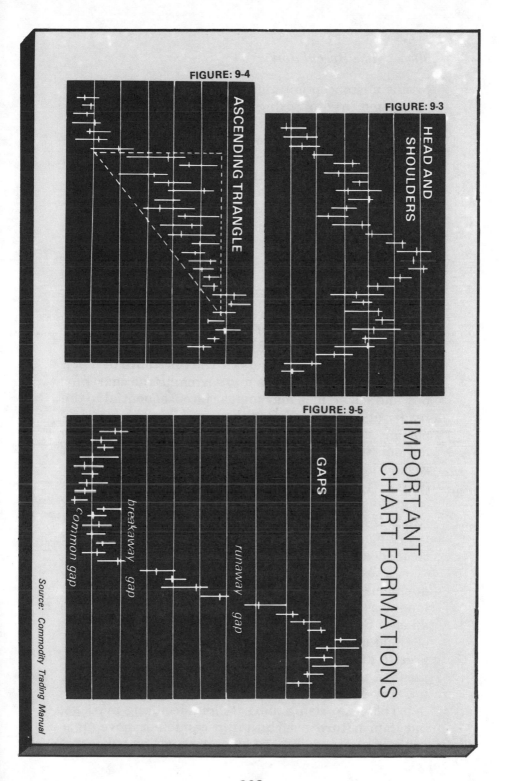

IMPORTANT
CHART FORMATIONS

FIGURE: 9-4

ASCENDING TRIANGLE

FIGURE: 9-3

HEAD AND
SHOULDERS

FIGURE: 9-5

GAPS

common gap

breakaway gap

runaway gap

Source: Commodity Trading Manual

to this misconception until they are either wiped out or become tired of losing money. To oversimplify for the sake of emphasis, a speculator should be long when prices are rising, and short when they are falling. So far as charts help him to attain this happy condition, they constitute valuable trading tools. But at the point that a trader becomes consumed with deciphering secret messages from what often may be random formations, it is usually time for him to take a vacation.

Verifying Market Trends

A more limited and, for many traders, a more realistic application of chart analysis is to verify the existence of a particular trend, hence the position (long or short) a trader should be holding, and provide an early alert to a trend reversal. The difference between this sort of trend analysis and searching the charts for buy and sell signals may appear inconsequential to the reader at first glance. But there is, in fact, a very important distinction. The signal watcher is trying to fathom what the market will do tomorrow and next week. The trend analyst believes that he has a better chance of making money by concentrating his efforts on getting a clear picture of what the market is doing today. If it is rising, he knows he should be long. If it is falling he should be short. If he does not have any clear idea of the trend, he should be on the sidelines.

As usual, such dogmatic statements raise more questions than they answer. What is a trend? How long does it last? How do we know when it comes to an end? Before a trader is able to incorporate a system of trend analysis into his plan, he must have a more precise answer to such questions than a mere statement of the obvious that, when prices are not going up, they are going down.

There are rising markets and declining markets, but their nature is such that prices do not move up or down in unbroken progression. A rising, or bull, mar-

ket is interrupted by periods of price weakness or reactions, just as bear, or declining, markets experience
rallies or periods of price strength. For the purpose of
trend analysis, a rising market is defined as one in
which each upward movement attains a higher price
level than the one preceding it, and each reaction
comes to a halt at a point above the low point of the
prior weakness. Conversely, in a declining market,
each downward leg falls to a new low level, while each
attempt at price recovery falls short of the one before.

Already we see complications emerging. A glance
at the charts in Figure 9-6 reveals that we are dealing
not only with primary uptrends and downtrends, but
with a succession of intermittent secondary trends as
well. The real secret of futures trading, if there is any
such thing, lies in determining which is which. We can
look at the chart on the left and say yes, of course, A-
G is a clear uptrend, interrupted by minor reactions
B-C, D-E and F-G. Likewise in the righthand chart,

FIGURE: 9-6

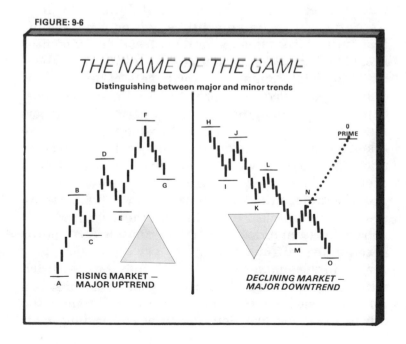

THE NAME OF THE GAME

Distinguishing between major and minor trends

RISING MARKET —
MAJOR UPTREND

DECLINING MARKET —
MAJOR DOWNTREND

line H-O represents a downtrend, broken periodically
by minor rallies I-J, K-L, and M-N. As usual, every-
thing is crystal clear after the fact. But what if, for
example, instead of turning down and falling obedi-
ently to point O, line M-N continues to advance to O'?
How far do we watch it rise before suspecting something has changed, that M-N is not merely a minor
rally in a major downtrend, and that, if we happen to
be short whatever contract the chart represents, we
may be in for trouble? That is essentially what futures
trading is all about.

The first task, then, is to distinguish between major and minor trends. A *major trend* may endure from
several months to several years, while a *minor trend*
could last for a few days to a few weeks. The major
trend could advance or decline 300 or more basis points
or 10 percentage points. Minor trends might show a
price change ranging from a few basis points or 32nds
to a considerably greater amount.

A chart of the September 1978 Ginnie Mae contract between September 1977 and June 1978 illustrates the concept in an actual situation. That Ginnie
Mae futures were in a major downtrend for 10 months
is evident, as the contract price fell steadily from about
97-00 to 90-00. Again, with the benefit of hindsight, it
clearly would have been profitable to have been short
Ginnie Maes through most of that period. The important question for our purpose is how long would it have
taken a chartist to decide that a major downtrend was
under way, and how could he determine when it was
over?

The minor rallies within the 10-month downtrend
are, themselves, clear enough. That they occurred with
no regularity and ran for varying times and distances
is confirmed by Table 9-1.

As in the simulated downtrend in Figure 9-6, each
minor uptrend failed to match the peak of the previous
rally, and each subsequent price decline brought the
contract to a new low. Some questions of trading strat-

Table 9-1. Minor Rallies in Ginnie Mae Futures, September 1977-June 1978.

Sept. 12 -Sept. 27	11 days	$17/_{32}$nds
Oct. 13 -Oct. 24	8 days	$21/_{32}$nds
Nov. 4 -Nov. 23	14 days	$28/_{32}$nds
Jan. 13 -Jan. 31	13 days	$12/_{32}$nds
Feb. 17 -Mar. 20	21 days	$1 8/_{32}$nds
Apr. 13 -Apr. 17	3 days	$25/_{32}$nds
June 1 -June 5	3 days	$15/_{32}$nds

egy now begin to emerge. Should one attempt to trade on the basis of the minor trends, or elect to ride them out and stay with the major trend? There is no hard and fast rule. But in the Ginnie Mae experience from September 1977 to June 1978, there is no doubt but that traders who held a short position throughout the 10-month period did substantially better than those who tried to trade the long side during the minor up-trends. The best of both worlds would have been to cover short positions and go long as the minor trend turned up, then liquidate and sell short again at the peak of each rally. Such agility calls for a degree of trading skill very few possess, however, and most speculators who attempt it find themselves getting "whip-sawed" in numerous false moves and dissipating their trading capital in losses and brokerage commissions.

Assuming a trader had the astuteness or good luck to go short Ginnie Mae futures during the fall of 1977, how would he have known when it had come time to take his profits? That question reverts to the cardinal trading rule of limiting losses and letting profits run. To compound their major mistake of allowing losses to go too far against them, many traders get so nervous about giving back what profits they do have that they liquidate their favorable positions too soon. The record shows that major trends often last much longer than most traders expect, and that many of them, either through an inability to distinguish between a major and minor trend or sheer "jumpiness," pass up what might have been the kind of profit they dream about.

The *trendline* formed by connecting the reaction bottoms of an uptrend or the rally tops of a downtrend is a most important device in differentiating between major and minor trends. The first consequential sign of a major trend reversal is the penetration of a trendline by a minor rally or correction. Returning to the September 1978 Ginnie Mae example, the line joining the Sept. 2-6 and 27-30, 1977, rally tops gave the first intimation of a downtrend in the making, prompting some traders to begin taking short positions in the 96-24 to 96-28 range during the first week of October. Others held back until they saw confirmation in a third rally top brushing against the trendline and falling back on Nov. 23-25. They began their selling at places between 96-02 and 96-08 during the first week of December.

The price decline in Ginnie Mae futures accelerated between mid-December and mid-January. The strongest minor uptrend during the first half of 1978 was the 1¼-point advance in the four weeks between Feb. 17 and March 20. Following the resumption of the downtrend, it became evident that the major trendline would have to be adjusted downward to fit the steeper slope, producing a curved trendline that is characteristic of an accelerating rate of price decline or advance. Traders who waited for a rally back to the original straight trendline to establish their short positions would have missed a good selling opportunity, with the subsequent March-June decline equaling the one from the previous September to February.

It is necessary to go back to the second half of 1976 to locate an equally distinct major uptrend for illustrative purposes. Selecting the March 1977 T-bill contract as our example, we see its price rise so sharply between June and December that it is more difficult to identify the minor trends than those in the 1977-78 Ginnie Mae bear market.

Most of the reactions were lateral movements as the market paused to consolidate its gains before con-

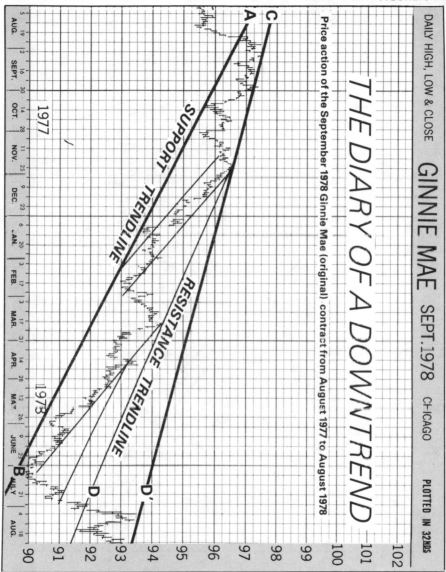

DAILY HIGH, LOW & CLOSE GINNIE MAE SEPT. 1978 CHICAGO PLOTTED IN 32NDS

THE DIARY OF A DOWNTREND

Price action of the September 1978 Ginnie Mae (original) contract from August 1977 to August 1978

Source: Commodity Research Bureau

299

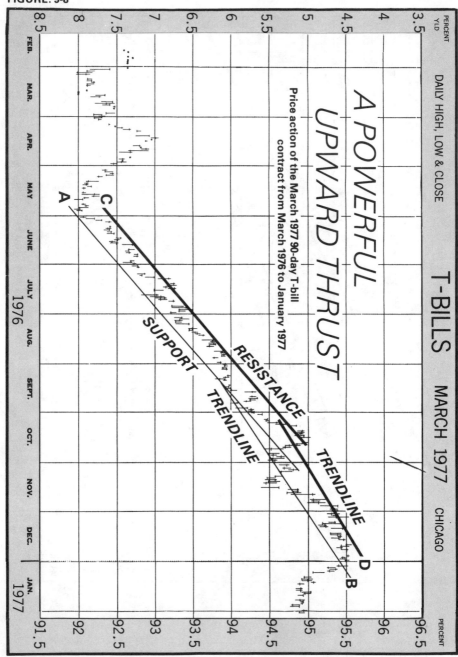

FIGURE: 9-8

A POWERFUL UPWARD THRUST

Price action of the March 1977 90-day T-bill contract from March 1976 to January 1977

T-BILLS MARCH 1977 CHICAGO

DAILY HIGH, LOW & CLOSE

Source: Commodity Research Bureau

tinuing the advance. There appear to be only four clear-cut minor corrections during a rise of some 350 basis points over the seven-month period: July 3-19, 43 basis points; Sept. 22-24, 33 basis points; Oct. 18-22, 60 basis points; Nov. 5-12, 42 basis points. There can be no doubt that staying with the major trend was the correct strategy in this instance. Only one trendline penetration of any consequence occurred during the second week of November, and was followed immediately by an apparent runaway gap into the concluding stage of the advance. The November correction did retard the overall rate of ascent, however, bending the trendline to a less steep angle.

Assessing Countertrends

Once he has drawn a discernible trendline, the chartist is concerned with estimating the extent to which minor countertrends are likely to run against the major trend. That is accomplished by determining the *trend channel*, the area between the trendline and another line drawn either through the rally tops of an uptrend or the reaction bottoms in a downtrend. Figures 9-7 and 9-8 display the trend channels of the March 1977 T-bill uptrend and the September 1978 Ginnie Mae downtrend by adding this secondary line which is often, but not always, parallel to the major trendline. It should be noted not only that the T-bill price rise is sharper than the Ginnie Mae's decline, but also that its trend channel is considerably narrower, allowing little room for maneuver by traders attempting to move with the minor trends.

The two lines that mark the trend channel (as important a navigational aid for futures trading as it is for boating) also define the critical levels of price *support* and *resistance*. Again, the trouble with using old charts to illustrate these concepts is that they give an impression of certainty and precision that does not exist in the futures market. It is clear enough after the fact that, in both the Ginnie Mae downtrend and the T-bill uptrend, lines A-B denoted some sort of support level, as each downward "leg" held at the line and turned up. In like manner, Lines C-D signify resistance, since each rally ran out of steam as it touched the line and fell back. So, all the chartist would have needed to do was to extend the trendline C-D, and each time a price rally met resistance there, sell the September 1978 Ginnie Mae contract; or, a little more than a year earlier to project line A-B, and go long March 1977 T-bills when the contract found support there. Almost simple enough for the dart-throwing chimpanzee the random-walkers talk about, right? Wrong!

There is something of a Catch-22 in this neat arrangement. The catch is that support and resistance lines are what they are supposed to be only so long as the market respects them as such. Once a price falls below a support level or rises through resistance, the chartist literally goes back to his drawing board and searches for the next support or resistance line. Just as the fundamentalists in Chapter Eight repeatedly were asking "Is the Fed tightening again?" their chart-oriented counterparts were wondering whether the contract price would hold at such and such a support level. In truth, no one knows for certain until the line holds or it doesn't. Admittedly a murky state of affairs, but one the trader has chosen to involve himself in.

Imperfect and misleading though this type of trend analysis all too often is, it offers traders the best chance, in the opinion of the author, to make consistent profits in the futures market. This opinion is shared by many professionals, and is reduced to the second inviolate maxim of futures trading: *Always trade with, never against, the market trend.*

To recapitulate, the first objective of trend analysis is to identify the major and minor trends (through the trendline and trend channel), and the second is to recognize a trend reversal as early as possible (when the trendline is violated). Just as many traders act precipitously in liquidating their profitable positions too soon, others overstay and give their profits back as the market changes direction. In effect, the trick lies in determining when a minor trend stops being that, and becomes the first segment of a new major trend.

A Case History

The best way to illustrate is by recreating an actual transaction as it unfolded. During October 1977, government bond futures were decidedly weak. The September 1978 contract had dropped from the 102 level more than two percentage points to below 100, and was staging a recovery as we moved into November. Since the evidence was not yet decisive that a major downtrend was underway, our feeling was that it would be advisable to wait and see how far the rally would carry before making any commitments. By the end of the month, the September 1978 contract had worked its way back to 101 and then resumed its decline. We now had two points (A and B) through which to draw a provisional trendline, and it most certainly had a downward slope.

By mid-December, September 1978 bond futures had fallen back to 100, a major downtrend had been confirmed, and a short position appeared to be in order. The first qualification of our trading plan had been met—we were selling in a downtrend. That left two further requirements, a profit objective and a risk limit. The lower boundary of the trend channel, line C-D, gave us a rough idea of our prospects if the market moved in our favor. An objective in the area of 96-00 to 97-00 appeared to be attainable. Well and good, but we knew we must also prepare for the worst. The projected resistance line was at this time at about 100-24, but it seemed advisable in placing buy stop orders to allow some leeway to avoid their being triggered by the occasional "spike" which pierces the trendline for

FIGURE: 9-9

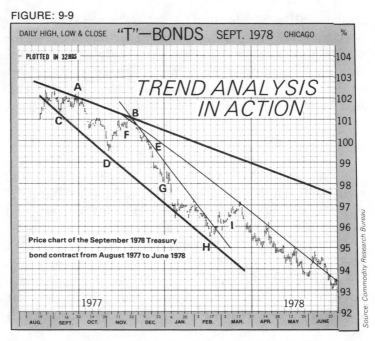

DAILY HIGH, LOW & CLOSE "T"—BONDS SEPT. 1978 CHICAGO   %

TREND ANALYSIS IN ACTION

Price chart of the September 1978 Treasury
bond contract from August 1977 to June 1978

Source: Commodity Research Bureau

a brief period but otherwise leaves it intact. Since the previous rally (D-B) was arrested at 101, our premise of a major downtrend, i.e., successively lower rally tops, would be voided if a subsequent minor uptrend reached that level. Our decision points, therefore, were:

Entry (short)	—	100-00
Objective	—	97-00
Stop (buy)	—	101-00

Disregarding commissions, our parameters of risking $1,000 to make $3,000 per contract seemed to comprise an attractive speculation.

Our best expectations were soon realized. Bond futures fell at an accelerating rate. Within a week of our short sales they were at 99-00. By the second week of January, the initial objective had been attained. The question at that juncture was whether to cover the short contracts or lower our objective as the downtrend showed no sign of abating. To the contrary, the runa-

way gap between 97-22 and 97-00 gave every indication of further weakness.

Our decision was to remain short, but to lock up
some profits by lowering our buy stop orders from their
original 101 level. But to where? Dropping them to the
trendline A-B would not have accomplished a great
deal, since it was only ½ point or so below the initial
stop level. Since the downtrend had clearly accelerated
since we drew trendline A-B, we returned to the chart
and drew line B-E between the November rally top
and our sell point. This much steeper trendline suggested possible resistance to any minor rally in the 98-
00 area. We accordingly reduced our buy stop orders
from 101 to 98, locking up in the process two points of
our paper profit, and agreed to keep moving them
down to within one point of the current market price.
The market reached a low of 95-16 for that downward
leg by mid-February, stabilized between there and 96-
00 for several trading sessions, and moved through the
minor trendline B-E on a breakaway gap, this time
moving upward. Our stops, having been lowered once
again to 96-16, were executed the following day, giving
us profits before commissions of 3½ points.

The question now was at what point should we
entertain going back into the market, and on what
side? We decided against reversing our position by
going long on the grounds that the market was still in
a major downtrend, and concentrated on selecting a
suitable point at which to re-establish our short positions. According to the original trendline A-B, the current rally could extend to 98-16 and the major trend
would remain intact. On the other hand, there was
some question whether A-B was still a valid resistance
line in light of the sharp break in bond futures between December and February. A back-up plan was
needed in the event the rally did not carry as far as
98-16. By mid-March, approximately three weeks after
our initial short positions were stopped out, the September 1978 contract was in a minor uptrend, with its

own trend channel bounded by a minor support line
H-I and minor resistance J-K. Prior to the March 20,
market opening, our analysis of the major and minor
trends (which appeared to be going in opposing directions) took the following form:

˙Table 9-2. Trend Analysis Summary   Sept. 1978
Bond Futures, March 20, 1978

Last Price	Trend		Support		Resistance		Trend Channel		Price Objective	
	Major	Minor	Major	Minor	Major	Minor	Top	Bot-tom	Major	Minor
96-25	Down	Up	94-10	96-24	98-16	97-08	97-06	96-24	98-16	97-08

Our analysis indicated that if the price held above
the 96-24 level it would have a chance of reaching the
major trendline at 98-16, but if it could not find support at 96-24, we had best go short then and there. The
latter instance was what actually occurred. On the
22nd, the September contract fell below the minor
trend channel marking the end of the minor rally. Two
days later the price had dropped back to 96-00, where
we managed to make some short sales in a rapidly
falling market. In retrospect, we were no better off
than had we kept our original short position. On the
other hand, we were relieved that we had been able to
reinstate our shorts at a reasonable price. A week later
the September contract fell below its previous 95-16
low, and continued its decline for the next fifteen
weeks.

Technical analysts work on the assumption that
any given price change has greater predictive significance when it occurs in the face of heavy trading activity. As an adjunct to tracking trendlines and trend
channels, therefore, they probe the related volume and
open interest figures for further insight into the dynamics of market behavior. Volume and open interest
that gradually increase as an uptrend unfolds are, as
a consequence, taken to be indicators of continued
strength as new long positions generate growing prof-

its and increased buying power. Conversely, higher volume and open interest during a declining market are taken as evidence that shorts are the preponderant force either as speculative sellers or as short hedgers, hence are presumed to signal further weakness. A decline in the open interest during periods of rising prices is a bearish indicator insofar as it implies the covering of short positions rather than fresh buying. This suggests a technically weak market where shorts are buying their contracts back from longs. Open interest that contracts as prices fall is a sign of potential strength, as it marks the liquidation of short positions, indicating the shorts' belief that the decline has about run its course.

In summary, if price and open interest move in the same direction, the market is considered to be technically strong. If one is rising while the other declines, it is taken as a sign of relative weakness. A sharp rise in volume and open interest during the early stages of a major trend seem to be more indicative of its continuation than when the trend is farther along. The appearance of high volume during the latter stages of an established trend, particularly in conjunction with an exhaustion gap, often signals an imminent reversal.

Five Steps for Speculators

We can, at this point, recapitulate the steps a trader must take *before* assuming any speculative position:

1. Both the major and the minor trend must be identified and taken into account in arriving at a trading decision. The type of trend analysis summarized in Table 9-2 should be performed at least weekly and as often as daily during periods of exceptional price volatility.

    By way of illustration, any trader who bought into the February-March, 1978 rally in government bond futures would have been stepping into a "bear trap"[6] unless he was aware that he was moving against the major downtrend and took appropriate precautions, which in this case meant a close stop.

2. Major and minor resistance and support levels must be identified.

Traders who had accrued good profits on short Ginnie Mae positions by the end of June 1978 would have seen three months' gains evaporate within five trading sessions had they neglected to keep close watch on the major resistance line and failed to place their stop orders accordingly.

3. The major and minor trend channels must be outlined by drawing the appropriate secondary boundaries above or below the major and minor trendline.

Violation of the March 1977 T-bill major trend channel, first through the upper, then the lower, limit in October-November 1976 gave longs their first intimation that the vigorous advance since June was running out of steam. By the same token, penetration of the minor trend channel of the September 1978 government bond rally near the end of March signaled the resumption of the major downtrend, giving traders sufficient opportunity to liquidate any long positions and get back on the short side of the market.

4. Major and minor price objectives must be established on the basis of the foregoing assessments. There may be a valid reason for changing the objective after a position is initiated,

---

[6]Traders who buy prematurely on the assumption that a major downtrend is in the process of a turnaround fall into such a "bear trap." What they take to be the reversal of the bear market turns out to be merely a short-lived rally, hence they find that they went long at a time when, if anything, they should have taken the opportunity to sell on temporary strength.

but stepping into the market without a goal in mind (and on paper) is courting trouble.

The success or failure of a contract to reach a minor price objective usually is a decisive indication of the attainability of the major objective. Traders who awaited the achievement of the minor objective before going long during the February-March 1978 bond futures rally were right to hold back. September 1978 bonds came within 2/32nds of the minor objective and then fell away, never returning to that level during the remaining life of the contract.

When a major price objective is reached, either the paper profit should be realized through liquidation of the position, or the protective stop order should be moved sufficiently close to the current market price to secure at least partial profits.

5. A contingent stop order must be entered at a predetermined risk limitation point above the entry price of a short position or below the price of a long position, whichever is appropriate. There should be no exceptions to this rule. As was stated earlier, all traders fervently agree that stops are indispensable, but too many of them go to great pains to justify making an exception "just this one time." Every trader has at one time or another experienced the frustration of being "stopped out" of what ultimately would have become a highly profitable position. That, unfortunately, is part of the game.

There are several corollaries to these five "musts" which, when observed, can help futures traders to improve their performance. They always should resist the temptation to anticipate reversals in the major trend. As will be related shortly in conjunction with the market action in T-bill futures in the fourth quarter of 1978, both major bull and bear trends tend to have a greater longevity than most traders expect, and attempts to call the turn usually are ill-fated. This is merely another way of reiterating the injunction never to trade against the prevailing trend. Assuming a position solely on the grounds that prices are too cheap to go much lower or too high to rise much further can be a rewarding strategy for long-term investors. It all too often leads to disaster for futures traders. Go along with the market rather than trying to buck it.

While traders properly gravitate to "where the action is" they ought not to ignore dull and inactive markets entirely. Futures prices can erupt from a quiescent state with astonishing suddenness. While patience and restraint should be exercised when a contract exhibits no discernible trend, support and resistance levels and volume and open interest figures should be monitored for early indications that a significant move is getting under way.

It has frequently been remarked that the worst thing that can happen to a novice trader is that his initial foray into the futures market is successful, breeding the overconfidence that will lead to his ultimate downfall. Whatever the merit of that particular homily, it is in any event true that traders who achieve consistent success do so by retaining a healthy measure of caution and awareness of the ever-present risks. As was stated in an earlier chapter, a contract can experience limit moves several days in succession, inflicting serious paper losses on traders who are on the wrong side and are unable to liquidate their positions. Short of that, there may be a gap opening or a sharp intraday price swing, during which positions are taken and stopped out at a loss within moments of one another. When trading becomes disorderly, or price movement too volatile, exchange officials can and do change the rules on short notice. Certain kinds of contingent or stop orders may be disallowed, new positions banned altogether, trading limits revoked or margin requirements sharply increased. Such restrictions are usually applied to the "spot" or nearby-delivery contracts, which speculative traders are advised as a rule to avoid, either liquidating positions outright as they move into the delivery month, or "rolling them over" to a more distant contract. The nearby contract is best left to the large-scale hedgers who, in their maneuvering to make or avoid delivery, are often the primary cause of the unusual trading activity the officials are endeavoring to curtail.

A Review of 1978

It is instructive to conclude this chapter by tracing the movement of one contract—December 1978 T-bills—over the course of that year. To determine the major trend of that contract through the first half of 1978, however, it is necessary to follow the chart from June 1977, when the major downtrend began.

So far as the selection of an appropriate trading strategy was concerned, 1978 was divided into three distinct segments. The major trend between December 1977 and June 1978 was gradually, but consistently, lower, punctuated by interim rallies of four to six weeks' duration. There were three opportunities—Nov. 25 to Dec. 5, April 14 to 19, and June 6 and 7—to make short sales at the resistance line for potential profits of 40 to 60 basis points. The second market segment—the only major uptrend of the year—was a brief, but dynamic, rally of 70 basis points from mid-July to mid-August, establishing at its peak the contract high that year of 92.80. That summer uptrend was followed by a price decline which became increasingly sharp, following the cash market as it moved through its previous record highs set in 1974.

A typical cycle during the first half of 1978 was a sharp break in futures prices induced by Federal Reserve tightening, followed by a four-week recovery of 20-30 basis points. A strategy of going long after the Fed's open market operations drove futures prices

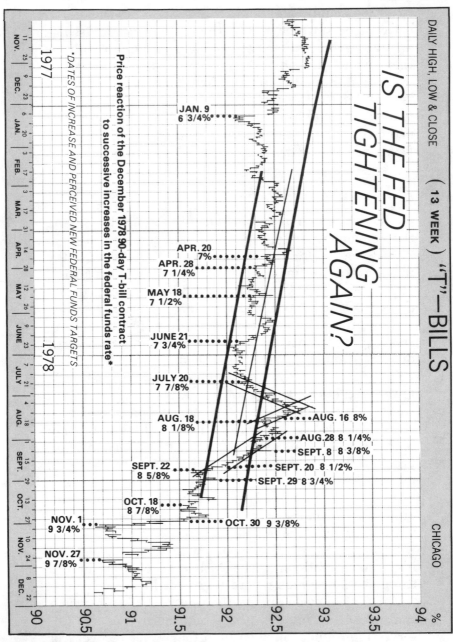

Source: Commodity Research Bureau

lower would have yielded moderate returns as prices rebounded, but it became increasingly risky to attempt as the year wore on. It would have been more rewarding to stick to the principle of trading with the major trend rather than against it, and sell each time the contract approached the resistance line with a buy stop order 10 to 20 basis points above.

The first suggestion that a new development was afoot came on July 24, when the minor trend channel was penetrated at its upper boundary. The major trendline was decisively broken four trading sessions later, which was considered confirmation that the 12-month downtrend had been reversed. Short positions taken at the trendline as earlier would have been closed out within the week by the execution of stop orders when the resistance did not hold as it had at each earlier test.

In retrospect, the July-August rally was a "bear trap." Penetration of the major downtrend was a signal to those shorts who had not been stopped out to cover their positions. The first indications of a trend reversal, namely penetration of minor and major resistance, was accompanied by talk of a "buying panic" in the cash market, wherein many traders, afraid of missing the boat, began buying before they had conclusive confirmation that an enduring uptrend had, in fact, commenced.

There were, however, ample signals to indicate that the downtrend was resuming and to alert futures traders to get back on the short side in time to profit from the sharpest move of the year. A chartist tracking the market would have identified at least five sell signals after early August, and would have been justified in taking a short position on the basis of any of them. They were:

1. Aug. 10 (92.70)—uptrend channel violated on downside.
2. Aug. 28 (92.40)—second rally attempt fails, downtrend resumes.

3. Sept. 8 (92.30)—former major resistance, now potential support, does not hold.
4. Sept. 22 (91.75)—drops through former minor support.
5. Oct. 30 (91.50)—completes triple top, breaks 91.50 level.

Though the Oct. 30 plunge of 35 basis points did occur as the December 1978 contract broke through the neckline of the triple top formation, the analyst did not need to scrutinize his chart for any enigmatic formations to see what was going on. The most convincing and, as it turned out, the most reliable sell signal was that the market dropped without hesitation through a succession of likely support levels. This sharp downtrend was first apparent as early as mid-August (with the wonderful benefit of hindsight, of course) and was reasonably confirmed by the end of the month. It took no great perception to recognize that the market was dropping and that shorts were making money.

The deterrent that prevented traders from acting on what their eyes told them was their subjective belief that futures prices were too low, and that short-term interest rates would not make history by surpassing their 1974 highs. That argument seemed very convincing at the time, with December T-bill futures at 91.50, but those traders who ignored the rule against trading counter to the prevailing trend and went long because they believed prices "couldn't go any lower" were stopped out during the following day's 35 basis-point drop. Others who were so swayed by their convictions that they decided to "watch" the market instead of entering a sell stop order at a reasonable level below 91.50, suffered an even greater shock as their long positions fell another 80 basis points within three days. As was stated at the outset of this chapter, it is far easier to set down rules of proper trading conduct than it is to obey them in practice.

Chapter Ten

The Hedgers

This book adheres to the convention of categorizing futures traders as either speculators or hedgers. It is useful to make this distinction to explain the risk-shifting rationale of the market mechanism. But the differences between the two groups are more theoretical than actual. Both enter the market for the purpose of making a profit, and both must assume certain risks in order to do so.

Professor Hieronymus defines the issue in the following terms:

> It is sometimes said that hedging is the opposite of speculation. This is not so. They are different kinds of the same thing. The thing that is usually defined as speculation—that is, long or short positions in futures contracts—is speculation in changes in price level. The thing we identify as hedging—long cash and short futures or vice versa—is speculation in price relationships. Hedging and speculation are not opposite. In fact, they are conceptually similar. They are just different kinds of speculation.[1]

---

[1]*Economics of Futures Trading,* p. 151.

315

Whether his inclination is to study the supply and demand for credit, watch for changes in Federal Reserve policy or follow price charts for indications of trend reversals, the continuing quest of the outright speculative futures trader is to anticipate changes in the absolute level of prices—actually, in this case, interest rates—and to buy or sell accordingly. That, to succumb to an irresistible pun, is the long and short of it.

Individuals who are not themselves involved with hedging situations in an actual business context find it a more difficult concept to grasp. The expression "to hedge one's bets" has assumed common usage in our language. Defined by Webster's as "reducing the risk of a wager by making a bet against the side one has bet on," the term has come to have an application beyond the casino or sports arena. The dictionary offers a second definition which is presumably more relevant to our purpose: "to counterbalance a sale or purchase of one security by making a purchase or sale of another." The operative word is "counterbalance." Note that this definition first refers to "sale or purchase" and then reverses their order. Though the dictionary includes no comparable definition specifically applicable to futures trading, we can adapt the foregoing to improvise our own: to offset the price risk of owning or having sold (short) without owning a particular commodity through the sale or purchase of equivalent futures contracts for that commodity.

Hedging to Enhance Profits

Hedging is a full-time commercial operation in which businesses engage for the purpose of enhancing their profitability. Though private investors of substantial means occasionally may employ to their advantage several of the techniques described in this chapter, they are intended in the first instance to be used by those financial institutions, industrial corporations and institutional investors which invest and/

or borrow large amounts of capital in the conduct of their corporate affairs and for whom interest rate change is, therefore, a matter of prime consequence.

In tracing the evolution of "to arrive" to forward and then to uniform futures contracts, Chapter One related how the organized futures markets developed during the last century as a means of protecting farmers, merchants, processors and end users from the price risks attendant to producing, storing, financing, shipping, converting or otherwise handling grain and cotton, among other commodities. Farmers in central Illinois sold futures at the Chicago Board of Trade to hedge against a decline in corn prices while their cash crop was stored in cribs awaiting shipment to the terminal market. New York exporters who had contracted to sell cotton in Liverpool could buy futures on the local exchange to counterbalance any price increase that might occur prior to their purchase of the actual commodity for shipment. In each instance the growers or merchants took positions in the futures market *equal and opposite* to their positions in the cash commodity, long corn or short cotton. In each case, the futures market transaction was a *temporary substitute* for an eventual sale or purchase in the cash market which would conclude that particular piece of business for the farmer or exporter.

The Illinois farmer would have been delighted to see the price of corn rise while his crop was in storage, just as the exporter in New York would have been pleased had cotton prices dropped before he had to buy to fulfill his contractual obligation. The fact that neither was willing to speculate (that word keeps cropping up) the price of his respective commodity actually would move in his favor prompted him to obtain coverage in the futures market for the time his cash position remained open.

In a sense, the futures market provided a form of price insurance by which the farmer and exporter transferred the price risks of owning corn or being short cotton to traders who bought corn and sold cotton contracts with the expectations that the prices would move to their advantage.[2] The important point is that all hedge transactions are by definition made in conjunction with an existing or contemplated cash position in that particular commodity. For the farmer to have sold futures without having the actual crop in his possession or the exporter to buy them without a firm contract to sell cash cotton would have been no different than the trades of the outright speculators who took the opposite sides of those sales and purchases.

Moving on to the present day, the agricultural analogy is germane to the use of interest rate futures in the credit markets. Corporate issuers of commercial paper and long-term bonds and mortgage bankers who originate mortgages which are pooled and packaged in the form of Ginnie Mae securities are, in a sense, "farmers" who are vulnerable to a decline in the price of their "crops" before they can be moved to market. Dealers and institutional investors who hold fixed-income securities in their permanent portfolios or as inventory for subsequent resale are in a position not unlike that of a grain elevator operator. Savings and loan associations that commit to sell mortgages at a firm price and portfolio managers awaiting the receipt of certain funds to make a planned investment are as much exposed to rising prices as the exporter who contracts to ship cotton abroad at a definite price before he has it in hand.

Those corporations and financial institutions which either own fixed-income securities or are in the business of creating them for sale to investors normally would cover themselves against the adverse price consequences of rising interest rates by selling

---

[2]Hieronymus contends that "insurance" is an inaccurate term, insofar as outright price risk is transferred from one party to another in toto, rather than being diffused among a large group of risk-bearers on an actuarially determined basis. He is, of course, right, but the primary point remains valid that certain risks in fact may be transferred by means of a futures transaction.

the appropriate futures contracts, thereby establishing a *short hedge* (long cash securities, short futures). Dealers or institutions which make commitments to sell at predetermined prices securities they do not yet own and portfolio managers who plan to make certain investments at a later date would offset the risk of paying higher prices resulting from a decline in rates by buying futures, thus initiating a *long hedge* (short cash securities, long futures). Establishing a long hedge is tantamount to "locking in" a specific rate of return on a prospective investment, just as the short hedge places a ceiling on interest expense for scheduled borrowing transactions.

By assuming these offsetting positions, the hedger seeks to make in one market the equivalent of what he stands to lose in the other, no matter in which direction interest rates and, conversely, market prices, move. The prerequisite for this type of counterbalancing operation is that prices in the two markets move in the same direction by the same amount.

FIGURE: 10-1

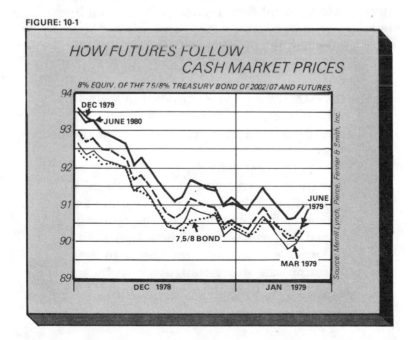

When cash and futures prices, be they for corn, cotton or T-bills, follow identical patterns, they allow the formation of a "perfect" hedge, since any dollar loss in one market will be matched by an equal dollar gain in the other.

Perfect hedges are more often observed in textbook illustrations than under actual trading conditions. Although the prices are essentially the same, the only ostensible difference between them being the time factor, the two markets in fact do not display absolute correlation. With that caveat in mind, it is nevertheless useful to begin our discussion with an example of a perfect hedge, if for no other purpose than to describe the generally unattainable ideal.

Perfect Hedges

In the first instance, the corporate treasurer of International Widget is advised on Jan. 15 of the current year that his company will receive payment the following May 15 of $10 million, which he will invest immediately in 90-day Treasury bills, pending disbursement later in the year. Since his expectation is that short-term interest rates will fall between January and May, he looks to the futures market to assure his rate of return four months prior to his making the actual investment and accordingly buys 10 June 90-day T-bill contracts.

Table 10-1 summarizes the outcome of the hedge transaction:

The hypothetical long hedge computation illustrates how the treasurer was able to "lock-in" a 7.60% discount yield on a three-month investment through the purchase of futures when the discount on 90-day bills dropped 80 basis points (7.60% to 6.80%). As the market price for cash bills increased to reflect the lower discount, the June contract rose by an equal amount, satisfying the conditions for a perfect hedge.

Table 10-1.   Hypothetical Long Hedge in 90-Day T-Bills.

Cash	Futures
January 15	
Actual 90-day T-bills maturing April 15	Buys 10 June 90-day T-bill contracts 91.90
Discount 7.60%	Discount equivalent 8.10%
No transaction	
May 15	
Buys $10 million 90-day T-bills maturing August 15	Sells 10 June 90-day T-bill contracts 92.70
Discount 6.80%	Discount equivalent 7.30% (Commissions not included in illustration)
Opportunity loss: 80 basis points or $20,000 Hedged discount 7.60%	Profit: 80 basis points or $20,000

Buying the June futures at a 91.90 index price did not fix a discount of 8.10% because the position was liquidated more than a month before the delivery date. If the cash 90-day discount instead had risen by 80 basis points between January and May, the June contract would have had to decline in price by the same amount for it to remain a perfect hedge. If that had occurred, the net result—an effective discount of 7.60% on the T-bills purchased on May 15—would have been the same.

A short hedge involves the sale of futures to offset depreciation in the market value of fixed-income securities caused by an increase in interest rates. Table 10-2 illustrates how such a hedge could protect the value of an investment in U.S. Treasury bonds.

The position was properly hedged, being long $100,000 in Treasury bonds and short one December contract representing an equivalent face value. Again the outcome was ideal insofar as the $3,750 depreciation in the bonds caused by a 40 basis-point increase in yield was matched to the dollar by a profit in the short futures position.

Table 10-2.   Hypothetical Short Hedge in U.S. Treasury Bonds.

Cash	*Futures*
June 1	
Owns $100,000 U.S. Treasury 7⅞'s of 1995 at 98-08 to yield 8.179%	Sells 1 December bond contract 97-16 to yield 8.257%
No transaction	
December 1	
U.S. Treasury 7⅞'s of 1995 at 94-16 to yield 8.580%	Buys 1 December bond contract 93-24 to yield 8.663%
No transaction	
Unrealized loss: $3^{24}/_{32}$nds or $3,750	Profit: $3^{24}/_{32}$nds or $3,750

Chapter Four dwelt at some length on the specified procedure for delivering securities in settlement of expiring contracts. It was stated at that point, however, that the overwhelming majority of futures positions opened for either hedging or outright speculative purposes are liquidated through an offsetting market transaction, rather than by actual delivery. The foregoing long and short hedge illustrations serve to reinforce the point.

In the case of the long T-bill hedge, had the company maintained the position through the expiration of the June contract, it would have been obliged to accept delivery of and pay in full for $10 million in 90-day bills. But it was the treasurer's intent to make his actual bill purchase when the funds became available in mid-May. If he proceeded to buy cash bills on May 15 as planned and remained long the 10 contracts, he no longer would be hedged but would in fact have "doubled up," holding $10 million in cash bills and an equal amount in futures, both on the long side. Instead, as is customary in "unwinding" hedges, the futures position was liquidated when the actual bills were purchased in the dealer market at the then prevailing cash discount of 6.80%. It was by applying the $20,000 profit on the futures transaction against the purchase price that the discount equivalent of 7.60% was obtained.[3]

The originator of the short hedge would have been required to deliver $100,000 face value Treasury bonds that met the contract specifications, had he not closed the futures position out through an offsetting purchase. In practice, had he elected to dispose of his actual bonds (which the example does not indicate) he still would have bought the December contract in at the same time that he sold his bonds in the secondary market. In both instances the futures market was used for the purpose of fixing a price, therefore a yield, and not to effect delivery from either the short or long side.

These textbook examples were so devised as to show offsetting dollar-for-dollar profits and losses in each case. As stated earlier, such perfect hedges rarely occur in the real world. Observe how the results would have been affected if, instead of cash and futures discounts both declining 80 basis points, the discount equivalent of the June T-bill contract fell (as the index rose) 90 basis points and the cash discount 70 basis points. Now there is a complication in the outcome of the hedge, as cash rates fall 10 points less than before while the futures side shows an additional 10-point profit. If, in the case of the short hedge, the futures side fell $3^{16}/_{32}$nds in price while the actual bonds declined four points, the hedge would have been only 75% effective, failing to cover a loss of $^{16}/_{32}$nds or $500.

The fact that cash and futures prices usually move in close harmony makes the futures contract a viable and potentially valuable hedging instrument. But the extent to which they fail to achieve perfect correlation

---

[3]Use of the formula in Chapter Two, p. 36 would produce the result

Cash Discount on $10 Million 90-Day Bills at 6.80%		Futures Profit		Effective Discount		Hedged Yield of
$170,000	+	$20,000	=	$190,000	or	7.60%

imparts a greater degree of uncertainty, hence risk, than the hypothetical calculations cited above suggest.

The Basis

The relationship between cash and futures prices—and yields in the case of the interest rate complex—is the key to each and every hedging situation. This relationship is referred to in the commodity markets as the *basis*. As stated by Hieronymus in the passage quoted earlier, while outright speculators concentrate on the absolute level of futures prices and their immediate trend, hedgers are preoccupied with the basis and the factors which determine it.

Returning to our earlier textbook examples, the difference between cash 90-day T-bills and the June futures contract was 50 basis points (8.10%-7.60%) when the long hedge was initiated on Jan. 15. In futures market terminology, the basis[4] was "50 under June." As an illustration of a perfect long hedge, the basis was still 50 under June when the hedge was terminated on May 15 (7.30%-6.80%), resulting in a futures gain precisely equal to the cash market opportunity loss. When the illustration is revised to show an additional $5,000 gain on the hedge, the change implies a shift in the basis from 50 under to 30 under June (7.20%-6.90%). In this instance, the 20-point narrowing of the price difference works to the hedger's advantage insofar as the price increase in the June contract more than offsets the opportunity loss on the cash side.

When the short hedge is debased from perfection, the $16/32$nds basis change from $24/32$nds under the December bond contract to $8/32$nds under works counter to the hedge objective in that the long position in cash

---

[4]This use of the word "basis" is not to be confused with "basis point," or .01%.

bonds depreciates $500 more than the comparable price drop in the December bond contract.

These modified examples bear out Hieronymus' contention that the hedging of cash positions in the futures market involves speculation, though of a different magnitude than that described in the previous chapter. Changes in the cash-futures basis which cannot be predicted impart an element of risk to what may at first glance appear to be a cut and dried operation. On the other hand, the same basis changes present profit opportunities to those firms which arc prepared to allocate the required resources to identify and trace the price relationships which affect their operations and to develop a hedge program that aggressively seeks to take advantage of these changes. To put it in Hieronymus' terms:

> What then is a perfect hedge? If we accept the notion that hedgers hedge to make profits, it follows that a bad hedge is one that loses money and a good hedge is one that makes money. Extending this, a perfect hedge is one that makes all of the money.[5]

The first step, therefore, in the formulation of a hedging program that is effective under actual trading conditions is understanding the factors that cause the basis to change. It has already been noted that until futures and cash prices start to converge during the final weeks of the contract, futures tend to display a life of their own, which sometimes deviates sharply from the prevailing cash market interest rates. We now can identify this phenomenon as variation in the basis, which is a matter of critical importance to prospective hedgers.

Within the interest rate complex, as in other commodity futures, the independent behavior of futures prices stems chiefly from factors pertaining to differ-

---

[5]Hieronymus, op. cit., p. 151.

ences in time and delivery grade. The pattern of consecutive delivery-month prices is generally one of increasingly greater discounts from or premiums over the cash price, depending in large part upon the absolute trend in interest rates and the relationship of short- to long-term rates.

When the yield curve is positive, reflecting an expected rise in interest rates, the price of each successive delivery month is lower than the one preceding it. As the curve turns negative with the growing expectation that rates are about to decline, futures prices become progressively higher by delivery month. As time elapses and each month approaches the cash rate, these structural discounts or premiums are steadily consumed, giving the basis an upward or downward bias.

The relationship of short- to long-term rates also influences the basis, inasmuch as it determines dealers' net costs of carrying securities in inventory. During periods that short-term rates are below long-term, there is a so-called "positive carry," meaning that dealers earn more in interest income while holding bonds and Ginnie Maes pending resale than they must pay to finance them. Since they are being compensated on balance for holding securities, dealers tend to quote lower prices on deferred sales, contributing to discounts on distant contracts. When long-term rates fall below short-term, there is a "negative carry," which prompts dealers to quote higher prices on deferred sales to offset their higher financing costs, adding to premiums on the futures contracts.

Financial managers must take the premium or discount structure of futures markets into account in making hedge decisions. A short hedge ordinarily will show better results in a discount market (cash prices below futures) as futures prices decline relative to cash with the passage of time, just as a premium market (cash above futures) normally favors a long hedge with futures rising toward the spot price as the contracts approach delivery date.

The contract specifications for the various interest rate futures allow some tolerance in the maturity and coupon rates of the securities which comprise good delivery. Although the final settlement price is adjusted to reflect these differences, variations in the precise securities eligible for tender influence the basis. Changes in the current or anticipated supply and demand affecting deliverable securities also are reflected in the basis. Extensive purchases of cash Treasury bills by foreign central banks as a consequence of their U.S. dollar support operations, for example, may drive the cash discount down without materially affecting the equivalent discount on deferred contracts, causing at least a temporary narrowing or widening of the basis, depending upon whether cash prices are at a premium or discount to futures at the time.

Above all, it is outright speculative activity which imparts to futures prices something of a separate existence before they approach the spot month. Technical analysts responding to chart signals, Fed watchers tracking money supply figures, or floor traders triggering resting stop orders may cause futures prices to behave in an exaggerated manner relative to cash market activity or even force them to move in the opposite direction for a brief period, causing significant changes in the basis.

'Aggressive' Hedgers: Trading the Basis

All of these elements lend a measure of uncertainty to cash-futures relationships, which prompts the attitude that hedging is "a different kind of speculating." The prospective hedger is satisfied, however, that he is reducing his overall risk exposure by substituting for the risk of an uncovered cash position the

measurably smaller one of a variation in the basis.[6]
More aggressive practitioners of the hedging art proceed beyond the purely defensive posture of reducing
risk insofar as possible, and seek to make a positive
contribution to operating profits by successfully "trading the basis."

A long hedge also is described as being "short the
basis" in that a long futures position signifies a short
position on the cash side. To trade the basis profitably
in this instance, it must "weaken," meaning that the
cash price must decline more or appreciate less than
that of the futures contract. A market in which cash
is at a premium to futures implies a weakening basis,
since futures must strengthen relative to cash as the
delivery date approaches. Conversely, a short hedge is
tantamount to being "long the basis." The short hedger
benefits when the cash price is at a discount and the
basis strengthens as cash and futures prices converge
at the contract's expiration.

An aggressive short hedger, therefore, will try to
place his hedge when the basis is weak relative to past
performance and likely to strengthen during the period the hedge is in force. The optimum time to initiate
a long hedge, on the other hand, is when the basis is
strong and any subsequent weakening will accrue to
the long hedger's advantage. Neither the long nor the
short hedger should rely solely on a premium or discount market, however, since the other forces that influence the basis can disrupt the steady convergence
of cash and futures prices up to and including the delivery month.

---

[6]Reverting to the earlier examples, the short hedger in the revised
example was better off in suffering a basis loss of $16/32$nds, or $500, than
the four-point, or $4,000, loss he would have incurred had the bond position
been left unhedged.

Basis Charts

Hedgers must have a rational framework within which to evaluate the basis and determine the most opportune time to accomplish their objective. To this end they maintain daily records of relevant basis changes and display the resulting data on charts which are as much analytical tools for "managed hedging" as conventional line and point and figure charts are for outright speculation. There are several methods of maintaining a basis chart, all of which employ the device of plotting one price above or below a horizontal line representing a second price. One method is to make the cash price (interest rate) the base line and plot the futures price (interest rate) relative to it. Or, the relationship may be reversed, with a deferred contract as the base line and the cash price charted against it. Yet a third alternative is to plot the cash price against each nearby contract until it matures, and then switch over to the next nearby contract, a method most closely resembling hedging as it is practiced in the market.

Figure 10-2 compares the two latter methods of keeping basis charts, showing on the same grid the cash 90-day T-bill discount throughout 1978 plotted against (A) the December 1978 contract and (B) each nearby contract—March, June, September and December 1978—to its expiration.

The cash to December 1978 basis chart reveals that the basis remained relatively constant from January to mid-May, ranging between 150 and 130 basis points under December. Since the cash rate itself fluctuated within a narrow band of 6.20% to 6.50%, a short hedge in retrospect would not have been especially advantageous, since the maximum movement in the cash rate was only 10 basis points greater than the basis change during the 4½-month period. For the balance of the year, going long the basis in the form of a short

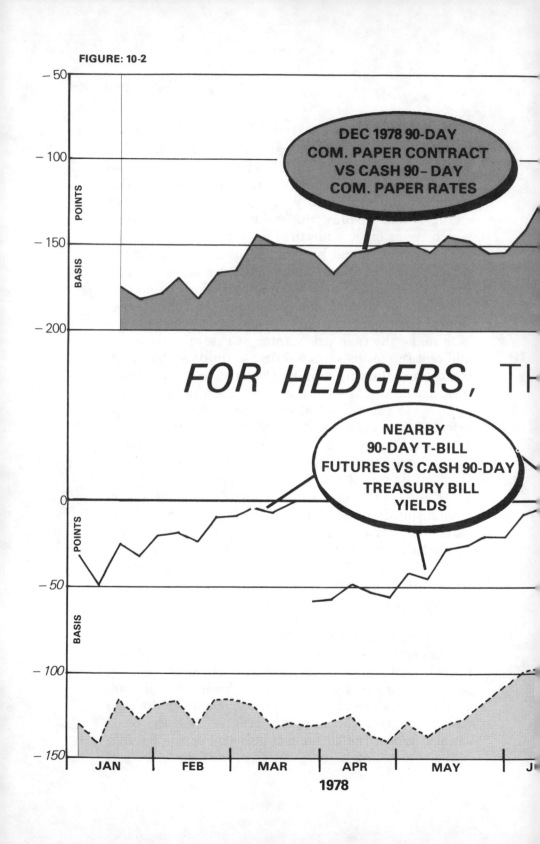

FIGURE: 10-2

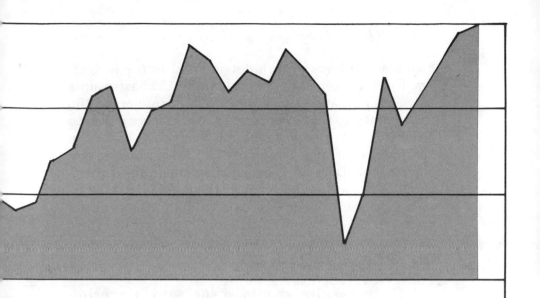

BASIS IS THE THING
Different methods of
drawing basis charts

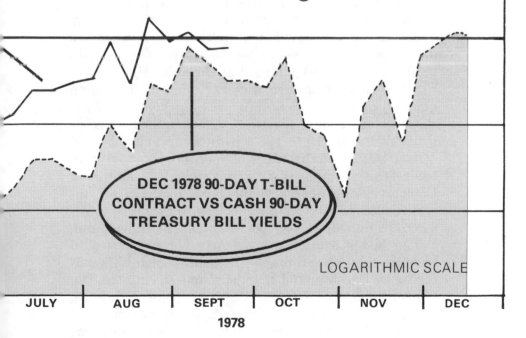

DEC 1978 90-DAY T-BILL
CONTRACT VS CASH 90-DAY
TREASURY BILL YIELDS

LOGARITHMIC SCALE

| JULY | AUG | SEPT | OCT | NOV | DEC |

1978

hedge would have proven detrimental to the hedger. The basis weakened by approximately 120 basis points between May and October, while cash rates rose 180 basis points, so that a short hedge would have provided protection only to the extent of ⅓ the potential loss on an unhedged 90-day T-bill position. A long hedger employing the December contract would have experienced the opposite, therefore more favorable result. As cash rates rose the 180 basis points and the contract price fell 60, he would still have captured ⅔ of the increase, even though he was hedged, since by weakening (in price) the basis was moving in his favor even though the futures position was incurring a loss.

These results should dispel any lingering thoughts that hedging is a riskless activity. Even so, the basis risk would have been reduced materially by conducting any hedging operations in the nearby contract, which displayed a more limited and consistent basis change for at least the first three quarters of the year. The basis moved in each quarter from about 50 to zero, alerting a prospective hedger that there would be a potential 50 basis-point loss in placing a short hedge as the basis weakened by that amount. On the other hand, there would be an equivalent built-in profit on a long hedge placed at the same time.

The regular pattern was disrupted in the fourth quarter, as both cash and futures markets displayed sharp volatility and the nearby basis uncharacteristically rose from 10 to 120 within five weeks, a vivid demonstration of the effect of speculative activity on basis relationships. During the turbulent month of October a long hedger would have incurred an unrealized loss of over 100 basis points, or nearly as much as on an unhedged long position. On the other hand, a long hedge established in early November would have been highly profitable. By selling cash bills maturing in late March 1979 short and buying the December 1978 contract at a 120 basis-point difference, the hedger was assured of a profit by that amount, as the basis closed to zero by delivery day six weeks later.

It is clear from the foregoing that a "basis trader," or profit-oriented hedger, must be selective in choosing the most advantageous delivery month, when to place his hedge and under what conditions he should close it out. In general terms, he has the three options of making or accepting delivery in settlement of his futures position which as indicated is rarely done; simultaneously, liquidating cash and futures positions in their respective markets, or rolling the futures position over by covering the expiring contract before delivery day and taking an identical position in the next delivery month.

To Hedge or Not to Hedge

Long before it addresses itself to such tactical considerations, corporate management must determine whether hedging interest rate risks is a necessary or desirable undertaking from its perspective and, if the decision is affirmative, establish general policies governing the company's activity in this area. Central to the policy decision is the estimated impact of possible interest rate changes on the firm's earnings, and of management's attitude toward this type of risk. What is the company's present or anticipated position in fixed-income securities or money market instruments? What is the size of projected borrowing and/or investment over the coming year, and what will be the net position? Assuming, say, a 2% rise or decline in short- and long-term interest rates, what would be the impact on corporate earnings in either instance? Would any potentially adverse change be acceptable as a customary part of doing business? If the perceived risks are insignificant or fall within tolerable limits, and are thought likely to average out over time, there may be no compelling incentive for the company to embark upon interest rate hedging operations.

If, on the other hand, large variations in rates such as have occurred in the money and capital markets over the past decade are liable to have a marked effect on investment income and/or borrowing cost, the company is vulnerable to such rate swings and should consider itself a hedge candidate. If that is the case, the follow-on question is, what type of hedging strategy should the company adopt? Should it regard itself as a "pure" hedger in the textbook sense, estimating its risk exposure as closely as possible and taking the prescribed action in the futures market to offset it? Or should it take a more selective approach, using futures when the basis appears to offer a profit opportunity over and above straight price or rate protection when the futures market projects yields which vary from management's own forecast?

The strategy that is employed will influence (and in turn be influenced by) the organizational "fit" of the hedging function within the business structure. Some firms look upon their hedge operations as distinct profit centers and expect them to be self-sustaining. Those that emphasize the protective or defensive approach consider hedging to be a support function and do not look to it to show profits per se.

Management's criteria for measuring performance are also a reflection of its basic attitude regarding risk management. Companies that are solely concerned with price protection are inclined to measure their aggregate borrowing cost or investment return. The profit-oriented hedgers are under greater compulsion to justify their existence. An assistant treasurer of a major industrial corporation described his company's attitude in the following manner: "Our purpose in hedging is to eliminate as much as possible unforeseen costs due to changing interest rates; therefore, the timing and proper placement and removal of the hedge is more important than the futures gain or loss at closeout." Many firms are still in the early stages of experimentation with an interest rate hedge program, and have yet to develop specific criteria for measuring trading success other than to develop rough "guesstimates" of what results would be with and without hedging.

Developing a Hedge Plan

Once the advisability of hedging is accepted by senior management and a fundamental philosophy is adopted, the first task of the individual assigned to implement the program is to commit to writing a policy statement and operating plan outlining in clear terms what he will seek to accomplish. Before and throughout the plan's execution, the following steps will enhance the likelihood of a successful outcome.

1. A decision should be made at the outset whether the objective of the hedge strategy is to provide straight price protection by locking in a specific rate, or to engage in "basis trading." If the hedge manager is given discretion to follow the latter course, a list of guidelines and limitations should be drafted.
2. In either case, the adopted plan should be initiated slowly and on a small scale. The emphasis during the initial transactions should be on mastering the mechanics of trading, testing the decision rules and identifying potential problems—in effect a pilot program. Even after the plan becomes fully operational, positions should be assumed gradually and on a scaled basis.
3. The hedge manager should acquaint himself thoroughly with the various basis relationships with which he is concerned, and become accustomed to analyzing the market in terms of the basis.
4. All levels of management up to and including the board of directors should be made familiar with the plan and be kept informed of its progress.
5. The hedging firm's bankers, accountants and brokers should also be advised of the plan and consulted as often as the situation warrants.
6. If the policy decision was to practice selective hedging, i.e., basis trading, the hedge manager should conduct a daily trend analysis similar to that required of speculative traders with the qualification

that here the applicable basis is the overriding consideration.

7. A system of procedures, record keeping and reporting should be developed as early as possible and refined until satisfactory to all parties involved in the hedging operation.

The guidelines for futures market activity set forth for national banks and federally chartered savings and loan associations by their respective regulatory agencies provide useful models for other organizations gearing up to undertake a hedging program. The Comptroller of the Currency requires national banks subject to the jurisdiction of his office to submit written proposals listing the personnel authorized to trade futures for the bank's account, position limits imposed on them, procedures designed to prevent unauthorized trading and a description of internal audit and control procedures. Each proposal must be accompanied by copies of the bank's internal forms disclosing all futures activity, open positions, the result of each completed trade and the aggregate profits and losses for futures transactions. Regulated banks are limited to pure hedge transactions "to substantially reduce the risk of loss resulting from interest rate fluctuations." To insure that each futures position is taken in conjunction with a related cash transaction, the reporting bank is required to supply documentation of the type and amount of each expected cash transaction that did not materialize.

Whereas national banks whose proposals are approved by the Comptroller's office are authorized to deal in T-bill and Ginnie Mae contracts, savings and loan associations subject to the Federal Home Loan Bank Board are limited to trading the latter, since it is the futures contract expressly designed to reduce risk in the mortgage market. S&Ls also are required to match all futures transactions against existing mortgage-related investments or commitments to buy or deliver same at a fixed interest rate, or fixed price, over a 12-month period and keep a written record of these matched trades. Like the banks, they must install suitable internal control procedures and submit a written policy statement of their guidelines for determining when and under what conditions the futures market should be used, position limits and procedures to secure the approval by the board of directors or a designated officer for each transaction.

The accounting treatment for hedge transactions is relatively straightforward. Inasmuch as futures contracts are commitments rather than investments, they are booked as a memorandum entry rather than entered in the general ledger. The initial margin deposit for a long or short position is debited to a margin debit account and cash is credited by a like figure. Similar entries are made when adverse market action necessitates additional maintenance margin deposits. Realized profits and losses are posted to the deferred profit or loss account and accumulated or written off over the average life of the mortgages or T-bills which were hedged. Any unrealized gains or losses on open positions at the end of the accounting period are entered as maintenance margin deposits identifying those gains and losses matched against related cash market transactions. When an anticipated cash transaction does not occur, the futures position is treated as a speculation with the ensuing profit or loss reflected in the current income statement.

For accounting purposes all open positions are entered as being closed on the hedger's books on the assigned closing date, even when they are in fact "rolled over" to the next distant contract. Table 10-3 presents illustrative journal entries for such hedge transactions.[7] The appropriate tax treatment of futures transactions by financial institutions remains in some re-

---

[7]For a detailed discussion of the accounting treatment of a hedging operation see Arthur Andersen & Co., *Interest Rate Futures Contracts—Accounting and Control Techniques for Banks,* Chicago, 1978.

spects open to interpretation. Each institution or corporation should consult its tax advisor on the proper tax treatment of such dealings. Initial and maintenance margin deposits are carried in the hedger's financial statements as "other assets," except when Ginnie Mae contracts are matched with mortgage loans held for sale. Any related amounts due to or from brokers are shown as miscellaneous receivables or payables.

The Southeastern Mortgage Co. Case

Mortgage bankers are in the business of originating mortgage loans for resale to permanent investors. Unlike savings and loan associations which also provide funds to the mortgage market but can put loans they originate in their own investment portfolios, mortgage banking firms typically operate on a limited capital base and depend upon the frequent turnover of a highly leveraged (that is, heavily financed) inventory to maintain their profitability. As a consequence, even a minor price depreciation in inventory induced by a rise in interest rates can seriously impair a firm's capital and jeopardize its future prospects. It is this extreme vulnerability to interest rate risk that first drew the attention of Board of Trade planners to the mortgage market as the financial sector most in need of a hedging capability, and eventually led to the development of the original Ginnie Mae contract.

The rationale of a mortgage-related short hedge is that, while a mortgage banker (or an S&L) is in the process of assembling a mortgage pool or, having done so, is "warehousing" it pending resale, a rise in interest rates in the mortgage market could well impose an inventory loss that more than eradicates the company's anticipated profits from origination and servicing fees, its basic source of income. If by selling Ginnie Mae futures contracts the mortgage banker is able to offset any potential decline in inventory value,

Table 10-3. Hypothetical Journal Entries for Short Hedge.

I. Recording the hedge.
  8/15/78   Sold 10 June 1979 Treasury Bond contracts at 93-12

  Only a memorandum entry of this futures transaction in the register of outstanding contracts is required.

II. Recording the initial margin deposit.
  8/15/78   Initial margin deposit $10,000
  Cash $10,000

  To record initial margin deposit on sale of futures contracts—10 contracts at $1,000 per contract

III. Required additional maintenance margin deposit.
  9/4/78   The June 1979 bond contract has risen to 95-00

  Maintenance margin deposit $16,250
  Cash $16,250

  To record additional maintenance margin deposit $(1^{20}/_{32}nds \times \$31.25 \times 10 = \$16,250)$

IV. Decrease in required maintenance margin deposit.
  10/6/78   June 1979 bond futures decline to 93-16

  Cash (or Accounts
  Receivable broker) $15,000
  Maintenance margin deposit $15,000

  To record reduction in maintenance margin deposit $(1 ^{16}/_{32}nds \times \$31.25 \times 10 = \$15,000)$

V. Gain on closing futures position
  11/9/78   Repurchased 10 June 1979 bond contracts at 92-10 for gain of $1^2/_{32}nds$ or $10,625.00 less commissions of $60 per contract

  Accounts receivable—broker
  (or cash) $21,275
  Initial margin deposit $10,000
  Maintenance margin deposit   1,250
  Deferred income
      or
  Gain on sale of loans   10,025

  To record gain on closing of short position
  $(\$10,625 - 600 = \$10,025)$

  Memorandum account contra-
      Trading account June 1979 bonds/short $1,000,000
  Memorandum account-
      Trading account June 1979 bonds/short $1,000,000

his anticipated profit from the completed transaction should remain unimpaired. Consistent with the examples cited earlier in the chapter, any loss incurred in selling the mortgage pool at a discount from the purchase price will be matched by an equivalent profit on the short Ginnie Mae futures position.

As in the case of the general examples, the effectiveness of the hedge would be determined by changes in the basis during the time it is in force. Therefore, we are again dealing with such factors as convergence, carrying costs and speculative activity. If the mortgage banker does in fact enjoy a positive carry by virtue of access to favorable financing terms, his warehousing profit—i.e. long-term minus short-term interest rates—should approximate the convergence loss implicit in a short hedge, limiting the basis risk during reasonably placid markets. Theoretically, at least, any adverse weakening of the basis due to convergence during the life of the hedge should be matched by the amount of positive carry for that period.

If the mortgage banker is hedging like entities, in this instance futures against cash Ginnie Maes, this straight basis risk is his sole concern. Should he attempt to undertake a "cross-hedge"—protecting a long position in conventional mortgages by a short hedge in Ginnie Mae futures—the problem becomes more complex in that he must then contend with the likelihood that rates on conventional mortgage loans and Ginnie Maes will not follow identical paths. In fact, instances when the two rates briefly move in opposite directions are not infrequent, raising the magnitude of risk beyond that contained in a straight "like for like" hedge.

The Southeastern Mortgage Co. case recapitulates a straight hedge initiated over eight days from Nov. 9 to 17, 1976, as the company originated VA/FHA mortgages for inclusion in a Ginnie Mae pool. Ten March 1977 Ginnie Mae contracts were sold at

**Table 10-4. Southeastern Mortgage Co.
Summary of Ginnie Mae Hedge
Nov. 9–Dec. 6, 1976.**

Date Sold	March 1977 Contracts	Price	Decimal Equivalent	Amount
11/9	3	96-20	96.62500	$289,875.00
11/11	1	96-26	96.81250	96,812.50
11/12	1	97-00	97.00000	97,000.00
11/15	1	96-28	96.87500	96,875.00
11/16	2	97-09	97.28125	194,562.50
11/17	2	97-13	97.40625	194,812.50
				$969,937.50

Date Purchased				
12/6	10	100-11	100.34375	$1,003,437.50
		Commission 10 × 60		600.00
				1,004,037.50
		Net Loss on Futures		($34,100.00)

Gain from sale of Ginnie Mae pool.

Sales price	99.59375		$1,015.607.20
Average closing price	96.19396		980,938.00
	Net Gain on Cash		34,669.20
	Net Gain on Hedge		569.20

various prices ranging from 96-20 to 97-13, matching the individual mortgages that were accumulated in a $1 million pool. Less than a month later the hedge was "unwound" and the contracts bought in when the pool was placed with a permanent investor.

The completed hedge transaction is summarized in Table 10-4, which shows that the net loss of $34,100 incurred on the futures side was more than offset by a net gain of $34,669.20 from the sale of the pool. But the resulting $569.20 net gain from the hedge was secondary to the fact that by carrying a hedged position Southeastern was able to protect origination and standby fees totaling $21,875, an amount that would have been lost had mortgage rates risen some 30 basis points during the time that the company was at risk with that particular pool.

Table 10-5 carries the analysis a step further by itemizing the hedge position each day that it was in

Table 10-5. Southeastern Mortgage Company Daily Hedge Summary.

Date	Cash Dollar Amount	Average Price	Sale Month Price	Gain (Loss)	Average Futures Price	Closing Price	Commission	Gain (Loss)	Exposure	Basis
					(converted to hundreds)					
11/9	277	96	95.25	(2078)	96.63	96.66	(180)	(270)	(2278)	1.41
11/10	307	96	95.31	(2118)	96.63	96.84	(180)	(810)	(2928)	1.53
11/11	365	96	95.31	(2519)	96.68	96.84	(240)	(880)	(3399)	1.53
11/12	441	96	95.63	(1632)	96.74	97.00	(300)	(1600)	(3232)	1.37
11/15	601	96	95.56	(3560)	96.76	96.97	(360)	(1620)	(5180)	1.41
11/16	809	96	95.75	(1503)	96.89	97.41	(480)	(4640)	(6143)	1.66
11/17	1004	96.10	96.25	1506	96.99	97.56	(600)	(6300)	(4794)	1.31
11/18	1004	96.10	95.88	(2209)	96.99	97.50	(600)	(5700)	(7909)	1.62
11/19	1004	96.10	96.50	4016	96.99	98.00	(600)	(10700)	(6684)	1.50
11/22	1004	96.10	96.94	8434	96.99	98.53	(600)	(16000)	(7566)	1.59
11/23	1004	96.10	97.06	9638	96.99	98.53	(600)	(16000)	(6362)	1.52
11/24	1004	96.10	97.25	11546	96.99	98.81	(600)	(18800)	(7254)	1.56
11/26	1004	96.10	98.03	19377	96.99	99.56	(600)	(26300)	(6923)	1.53
11/29	1004	96.10	98.28	21800	96.99	99.56	(600)	(26300)	(4500)	1.28
11/30	1004	96.10	98.38	22800	96.99	99.47	(600)	(25400)	(2600)	1.09
12/1	1004	96.10	98.51	24100	96.99	99.69	(600)	(27600)	(3500)	1.18
12/2	1004	96.10	99.44	23494	96.99	99.97	(600)	(30400)	(6906)	1.53
12/3	1004	96.10	99.50	34136	96.99	100.44	(600)	(35100)	(964)	.94
12/4	1004	96.10	99.59	35040	96.99	100.34	(600)	(34100)	940	.75

force. The column at the far right shows a variation in the cash-futures basis of nearly a full percentage point from 1.66 to .75 (32nds converted to hundreds). By maintaining such an ongoing analysis, the hedge manager can monitor daily changes in a particular basis relationship and exercise his judgment as to the most opportune time to initiate and terminate his hedge.

In addition to keeping a close eye on the basis, a successful hedger works with a definite interest rate forecast in mind, especially if his objective is the aggressive type of hedging described earlier in this chapter. The difference between pure hedging and trading the basis can be demonstrated within the context of the Southeastern case. If, in the opinion of the hedge manager, interest rates on VA/FHA loans were likely to decline while the mortgages were being "warehoused," the company might elect to carry an unhedged or partially hedged position to accrue the additional gain it stands to realize from the re-sale of the mortgages at a higher price. If, on the other hand, progressively higher interest rates are forecast, Southeastern might sell more futures contracts that would be indicated by its current level of mortgage production, with a view toward securing additional profits on loans originated at a later date.

The extent to which a particular inventory is underhedged or overhedged depends in the main on management's interest rate expectations and those quoted in the futures market, once again underscoring the importance of the basis in conducting such an operation.

The Amalgamated Manufacturing Corp. Case

In June 1978 the treasurer of Amalgamated Manufacturing reviewed his company's plan to issue $50 million in commercial paper the following December. Proceeding from his forecast of rising short-term rates through the balance of the year, consideration was given to hedging the cost of the company's upcoming borrowing through the purchase of an appropriate number of 90-day commercial paper contracts.[8] The situation, on June 15, was as follows:

September commercial paper futures	8.55%
December commercial paper futures	8.75%
Cash 90-day commercial paper	7.50%
Basis cash under December	125

Aware that cash and futures rates would begin to converge as the December delivery date approached, Amalgamated's treasurer faced the choice of buying the December contract and having the strengthening basis work against him or buying the September contract and rolling the position over prior to its expiration. Cash rates would have to rise by more than 125 basis points from their June level before a hedge in the December contract became effective. If they increased by a lesser amount, remained unchanged or declined, Amalgamated's effective borrowing cost would still be "locked in" at 8.75%.

The treasurer felt that commercial paper rates would rise above that level by his projected borrowing date and decided to proceed with the December hedge. It proved in retrospect to have been an opportune step, as rates were considerably higher than 8.75% by mid-December. In the actual event the company issued its commercial paper at a 10.25% discount and liquidated its futures position at a 150 basis-point profit.

The effective discount calculation proceeds as follows:

---

[8]Buying futures for what would normally be a short hedge is the consequence of the quotation method of the Board of Trade's 90-day commercial paper contract before it was revised. As was pointed out in page 59 footnote 3, the outcome of the case is materially unchanged by the redefinition of contract terms.

Table 10-6. Amalgamated Manufacturing's Commercial Paper Hedges.

June 15

Cash	Futures
No transaction	Buy 50 December C.P. at 8.75%
Commercial paper discount 7.50%	Deposit initial margin $50,000

December 15

Cash	Futures
Issue $50 million 90-day commercial paper 10.25%	Sell 50 December C.P. at 10.30% recover margin

Face value	$50,000,000	Gross futures gain	$193,750
Discount	1,281,250	155 × 25 × 50	
Proceeds	48,718,750	Less commissions	3,000
		Less interest on margin	2,500
		Net futures profit	$188,250

Commercial paper proceeds + net futures profit = hedged proceeds
$48,718,750 + $188,250 = $48,907,000
Hedged discount = $1,093,000 or 8.74%

Because the futures market already was anticipating a substantial increase in short-term rates at mid-year, it was not possible at that point to secure total protection from the June-December surge. Even so, a hedged rate of 8.75% turned out to be preferable to incurring a borrowing cost of 10.25%. Despite the adverse move in the basis, the short hedge was successful in offsetting more than one-half of Amalgamated's increased borrowing cost (10.25%-7.50%).

Construction Workers Pension Fund Case

The $160 million pension fund portfolio of the Construction Workers International union was 50% invested in medium-term bonds at the beginning of 1978, of which again half were U.S. Treasury issues. Bond values had suffered some deterioration during the year just ended, and with a forecast of a continued rise in long-term interest rates, the fund's managers were apprehensive of further price erosion. Their alternatives were to increase the equity portion of the fund at the expense of the fixed-income segment, shorten bond maturities to reduce the price effect of rising rates or hedge all or part of the bond holdings in the futures market. The first two options were rejected in light of an equally bearish outlook for stock prices, and the fact that current interest income was already uncomfortably close to falling short of the fund's minimum contractual requirements.

The fund's managers accordingly sought and received authorization from the trustees to implement a program of selective futures hedging to offset continuing depreciation of the bond portfolio and maintain a high level of current income. The strategy adopted was to sell government bond futures equal in value to the portfolio's holdings of Treasury bonds and leave the corporate segment unhedged. The managers felt that prudence dictated their gradual entry into the futures market, and they preferred to derive their initial experience with a straight hedge before undertaking a more complex cross hedge between corporate issues and Treasury bond futures.

Between January and March 1978, 400 Treasury bond contracts spanning several delivery months were sold. The purpose of dispersing delivery dates was to allow easier liquidation when the time came to terminate the hedge. A comparison between the hedged and unhedged portions of the bond portfolio at year-end thoroughly justified the hedge strategy. The corporate segment, valued at approximately $40 million in January, had depreciated some 9%, or $3.6 million, by year-end. Although the Treasury bonds declined by a comparable amount, roughly equivalent profits in the short futures positions kept the aggregate value of the hedged segment intact.

Moreover, as the general level of long-term interest rates increased throughout the year, new bonds were coming to the cash market with coupons reflecting the higher rates. While their reluctance to incur realized capital losses deterred the managers from switching into newly offered bonds paying a higher current return, the short hedge freed them from that constraint with the Treasury bonds. Including realized and unrealized futures profits, the market value of the hedged half of the bond portfolio stood about 9½% above that of the unhedged segment by Dec. 31, by which time current income from the Treasury bonds had been raised over 10% as a result of judicious swaps which could be made without the need to book realized losses.

Under the guidelines set forth in the hedge plan, the pension fund's managers would discontinue their sale of futures when it appeared to them that the long-term rate cycle had turned downward. The benefits gained from the earlier hedges would continue to be reflected in the fund's performance, however, as the capital that was kept intact would appreciate from a larger base when bond prices began their recovery.

The "Strip Buy" Strategy

The three preceding cases illustrated short hedges (or the equivalent in the instance of the original 90-day commercial paper contract) employed to protect a prospective institutional borrower or owner of fixed-income securities from the adverse price consequences of rising interest rates. The long hedge, as described earlier in the chapter, is created through the purchase of futures to neutralize the reduction of income from falling interest rates.

The drawback of both the short and long hedges is that the futures market invariably discounts the prevailing consensus concerning the outlook for interest rates. Any increase or decrease in rates, therefore, can be effectively hedged only to the extent that it surpasses the level indicated by currently quoted futures prices. Once again, it is a question of convergence and a chánging basis.

A strategy which falls midway between a conventional long hedge and the sort of arbitrage operations discussed in the following chapter involves the use of a series of successive futures contracts to secure a higher rate of return than what is available from a comparable cash market investment. Though it may take a variety of forms, the so-called "strip buy" is easiest to conceive when comparing the discount on a cash 12-month Treasury bill with that which may be obtained by buying the combination of a cash 90-day T-bill and three consecutive futures contracts. This cash-futures strip represents a comparable investment because each expiring contract ensures delivery at the designated rate of a new 90-day bill the day the previous 90-day bill matures. An investor thereby substitutes for a year bill a series of four 90-day bills whose average return can be computed the day the contracts are purchased. If the strip provides a higher yield, it is the more attractive investment alternative.

To illustrate, the following discounts were quoted in the cash and futures markets on Sept. 22, 1977:

		% Discount
Cash Market		
9/19/78 Treasury bill (one year)		6.23
12/22/77 Treasury bill (90 days)		5.96
Futures Market		
December 1977	T-bill contract	6.22
March 1978	T-bill contract	6.52
June 1978	T-bill contract	6.81

On Sept. 22, therefore, a corporation or institutional investor which intended to put funds into the Treasury bill market for one year had the option of buying the 12-month bill at 6.23% discount or the 90 day bill maturing Dec. 22, 1977, and the December 1977 and March and June 1978 contracts which, according to the following calculation, would provide an average return of 6.38%, or a 15 basis-point improvement over the return on the year bill:

$$\frac{90\ (5.96) + 90\ (6.22) + 90\ (6.52) + 90\ (6.81)}{360} = 6.38$$

A yield pickup of 15 basis points on $1 million invested for one year is $1,500. From that amount commissions and other costs must be subtracted to derive the net gain.

To carry out the strip strategy on those dates which do not coincide with the quarterly futures delivery dates, a fourth contract may be purchased, giving an investor the option of taking delivery of another 90-day bill and selling it at the end of the 360-day period or liquidating the fourth contract prior to its expiration and purchasing in the cash market a bill with the correct maturity.

The cash-futures strip does not invariably produce an average yield superior to that of the cash bill. For example, the discount on the cash one-year bill upon the maturity of the June 1978 contract was about 10 basis points above what could then be obtained from the comparable strip investment. The advantage, if any, offered by either alternative is determined by the respective slopes of the cash and futures yield curves at the time the investment is to be made. Investors contemplating the strip strategy should monitor both markets continuously to identify any advantages as they may occur. The strategy is not limited to Treasury bill investments of one year or less. Since T-bill futures are traded for eight successive quarterly expiration dates, it may be applied to investments in U.S. Treasury notes extending out two years. The introduction of a four-year note contract gives the strip strategy an even wider application.

Chapter Eleven
Spreaders and Arbitrageurs

This chapter elaborates upon and proposes further applications of material introduced earlier in the book. Chapters Five and Six outlined the primary reasons why different securities offer different yields, and examined in some detail the ways in which these differences change over the course of an interest rate cycle. They also demonstrated how the differences in yield between various maturities of the same security change with every shift in the slope and position of the yield curve. Chapter Ten took up the subject of yield differentials in another context as part of its description of the means whereby firms may utilize the price/yield relationships between cash instruments and futures contracts to minimize the interest rate risk implicit in owning or otherwise dealing in fixed-income securities.

The expression "spread," therefore, has somewhat different though certainly related connotations in the credit and futures markets. In either sense, it is a central concept which is essential for traders of interest rate futures, be it for hedging or outright speculative purposes, to understand and apply. When used as a noun, the word refers to the price or yield differentials between two or more securities or futures contracts. As a verb, i.e. to spread, it denotes a trading technique whose objective is to secure profits by correctly anticipating changes in these differentials. Much that was said about hedging in the previous chapter, therefore, applies to spreading as well. While hedging entails assuming opposite positions in the cash and futures markets, a futures market spread involves simultaneous long and short positions in related futures contracts. In other words, a hedge is a particular type of spread in which one of the "legs" happens to be a position in the cash market. There are as many other spreading possibilities within the interest rate complex as there are delivery months of the various contracts.

Newcomers to the futures markets are sometimes confused by indiscriminate references to spreads, straddles and arbitrage. The first two terms are generally held to be synonymous, and will be so used here. By custom, the word spread is favored in the grain trade, while one hears the expression straddle more frequently in other futures markets within the U.S. and abroad. Arbitrage is in the strictest sense a different type of operation, and will be treated as such in this chapter.

The Nature of Spreading

Unlike the commercial hedging operations undertaken by commodity producers or processors, spreading is normally the province of floor scalpers and "outside" speculative traders who are not involved in the cash market as part of their regular business. But the motive is in each instance the same—the diminution of risk. Spreaders regard their specialty as a more conservative method of trading for the very reason that hedgers judge basis risk to be less than that of an open long or short position, namely the tendency of cash and successive futures to move up and down more or less in tandem.

The reduced risk inherent in offsetting positions in the same or related futures allows the exchanges and their members to set lower margin requirements and commission rates on spread transactions than on outright positions in the same contracts, another feature of spreading which is attractive to traders. At the time that the margins listed in Table 4-1, page 119, were in force, a two-contract spread position in 90-day T-bills would have entailed an initial margin deposit of $300, as opposed to the exchange minimum of $800 to assume a net long or short position. Be aware of this caveat, however: The attitude of some traders that they can control a greater number of contracts in a spread position for the same dollar outlay subjects them to the danger of overreaching themselves.

The three fundamental types of spread positions are the intermonth, intermarket, and intercommodity spreads. Like the 90-day T-bill spread described in Chapter Six[1], an intermonth spread consists of concurrent long and short positions in two delivery months of the same contract. An intermarket spread is placed between similar contracts traded on different futures exchanges. An example of such a spread would be opposite positions in Ginnie Mae certificate delivery contracts traded at the Chicago Board of Trade and the American Commodity Exchange in New York. Intercommodity spreads are taken between contracts for different maturities of like securities, i.e. 90-day vs. one-year T-bills or between different securities such as T-bills and commercial paper or bonds and Ginnie Maes.

These three categories need not be mutually exclusive. A long position in March 90-day T-bills vs. a short one in September 90-day commercial paper would be, for example, both an intermonth and an intercommodity spread. There must be, however, a bona fide relationship between the yields on the two securities for it to comprise an authentic spread. Lacking

---

[1]Page 206.

such a connection, they are just two positions that happened to be taken at the same time.

Of the three types, intermonth spreads are most commonly taken by traders who believe that the same factors which cause changes in the basis between cash and futures will also affect the price/yield relationship between the various delivery months of that contract. Such factors are usually those which arise from differences in time, delivery grade and, in some cases, location of available supplies.

Nearby vs. Distant Contracts

It was noted in the preceding chapter that the maturity structure of a particular contract normally consists at any time of successive premiums or discounts from delivery month to delivery month, which tend to taper as the contract approaches its expiration date. When the nearby contracts sell at a price discount (yield premium) to the deferred months, the logical spread position is to be long the near month and short the distant to gain the benefit of the contraction of the discount with the passage of time. The spreader's risk in this instance is that the discount may grow wider while the position is in force. When the near month sells at a price premium (yield discount) over distant contracts, the inverse position— short the nearby and long the deferred—is in order unless the trader has reason to believe there are potential factors which will make the premium even greater.

In futures markets for storable commodities such as grains and metals, the structure in which each delivery month is priced at a discount to the one following is known as a "carrying charge" market, where the price difference from one contract expiration to the next reflects the storage, financing and insurance costs of holding the physical commodity during that three-month period, or whatever the interval between contracts happens to be. Also referred to as a contango market,[2] such a price structure occasionally provides futures traders with an opportunity to place a so-called "no-risk spread" by buying a nearby contract and selling a deferred month at or near full carrying charges. The purported absence of risk in this particular transaction stems from the assumption that hedgers would seize the chance to reduce their storage charges by selling the distant contracts whenever their price rose above carrying charges and, if need be, settle their short positions at maturity by making actual delivery from their inventories. The so-called negative carry market has no such restraining element which serves to limit the premium at which near months sell over the distant.

Fixed-income securities are not subject to the same type of carrying charges as either storable or perishable commodities. Since safekeeping, insurance and transportation charges are not significant items in relation to the face value involved, net financing expense—the difference between interest received and paid—comprises the major cost of carry in the interest rate futures complex. Just as expectations concerning the behavior of interest rates influence the absolute level of futures prices, they are as much a determinant of the price spreads between delivery months. The mirror image of a positive yield curve reflecting the expectation of rising interest rates is a premium market where nearby contracts sell at higher prices (lower yields) than the deferred contracts. As cash rates rise amid a growing consensus that they will increase even more, the price premium (or yield discount) of nearby contracts over deferreds is likely to expand, making a

---

[2]The term is borrowed from the settlement procedure on the London Stock Exchange and is believed to be a modification of *continue*. It refers to the consideration paid by a buyer to a seller for delaying full payment until the next fortnightly settlement period. Payment from a seller to a buyer for extending the delivery date is called *backwardation,* or, in futures usage, inverse carrying charges.

long-nearby—short-distant the most advantageous spread position.

As cash rates approach what is presumed to be a cyclical peak, the price premium of nearby over distant delivery months starts to contract as traders step up their buying of deferred contracts in anticipation of an eventual decline in rates. The advantage then shifts to the reverse spread position—short the near and long the distant months—as the latter display relative strength, converting the nearby premiums to discounts.

Table 11-1 contains a tabulation of 1978 monthly averages of daily 90-day Treasury bill discounts in the cash and futures markets based upon closing IMM index prices.[3] The figures reflect in statistical form the same changes that were graphically presented in the diagram of yield curve shifts in Chapter Six.[4] A side-by-side comparison of the two exhibits discloses that, as the futures curve assumes a sharper upward slope, the price/yield spreads between delivery months tends to expand; but, as the near end moves higher up the yield axis, causing the curve to flatten out and then turn into a humped configuration (indicating the market's belief that short-term rates are at or near a peak), the spreads begin to contract, and the distant contracts begin moving to a price premium (yield discount) over the near or intermediate deliveries.

The same sequence was the background to the intermonth spread described in Chapter Six, where a December 1978 T-bill contract was sold in April at a 94 basis-point premium over the long position in December 1979 T-bills. By the following November, the spread between the near and distant December con-

---

[3]Futures prices are expressed in terms of their equivalent discount yields to provide a clearer comparison with cash rates. In considering the spreads between delivery months stated in parentheses, readers are reminded that a yield discount from month to month is the equivalent of a price premium and, conversely, a higher yield indicates a price discount.

[4]Page 204.

Table 11-1. Cash and Futures Discounts and (Spreads)
90-day Treasury Bills—International Monetary Market
Monthly Averages of Daily Closing Discounts Based on IMM Index

Month	Cash Discount	March 1978	June 1978	Sept. 1978	Dec. 1978	March 1979	June 1979	Sept. 1979	Dec. 1979	March 1980	June 1980	Sept. 1980
1978												
Jan.	6.40	(33)6.73	(39)7.12	(30)7.42	(25)7.67	(22)7.89	(18)8.07	(17)8.24	(14)8.38			
Feb.	6.45	(16)6.61	(53)7.14	(23)7.37	(26)7.63	(23)7.86	(19)8.05	(19)8.24	(16)8.40			
Mar.	6.30	(3)6.33	(50)6.83	(40)7.23	(30)7.53	(26)7.79	(24)8.03	(19)8.22	(18)8.40			
Apr.	6.29		(50)6.79	(47)7.26	(32)7.58	(26)7.84	(22)8.06	(21)8.27	(19)8.46	(16)8.62		
May	6.42		(33)6.75	(58)7.33	(39)7.72	(29)8.01	(25)8.26	(22)8.48	(19)8.67	(19)8.86		
June	6.71		(-2)6.69	(61)7.30	(43)7.73	(31)8.04	(24)8.28	(22)8.50	(20)8.70	(20)8.90	(19)9.19	
July	7.04			(31)7.35	(44)7.79	(33)8.12	(25)8.37	(23)8.60	(20)8.80	(20)9.00	(19)9.01	
Aug.	7.02			(7)7.09	(41)7.50	(33)7.83	(29)8.12	(25)8.37	(23)8.60	(22)8.82	(8)8.57	
Sept.	7.82			(-8)7.74	(24)7.98	(12)8.10	(10)8.20	(10)8.30	(10)8.40	(9)8.49	(4)9.00	(5)9.05
Oct.	7.95				(43)9.01	(26)8.65	(13)8.78	(9)8.87	(4)8.91	(5)8.96	(-5)9.01	(-2)8.99
Nov.	8.58				(-6)9.01	(27)9.28	(5)9.33	(-8)9.25	(-10)9.15	(-9)9.06	(-6)9.17	(-1)9.16
Dec.	9.07					(39)9.40	(11)9.51	(-3)9.48	(-12)9.36	(-13)9.23		

356

tracts had narrowed to 40 basis points, allowing the position to be "unwound" at a 54 basis-point or $1,350 profit before commission charges on an initial margin commitment of $500. If the reverse spread had been placed in April—long nearby, short distant—the position would have incurred a comparable loss during the same holding period, sufficient evidence that there is still ample risk implicit in spread positions, against which safeguards, i.e. stops, should be taken. A record of price relationships such as that contained in Table 11-1 should be maintained and studied as assiduously as traders carrying outright positions examine their trend charts.

The actual outcome of the short December 1978—long December 1979 intermonth spread was a cyclical development, inasmuch as it occurred as a consequence of the market's assessment over a seven-month period that short-term interest rates were approaching their peak. More fleeting changes in intermonth spread relationships occur as successive delivery months reflect in varying degrees what is transpiring in the cash market. The spread trader's decisions are based in this instance not so much upon his opinion regarding the cyclical outlook for interest rates as upon his appraisal of the extent to which what may be purely temporary supply-demand dislocations may affect the prices of successive delivery months in the futures market. When a specific event—foreign central bank purchases of Treasury bills, for example—exerts a bullish or upward influence on cash market prices, a long-nearby—short-deferred month spread would be indicated, inasmuch as the one or two delivery dates nearest the spot month are the ones which are the most directly affected. Conversely, a bearish development in the cash market would favor a short-nearby—long-deferred spread position.

Much of the "scalp" trading on the exchange floor involves this type of spreading operation. In many instances a local will accept a bid or offer in the pit, and immediately offset it with an opposite position in another delivery month to reduce his risk exposure. This sort of on-going spread activity serves to keep the price differences between contract months within fairly consistent limits as a matter of course, and is anticipated by outside traders who watch for temporary deviations from normal spreads to place positions before counter trading restores the earlier spread. They are at a time disadvantage to traders who are physically in the pit, however, and the commissions charged makes it infeasible for them to trade for the one or two "ticks" that are profitable for a member.

Spreading the Markets

Intermarket spread positions are taken between similar contracts traded on different commodity exchanges. In the grain markets, for example, wheat futures are traded in Chicago, Kansas City and Minneapolis, providing occasional spread opportunities when prices in these markets vary from their usual relationships. Similar situations may arise among such "international" commodities as cocoa, sugar, and silver, for which futures markets exist in London as well as in New York.

The only comparable intermarket spread opportunity available in the interest rate futures complex by mid-1979 was that between the Ginnie Mae certificate delivery contract traded on the Chicago Board of Trade and the American Commodity Exchange contract traded in New York. There has yet to be compiled a sufficient price history for the two contracts to draw firm conclusions, since both were introduced in September 1978, but the data summarized in Table 11-2 suggest that the markets are too closely aligned for non-members to derive significant spreading opportunities between them. Moreover, since the stipulated delivery months for the Board of Trade and ACE contracts do not coincide, a long position taken in one

Table 11-2. June 1979 CBT Certificate Delivery Versus May 1979 ACE Ginnie Mae Contract Weekly Closing Prices.

1978	CBT GNMA June 1979	ACE GNMA May 1979	CBT Over ACE
Sept. 13	91-25	92-00	−7
20	91-01	91-00	1
27	90-28	90-25	3
Oct. 4	90-18	90-21	−3
11	91-05	91-01	4
18	90-16	90-16	—
25	90-05	90-05	—
Nov. 1	89-25	89-21	4
8	89-25	89-24	1
15	90-19	90-15	4
22	90-17	90-11	6
29	89-31	89-25	6
Dec. 6	90-01	89-28	5
13	89-10	89-06	4
20	88-02	87-27	7
27	88-10	88-05	5

market against a short position in the other would of necessity consist of an intermonth as well as an inter-market spread.

A drawback to this as well as other spread positions taken between different exchanges lies in forc-going the reduced margins and commission rates available on spreads placed within the same market. On the basis of the weekly closing prices in Table 11-2, this particular spread would appear to be better suited to floor traders on either exchange who have the advantage of saving commissions on at least one of the legs.

A similar spread which is better suited to "commercials" than to private traders is one between Ginnie Mae futures contracts and what are known as cash market forward commitments of the same maturity. It is difficult for individual accounts to undertake this spread because one of the legs is placed in the dealer forward market, to which private traders do not normally have access.

The condition governing this spread is that Ginnie Mae securities may be bought and sold for future delivery in both markets, with case forward and futures prices converging at their common maturity. By superimposing the two prices we see that when futures were sold at a price equal to or greater than the purchase price of an equivalent cash forward contract, there usually has been an opportunity to "unwind" the spread at a gross profit of $^{16}/_{32}$nds or $500 per contract. Conversely, when the spread opens in the other direction, a long position in futures $^{24}/_{32}$nds below a short position in cash forwards has generated profits as the two prices converged at delivery date. The principal risk in either instance is that the spread may open or close beyond its regular parameters. But, based upon the relevant price history, it would appear that such risks are limited when the spread is initiated at either of the extremities indicated by the chart—that is to say, short futures and long cash forwards when futures are equal to or above cash prices; long futures and short cash forwards when futures are $^{16}/_{32}$nds or more below cash.

Like other spread situations, the futures–cash forward Ginnie Mae spread involves four separate transactions to place and ultimately terminate the opposite positions. The $1 million unit of trading in the cash forward market dictates the sale or purchase of 10 futures contracts against each forward commitment assumed in the spread. Margin deposits generally have not been required in making cash transactions for forward delivery, and the dealer's compensation is built into the bid-asked differential (or spread, as the pros call it, a term which risks totally confusing the discussion) rather than a stated commission. In addition to being implemented on its own merits, the futures–

cash Ginnie Mae spread is undertaken by thrift institutions and mortgage bankers as one of the selective
hedging operations described in Chapter Ten.

Apples vs. Oranges

Intercommodity spreads, the third major classification, are taken between two different though related
contracts. The possibilities in the interest rate complex
are numerous, since all of the contracts are by definition sensitive to changes in long-term or short-term
interest rates.

The two legs of the spread might consist of positions in contracts for different securities or different
maturities of the same instrument. The comparative
behavior of 90-day Treasury bill and commercial paper
yields was traced in Chapter Six, where it was averred
that commercial paper rates tend to move faster and
farther than rates on T-bills of the same maturity during the latter stages of a cyclical trend. Under such
circumstances, an appropriate intercommodity spread
during the final months of a cyclical uptrend, as borne
out by the experience of the latter half of 1978, would
have been to go long both T-bill and commercial paper
futures, just as short positions in both contracts would
be in order as rates approach the trough of a cyclical
downturn.[5]

According to the price data in Table 6-4 on page
188, a long 90-day T-bill—long 90-day commercial paper spread might have been initiated on June 5, at a
90 basis-point yield premium, commercial paper over
T-bills. By Nov. 20, the spread had opened up to 237
basis points, accruing a profit of 147 basis points, or

---

[5]This is no longer so since the redefinition of the 90-day commercial
paper contract. Under the present terms of the contract, a T-bill–C.P.
spread would be established like any other—long one contract, short the
other. To repeat, the distinction between the original contract and the
current one is chiefly a matter of mechanics.

$3,675 before commissions on each two-contract spread position. Assuming the spread was initiated and "unwound" on those two rates, the profit calculation would have appeared as follows:

Table 11-3.   T-bill and Commercial Paper Spread.

		Commercial Paper over T-bills
June 5, 1978		
Buy 1 Dec. 1978 T-bills at 92.28 (7.72% discount)	Buy 1 Dec. 1978 commercial paper at 8.62% discount	90 basis points
November 20, 1978		
Sell 1 Dec. 1978 T-bills at 91.17 (8.83% discount)	Sell 1 Dec. 1978 commercial paper at 11.20% discount	237 points
Loss $2,775 (111 × $25 × 1)	Profit $6,450 (258 × $25 × 1)	Spread Profit $3,675 (147 × $25 × 1)

Chapter Six also tracked the change in spread between 90-day and one-year T-bills between 1969 and 1978. According to the theoretical analysis, as short-term interest rates approach a cyclical peak, the yield curve becomes humped or negative, meaning that yields on the shortest maturities are rising faster than those on longer maturities. The approiriate spread in such a situation would be to go short the 90-day and long the one-year bill contract.

Like the ACE and Board of Trade Ginnie Mae certificate delivery contracts, which commenced trading at about the same time, the price history of the IMM's one-year T-bill contract since its introduction in late 1978 is not extensive enough to justify making trading decisions on the strength of it. The data that was available by year-end, however, did conform to the theoretical expectation.

Table 11-4 shows that the 90-day to one-year bill yield spread (June 1979 contracts) opened from nine

**Table 11-4. International Monetary Market
June 1979 90-Day T-Bills
Versus June 1979 One-Year T-Bills
September-December 1978, Weekly
Closing Prices.**

	June 1979 90-day T-bills	June 1979 One-Year T-bills	90-day to One-Year Yield Spread
Sept. 13	91.94 (8.06)	91.85 (8.15)	−9
20	91.76 (8.24)	91.76 (8.24)	even
27	91.42 (8.58)	91.67 (8.33)	25
Oct. 4	91.41 (8.59)	91.59 (8.41)	18
11	91.38 (8.62)	91.57 (8.43)	19
18	91.23 (8.77)	91.46 (8.54)	23
25	91.21 (8.79)	91.41 (8.59)	20
Nov. 1	90.62 (9.38)	90.80 (9.20)	18
8	90.41 (9.59)	90.75 (9.25)	34
15	90.91 (9.09)	91.02 (8.98)	11
22	90.77 (9.23)	91.10 (8.90)	33
29	90.65 (9.35)	90.96 (9.04)	31
Dec. 6	90.69 (9.31)	90.87 (9.13)	18
13	90.65 (9.35)	90.85 (9.15)	20
20	90.21 (9.79)	90.42 (9.58)	21
27	90.34 (9.66)	90.52 (9.48)	18

basis points under to 33 over between mid-September and late November, then narrowed to 18 over by year-end. The standard profit calculation indicates that a short 90-day, long one-year bill spread during that 3½ month period would have generated a profit before commissions of about 40 basis points, or $1,000, per contract if unwound at its optimum point during the last week of November, and about a 30 basis-point, or $750, profit if the spread were carried through year-end.[6] On the requisite spread margin of $500, these gains represented profits of 200% and 150% respec-

---

[6]Since the contract sizes of the 90-day and one-year contracts are $1 million and $250,000, respectively, the value of a basis point is in each case $25, making the calculation the same as for those contracts involving the same maturities.

tively, very nice results indeed for what are considered to be limited risk situations.

The foregoing examples illustrate but a few of the possible spread relationships that may be explored. The Treasury bond–Ginnie Mae spread cited in Chapter Six[7] offers yet another candidate. As additional new contracts receive regulatory approval and commence trading, the permutations and combinations will multiply exponentially.

The Butterfly Spread

A somewhat more complex spreading technique more frequently employed by "scalpers" and other professional traders than by outside speculators is the butterfly spread, so-named for a diagram of its component positions. A "butterfly" is a combination of two spreads, placed simultaneously in the belief that together they further reduce the risk of an ordinary spread position. It is established by assuming a short or long position in a nearby contract and the opposite position in a distant delivery month, then doubling up in a middle month so that the total number of long contracts equals the total shorts. Where a regular spread trader acts in the belief that two prices are out of line, a butterfly spreader moves on his supposition that one spread relationship is out of line with another.

Selecting our price and spread information from Table 11-1, we can draw diagrams of a hypothetical butterfly spread for June and August 1978 and see how such a spread would have fared over that period. The diagram opposite, Figure 11-1, shows a long December 1978–short June 1979 T-bill spread at a 55 basis point difference, and a concurrent long June 1979–short December 1979 spread at a 42 basis point

---

[7]Page 191.

FIGURE: 11-1

365

difference. Carrying the "butterfly" into August, the long December–short June widens to 62 basis points, and the long June–short December widens as well to 48 basis points.

It so happened that because of the aforementioned turnaround of the yield curve during those months, both legs (or "wings" in this instance) registered a profit even though the usual outcome of a butterfly spread is that the two relationships show a similar but opposite change, rendering a minimal net profit or loss.

Though a butterfly spread probably does reduce risk, its profit potential is proportionately limited. Like the Chicago–New York Ginnie Mae spread, such a spread position is better suited to exchange members who do not pay commissions and therefore find it profitable to trade sizeable positions for two or three "ticks."

Tax Spreads

Conventional and butterfly spreads have in the past been undertaken by traders for the primary purpose of securing such tax benefits as deferring a tax liability to a later period, converting ordinary income and short-term capital gains into long-term gains, converting a capital loss into an ordinary loss, and extending an expiring corporate tax loss carry-forward.

T-bill futures gained particular attention in this regard during the first three years of their trading life due to a singular tax ruling that the discount earned on cash Treasury bills is considered ordinary income. The assumed extension of ordinary income and loss treatment to futures transactions, in addition to the above-mentioned advantages, stimulated spreading in T-bill futures solely for tax reasons until a formal IRS ruling in late 1978 declared these contracts to be capital assets and designated any profit or loss incurred in dealing in them a capital gain or loss, despite the ordinary income treatment accorded profits from the purchase of cash bills. In the same ruling, which is subject to appeal, the practice of using futures market spreads of any type to secure favorable tax consequences was disallowed. Whatever the final resolution of the tax-spread issue, such activity falls outside the scope of this book. No transactions should be undertaken in the futures market for tax reasons before consulting expert counsel and a broker experienced in this manner of trading.

Arbitrage and Quasi-Arbitrage

As was stated at the outset of this chapter, the use of the term yield arbitrage to describe the type of spreading activity discussed thus far is not strictly correct. The standard definition of an arbitrage is the purchase of an asset in one market and its immediate resale for a profit in another, i.e. buying General Motors common stock on the New York Stock Exchange and selling it on the Pacific Stock Exchange, or buying Swiss francs in Zurich against their simultaneous resale in London. Spreading between like or different futures contracts is based upon an anticipated change in the relationship between two prices over a period of time, rather than the opportunity to secure an immediate profit by capturing the existing difference between them. Therefore, a futures spread in most instances contains an element of risk that a so-called "pure" arbitrage does not entail. The Ginnie Mae futures–cash forward spread might be termed a "quasi-arbitrage" in the sense that the same assets are being bought and sold in different markets. Inasmuch as the complete transaction is not immediately consummated, but rather hinges on the narrowing or widening of the price spread over a period of weeks or months however, it falls short of the classic arbitrage as defined above.

Another type of quasi-arbitrage involving the use

of interest rate futures comes closer to the ideal of a riskless transaction. Known as the "hedged yield curve ride," it, like the cash-futures strip buy strategy described in the preceding chapter, employs futures contracts to secure a yield higher than the one available on a comparable cash investment.

Reference was made earlier in the book to the conventional yield curve ride, in which a money market investor undertakes to increase his rate of return by purchasing an instrument with a longer life than his planned period of investment with the intention of selling it prior to its maturity date. The example cited in Chapter Five involved the purchase and sale after 90 days of a 180-day Treasury bill in lieu of buying and holding to maturity a 90-day bill.[8] Though the investment period of the two alternatives is the same—three months—and the securities are identical save their maturity, there is an incremental return to be gained from owning the longer maturity as it moves down the steepest part of the yield curve. The risk inherent in this technique is the one normally associated with extending maturities, namely that any increase in short-term interest rates during the holding period would not only eradicate the purported yield advantage, but might also result in a net loss if rates rose sharply enough. As was noted during the earlier description of the cash market, there is no interest rate risk when a Treasury bill is held to maturity because the investor is assured of receiving the entire discount (yield) when the instrument is redeemed at par. The investment trade-off made by a "yield curve rider" is one of deliberately exposing himself to interest rate risk for the sake of earning a higher return.

The sale of an appropriate futures contract at the time the longer-term instrument is purchased serves

---

[8]P. 173. In the following discussion, we again take the liberty of using maturities of 90 and 180 days for simplicity of illustration in order to spare readers the added complication of computing discounts for the actual 91 and 182 day maturities on three- and six-month bills.

to offset this risk. The combined transaction also constitutes something of an arbitrage in that it provides for the sale of an asset at a firm price in the futures market at the same time that it is purchased in the cash market. Unlike the spreads discussed thus far, the gain from the transaction is fixed from the outset. As in the earlier cases, the concept is best illustrated by an actual example:

On June 22, 1978, the discounts on three- and six-month Treasury bills were 6.82% and 7.32%, respectively. The September 1978 T-bill contract settled that day at 92.60, reflecting a 7.40% discount on three-month bills to be issued Sept. 22 and maturing the following Dec. 21. The available alternatives for a three-month investment in Treasury bills as of June 22 were, therefore, to:

Table 11-5.   Three Month Investment Alternative June 22, 1978.

1. Buy three-month bills and hold them to their 9/21/78 maturity, thereby earning	6.82%
or	
2. Buy six-month bills dated 12/21/78 at a current discount of	7.32%
with the intention of selling them in 90 days	
and	
sell September 1978 T-bill futures at 92.60, reflecting a discount of	7.40%

A comparison of the respective yields indicated that the long six-month bill, short September 1978 futures alternative offered a yield advantage of 50 basis points over the three-month bill (7.32%-6.82%), of which 8 basis points (7.40%-7.32%) were surrendered on the futures sale at the higher yield (lower price). The net benefit disregarding commissions to be derived from Alternative Two was, therefore, 42 basis points or a $1,050 gain on each $1 million invested in that manner.

Breaking the transactions down according to prin-

**Table 11-6.　Yield Comparisons
90-Day Bill vs 180-Day Bill
With Futures Hedge,
June 22-Sept. 21, 1978.**

Alternative One

June 22—Buy $1 million 90-day bills @　　　　　　　6.82%

　　Cost = $982,950　　　Discount = $17,050

　Sept. 21 Bills mature at par

　　　　　　　　　　　Discount =　　　　　0

　　　　　　　　　　　Profit　　　　$17,050

　　Discount yield

　　for 90 days = $17,050 ÷ $1 million $\times \dfrac{360}{90}$ =

　　　　　　　　　　　　　　　　　　　　　6.82%

Alternative Two

June 22—Buy $1 million 180-day bills @　　　　　　7.32%

　　Cost = $963,400　　　Discount = $36,600

　　Sell 1 September 1978 T-bill

　　　　contract at 92.60　or　　　　　　　　7.40%

　Sept. 21　Deliver $1 million 90-day bills at　　　7.40%

　　　on Futures short position

　　Proceeds = $981,500　Discount =　　　$18,500

　　　　　　　　　　　Profit　　　$18,100

　　Discount yield

　　for 90 days = $18,100 ÷ $1 million $\times \dfrac{360}{90}$ =

　　　　　　　　　　　　　　　　　　　　7.24%

Net Result

　　$18,100 − $17,050 = $1,050

　　or 42 basis points (7.24%-6.82%)

　　on $1 million for 90 days.

cipal amounts and dollar discounts, the yield calculations in Table 11-6 demonstrate the same result.

For ease of comparison, the maturity date of the three-month bill in the above example coincided with the delivery date of the futures contract, by which time the original six-month bill, with 90 days left to its maturity, had become a deliverable security. The following formula may be used to compute the hedged discount yield on securities to be sold on non-delivery dates:

$$\begin{array}{c}\text{Cash}\\\text{Cost}\\\text{Yield}\end{array} + \left[\begin{array}{c}\text{Days remaining}\\\underline{\text{to maturity when sold}}\\\text{Days held}\end{array} \times \left(\begin{array}{cc}\text{Cash} & \text{Futures}\\\text{Cost} - & \text{Sale}\\\text{Yield} & \text{Yield}\end{array}\right)\right] = \begin{array}{c}\text{Hedged}\\\text{Discount}\\\text{Yield}\end{array}$$

Proving the formula with the figures from the earlier example, we have:

$$7.32\% + \left[\frac{90}{90} \times (7.32\% - 7.40\%)\right] = 7.24\%$$

or 42 basis points greater than Alternative One as shown above.

The hedged ride strategy may be applied profitably whenever the yield spread between the longer and shorter maturities is greater than the spread between the yield on the longer bill and that of the next futures delivery month. The strategy is as valid for other combinations of alternate investments where there is a yield advantage to be gained from extending maturities.

Some Do's and Don't's

There has evolved over time a list of "Do's and Don't's" that have been helpful to futures traders in placing profitable spread positions and avoiding the most common pitfalls.

Beginning on the negative side, some neophyte spreaders attempt to obtain more favorable positions by placing or unwinding their spreads "one leg at a time" rather than simultaneously as proper trading practice requires. Though their intent is to secure the best of the two worlds of outright speculation and spreading, they often find themselves saddled with the worst of both worlds. At the same time, they are losing the benefits of reduced spread margins and commissions. A spread should not be initiated until the desired price difference is immediately obtainable. Attempting to place or undo it piecemeal usually leads to unfavorable consequences.

Other traders suddenly decide to become spreaders when they are confronted with a paper loss in an outright long or short position which they are unwilling to realize. They seem to believe, presumably more out of desperation than logic, that taking an offsetting position at that late date will somehow help them to maneuver their way out of a losing position. What it really does is lock in a loss for the time the spread is in force, and in the process exchange one problem for two.

Other traders are motivated to enter into spread positions solely on account of the reduced margin requirements, believing that their profit potential is enhanced by their taking on, say, a three-contract spread as opposed to an outright position in a single contract. If the spread is not well chosen on its own merits, it may very well be that the risk of the larger position outweighs any anticipated increased profit potential.

The choice of the most appropriate delivery months in which to place the two legs of a spread is as important a decision as determining the basic position. Many traders select like months, i.e. December to December, for intermonth or intercommodity spreads without giving the matter sufficient thought or because those are the months plotted in the particular spread chart they happen to be following.

Turning to the positive considerations, spread positions should be researched as carefully as outright trades, with the spreader very clear as to the reasons why he is taking a certain position. Past and current relationships, such as those tabulated in Table 11-1 should be studied for indications as to whether a particular relationship is consistent with or is a deviation from its historical norm.

Traders should become accustomed to thinking in terms of price differences and referring to spread charts as consistently as hedgers do to their basis charts. They should be aware of the extent to which spreads have changed during past interest rate cycles and know, for example, that the Ginnie Mae futures–cash forward relationship usually moves from parity to a $^{24}/_{32}$nds spread.

Finally, a spread should stand on its own two legs, so to speak. The decision to assume a specific spread should be made only after a thorough analysis of that particular relationship, not because a certain long or short position appears promising and the trader has read or heard that he can achieve the same results with less risk by doing the trade in the form of a spread. A closer examination might reveal that the potential risk-return ratio, relative to the amount of margin required, is more favorable with an outright position than with a spread which is the result of an afterthought.

Chapter Twelve
The Future for Futures

At the close of 1978 there was little doubt that interest rate futures had become the hot new market for a growing number of participants. Its development over the course of the first three years had surprised even its most optimistic proponents, as the exchanges repeatedly reported record volume figures and the cost of floor-trading privileges soared to astonishing levels.

Though the surge in activity and its attendant publicity suggested a headlong rush by traders and institutions to get in on a good thing, such has not necessarily been the case. By and large, the participants, brokers and customers alike, have exhibited a level of professionalism that bodes well for the market's sustained viability.

Absorbing the concepts underlying the new instruments and gaining the initial experience of trading them has been in most instances a time-consuming affair. Both Chicago exchanges have from the outset conducted extensive educational and marketing programs to promote the idea of hedging interest rate risk within the financial community. Expertise needed to be developed within the member firms themselves, and their own representatives trained to acquaint existing and prospective clients with the fundamentals and mechanics of the market.

Seasoned commodity traders were faced with mas-

374

tering the intricacies of the money, bond and mortgage markets, while corporate financial executives and institutional investment managers were for the first time exposed to a marketplace with which they had no prior experience. Participants in two previously disparate markets had to learn a common language and become accustomed to doing business with one another. On the corporate side, senior management and directors needed to be persuaded that futures trading was a suitable undertaking, and various regulatory agencies satisfied that appropriate precautions had been taken to prevent speculation and unauthorized trading. In short, the market needed to pass close scrutiny at many levels before the first transactions could be initiated.

Participation by Banks

National banks have been expressly authorized to deal in interest rate futures since 1976, providing they submit to the Comptroller of the Currency an acceptable plan outlining their proposed trading guidelines and procedures, and confine their participation to reducing the risk of interest rate fluctuations—translation: no speculation.[1] By early 1979, proposals from 33 national banks had been approved by the Comptroller's office. Of that number, approximately half by then had commenced active participation in the futures market.

Banks have two principal incentives to deal in the futures market. A short hedge placed during bear bond markets (a most appropriate investment strategy throughout 1978) offsets depreciation in portfolio values. In like manner, banks that conduct dealer operations have the opportunity to increase their trading profits inasmuch as the opportunity to hedge permits them to carry larger inventory positions without in-

---

[1]Comptroller of the Currency, Banking Circular No. 79, Nov. 2, 1976.

curring comparably greater risks. The reduction in risk also allows the traders to tighten the spreads between their bid and offer quotations, providing more attractive prices for prospective buyers and sellers alike.

The second application, either as a long or short hedge, is to lock up a specific yield on projected investments or set a limit on the bank's own borrowing cost, usually on the sale of its certificates of deposit. When the bank has determined the amount and timing of its projected CD sales, it may sell an appropriate number of futures contracts and buy them in as the CDs are sold, thereby fixing as nearly as the correlation between CD and T-bill rates will allow the bank's effective borrowing rate.

Thrift institutions were authorized in early 1978 to sell small denomination six-month certificates of deposit at rates tied to the 90-day T-bill discount. Initially offered in April at 6.75%, the certificates were due to be renewed the following October, by which time the 90-day bill rate had risen to 8%. The sale of T-bill futures at the time the original certificates were offered averted the necessity of paying the added interest cost when it came time to refund the certificates.

Of twelve banks surveyed at the end of 1978, nine had been active in the futures market for a year or longer. Six out of the twelve had made at least one transaction in each of the available contracts, the remainder confining their activity to either T-bill or Ginnie Mae contracts, depending upon the purpose of the hedge. As determined by the size of the institution and the position to be hedged, individual transactions usually ranged between 10 and 50 contracts. In the case of the dealer banks, however, the average transaction size was considerably greater, sometimes amounting to hundreds of contracts.

The objectives were in all cases either to hedge an existing portfolio position, or to fix a future rate of return or borrowing cost as an element in a bank's asset-liability management. Several banks had utilized the strip-buy strategy of taking long positions in a series of successive contracts to obtain a better rate than that available on a cash instrument of comparable maturity. The respondents believed their hedging operations to be successful in most cases, and were on balance satisfied with the results of their participation in the futures market. Margin and commission costs were not considered to be significant factors in relation to the interest and/or capital value preserved by hedging.

As spokesman for an institutional participant, William Maher, a vice president of New York's Citibank, thinks that an enduring state of economic uncertainty, coupled with the resulting volatility of interest rates, will impel an increasing number of financial institutions to seek relief in the futures market. Citing their utility in the execution of certain investment decisions, he notes in particular the opportunity afforded by futures to secure attractive yields on long-term bonds when interest rates are high without incurring the negative cost of carry (short-term rates above long-term) that often prevails during such periods.

Citibank has used interest rate futures since 1976 in conjunction with its investment portfolio. Though the bank has dealt in all of the outstanding contracts at one time or another, its highest level of activity has been in the 90-day T-bill contract. Maher is in most respects satisfied with the operation of the market and the conduct of its participants, and anticipates that Citibank will continue to be an active user so long as there exists a need to obtain price and yield protection.

James G. Wilson, senior vice president of Equibank in Pittsburgh, holds an equally optimistic view of the outlook for financial futures. Believing that they have already proven themselves to be important tools for asset-liability management, the head of the bank's investment department predicts a growth in their use comparable to that of negotiable certificates of deposit since their introduction in 1961. Equibank was first attracted to the futures market by the large discount (higher yields) offered by T-bill futures relative to cash rates in mid-1976.[2] Having at that time purchased strips of successive delivery dates, the bank realized substantial profits on the futures side of its long hedge as T-bill contracts moved sharply higher during the second half, allowing it to secure a yield level that was not seen in the cash market until over a year later. From its initial long hedge position in 90-day bill futures, the bank has dealt in the other contracts as well, moving beyond locking up a specific rate to capitalizing upon favorable changes in certain cash-to-futures relationships (trading the basis). The use of futures has not been limited to dealer or money center banks. Broadway National Bank of San Antonio sold Ginnie Mae contracts as it issued commitments to builders to purchase mortgages at specified prices. Gregory Crane, executive vice president, noted the difficulties encountered in placing short hedges when futures prices were selling at a discount to cash. The convergence of the two over time—described in Chapter Ten as a weakening basis—worked to the detriment of the hedge, underscoring the critical effect of basis changes on any type of hedging operation.

Mortgage Bankers and S&Ls

Mortgage bankers and savings and loan associations that produce a large number of mortgages use Ginnie Mae futures in a comparable manner. Their need to hedge is possibly more compelling than that of commercial banks. Without doing so, the industry practice of making advance commitments to buy or sell whole mortgages or mortgage-backed securities at

---

[2]The reader can refer back to Chapter Six, p. 210.

firm prices leaves an institution fully exposed to the risk of loss during the time required to conclude the other side of the transaction.

Customarily operating on a narrow and highly leveraged equity base, mortgage bankers are more vulnerable to interest rate swings than savings and loans, which have the questionable option of burying their rate miscalculations in their investment portfolios. As a consequence, mortgage bankers are as a group the most extensive users of Ginnie Mae futures. By the end of 1978, there were an estimated 50 mortgage banking firms which had used the futures market to some extent, of which as many as 10 were participating on a particularly large scale.

Fidelity Bond and Mortgage Corp. of Philadelphia has been involved in the market as a hedger since mid-1977. According to Hugh J. Campbell, Jr., vice president and hedge specialist at Fidelity, the Board of Trade's Ginnie Mae CDR contract is but one of several alternatives at the mortgage banking firm's disposal to hedge its production of government-insured (VA and FHA) mortgages. Whether he elects to go to the futures market in favor of making a mandatory or optional sale of individual mortgage loans, selling Ginnie Mae securities for immediate or forward delivery on a mandatory or optional "standby" basis, or obtaining a four-month commitment from Federal National Mortgage Association (Fannie Mae) will depend upon the comparative prices prevailing in any of these markets when a hedging decision is required.

In exercising his judgment as to the most advantageous time and vehicle with which to achieve a hedged position, Campbell is in effect "trading the basis." With changes in the cash-futures basis having narrowed considerably since the beginning of 1978, he regards an $8/32$nds futures premium over cash an optimum level at which to place a short hedge, and will be content to "unwind" the hedge if futures drop to a slight discount to cash. Otherwise, he is prepared to go through with the delivery procedure if it affords him a price advantage.

Campbell notes that the ambiguity of the original Ginnie Mae CDR contract, the purported drawback which prompted the creation of the Board of Trade and American Commodity Exchange certificate delivery contracts, is the feature which makes it an attractive vehicle for trading the basis. His view underscores the difference in attitude between purely defensive hedgers for whom basis change is an unwanted complication and those like himself who regard it as a profit opportunity.

Savings and loan associations have access to the same alternatives with which to hedge existing and anticipated mortgage commitments. As a group they have not used the Ginnie Mae futures market as extensively as have the mortgage bankers. Those S&Ls that have become involved, however, report highly favorable results. Westchester Federal Savings of New Rochelle, N.Y., initiated its first position to assure itself of what was considered an attractive yield on the planned reinvestment of $10 million CDs scheduled to mature in 1977. The association's long hedge strategy called for the purchase of 100 Ginnie Mae contracts with delivery dates which coincided with the maturities of the CDs in the portfolio.

During the time the long hedge was in place, the portfolio managers became more cognizant of the changing basis relationships between cash and futures prices in the two Ginnie Mae markets, and began placing their hedge positions at points where ensuing changes in the basis were most likely to work in their favor. A short hedge would be undertaken when the basis had closed to a historically narrow level, then reversed to a long hedge when the spread opened out to the wide side of its customary range.

Over the course of its first year in the futures market, Westchester Federal's hedging objective evolved from securing straight yield protection on an anticipated investment, to a profit center approach in which trades were undertaken to derive gains from disparities between the two related markets. According to John E. Dowling, president, the latter strategy has contributed markedly to realization of the association's earnings projections, more than justifying the commitment of time and resources.

Non-Financial Institutions

Non-financial corporations also have been slower than banks in availing themselves of the futures market. Whether their hesitation has been due to the relatively thin market for 90-day commercial paper futures or whether trading volume in that particular contract has not developed as quickly as the others on account of corporate disinterest, is something of a chicken-and-egg proposition.

Chicago-based Walter E. Heller & Co., Inc., a leading commercial and consumer finance company with $1.2 billion of its own commercial paper outstanding, has been engaged in trading commercial paper futures since their inception. According to F. D. Pedersen, vice president, financial, the company's objective is the straightforward hedging of borrowing costs on its commercial paper issues rather than the type of basis trading undertaken at Fidelity Bond and Mortgage and at Westchester Federal. Heller occupies a somewhat unique position in the market since, as one of the 41 approved issuers of contract-grade paper, it has the option of delivering its own paper in settlement of long positions.

Although the company's level of activity in the futures market is minuscule in comparison to the size of its actual paper issues, it is hampered by the illiquidity of the 90-day paper contract, often finding it difficult to move out of a position within a reasonable period without unduly affecting the price. The same problem occurs when unwinding spreads between commercial paper and T-bill futures. When it comes time to unwind, Pedersen states, there is often no one ready to take the other side of the commercial paper trade. Even with the company's prerogative of delivering its own paper, the 90-day maturity of the contract does not necessarily correlate well with the 20- to 30-day paper which are its most frequently issued maturities in the cash market. Though Heller will not be one of four approved issuers under the terms of the Board of Trade's proposed 30-day contract, Pedersen thinks that the availability of the shorter maturity will encourage more hedger participation, leading to a level of volume the present contract has not attained.

Some corporate borrowers have preferred to place their hedges by means of the 90-day T-bill contract. There is a feeling that the greater volume and liquidity of trading in that contract compensates for the disadvantage of cross-hedging, namely the larger basis risk than exists when hedging between like instruments.

Big Broker-Dealer Firms

The large broker-dealer firms trade futures for their own account to hedge securities inventories as well as execute orders for their institutional and retail customers. During the initial years a number of exchange members found themselves unprepared to educate and service clients who were interested in the new market. As with others, development was impeded by the interfacing of two theretofore distinct departments, commodity futures and fixed-income securities. Brokers had abundant expertise in both areas, but co-ordinating and integrating the two proved to be a time-consuming process.

While some firms chose their bond-trading departments in which to locate their newly established financial futures units, others preferred to contain the new function within their commodity divisions. A logical approach was to recruit specialists from both departments, having each merge his specialized knowledge into a team effort. Beyond the actual trading operations, the research and marketing efforts also needed to straddle, to use an apt expression, the two disciplines. The charting and related technical analysis, generally held to be a more integral part of futures trading than of fixed-income investment, usually came from the commodity side. Fundamental research, drawn for the most part from the bond and money markets, in all likelihood would be performed by analysts from those departments.

In the area of marketing, the most frequent point of contact with prospective hedge accounts for most firms would be their institutional sales departments. But here again, few if any institutional salespersons were knowledgeable about futures trading, and their commodity counterparts were equally unaccustomed to calling on banks, insurance companies and the like. Some firms had the salesman assigned to cover a particular account bring the financial futures specialist into the picture if the client indicated serious interest in the market. Other houses set out to establish and train a group of marketing specialists to solicit and service accounts on their own initiative, as well as providing support for other marketing personnel.

On the retail, or individual account side, the firm's most likely financial futures prospects were those existing commodity customers already being serviced by representatives in the branches who could call on their home office specialists for operational support and research information. Some firms offered managed-account programs in which clients authorize the account manager to take futures positions, including interest rate contracts, and liquidate them at his discretion.

Typical in structure, if not in size, is Merrill Lynch's approach to developing the interest rate futures market. The investment firm employs its own floor brokers at the Board of Trade and IMM, and in addition uses independent brokers when trading becomes especially active. Its private wire network connects the branch offices in the U.S. and abroad with both Chicago exchanges, as well as with the ACE trading floor in New York. Many of the branches are staffed with at least one commodity account executive who is qualified to discuss the interest rate complex with clients and enter any orders they agree upon. Daily market comments are sent over the Merrill Lynch newswire before the opening, and important developments which break during trading hours are announced over a system-wide speaker-phone hookup, affording account executives and their customers throughout the country equal access to timely information.

Research is conducted on a dual basis with a financial instrument unit in Chicago covering activity on the two trading floors, and the firm's money market and technical units in New York monitoring the cash markets. In addition to their own research, the Chicago and New York units may draw upon Merrill Lynch Government Securities Inc., the firm's dealer operation, for analytical and trading data.

Like the dealer banks and other non-bank dealers, Merrill Lynch Government Securities is a major user of interest rate futures to hedge its own inventory positions. As do other firms that execute futures transactions for their own account, as well as for customers, Merrill Lynch strictly segregates its broker and dealer functions. Hedge orders from the government securities division are placed on an equal footing with customer orders. Whenever there is a possible conflict over precedence, customer orders are given priority.

The Flow of Data

Access to current prices and related data is critical when dealing in such markets as interest rate futures, which can and do move with disquieting speed. Timely information also is essential in identifying and acting upon favorable spread or hedging opportunities which may be attainable only for the briefest period when two or more prices momentarily diverge, and then return to their usual relationship, as other market-watchers spot the disparity and hasten to take the appropriate action. When traders are confronted with such rapidly moving markets, the rudimentary sort of spread tables presented in the foregoing chapters will not suffice in guiding their execution of the more complex strategies.

A number of remote access data computing firms supply their customers with real-time price quotations, as well as an extensive price history against which market participants can gauge the validity of current transactions. Rapidata, a national firm headquartered in Fairfield, N.J., markets in conjunction with Telerate Systems Inc. such a combination of immediate and historical price information. To supplement current price quotations for all interest rate futures contracts from the two trading floors, the Telerate Historical Data Base provides cash price and yield information on almost all relevant money market instruments and U.S. government securities on a daily basis from 1975 and monthly since 1950. The data base also contains an array of money market, commercial banking, Federal Reserve and flow-of-funds statistics useful in conducting the type of supply-demand analysis described in Chapter Six.

Rapidata's proprietary contribution to the data package is PROBE, the company's time series statistical analysis system. Among its varied applications relating to financial reporting and analysis, the PROBE language generates cash-futures price data in a format designed to aid hedgers and spreaders in assessing a particular basis or spread relationship within the context of its historical boundaries. The system incorporates several statistical forecasting methods of varying complexity, ranging from simple regression analysis that can be understood and applied by traders without extensive training and experience in statistics to more advanced techniques. PROBE also provides for the cathode terminal electronic display of basis and spread charts, and the conduct of matrix analysis within parameters elected by the system's user.

An Idea Whose Time Came

The reaction of market observers to the extraordinary increase in trading volume during what is, in the case of most newly introduced contracts, a period of gradual growth and gestation has ranged from a booster-like "The surface hasn't been scratched yet" to the cynical "It's just another one of Wall Street's marketing gimmicks," although in this instance Wall Street per se was belatedly trying to climb aboard the bandwagon. Some congenital naysayers worried about the financial structure of the country being undermined by speculation in and possible manipulation of U.S. government securities for the purpose of influencing futures prices.

What is the future for interest rate futures? As with the forecasting of interest rates themselves, or the weather for that matter, the best one can offer is a hopefully well-informed opinion. Stripping away the hyperbole, the record of the first three years suggests that collectively they represent an idea whose time has come. As has often occurred during the history of innovation, the creators of the original Ginnie Mae contract may have achieved a more significant breakthrough than even they ever anticipated. *The New York Times,* not often given to overstatement, theorized that the new instruments could affect the way business is done in every sector of the money and capital markets.[3] One need not go far beyond that to pres-

---

[3]Financial Futures: New Hedge, Dec. 28, 1978, p. D-1.

ent a case for their becoming the most consequential new financial vehicle since the development of the mutual fund 50 years earlier.

Brokers and the exchanges themselves have been diligent in promoting the merits of the market for prospective hedgers and speculators. But their internal assessment, namely the price of a floor membership, is even more telling. Like any other investment, the price a prospective member is prepared to pay for the privilege of trading on the exchange floor is an indication of the return he hopes to secure on his outlay. At the going rates of $95,000 and $155,000 respectively, the cost of Board of Trade financial instrument and IMM memberships at year-end 1978 underscored the opinion of market insiders that there is where the trading action, hence commissions and profits, is and where it is likely to remain for some time.

The proposals by the two Chicago exchanges to add to their lists of interest rate contracts, and the eagerness of other exchanges to establish similar markets of their own have stimulated the bandwagon aura noted above. The New York Stock Exchange, its own pre-eminence as the country's, if not the world's, leading securities market threatened by competitive pressures on many sides, announced its intent to establish a financial instrument futures facility, The New York Futures Exchange, by 1980, on which interest rate as well as foreign currency contracts would be traded.

It was to be expected that, faced with investor disenchantment with their traditional wares, loss of the price protection of a fixed-commission schedule and competitive problems of their own, other exchanges and their membership would be eager to seize upon a new source of revenue. Equally understandable is the desire of the Chicago exchanges to remain the primary markets for the instruments they pioneered.

Amidst this somewhat feverish maneuvering for competitive advantage, the inevitable bad apples are sure to emerge from the bottom of the barrel with the intent of cashing in on a hot new game. However, a remarkable facet of the mushrooming of the market has been that its rapid growth has occurred without any vestige to date of scandal or questionable dealing, a commendation for the exchanges and their memberships as well as for the regulatory authorities. As volatile and capricious, therefore risky, as the market can be, there has never been any suggestion of impropriety by the brokers or their customers. It may very well be that the level of financial and trading sophistication that success in this market demands has kept the gullible and the slick operators who prey upon them away.

Besides the addition of new instruments to the original Ginnie Mae and 90-day T-bill contracts, a large part of the growth of trading volume in 1978 was the result of speculators' responding to the rise of short- and long-term interest rates to record highs. No futures market has endured for very long, however, let alone flourished to the extent the interest rate complex has done, purely on speculative activity. Without a minimum level of use by bona fide hedgers, a market will atrophy and in time disappear.

A survey of open positions taken by the Commodity Futures Trading Commission as of Nov. 30, 1977, indicated that over 40% of total Ginnie Mae positions and over 25% of those in the 90-day T-bill contract were held in what were designated as hedge accounts. On the same date hedgers were identified as being parties to nearly 60% of the open interest in government bond futures.[4] At the time of the survey, more than 130 securities dealers and banking institutions had initiated positions in at least one of the contracts within the interest rate complex, a substantial increase over the number of institutions active in the market as hedgers a year earlier. Those who claimed

---

[4]Ronald B. Hobson, Futures Trading in Financial Instruments, Division of Economics and Education, Commodity Futures Trading Commission, Washington, D.C. October 1978.

the surface had barely been scratched were referring to the minuscule percentage these figures represented of the total number of such institutions that might eventually enter the market.

The Regulatory Battle

The success of the market also gave rise to what was billed in the futures industry as The Great Regulatory Battle of 1978. As the federal agency mandated to oversee trading activity on the exchanges and related conduct by the members, the Commodity Futures Trading Commission has the authority to review proposed new contracts and determine before granting approval to trade them whether they fulfill a bona fide economic purpose and thereby serve the public interest. During the start-up phase of the Ginnie Mae and 90-day T-bill contracts, other agencies seemed to pay scant attention to what they may at the time have regarded as an experiment of no great importance. The indifferent attitudes of the Treasury Department, Federal Reserve and Securities and Exchange Commission changed, however, when the activity in the financial contracts no longer could be overlooked. All three agencies expressed concern that continued growth in the volume of futures trading could have an adverse effect on the securities underlying the contracts and, as a consequence, on the government securities market as a whole. They therefore took the position that one of the three should assume jurisdiction over the new market or, failing that, share responsibility with the CFTC on the grounds that the new contracts go beyond the accepted sense of commodity futures.

The bid by the Treasury, Fed and SEC came when the enabling legislation under which the futures commission operated was due for congressional renewal, and the agency's own future was for a time in doubt as critics charged it with being incapable of properly supervising the traditional commodity markets, let alone the new financial commodities. The issue was resolved to the commission's satisfaction when Congress extended its mandate and reaffirmed its sole jurisdiction over all futures trading on regulated exchanges. At the same time, however, the CFTC was directed to take under advisement the views of the other agencies concerned in deciding whether and with what qualifications any proposed additional contracts should be approved.

Following the settlement of the jurisdictional dispute, the Secretary of the Treasury requested that the futures commission take a "go-slow" attitude toward approving any additional interest rate contracts on the grounds that the burgeoning volume of trading could lead to manipulation in the cash government securities market. The Secretary's concern was that holders of large futures positions might attempt to influence prices by inciting artificial movement in the cash market. His reasoning was that, despite the vast volume of outstanding Treasury securities, it might be possible to engineer a temporary shortage or oversupply of those issues that constitute good delivery, leading to a desired change in the futures price.

Where it is difficult to envisage any private manipulation in the Treasury bill market in the face of the massive scale of the Federal Reserve's open market operations, it is conceivable that a thin outstanding supply or "float" of certain notes or long-term bonds might open the door to price manipulation. The mere possibility of such rigging might compel the Treasury to plan their financings in a way that they would otherwise not choose to do.

To provide the CFTC with further information on which to base its decision on the IMM's four-year note and other proposed contracts prior to their approval, the Treasury and Federal Reserve conducted their own surveys of the futures market for the purpose of ascertaining the effect of futures trading on price volatility in the cash market and the vulnerability of the latter to the type of manipulation described above.

Other Questions

A greater inhibition than the remote possibility of market manipulation has been the uncertainty in many instances whether the use of futures is an appropriate activity for fiduciary and public institutions. As stated earlier, the regulatory agencies charged with the supervision of national banks and federal savings and loan associations have approved, subject to certain guidelines and limitations, their dealing in interest rate futures. State-chartered banks and S&Ls have in most cases received no such authorization, leaving their participation subject to individual rulings by state banking commissions and other concerned agencies.

Legislative action may prove necessary to allow state and municipal treasuries and finance departments to hedge against the same market risks and interest costs to which private institutions are subject. Such enabling legislation was passed in California following an opinion by the state attorney general that the treasurer did not possess the authority to deal in futures contracts under the then-existing law.

The issue of the suitability of futures trading in any institutional context comes down to the matter of risk, specifically whether the use of futures increases or reduces it under a given set of circumstances. The extended discussion throughout the foregoing chapters should, if nothing else, have made it clear that there is a broad variety of applications to which these instruments may be put. Some applications are well-suited to, and in fact can materially contribute to, the realization of conservative investment strategies, just as others are patently inappropriate. It is the responsibility of the financial or investment manager to acquaint himself with the possibilities and limitations of a particular application or trading technique before determining whether it is fitted to the situation with which he is confronted. It is likewise the obligation of regulatory bodies to go beyond a knee-jerk reaction that futures are highly speculative, hence beyond the pale so far as prudent money management is concerned, and endeavor to apply the same criteria of risk evaluation.

The experience of recent years repeatedly has confirmed that we occupy a risk-ridden world, in the investment sphere as elsewhere. If it can be demonstrated that the financial risk of entering into a futures contract is measurably less than the risk of not doing so, the question of suitability should be rethought.

Interest rate futures are neither tools of the devil nor are they a panacea for all financial and investment ills. They have not made, and are not likely to make, risk obsolete. Their primary value, or economic utility if you will, is to provide additional flexibility in the management of certain types of risk, and (along the way) offer opportunities for profit to those who are accomplished in their use, as well certainly as losses for those not so adept. In the end, profits equal losses as in any market. Their distribution, however, is not necessarily, and probably never will be equal. There are few winners in any game.

The growth of the market, and the generally favorable opinion of those who have become involved with it, are very convincing answers to the question of whether it serves an economic purpose. Markets do not double and re-double in size merely because they feature an interesting new trading vehicle. Nor can they over the long run be planned or engineered. They exist so long as they satisfy needs. The record of the first three years suggests in a most emphatic manner that interest rate futures are satisfying a variety of needs of a growing number of participants. Whether they will become a permanent part of the financial landscape is impossible to predict with assurance. To hedge our forecast, the day may return when a 1% rise or fall in interest rates is once again considered a move of major magnitude. Until then, it is more than likely that the market will continue to thrive.

Appendix A
Bibliography and Suggested Additional Reading

Books

Credit and Capital Markets

Bonello, Frank J. *The Formulation of Expected Interest Rates—An Examination of Alternative Hypotheses*. East Lansing, Graduate School of Business Administration, Michigan State University, 1969.

Bradley, Stephen P. and Dwight B. Crane. *Management of Bank Portfolios*. New York, John Wiley & Sons, Inc., 1975.

Cohen, Jerome B., Edward D. Zinbarg and Arthur Zeikel. *Investment Analysis and Portfolio Management*. Homewood, Ill., Richard D. Irwin, Inc., 1977.

Conrad, Joseph W. *The Behavior of Interest Rates—A Progress Report*. New York, National Bureau of Economic Research, 1966.

Cook, Timothy Q. (Ed.). *Instruments of the Money Market*. Richmond, Va., Federal Reserve Bank of Richmond, 1977.

Darst, David M. *The Complete Bond Book—A Guide to All Types of Fixed-Income Securities*. New York, McGraw-Hill, Inc., 1975.

Duesenberry, James S. *Money and Credit: Impact and Control*. Englewood Cliffs, N.J., Prentice-Hall, Inc., 1964.

First Boston Corporation. *Handbook of the Securities of the United States Government and Federal Agencies and Related Money Market Instruments*. New York, 1978.

Friedman, Milton and Anna J. Schwartz. *A Monetary History of the United States, 1867-1960*. Princeton, N.J., Princeton University Press, 1963.

GNMA Mortgage-Backed Securities Dealers Association. *The Ginnie Mae Manual*. Homewood, Ill., Dow Jones-Irwin, 1978.

Guttentag, Jack M. and Philip Cagan (Ed.). *Essays on Interest Rates*. Volume I. New York, National Bureau of Economic Research, 1969.

Hawk, William A. *The U.S. Government Securities Market.* Chicago, Harris Trust and Savings Bank, 1976.

Henning, Charles N., William Pigott and Robert Haney Scott. *Financial Markets and the Economy.* Englewood Cliffs, N.J., Prentice-Hall, Inc., 1975.

Homer, Sidney. *A History of Interest Rates.* New Brunswick, N.J., Rutgers University Press, 1963.

————, *The Bond Buyer's Primer.* New York, Salomon Brothers, 1968.

————, *The Great American Bond Market—Selected Speeches,* Homewood, Ill., Dow Jones-Irwin, 1979.

———— and Richard I. Johannesen. *The Price of Money 1946-1969, An Analytical Study of United States and Foreign Interest Rates.* New Brunswick, N.J., Rutgers University Press, 1969.

———— and Martin L. Leibowitz. *Inside the Yield Book—New Tools for Bond Market Strategy.* Englewood Cliffs, N.J., Prentice-Hall, Inc. and New York, New York Institute of Finance, 1972.

Lindow, Wesley. *Inside the Money Market.* New York, Random House, 1972.

Malkiel, Burton G. *The Term Structure of Interest Rates—Expectations and Behavior Patterns.* Princeton, N.J., Princeton University Press, 1966.

Meiselman, David. *The Term Structure of Interest Rates.* Englewood Cliffs, N.J., Prentice-Hall, Inc., 1962.

Ritter, Lawrence S. and William L. Silber. *Principles of Money, Banking, and Financial Markets.* New York, Basic Books, Inc., 1974.

Roll, Richard. *The Behavior of Interest Rates—An Application of the Efficient Market Model to U.S. Treasury Bills.* New York, Basic Books, Inc., 1970.

Roosa, Robert V. *Federal Reserve Operations in the Money and Government Securities Markets.* New York, Federal Reserve Bank of New York, 1956.

Senft, Dexter E. *Inside Pass-Through Securities.* New York, First Boston Corporation, 1978.

Sprinkel, Beryl W. *Money and Markets—A Monetarist View.* Homewood, Ill., Richard D. Irwin, Inc., 1971.

Stigum, Marcia. *How to Turn Your Money Into More Money Quickly and Safely.* Homewood, Ill., Dow Jones-Irwin, 1976.

————, *The Money Market: Myth, Reality and Practice.* Homewood, Ill., Dow Jones-Irwin, 1979.

Wrightsman, Dwayne. *An Introduction to Monetary Theory and Policy.* New York, The Free Press, 1971.

Futures Markets

Amex Commodities Exchange, Inc. *Rules of the ACE GNMA Futures Contract.* New York, 1978.

————, *Trading in the ACE GNMA Futures Contract,* New York, 1978.

Arthur Andersen & Co. *Interest Rate Futures Contracts—Accounting and Control Techniques for Banks.* Chicago, 1978.

Arthur, Henry B. *Commodity Futures as a Business Management Tool.* Cambridge, Mass., Graduate School of Business Administration, Harvard University, 1971.

Baer, J. B. and O. G. Saxon. *Commodity Exchanges and Futures Trading.* New York, Harper & Row, 1947.

Berlin, Bruce S. *Corporate Use of Commodity Futures.* New York, The Conference Board, 1972.

Chicago Board of Trade. *Commodity Trading Manual.* Chicago, 1976.

———, *Statistical Annual.* Chicago, 1978.

———, *An Introduction to the Interest Rate Futures Market.* Chicago, 1977.

———, *Hedging Interest Rate Risks.* Chicago, 1977.

———, *Making and Taking Delivery on Interest Rate Futures Contracts,* Chicago, 1977.

Chicago Mercantile Exchange. *Opportunities in T-Bills.* Chicago, 1975.

———, *IMM Treasury Bill Futures Contract Specifications.* Chicago, 1975.

Commodity Futures Trading Commission. *Financial Futures Markets and Federal Regulation.* Washington, D.C., 1978.

Commodity Research Bureau, Inc. *Commodity Year Book.* New York, Published annually.

Gold, Gerald. *Modern Commodity Futures Trading.* New York, Commodity Research Bureau, Inc., 1972.

Gould, Bruce E. *Dow Jones Guide to Commodities Trading.* Homewood, Ill., Dow Jones-Irwin, 1973.

Hieronymus, Thomas A. *Economics of Futures Trading for Commercial and Personal Profit.* New York, Commodity Research Bureau, Inc., 1971.

Hobson, Ronald B. *Futures Trading in Financial Instruments.* Washington, D.C., Commodity Futures Trading Commission, 1978.

Kroll, Stanley and Irwin Shishko. *The Commodity Futures Market Guide.* New York, Harper & Row, 1973.

Loosigian, A. M. & Co. *An Introduction to the T-Bill Futures Market.* Stamford, Conn., 1976.

Teweles, Richard J., Charles V. Harlow and Herbert L. Stone. *The Commodity Futures Trading Guide; The Science and Art of Sound Commodity Trading.* New York, McGraw-Hill, Inc., 1969.

Additional Books on Specific Topics

Cootner, Paul H. (Ed.). *The Random Character of Stock Market Prices.* Cambridge, Mass., The MIT Press, 1964.

Edwards, R. D. and John Magee, Jr. *Technical Analysis of Stock Trends.* Springfield, Mass., Stock Trend Service, 5th edition, 1973.

Klein, Frederick C. and John A. Prestbo. *News and The Market.* Chicago, Henry Regnery Company, 1974.

Silk, Leonard S. and M. Louise Curley. *A Primer on Business Forecasting.* New York, Random House, 1970.

Articles

Ederington, Lewis. "The New Futures Markets and Financial Instruments as Hedging Instruments," *Journal of Finance.* December 1978, pp. 16-20.

Ganis, David R. "All About the GNMA Mortgage-Backed Securities Market," *Real Estate Review.* Winter, 1973, pp. 55-60.

———, "GNMA Futures Market Has Advantages, But Not a Way To Make Or Take Delivery," *The Mortgage Banker,* January 1976, pp. 16-23.

———, "Cash Market Or Futures Market? Which One Is Better for Mortgage Bankers?" *The Mortgage Banker.* November 1978, pp. 7-11.

Kasriel, Paul. "Hedging Interest Rate Fluctuations," *Business Conditions.* Federal Reserve Bank of Chicago, April 1976, pp. 3-10.

Puglisi, Donald. "Is the Futures Market for Treasury Bills Efficient?" *Journal of Portfolio Management.* Winter, 1978. pp. 64-67.

Rattner, R. Lillian. "Another Look At Hedging in the GNMA Futures Market," *Savings Bank Journal.* April 1977, pp. 35-50.

Stevens, Neil A. "A Mortgage Futures Market: Its Development, Uses, Benefits and Costs," *Federal Reserve Bank of St. Louis Review,* April 1976, pp. 20-27.

Other Sources of Information

The Chicago Board of Trade and International Monetary Market publish and distribute upon request interest rate futures market newsletters.

The respective addresses are:

Financial Instruments Marketing Department
Chicago Board of Trade
LaSalle at Jackson
Chicago Il. 60604   Tel: 312/435-3500

International Monetary Market
444 West Jackson Boulevard
Chicago, Il. 60606   Tel: 312/648-1000

Daily futures price quotations and accompanying commentaries are carried in *The Wall Street Journal, New York Times, Journal of Commerce* and other major newspapers.

These magazines cover futures market activity on a regular basis:

Barron's—22 Cortlandt St., New York, N.Y. 10007   Tel: 212/285-5243

Forbes Magazine—60 Fifth Avenue, New York, N.Y. 10011   Tel: 212/675-7500

Financial World—919 Third Avenue, New York, N.Y. 10022   Tel: 212/826-4360

Commodities—219 Parkade, Cedar Falls, Iowa 50613   Tel: 319/277-6341

Other publications which upon occasion contain pertinent money and bond market information include:

American Banker—525 West 42nd St., New York, N.Y. 10036   Tel: 212/563-1900

Money Manager and *The Bond Buyer*—1 State Street Plaza, New York, N.Y. 10004   Tel: 212/943-8207

Securities Week—1221 Avenue of the Americas, New York, N.Y. 10020   Tel: 212/997-6410

Appendix B
Selected Cash and Futures Market Yields by Month, 1976-1978

1976

First of Month	CASH MARKET								FUTURES MARKETS (Nearby Contracts)		
	90-Day Bills	1-Year Bills	30-Day Comml. Paper	90-Day Comml. Paper	GNMA 8%	20-Year Treas. Bonds	Federal Funds	M$_1$ % Rate Change	90-Day Bill Futures	GNMA 8% Futures	Treas. Bond Futures
Jan.	5.18%	5.58%	5.38%	5.63%	8.57%	7.83%	4.87%	5.7%	5.35%	8.55%	
Feb.	4.71	5.57	4.63	5.00	8.35	7.85	4.77	8.1	4.91	8.43	
Mar.	5.00	6.01	4.88	5.25	8.37	7.80	4.84	5.6	5.44	8.56	
Apr.	4.96	5.78	4.88	5.13	8.37	7.90	4.82	8.8	5.67	8.43	
May	4.90	5.65	4.75	5.00	8.30	7.95	5.29	7.2	5.50	8.47	
June	5.48	6.08	5.50	5.75	8.65	8.12	5.48	0.8	5.66	8.60	
July	5.35	5.89	5.50	5.75	8.57	7.98	5.31	2.4	6.03	8.70	
Aug.	5.16	5.63	5.13	5.38	8.50	8.01	5.29	6.7	5.43	8.48	
Sept.	5.13	5.56	5.00	5.25	8.34	7.85	5.25	3.9	5.08	8.34	
Oct.	5.10	5.13	5.13	5.38	8.24	7.78	5.03	12.9	5.28	8.34	
Nov.	4.87	5.20	4.83	5.13	8.16	7.73	4.95	1.9	5.03	8.30	
Dec.	4.50	4.71	4.63	4.75	7.85	7.48	4.65	7.7	4.43	7.88	
Ave.	5.03%	5.57%	5.02%	5.28%	8.36%	7.86%	5.05%	6.0%	5.32%	8.42%	

Sources: Salomon Brothers *Analytical Record of Yields and Yield Spreads*
Federal Reserve Bulletin
The Wall Street Journal

1977			CASH MARKET						FUTURES MARKETS (Nearby Contracts)		
First of Month	90-day Bills	1-Year Bills	30-Day Comml. Paper	90-Day Comml. Paper	GNMA 8%	20-Year Treas. Bonds	Federal Funds	M₁ % Rate Change	90-Day Bill Futures	GNMA 8% Futures	Treas. Bond Futures
Jan.	4.33%	4.73%	4.50%	4.63%	7.68%	7.16%	4.61%	8.8%	4.60%	7.85%	
Feb.	4.72	5.35	4.63	4.88	8.07	7.68	4.68	5.3	5.12	8.25	
Mar.	4.70	5.23	4.63	4.75	8.19	7.74	4.69	7.6	4.82	8.29	
Apr.	4.53	5.16	4.63	4.75	8.16	7.69	4.73	13.9	5.12	8.27	
May	4.68	5.40	4.63	4.88	8.18	7.68	5.35	1.5	5.05	8.26	
June	5.02	5.41	5.30	5.40	8.16	7.65	5.39	7.1	5.05	8.11	
July	5.00	5.65	5.25	5.38	8.05	7.50	5.42	11.8	5.35	8.04	
Aug.	5.39	6.11	5.38	5.50	8.18	7.62	5.90	6.2	5.63	8.13	
Sept.	5.56	6.16	5.80	5.88	8.14	7.51	6.14	8.7	5.64	8.11	
Oct.	5.90	6.62	6.13	6.25	8.21	7.61	6.47	10.9	6.35	8.27	7.73
Nov.	6.21	6.54	6.38	6.55	8.36	7.80	6.51	0.4	6.43	8.37	7.92
Dec.	6.04	6.55	6.30	6.50	8.34	7.75	6.56	7.2	6.15	8.29	7.84
Ave.	5.17%	5.74%	5.30%	5.45%	8.14%	7.62%	5.54%	7.5%	5.44%	8.19%	7.83%

1978

	CASH MARKET								FUTURES MARKETS (Nearby Contracts)		
First of Month	90-Day Bills	1-Year Bills	30-Day Comml. Paper	90-Day Comml. Paper	GNMA 8%	20-Year Treas. Bonds	Federal Funds	M_1 % Rate Change	90-Day Bill Futures	GNMA 8% Futures	Treas. Bond Futures
Jan.	6.12%	6.55%	6.60%	6.63%	8.57%	7.95%	6.70%	9.6%	6.54%	8.59%	8.12%
Feb.	6.42	6.81	6.50	6.75	8.70	8.09	6.78	-1.1	6.61	8.72	8.28
Mar.	6.42	6.88	6.50	6.55	8.82	8.16	6.79	3.5	6.49	8.68	8.31
Apr.	6.47	6.96	6.55	6.55	8.86	8.28	6.89	19.0	6.94	8.89	8.42
May	6.34	7.28	6.70	6.88	8.93	8.31	7.36	8.0	6.85	8.90	8.47
June	6.65	7.53	7.13	7.25	9.18	8.47	7.60	7.5	6.74	9.11	8.58
July	7.01	7.79	7.65	7.80	9.32	8.63	7.81	4.8	7.40	9.40	8.74
Aug.	6.78	7.73	7.50	7.75	9.24	8.56	8.04	8.5	7.07	9.17	8.66
Sept.	7.53	8.01	7.80	8.00	9.07	8.38	8.45	13.8	7.57	8.99	8.48
Oct.	7.98	8.45	8.45	8.63	9.18	8.57	8.96	1.7	8.32	9.27	8.74
Nov.	8.75	9.20	9.13	9.30	9.50	8.86	9.76	-2.0	9.27	9.38	8.87
Dec.	9.00	9.44	9.88	10.25	9.34	8.73	10.03	1.7	8.95	9.43	8.77
Ave.	7.12%	7.72%	7.53%	7.75%	9.06%	8.42%	7.93%	6.3%	7.40%	9.04%	8.54%

Appendix C
Selected Formulas

1. Treasury Bill Discount

$$\frac{\text{Dollar}}{\text{Discount}} = \frac{\text{Face}}{\text{Amount}} \times \frac{\text{Discount}}{\text{Yield}} \times \frac{\text{Days to Maturity}}{360}$$

$$\$20{,}000 = \$1 \text{ million} \times .08 \times \frac{90}{360}$$

2. Purchase Price for Given Maturity and Discount Yield

$$\frac{\text{Purchase}}{\text{Price}} = \frac{\text{Face}}{\text{Amount}} - \frac{\text{Dollar}}{\text{Discount}}$$

$$\$980{,}000 = \$1 \text{ million} - \$20{,}000$$

The same calculation applies to smaller dollar amounts as well. The purchase of a bill with $10,000 face value at the same 8% discount, for example, is $9,800.

3. Bond Equivalent Yield

$$\frac{\text{Bond}}{\text{Equivalent}} = \frac{\text{Dollar Discount}}{\text{Purchase Price}} \times \frac{365}{\text{Days to Maturity}} \times 100$$

$$8.27\% = \frac{\$20{,}000}{\$980{,}000} \times \frac{365}{90} \times 100$$

Because interest on bonds and notes is computed on the basis of a 365-day year rather than the 360-day discount basis, the bond equivalent yield is always higher than the discount yield. Therefore, the 8% discount on the 90-day bill used in the calculation above works out to a 8.27% coupon equivalent.

4. Yield on A Treasury Bill Sold Before Maturity

$$\text{Yield} = \frac{\text{Sale Price} - \text{Purchase Price}}{\text{Purchase Price}} \times \frac{365}{\text{No. of days held}} \times 100$$

$$8.76\% = \frac{\$990,625 - \$980,000}{\$980,000} \times \frac{365}{45} \times 100$$

Hence, the above bill, if sold after 45 days at a 7.50 discount would provide the holder with a coupon equivalent yield of 8.76% for that period. This is another example of the yield curve ride discussed in Chapters Two and Eleven, with the added benefit of a general decline in interest rates during the 45-day holding period.

5. Current Coupon Yield

$$\frac{\text{Current}}{\text{Yield}} = \frac{\text{Coupon Rate}}{\text{Market Price}}$$

$$8.33\% = \frac{80}{960}$$

Thus a bond bearing an 8% coupon provides a current yield of 8.33% at a market price of 96.

6. Yield to Maturity (Approximate)

$$\text{Yield to Maturity} = \frac{\begin{array}{c}\text{Coupon} \\ \text{Rate}\end{array} \begin{array}{c}\text{Premium} \\ \text{or} \\ \text{Discount}\end{array} \text{ or } \div \begin{array}{c}\text{Years to} \\ \text{Maturity}\end{array}}{\dfrac{\text{Market}}{\text{Price}} + \dfrac{\text{Par}}{\text{Value}} \div 2}$$

$$8.37\% = \frac{80 + \left(\dfrac{40}{20}\right)}{(960 + 1000) \div 2} = \frac{82}{980}$$

Yield to maturity of the above bond, assuming a 20-year maturity, is 8.37%. The increase over current yield (8.37% − 8.33%) stems from the amortization of the 4-point discount over the 20-year term. If the bond were selling at a 4-point premium the YTM would be proportionately less than the current yield.

7. Dollar Discount for Delivery on 90-day T-bill Futures Contracts

$$\frac{\text{Dollar}}{\text{Discount}} = \left(100 - \frac{\text{Contract}}{\text{Index}}\right) \times \$1 \text{ million} \times \frac{90}{360}$$

$$\$21,000 = (100 - 91.60) \times \$1 \text{ million} \times \frac{90}{360}$$

8. Delivery Payment on 90-day T-Bill Contract

Payment = $1 million − Dollar Discount

$979,000 = $1 million − $21,000

If 91- or 92-day bills were delivered, as is allowed under the terms of the IMM contract, a further price adjustment would be necessary to provide for the different maturity.

9. Cash—Nearby Futures Equilibrium Price

Equilibrium
Futures Price $\quad = 100 -$
Of Nearby Contract

$$\frac{\begin{array}{l}\text{Basis Point} \\ \text{Difference} \\ \text{Between} \\ \text{Contracts}\end{array} \times \begin{array}{l}\text{Remaining Life} \\ \text{Nearby Futures}\end{array} + \begin{array}{l}\text{Discount} \\ \text{Yields} \\ \text{Deliverable} \\ \text{Bill}\end{array}}{\text{Remaining Life (Days) of Deliverable Bill}}$$

$$90.10 \quad = 100 - \frac{(9.70 - 9.40) \times 60 + 9.70}{90}$$

If, for example, September 90-day T-bill futures are priced at 90.30 when September 21 cash bills are priced at a 9.40 discount and December 21 cash bills are priced at a 9.70 discount, it is theoretically possible to secure a 20-basis point or $500 arbitrage profit by selling the September futures contract and buying the December 21 cash bill for eventual delivery purposes. The 90.10 equilibrium futures price is only a theoretical price, however, and the indicated 20-basis point disparity may not be realized under actual trading conditions.

10. Hedged Discount Yield on Treasury Bills Sold on Futures Non-delivery Dates

$$\begin{array}{l}\text{Hedged} \\ \text{Discount} \\ \text{Yield}\end{array} = \begin{array}{l}\text{Cash Bill} \\ \text{Cost Yield}\end{array} + \left[\frac{\begin{array}{l}\text{Days Remaining} \\ \text{To Maturity When Sold}\end{array}}{\text{Days Held}} \left(\begin{array}{l}\text{Cash Bill} \\ \text{Cost Yield}\end{array} - \begin{array}{l}\text{Futures} \\ \text{Sale} \\ \text{Yield}\end{array}\right)\right]$$

$$7.24 = 7.32 + \frac{90}{90} \times (7.32 - 7.40)$$

Repeating the hedged yield curve ride example cited in Chapter Eleven, Page 369, a combination of futures contract sold at the price equivalent of a 7.40 discount and the deliverable cash bill purchased at a 7.32 discount would lock-in a yield of 7.24% for three months, a 42-basis point improvement over the available yield on a 90-day bill as of the same purchase date.

Appendix D
Tables of Prices and Yields

1. Ginnie Mae 8% Prices and Related Yields

Price	Yield	Price	Yield	Price	Yield	Price	Yield	Price	Yield	Price	Yield	Price	Yield
89-00	9.572	91-00	9.259	93-00	8.954	95-00	8.659	97-00	8.371	99-00	8.092	101-00	7.820
89-01	9.567	91-01	9.254	93-01	8.950	95-01	8.654	97-01	8.367	99-01	8.088	101-01	7.816
89-02	9.562	91-02	9.249	93-02	8.945	95-02	8.649	97-02	8.362	99-02	8.083	101-02	7.812
89-03	9.557	91-03	9.244	93-03	8.940	95-03	8.645	97-03	8.358	99-03	8.079	101-03	7.807
89-04	9.552	91-04	9.239	93-04	8.935	95-04	8.640	97-04	8.354	99-04	8.075	101-04	7.803
89-05	9.547	91-05	9.234	93-05	8.931	95-05	8.636	97-05	8.349	99-05	8.070	101-05	7.799
89-06	9.543	91-06	9.230	93-06	8.926	95-06	8.631	97-06	8.345	99-06	8.066	101-06	7.795
89-07	9.538	91-07	9.225	93-07	8.921	95-07	8.627	97-07	8.340	99-07	8.062	101-07	7.791
89-08	9.533	91-08	9.220	93-08	8.917	95-08	8.622	97-08	8.336	99-08	8.058	101-08	7.787
89-09	9.528	91-09	9.215	93-09	8.912	95-09	8.618	97-09	8.332	99-09	8.053	101-09	7.782
89-10	9.523	91-10	9.210	93-10	8.907	95-10	8.613	97-10	8.327	99-10	8.049	101-10	7.778
89-11	9.518	91-11	9.206	93-11	8.903	95-11	8.609	97-11	8.323	99-11	8.045	101-11	7.774
89-12	9.513	91-12	9.201	93-12	8.898	95-12	8.604	97-12	8.318	99-12	8.040	101-12	7.770
89-13	9.508	91-13	9.196	93-13	8.893	95-13	8.600	97-13	8.314	99-13	8.036	101-13	7.766
89-14	9.503	91-14	9.191	93-14	8.889	95-14	8.595	97-14	8.310	99-14	8.032	101-14	7.761
89-15	9.498	91-15	9.186	93-15	8.884	95-15	8.591	97-15	8.305	99-15	8.028	101-15	7.757
89-16	9.493	91-16	9.182	93-16	8.879	95-16	8.586	97-16	8.301	99-16	8.023	101-16	7.753
89-17	9.488	91-17	9.177	93-17	8.875	95-17	8.581	97-17	8.296	99-17	8.019	101-17	7.749
89-18	9.483	91-18	9.172	93-18	8.870	95-18	8.577	97-18	8.292	99-18	8.015	101-18	7.745
89-19	9.478	91-19	9.167	93-19	8.866	95-19	8.572	97-19	8.288	99-19	8.010	101-19	7.741
89-20	9.473	91-20	9.163	93-20	8.861	95-20	8.568	97-20	8.283	99-20	8.006	101-20	7.737
89-21	9.468	91-21	9.158	93-21	8.856	95-21	8.563	97-21	8.279	99-21	8.002	101-21	7.732
89-22	9.463	91-22	9.153	93-22	8.852	95-22	8.559	97-22	8.274	99-22	7.998	101-22	7.728
89-23	9.458	91-23	9.148	93-23	8.847	95-23	8.554	97-23	8.270	99-23	7.993	101-23	7.724
89-24	9.454	91-24	9.143	93-24	8.842	95-24	8.550	97-24	8.266	99-24	7.989	101-24	7.720
89-25	9.449	91-25	9.139	93-25	8.838	95-25	8.545	97-25	8.261	99-25	7.985	101-25	7.716
89-26	9.444	91-26	9.134	93-26	8.833	95-26	8.541	97-26	8.257	99-26	7.981	101-26	7.712
89-27	9.439	91-27	9.129	93-27	8.828	95-27	8.536	97-27	8.252	99-27	7.976	101-27	7.707
89-28	9.434	91-28	9.124	93-28	8.824	95-28	8.532	97-28	8.248	99-28	7.972	101-28	7.703
89-29	9.429	91-29	9.120	93-29	8.819	95-29	8.527	97-29	8.244	99-29	7.968	101-29	7.699
89-30	9.424	91-30	9.115	93-30	8.815	95-30	8.523	97-30	8.239	99-30	7.964	101-30	7.695
89-31	9.419	91-31	9.110	93-31	8.810	95-31	8.518	97-31	8.235	99-31	7.959	101-31	7.691
90-00	9.414	92-00	9.105	94-00	8.805	96-00	8.514	98-00	8.231	100-00	7.955	102-00	7.687
90-01	9.409	92-01	9.101	94-01	8.801	96-01	8.509	98-01	8.226	100-01	7.951	102-01	7.683
90-02	9.404	92-02	9.096	94-02	8.796	96-02	8.505	98-02	8.222	100-02	7.947	102-02	7.678
90-03	9.400	92-03	9.091	94-03	8.791	96-03	8.500	98-03	8.218	100-03	7.942	102-03	7.674
90-04	9.395	92-04	9.086	94-04	8.787	96-04	8.496	98-04	8.213	100-04	7.938	102-04	7.670
90-05	9.390	92-05	9.082	94-05	8.782	96-05	8.492	98-05	8.209	100-05	7.934	102-05	7.666
90-06	9.385	92-06	9.077	94-06	8.778	96-06	8.487	98-06	8.204	100-06	7.930	102-06	7.662
90-07	9.380	92-07	9.072	94-07	8.773	96-07	8.483	98-07	8.200	100-07	7.925	102-07	7.658
90-08	9.375	92-08	9.067	94-08	8.768	96-08	8.478	98-08	8.196	100-08	7.921	102-08	7.654
90-09	9.370	92-09	9.063	94-09	8.764	96-09	8.474	98-09	8.191	100-09	7.917	102-09	7.650
90-10	9.365	92-10	9.058	94-10	8.759	96-10	8.469	98-10	8.187	100-10	7.913	102-10	7.645
90-11	9.360	92-11	9.053	94-11	8.755	96-11	8.465	98-11	8.183	100-11	7.908	102-11	7.641

1. Ginnie Mae 8% Prices and Related Yields (Continued)

90-12 9.356	92-12 9.048	94-12 8.750	96-12 8.460	98-12 8.178	100-12 7.904	102-12 7.637
90-13 9.351	92-13 9.044	94-13 8.745	96-13 8.456	98-13 8.174	100-13 7.900	102-13 7.633
90-14 9.346	92-14 9.039	94-14 8.741	96-14 8.451	98-14 8.170	100-14 7.896	102-14 7.629
90-15 9.341	92-15 9.034	94-15 8.736	96-15 8.447	98-15 8.165	100-15 7.892	102-15 7.625
90-16 9.336	92-16 9.029	94-16 8.732	96-16 8.442	98-16 8.161	100-16 7.887	102-16 7.621
90-17 9.331	92-17 9.025	94-17 8.727	96-17 8.438	98-17 8.157	100-17 7.883	102-17 7.617
90-18 9.326	92-18 9.020	94-18 8.723	96-18 8.433	98-18 8.152	100-18 7.879	102-18 7.613
90-19 9.322	92-19 9.015	94-19 8.718	96-19 8.429	98-19 8.148	100-19 7.875	102-19 7.608
90-20 9.317	92-20 9.011	94-20 8.713	96-20 8.425	98-20 8.144	100-20 7.870	102-20 7.604
90-21 9.312	92-21 9.006	94-21 8.709	96-21 8.420	98-21 8.139	100-21 7.866	102-21 7.600
90-22 9.307	92-22 9.001	94-22 8.704	96-22 8.416	98-22 8.135	100-22 7.862	102-22 7.596
90-23 9.302	92-23 8.996	94-23 8.700	96-23 8.411	98-23 8.131	100-23 7.858	102-23 7.592
90-24 9.297	92-24 8.992	94-24 8.695	96-24 8.407	98-24 8.126	100-24 7.854	102-24 7.588
90-25 9.292	92-25 8.987	94-25 8.691	96-25 8.402	98-25 8.122	100-25 7.849	102-25 7.584
90-26 9.288	92-26 8.982	94-26 8.686	96-26 8.398	98-26 8.118	100-26 7.845	102-26 7.580
90-27 9.283	92-27 8.978	94-27 8.681	96-27 8.393	98-27 8.113	100-27 7.841	102-27 7.576
90-28 9.278	92-28 8.973	94-28 8.677	96-28 8.389	98-28 8.109	100-28 7.837	102-28 7.572
90-29 9.273	92-29 8.968	94-29 8.672	96-29 8.385	98-29 8.105	100-29 7.833	102-29 7.567
90-30 9.268	92-30 8.964	94-30 8.668	96-30 8.380	98-30 8.101	100-30 7.828	102-30 7.563
90-31 9.263	92-31 8.959	94-31 8.663	96-31 8.376	98-31 8.096	100-31 7.824	102-31 7.559

Source: Financial Publishing Company

2. Decimal Equivalents of 32nds per $1,000

32nds	Per $1,000	32nds	Per $1,000
1	$ 31.25	17	$531.25
2	62.50	18	562.50
3	93.75	19	593.75
4	125.00	20	625.00
5	156.25	21	656.25
6	187.50	22	687.50
7	218.75	23	718.75
8	250.00	24	750.00
9	281.25	25	781.25
10	312.50	26	812.50
11	343.75	27	843.75
12	375.00	28	875.00
13	406.25	29	906.25
14	437.50	30	937.50
15	468.75	31	968.75
16	500.00	32	1000.00

3. Treasury Bond Prices and Yields 8% Coupon

85-00 to 87-31	88-00 to 90-31	91-00 to 93-31	94-00 to 96-31	97-00 to 99-31
85-00 9.714	88-00 9.336	91-00 8.977	98-00 8.635	97-00 8.310
85-01 9.710	88-01 9.332	91-01 8.973	94-01 8.632	97-01 8.307
85-02 9.706	88-02 9.328	91-02 8.969	94-02 8.628	97-02 8.304
85-03 9.702	88-03 9.324	91-03 8.966	94-03 8.625	97-03 8.300
85-04 9.698	88-04 9.320	91-04 8.962	94-04 8.621	97-04 8.297
85-05 9.694	88-05 9.316	91-05 8.958	94-05 8.618	97-05 8.294
85-06 9.690	88-06 9.313	91-06 8.955	94-06 8.614	97-06 8.290
85-07 9.686	88-07 9.309	91-07 8.951	94-07 8.611	97-07 8.287
85-08 9.682	88-08 9.305	91-08 8.947	94-08 8.608	97-08 8.284
85-09 9.678	88-09 9.301	91-09 8.944	94-09 8.604	97-09 8.280
85-10 9.674	88-10 9.297	91-10 8.940	94-10 8.601	97-10 8.277
85-11 9.670	88-11 9.294	91-11 8.937	94-11 8.597	97-11 8.274
85-12 9.666	88-12 9.290	91-12 8.933	94-12 8.594	97-12 8.271
85-13 9.662	88-13 9.286	91-13 8.929	94-13 8.590	97-13 8.267

3. Treasury Bond Prices and Yields 8% Coupon (Continued)

Price	Yield	Price	Yield	Price	Yield	Price	Yield	Price	Yield
85-14	9.658	88-14	9.282	91-14	8.926	94-14	8.587	97-14	8.264
85-15	9.654	88-15	9.278	91-15	8.922	94-15	8.583	97-15	8.261
85-16	9.650	88-16	9.274	91-16	8.918	94-16	8.580	97-16	8.257
85-17	9.646	88-17	9.271	91-17	8.915	94-17	8.577	97-17	8.254
85-18	9.642	88-18	9.267	91-18	8.911	94-18	8.573	97-18	8.251
85-19	9.638	88-19	9.263	91-19	8.908	94-19	8.570	97-19	8.248
85-20	9.634	88-20	9.259	91-20	8.904	94-20	8.566	97-20	8.244
85-21	9.630	88-21	9.255	91-21	8.900	94-21	8.563	97-21	8.241
85-22	9.626	88-22	9.252	91-22	8.897	94-22	8.559	97-22	8.238
85-23	9.622	88-23	9.248	91-23	8.893	94-23	8.556	97-23	8.235
85-24	9.618	88-24	9.244	91-24	8.890	94-24	8.553	97-24	8.231
85-25	9.614	88-25	9.240	91-25	8.886	94-25	8.549	97-25	8.228
85-26	9.610	88-26	9.237	91-26	8.882	94-26	8.546	97-26	8.225
85-27	9.606	88-27	9.233	91-27	8.879	94-27	8.542	97-27	8.221
85-28	9.602	88-28	9.229	91-28	8.875	94-28	8.539	97-28	8.218
85-29	9.598	88-29	9.225	91-29	8.872	94-29	8.535	97-29	8.215
85-30	9.594	88-30	9.221	91-30	8.868	94-30	8.532	97-30	8.212
85-31	9.590	88-31	9.218	91-31	8.864	94-31	8.529	97-31	8.208
86-00	9.586	89-00	9.214	92-00	8.861	95-00	8.525	98-00	8.205
86-01	9.582	89-01	9.210	92-01	8.857	95-01	8.522	98-01	8.202
86-02	9.578	89-02	9.206	92-02	8.854	95-02	8.518	98-02	8.199
86-03	9.574	89-03	9.203	92-03	8.850	95-03	8.515	98-03	8.195
86-04	9.570	89-04	9.199	92-04	8.847	95-04	8.512	98-04	8.192
86-05	9.566	89-05	9.195	92-05	8.843	95-05	8.508	98-05	8.189
86-06	9.562	89-06	9.191	92-06	8.839	95-06	8.505	98-06	8.186
86-07	9.558	89-07	9.188	92-07	8.836	95-07	8.501	98-07	8.182
86-08	9.554	89-08	9.184	92-08	8.832	95-08	8.498	98-08	8.179
86-09	9.550	89-09	9.180	92-09	8.829	95-09	8.495	98-09	8.176
86-10	9.546	89-10	9.176	92-10	8.825	95-10	8.491	98-10	8.173
86-11	9.542	89-11	9.172	92-11	8.822	95-11	8.488	98-11	8.169
86-12	9.538	89-12	9.169	92-12	8.818	95-12	8.484	98-12	8.166
86-13	9.534	89-13	9.165	92-13	8.814	95-13	8.481	98-13	8.163
86-14	9.530	89-14	9.161	92-14	8.811	95-14	8.478	98-14	8.160
86-15	9.526	89-15	9.158	92-15	8.807	95-15	8.474	98-15	8.157
86-16	9.522	89-16	9.154	92-16	8.804	95-16	8.471	98-16	8.153
86-17	9.518	89-17	9.150	92-17	8.800	95-17	8.467	98-17	8.150
86-18	9.515	89-18	9.146	92-18	8.797	95-18	8.464	98-18	8.147
86-19	9.511	89-19	9.143	92-19	8.793	95-29	8.461	98-19	8.144
86-20	9.507	89-20	9.139	92-20	8.790	95-20	8.457	98-20	8.140
86-21	9.503	89-21	9.135	92-21	8.786	95-21	8.454	98-21	8.137
86-22	9.499	89-22	9.131	92-22	8.782	95-22	8.450	98-22	8.134
86-23	9.495	89-23	9.128	92-23	8.779	95-23	8.447	98-23	8.131
86-24	9.491	89-24	9.124	92-24	8.775	95-24	8.444	98-24	8.128
86-25	9.487	89-25	9.120	92-25	8.772	95-25	8.440	98-25	8.124
86-26	9.483	89-26	9.116	92-26	8.768	95-26	8.437	98-26	8.121
86-27	9.479	89-27	9.113	92-27	8.765	95-27	8.434	98-27	8.118
86-28	9.475	89-28	9.109	92-28	8.761	95-28	8.430	98-28	8.115
86-29	9.471	89-29	9.105	92-29	8.758	95-29	8.427	98-29	8.111
86-30	9.467	89-30	9.102	92-30	8.754	95-30	8.424	98-30	8.108
86-31	9.463	89-31	9.098	92-31	8.751	95-31	8.420	98-31	8.105
87-00	9.460	90-00	9.094	93-00	8.747	96-00	8.417	99-00	8.102
87-01	9.456	90-01	9.090	93-01	8.744	96-01	8.413	99-01	8.099
87-02	9.452	90-02	9.087	93-02	8.740	96-02	8.410	99-02	8.095
87-03	9.448	90-03	9.083	93-03	8.737	96-03	8.407	99-03	8.092
87-04	9.444	90-04	9.079	93-04	8.733	96-04	8.403	99-04	8.089
87-05	9.440	90-05	9.076	93-05	8.730	96-05	8.400	99-05	8.086
87-06	9.436	90-06	9.072	93-06	8.726	96-06	8.397	99-06	8.083
87-07	9.432	90-07	9.068	93-07	8.722	96-07	8.393	99-07	8.079
87-08	9.428	90-08	9.065	93-08	8.719	96-08	8.390	99-08	8.076
87-09	9.425	90-09	9.061	93-09	8.715	96-09	8.387	99-09	8.073
87-10	9.421	90-10	9.057	93-10	8.712	96-10	8.383	99-10	8.070
87-11	9.417	90-11	9.054	93-11	8.708	96-11	8.380	99-11	8.067
87-12	9.413	90-12	9.050	93-12	8.705	96-12	8.377	99-12	8.063
87-13	9.409	90-13	9.046	93-13	8.701	96-13	8.373	99-13	8.060
87-14	9.405	90-14	9.042	93-14	8.698	96-14	8.370	99-14	8.057
87-15	9.401	90-15	9.039	93-15	8.694	96-15	8.367	99-15	8.054
87-16	9.397	90-16	9.035	93-16	8.691	96-16	8.363	99-16	8.051
87-17	9.393	90-17	9.031	93-17	8.687	96-17	8.360	99-17	8.048
87-18	9.390	90-18	9.028	93-18	8.684	96-18	8.357	99-18	8.044
87-19	9.386	90-19	9.024	93-19	8.680	96-19	8.353	99-19	8.041
87-20	9.382	90-20	9.020	93-20	8.677	96-20	8.350	99-20	8.038
87-21	9.378	90-21	9.017	93-21	8.673	96-21	8.347	99-21	8.035
87-22	9.374	90-22	9.013	93-22	8.670	96-22	8.343	99-22	8.032
87-23	9.370	90-23	9.009	93-23	8.667	96-23	8.340	99-23	8.028
87-24	9.366	90-24	9.006	93-24	8.663	96-24	8.337	99-24	8.025
87-25	9.363	90-25	9.002	93-25	8.660	96-25	8.333	99-25	8.022
87-26	9.359	90-26	8.998	93-26	8.656	96-26	8.330	99-26	8.019
87-27	9.355	90-27	8.995	93-27	8.653	96-27	8.327	99-27	8.016
87-28	9.351	90-28	8.991	93-28	8.649	96-28	8.323	99-28	8.013
87-29	9.347	90-29	8.987	93-29	8.646	96-29	8.320	99-29	8.009
87-30	9.343	90-30	8.984	93-30	8.642	96-30	8.317	99-30	8.006
87-31	9.339	90-31	8.980	93-31	8.639	96-31	8.313	99-31	8.003

| 85-00 to 87-31 | 88-00 to 90-31 | 91-00 to 93-31 | 94-00 to 95-31 | 97-00 to 99-31 |

3. Treasury Bond Prices and Yields 8% Coupon (Continued)

Treasury Bond Prices and Yields 8% Coupon

98-00 to 100-31 101-00 to 103-31 104-00 to 106-31 107-00 to 109-31 110

98-00 8.205	101-00 7.900	104-00 7.608	107-00 7.328
98-01 8.202	101-01 7.897	104-01 7.605	107-01 7.325
98-02 8.199	101-02 7.893	104-02 7.602	107-02 7.322
98-03 8.195	101-03 7.890	104-03 7.599	107-03 7.319
98-04 8.192	101-04 7.887	104-04 7.596	107-04 7.316
98-05 8.189	101-05 7.884	104-05 7.593	107-05 7.313
98-06 8.186	101-06 7.881	104-06 7.590	107-06 7.311
98-07 8.182	101-07 7.878	104-07 7.587	107-07 7.308
98-08 8.179	101-08 7.875	104-08 7.584	107-08 7.305
98-09 8.176	101-09 7.872	104-09 7.581	107-09 7.302
98-10 8.173	101-10 7.869	104-10 7.578	107-10 7.299
98-11 8.169	101-11 7.866	104-11 7.575	104-11 7.296
98-12 8.166	101-12 7.862	104-12 7.572	107-12 7.293
98-13 8.163	101-13 7.859	104-13 7.569	107-13 7.291
98-14 8.160	101-14 7.856	104-14 7.566	107-14 7.288
98-15 8.157	101-15 7.853	104-15 7.563	107-15 7.285
98-16 8.153	101-16 7.850	104-16 7.560	107-16 7.282
98-17 8.150	101-17 7.847	104-17 7.557	107-17 7.279
98-18 8.147	101-18 7.844	104-18 7.554	107-18 7.276
98-19 8.144	101-19 7.841	104-19 7.551	107-19 7.274
98-20 8.140	101-20 7.838	104-20 7.548	107-20 7.271
98-21 8.137	101-21 7.835	104-21 7.545	107-21 7.268
98-22 8.134	101-22 7.832	104-22 7.542	107-22 7.265
98-23 8.131	101-23 7.829	104-23 7.539	107-23 7.262
98-24 8.128	101-24 7.825	104-24 7.536	107-24 7.260
98-25 8.124	101-25 7.822	104-25 7.534	107-25 7.257
98-26 8.121	101-26 7.819	104-26 7.531	107-26 7.254
98-27 8.118	101-27 7.816	104-27 7.528	107-27 7.251
98-28 8.115	101-28 7.813	104-28 7.525	107-28 7.248
98-29 8.111	101-29 7.810	104-29 7.522	107-29 7.245
98-30 8.108	101-30 7.807	104-30 7.519	107-30 7.243
98-31 8.105	101-31 7.804	104-31 7.516	107-31 7.240
99-00 8.102	102-00 7.801	105-00 7.513	108-00 7.237
99-01 8.099	102-01 7.798	105-01 7.510	108-01 7.234
99-02 8.095	102-02 7.795	105-02 7.507	108-02 7.231
99-03 8.092	102-03 7.792	105-03 7.504	108-03 7.229
99-04 8.089	102-04 7.789	105-04 7.501	108-04 7.226
99-05 8.086	102-05 7.786	105-05 7.498	108-05 7.223
99-06 8.083	102-06 7.783	105-06 7.495	108-06 7.220
99-07 8.079	102-07 7.779	105-07 7.492	108-07 7.217
99-08 8.076	102-08 7.776	105-08 7.489	108-08 7.214
99-09 8.073	102-09 7.773	105-09 7.487	108-09 7.212
99-10 8.070	102-10 7.770	105-10 7.484	108-10 7.209
99-11 8.067	102-11 7.767	105-11 7.481	108-11 7.206
99-12 8.063	102-12 7.764	105-12 7.478	108-12 7.203
99-13 8.060	102-13 7.761	105-13 7.475	108-13 7.200
99-14 8.057	102-14 7.758	105-14 7.472	108-14 7.198
98-15 8.054	102-15 7.755	105-15 7.469	108-15 7.195
99-16 8.051	102-16 7.752	105-16 7.466	108-16 7.192
99-17 8.048	102-17 7.749	105-17 7.463	108-17 7.189
99-18 8.044	102-18 7.746	105-18 7.460	107-18 7.186
99-19 8.041	102-19 7.743	105-19 7.457	108-19 7.184
99-20 8.038	102-20 7.740	105-20 7.454	108-20 7.181
99-21 8.035	102-21 7.737	105-21 7.452	108-21 7.178
99-22 8.032	102-22 7.734	105-22 7.449	108-22 7.175
99-23 8.028	102-23 7.731	105-23 7.446	108-23 7.172
99-24 8.025	102-24 7.728	105-24 7.443	108-24 7.170
99-25 8.022	102-25 7.725	105-25 7.440	108-25 7.167
99-26 8.019	102-26 7.722	105-26 7.437	108-26 7.164
99-27 8.016	102-27 7.719	105-27 7.434	108-27 7.161
99-28 8.013	102-28 7.716	105-28 7.431	108-28 7.159
99-29 8.009	102-29 7.713	105-29 7.428	108-29 7.156
99-30 8.006	102-30 7.710	105-30 7.425	108-30 7.153
99-31 8.003	102-31 7.707	105-31 7.423	108-31 7.150
100-00 8.000	103-00 7.704	106-00 7.420	109-00 7.147
100-01 7.997	103-01 7.701	106-01 7.417	109-01 7.145
100-02 7.994	103-02 7.697	106-02 7.414	109-02 7.142
100-03 7.991	103-03 7.694	106-03 7.411	109-03 7.139
100-04 7.987	103-04 7.691	106-04 7.408	109-04 7.136
100-05 7.984	103-05 7.688	106-05 7.405	109-05 7.134
100-06 7.981	103-06 7.685	106-06 7.402	109-06 7.131
100-07 7.978	103-07 7.682	106-07 7.399	109-07 7.128
100-08 7.975	103-08 7.679	106-08 7.397	109-08 7.125
100-09 7.972	103-09 7.676	106-09 7.394	109-09 7.122
100-10 7.969	103-10 7.673	106-10 7.391	109-10 7.120
100-11 7.965	103-11 7.670	106-11 7.388	109-11 7.117
100-12 7.962	103-12 7.667	106-12 7.385	109-12 7.114
100-13 7.959	103-13 7.664	106-13 7.382	109-13 7.111
100-14 7.956	103-14 7.661	106-14 7.379	109-14 7.109

410

3. Treasury Bond Prices and Yields 8% Coupon (Continued)

100-15 7.953	103-15 7.658	106-15 7.376	109-15 7.106
100-16 7.950	102-16 7.655	106-16 7.373	109-16 7.103
100-17 7.947	103-17 7.652	106-17 7.371	109-17 7.100
100-18 7.943	103-18 7.649	106-18 7.368	109-18 7.098
100-19 7.940	103-19 7.646	106-19 7.365	109-19 7.095
100-20 7.937	103-20 7.643	106-20 7.362	109-20 7.092
100-21 7.934	103-21 7.640	106-21 7.359	109-21 7.089
100-22 7.931	103-22 7.637	106-22 7.356	109-22 7.087
100-23 7.928	103-23 7.634	106-23 7.353	109-23 7.084
100-24 7.925	103-24 7.631	106-24 7.351	109-24 7.081
100-25 7.922	103-25 7.628	106-25 7.348	108-25 7.078
100-26 7.918	103-26 7.625	106-26 7.345	108-26 7.076
100-27 7.915	103-27 7.622	106-27 7.342	109-27 7.073
100-28 7.912	103-28 7.619	106-28 7.339	109-28 7.070
100-29 7.909	103-29 7.616	106-29 7.336	109-29 7.067
100-30 7.906	103-30 7.614	106-30 7.333	109-30 7.065
100-31 7.903	103-31 7.611	106-31 7.331	109-31 7.062

98-00 to 100-31 101-00 to 103-31 104-00 to 106-31 107-00 to 109-31 110-00

4. Discount Rates and Equivalent Bond Yields

Discount rate (percent)	Equivalent bond yields at varying maturities							
	1 mo.	2 mo.	3 mo.	4 mo.	5 mo.	6 mo.	9 mo.	1 yr.
5	5.09	5.11	5.13	5.16	5.18	5.20	5.22	5.27
5⅛	5.22	5.24	5.26	5.29	5.31	5.33	5.36	5.41
5¼	5.35	5.37	5.39	5.42	5.44	5.47	5.49	5.55
5⅜	5.47	5.50	5.52	5.55	5.57	5.61	5.63	5.69
5½	5.60	5.63	5.65	5.68	5.71	5.74	5.76	5.83
5⅝	5.73	5.76	5.79	5.81	5.84	5.87	5.90	5.97
5¾	5.86	5.89	5.92	5.94	5.97	6.00	6.03	6.10
5⅞	5.99	6.02	6.05	6.08	6.11	6.14	6.17	6.24
6	6.11	6.15	6.18	6.21	6.24	6.27	6.31	6.38
6⅛	6.24	6.27	6.31	6.34	6.37	6.41	6.45	6.52
6¼	6.37	6.40	6.44	6.47	6.51	6.54	6.58	6.66
6⅜	6.50	6.53	6.57	6.60	6.64	6.68	6.72	6.80
6½	6.63	6.66	6.70	6.74	6.77	6.81	6.85	6.94
6⅝	6.75	6.79	6.83	6.87	6.91	6.95	6.99	7.08
6¾	6.88	6.92	6.96	7.00	7.04	7.08	7.13	7.22
6⅞	7.01	7.05	7.09	7.13	7.18	7.22	7.27	7.36
7	7.14	7.18	7.22	7.27	7.31	7.36	7.40	7.50
7⅛	7.27	7.31	7.36	7.40	7.45	7.49	7.54	7.65
7¼	7.40	7.44	7.49	7.53	7.58	7.63	7.68	7.79
7⅜	7.52	7.57	7.62	7.67	7.71	7.76	7.82	7.93
7½	7.65	7.70	7.75	7.80	7.85	7.90	7.96	8.07
7⅝	7.78	7.83	7.88	7.93	7.98	8.04	8.10	8.21
7¾	7.91	7.96	8.01	8.07	8.12	8.17	8.24	8.35
7⅞	8.04	8.09	8.14	8.20	8.26	8.31	8.38	8.49
8	8.17	8.22	8.28	8.33	8.39	8.45	8.51	8.63
8⅛	8.29	8.35	8.41	8.47	8.53	8.59	8.65	8.77
8¼	8.42	8.48	8.54	8.60	8.66	8.72	8.79	8.92
8⅜	8.55	8.61	8.67	8.74	8.80	8.86	8.93	9.07
8½	8.68	8.74	8.81	8.87	8.93	9.00	9.07	9.21
8⅝	8.81	8.87	8.94	9.00	9.07	9.14	9.21	9.35
8¾	8.94	9.00	9.07	9.14	9.21	9.28	9.35	9.50
8⅞	9.07	9.13	9.20	9.27	9.34	9.42	9.49	9.65

411

4. Discount Rates and Equivalent Bond Yields (Continued)

Discount rate (percent)	Equivalent bond yields at varying maturities							
	1 mo.	2 mo.	2 mo.	4 mo.	5 mo.	6 mo.	9 mo.	1 yr.
9	9.20	9.26	9.34	9.41	9.48	9.56	9.64	9.79
9⅛	9.33	9.39	9.47	9.54	9.62	9.69	9.78	9.94
9¼	9.45	9.52	9.60	9.67	9.75	9.83	9.92	10.08
9⅜	9.58	9.65	9.73	9.81	9.89	9.97	10.06	10.23
9½	9.71	9.79	9.87	9.95	10.03	10.11	10.20	10.38
9⅝	9.84	9.92	10.00	10.08	10.17	10.25	10.34	10.53
9¾	9.97	10.05	10.13	10.22	10.30	10.39	10.49	10.67
9⅞	10.10	10.18	10.27	10.35	10.44	10.53	10.63	10.82
10	10.22	10.31	10.40	10.49	10.58	10.67	10.77	10.97
10⅛	10.35	10.44	10.53	10.62	10.72	10.81	10.92	11.12
10¼	10.48	10.57	10.67	10.76	10.86	10.95	11.06	11.27
10⅜	10.61	10.70	10.80	10.89	10.99	11.09	11.20	11.42
10½	10.74	10.84	10.93	11.03	11.13	11.24	11.35	11.57
10⅝	10.87	10.97	11.07	11.17	11.27	11.38	11.49	11.72
10¾	11.00	11.10	11.20	11.30	11.41	11.52	11.64	11.87
10⅞	11.13	11.23	11.33	11.44	11.55	11.66	11.78	12.02

APPENDIX E

Contract Specifications and Trading Data

	Contract Amount	Value of Minimum Fluctuation	Delivery Grade	Exchange	Contract Traded Since	Delivery Months	Trading Hours	Maximum Daily Price Move*
90-Day U.S. Treasury Bills	$1 million face value at maturity	One basis point (.01%) or $25 per contract	90-day U.S. Treasury bills	International Monetary Market	January 1976	March, June September and December	9:10 a.m. to 2:40 p.m. EST	50 basis points
				Amex Commodities Exchange	June 1979	January, April July and October	9 a.m. to 3:30 p.m. EST	50 basis points
				Comex, Inc.	1979	February, May August and November		60 basis points
One-year U.S. Treasury Bills	$250,000 face value at maturity	One basis point (.01%) or $25 per contract	One-year U.S. Treasury bills	International Monetary Market	September 1978	March, June September and December	9:15 a.m. to 2:35 p.m. EST	50 basis points

*Above or below prior day's settlement price

413

Contract Specifications and Trading Data (Continued)

	Contract Amount	Value of Minimum Fluctuation	Delivery Grade	Exchange	Contract Traded Since	Delivery Months	Trading Hours	Maximum Daily Price Move°
30-Day Commercial Paper	$3 million face value at maturity	One basis point (.01%) or $25 per contract	C.P. rated A-1 by S&P, P-1 by Moody's	Chicago Board of Trade	May 1979	March, June September and December	9:30 a.m. to 2:00 p.m. EST	50 basis points
90-Day Commercial Paper	$1 million face value at maturity	One basis point (.01%) or $25 per contract	C.P. rated A-1 by S&P, P-1 by Moody's	Chicago Board of Trade	October 1977	March, June September and December	9:30 a.m. to 2:00 p.m. EST	50 basis points
Four-year U.S. Treasury Notes	$100,000 face value at maturity	1/64th point per 100 points or $15.625 per contract	U.S. Treasury notes of same issue	International Monetary Market	July 1979	February, May August and November	9:20 a.m. to 2:35 p.m. EST	¾ of 1% of par on 48/64ths
Four-to-six year U.S. Treasury Notes	$100,000 face value at maturity	1/32nd point per 100 points or $31.25 per contract	Notes of same issue with 4- to-6 year maturity priced at 8% equivalent	Chicago Board of Trade	June 1979	March, June September and December	9:30 a.m. to 2:00 p.m. EST	½ of 1% of par or 16/32nds.
U.S. Treasury Bonds	$100,000 par value	1/32nd point per 100 points or $31.25 per contract	Bonds of same issue at least 15 years to call or maturity priced at 8% equivalent	Chicago Board of Trade	September 1977	March, June September and December	9:30 a.m. to 2:00 p.m. EST	1% of par or 32/32nds

Contract Specifications and Trading Data (Continued)

	Contract Amount	Value of Minimum Fluctuation	Delivery Grade	Exchange	Contract Traded Since	Delivery Months	Trading Hours	Maximum Daily Price Move°
GNMA Mortgage Securities								
(Old-Depository Receipt)	$100,000 principal balance	1/32nd point per 100 points or $31.25 per contract	Pass-through securities at 8% at par under assumption of 30-year maturity prepaid in 12th year	Chicago Board of Trade	October 1975	March, June September and December	9:30 a.m. to 2:00 p.m. EST	¾ of 1% of par or 24/32nds
(New-Certificate Delivery)	$100,000 principal balance	1/32nd point per 100 points or $31.25 per contract	Pass-through securities at 8% at par under assumption of 30-year maturity prepaid in 12th year	Chicago Board of Trade	September 1978	March, June September and December	9:30 a.m. to 2:00 p.m. EST	¾ of 1% of par or 24/32nds
				Amex Commodities Exchange	September 1978	February, May August and November	9:00 a.m. to 3:45 p.m. EST	¾ of 1% of par or 24/32nds

*Above or below prior day's settlement price

415

Appendix F:
Glossary of Frequently Used Commodity Terms

Where words appear *italicized,* separate definitions of those words may be helpful to understanding and are provided in the appropriate alphabetical sequence.

Actuals—The physical or *cash commodity,* as distinguished from commodity *futures contracts* based upon the commodity.

Basis—(1) The relationship of a *cash price* to the price of a particular *futures contract.* (2) In certain other uses, "basis" is understood as a concise expression of what might more completely be expressed as "is based upon the following conditions." For example, "price basis delivered Chicago, Illinois, registered in owner's name ..." means that the price being quoted is based upon those conditions being met.

Bona fide hedger—A classification or definition which may be established by the *Commodity Futures Trading Commission* for regulation purposes. The definition typically includes the industries which are viewed as having a bona fide *hedging* potential in their use of *futures contracts;* the uses of futures contracts which can be classified as bona fide hedging by some or all of those industries; and the size or degree of *position* that would be classified as bona fide hedging for some or all such industries. All market positions except those falling under the definition of bona fide hedging are classified as speculative. Different daily *trading* and *position limits* and *margins* may apply to hedging and speculative trading. Anyone unsure of his status should consult his broker.

416

Broker—(1) A person paid a fee or commission for acting as an agent in making contracts, sales or purchases; (2) When used as floor broker, it means a person who actually executes someone else's trading orders on the trading floor of an exchange; (3) When used to mean account executive, it means the person who deals with customers and their orders in commission house offices. See also *Registered Commodity Representative.*

Cash (Commodity)—The physical commodity, as distinguished from *futures contracts* based upon the physical commodity; the commodity as acquired through a cash market.

Cash Market—A market in which transactions for purchase and sale of the physical commodity are made, under whatever terms are agreeable to buyer and seller and are legal under law and the rules of the market organization, if such exists. "Cash market" can refer to an organized, self-regulated central market, such as the cash grain sections of commodity exchanges that also have futures contract trading, or such as the central stockyards in the livestock industry. It can also refer to an over-the-counter type of market, in which buyers, sellers and/or dealers compete in decentralized locations, possibly under rules of an organized association. In still other uses, the term may refer to such other methods of purchasing and selling the physical commodity as are prevalent in the industries using that commodity. For example, an elevator company in town and neighboring farmers who feed livestock may comprise a corn grower's "cash market," even though no organized relationship exists between them. Likewise, one's "cash market" for Ginnie Maes may refer to a group of recognized dealers, such independent buyers or sellers as the party can find, or to a mixture of both, depending upon the circumstances in which the term is used. See also *spot* and *forward contract.*

Cash Price—A price quotation obtained in a *cash market.*

Charting—The use of graphs and charts in analysis of market behavior, so as to plot trends of price movements, average movements of price, volume and open interest, in the hope that such graphs and charts will help one to anticipate and profit from price trends. Contrasted with *fundamental analysis.*

Clearing House—An agency connected with a commodity exchange through which all futures contracts are made, *offset* or fulfilled through *delivery* of the commodity and through which financial settlement is made. It may be a fully chartered separate corporation, rather than a division of the exchange itself.

Closing Price—See *settlement price.*

Commodity Futures Trading Commission (CFTC)—A federal regulatory agency charged and empowered under the Commodity Futures Trading Commission Act of 1974 with regulation of futures trading in all commodities. The commission is comprised of five commissioners, one of whom is designated as chairman, all appointed by the President subject to Senate confirmation, and is independent of all cabinet departments.

Day Traders—*Speculators,* usually members of an exchange, who take positions in commodity futures and then *offset* them prior to the close of the same trading day.

Deferred Months—The more distant *delivery months* in which futures trading is taking place.

Delivery—This common word has unique connotations when used in connection with *futures contracts.* Basically, in such usage, delivery refers to the changing of ownership or control of a commodity under very specific terms and procedures established by the exchange upon which the contract is traded. Typically, the commodity must be placed in an approved warehouse, on-track boxcar or bank and inspected by approved personnel, after which the facility issues a warehouse receipt, shipping certificate or due bill, which becomes a transferable delivery instrument. Delivery of the delivery instrument typically must be preceded by delivery of a *Notice of Intention to Deliver,* made two days before delivery of the instrument. After receipt of the delivery instrument, the new owner typically can arrange with the storage facility to take possession of the physical commodity, can deliver the delivery instrument into the futures market in satisfaction of a *short position,* or can sell the delivery instrument to another market participant who can use it for delivery into the futures market in satisfaction of his short position or for cash.

Delivery Month—A calendar month during which delivery against a futures contract can be made.

Delivery Notice—See *Notice of Intention to Deliver.*

Delivery Points—Those locations and facilities designated by a commodity exchange at which stocks of a commodity may be delivered in fulfillment of a contract, under procedures established by the exchange.

Discretionary Account—An arrangement by which the holder of the account gives written power of attorney to another, often his broker, to make buying and selling decisions without notification to the holder; often referred to as a "managed account" or "controlled account."

First Notice Day—The first day on which *Notices of Intent to Deliver* the commodity in fulfillment of a given month's futures contract can be made by the seller to the *clearing house* and by the clearing house to a buyer.

Forward Contract—A cash market transaction in which two parties agree to the purchase and sale of a commodity at some future time under such conditions as the two agree. In contrast to a *futures contract,* the terms of a forward contract are not standardized; a forward contract is not transferable and usually can be cancelled only with the consent of the other party, which often must be obtained for consideration and under penalty; and forward contracts are not traded in federally designated contract markets. Essentially, forward contract refers to any cash market purchase or sale agreement for which delivery is not made "on the *spot.*"

Fundamental Analysis—An approach to market behavior which stresses the study of underlying factors of supply and demand in the commodity, in the belief that such analysis will enable one to profit from being able to anticipate price trends. Contrasted with *charting.*

Futures—See *futures contract.*

Futures Contract—A transferable agreement to make or take *delivery* of a standardized amount of a commodity, of standardized minimum quality grades, during a specific month, under terms and conditions established by the federally designated contract market upon which trading is conducted.

Hedging—The initiation of a position in a futures market which is intended as a temporary substitute for the sale or purchase of the actual commodity. See also *speculator, bona fide hedger.*

Limits—See *price limits; trading limits; variable limits,* or *reporting limit.*

Liquid Market—A market where selling and buying can be accomplished with ease, due to the presence of a large number of interested buyers and sellers willing and able to trade substantial quantities at small price differences.

Long—As a noun, one who has bought *futures contracts* (or the *cash commodity,* depending upon the market under discussion) and has not yet *offset* that position. As a verb (going long), the action of taking a position in which one has bought futures contracts (or the cash commodity) without taking the offsetting action. For example, if you had no position and you bought five contracts, you would be a "long." However, if your previous position was one of having sold five contracts (i.e., "being *short* five"), and you then bought five contracts to offset that position, your second action would not be referred to as going long because your position when the second action is concluded would be zero. Long also is used with similar meanings as an adjective or adverb.

Margin—An amount of money deposited by both buyers and sellers of futures contracts to ensure performance of the terms of the contract, i.e., the *delivery* or taking of delivery of the commodity or the cancellation of the position by a subsequent offsetting trade at such price as can be attained. Margin in commodities is not a payment of equity or down payment on the commodity itself but rather is in the nature of a performance bond or security deposit.

Margin Call—A call from a *clearing house* to a clearing member, or from a brokerage firm to a customer, to bring *margin* deposits up to a required minimum level.

Nearby—A *delivery month* of a futures contract that is in the near future, as contrasted with a *deferred* month which is farther into the future.

Net Position—The number of contracts a trader has bought or sold but not *offset* by opposite trades. For example, if a trader bought 10 December and then sold 15 December, his net position would be five *short*. If he then bought 10 more, he would then be five *long*. Similarly, the Net Position of a brokerage firm or clearing member can be calculated by determining the total it has bought and sold for its customers.

Notice of Intention to Deliver—A notice that must be presented by the seller to the *clearing house*. The clearing house then assigns the notice, and the subsequent delivery instrument to the longest-standing buyer on record. Under Chicago Board of Trade rules, such notices must be presented by 8:00 a.m. of the second business day prior to the day on which delivery is to be made.

Offset—The liquidation of a purchase of futures through sale of an equal number of contracts of the same delivery month, or the covering of a *short* sale of futures through the purchase of an equal number of contracts of the same delivery month. Either action cancels the obligation to make or take delivery of the commodity.

Open Interest—The total number of futures contracts of a given commodity which have not yet been *offset* by opposite futures transactions nor fulfilled by *delivery* of the commodity; the total number of open transactions. Each open transaction has a buyer and a seller, but for calculation of open interest, only one side of the contract is counted.

Position—A market commitment. For example, one who has bought futures contracts is said to have a *long* position, and conversely, a seller of futures contracts is said to have a *short* position. See also *Net Position*.

Position Limit—The maximum number of speculative futures contracts one can hold as determined by the *Commodity Futures Trading Commission* and/or the exchange upon which the contract is traded. See also *bona fide hedger, speculator*.

Position Trading—An approach to trading in which the trader either buys or sells contracts and holds them for an extended period of time, as distinguished from the *day trader*, who will normally initiate and offset his position within a single trading session.

Price Limits—The maximum price advance or decline from the previous day's *settlement price* permitted for a contract in one trading session by the rules of the exchange. See also *Variable Limits*.

Registered Commodity Representative (RCR)—A member or non-member of an exchange who is registered with the exchange to solicit and handle commodity customer business for his firm.

Reporting Limit, Reportable Position—The number of futures contracts, as determined by the exchange and/or the *Commodity Futures Trading Commission*, above which one must report daily to the exchange and/or the CFTC with regard to the size of one's position by commodity, by delivery month, and by purpose of the trading (i.e., *bona fide hedging* or *speculating*).

Scalper—A *speculator* who trades a large volume of contracts at small price differences in the hope of being able to earn an acceptable over-all profit at minimal risk. Although the name frequently gives just the opposite image, the scalper in fact is essential to the hedger, for the scalper's large volume of trading helps to create the *liquid market* vital to easy placing and lifting of hedges by commercial firms.

Settlement Price—The price established by a clearing house at the close of each trading session as the official price to be used in determining net gains or losses, *margin* requirements and the next day's *price limits,* and for other purposes. The term settlement price is also often used as an approximate equivalent

to the term "closing price." The "close" in futures trading refers to a very brief period of time at the end of the trading
day, during which transactions frequently take place quickly
and at a range of prices immediately before the bell. Therefore,
there frequently is no one "closing price," but a range of closing prices. The settlement price is the closing price if there is
only one closing price. When there is a closing range, it is as
near to the mid-point of the closing range as possible, consistent with the contract's price increments. Thus, the settlement
price can be used to provide a single reference point for analysis of closing market conditions.

Short—As a noun, one who has sold *futures contracts* (or the cash
commodity, depending upon the market under discussion) and
has not yet *offset* that position. As a verb, the action of taking
a position in which one has sold futures contracts (or made a
forward contract for sale of the cash commodity) without taking the offsetting action. For example, if you had no position
and you sold five contracts, your action would be "shorting the
futures," and you would then be a "short." However, if your
previous position was one of having bought five contracts (i.e.,
"being *long* five"), and you then sold five contracts to offset
that position, your second action would not be referred to as
"shorting," because your position when the second action was
concluded would be zero. Short is also used with similar meanings as an adjective and adverb.

Speculator—In an economic sense, one who attempts to anticipate
commodity price changes and to profit through the sale and
purchase or purchase and sale of commodity futures contracts
or of the physical commodity; in a legal sense, any commodity
futures trader not defined as a *bona fide hedger* by the *Commodity Futures Trading Commission*.

Spot—Refers to the characteristic of being available for immediate
(or nearly immediate) delivery. An outgrowth of the phrase
"on the spot," it usually refers to a *cash market* price for stocks
of the physical commodity that are available for immediate
delivery, or vice versa and depending upon the noun it modi-
fies, the stocks themselves that are available for delivery if an
acceptable price is quoted. Thus, cash market transactions are
usually grouped into two kinds: spot and *forward contracts*.
However, "spot" is also sometimes used in reference to the
futures contract of the current month, in which case trading
is still "futures" trading but *delivery* is possible at any time.

Spreading—The purchase of one *futures contract* and sale of another, in the expectation that the price relationships between
the two will change so that a subsequent *offsetting* sale and
purchase will yield a net profit. Examples include the purchase
of one *delivery month* and the sale of another in the same

commodity on the same exchange, or the purchase and sale of the same delivery month in the same commodity on different exchanges, or the purchase of one commodity and the sale of another (wheat vs. corn or corn vs. hogs), or the purchase of one commodity and the sale of the products of that commodity (soybeans vs. soybean oil and soybean meal). When the terms of the contract and all other relevant factors indicate that the price relationships between the contracts should be constant, but price discrepancies develop due to temporary supply-demand imbalances, spreading operations to take advantage of such discrepancies are sometimes called arbitrage. However, true spreading involves the making of judgments about price relationships which are subject to gradual change due to economic factors which vary over a period of time and is therefore a form of speculation.

Technical Analysis—An approach to analysis of futures markets and future trends of commodity prices which examines the technical factors of market activity. Technical analysts normally examine patterns of price change, rates of change, and changes in volume of trading and *open interest,* often by *charting,* in the hope of being able to predict and profit from future trends. Contrasted with *fundamental analysis.*

Trading Limit—The maximum number of contracts, as determined by an exchange and/or the *Commodity Futures Trading Commission,* that one may trade in a given trading day.

Tender—The act on the part of the seller of a futures contract of giving *notice* to the *clearing house* that he intends to *deliver* the commodity in satisfaction of the futures contract.

Variation Call—A call for additional margin deposits made by a *clearing house* to a clearing member while trading is in progress when current price trends have substantially reduced the protective value of the clearing member's margin deposits. Variation calls are payable within the hour.

Variable Limits—A Chicago Board of Trade *price limit* system which allows for larger than normally allowable price movements under certain circumstances. Those circumstances are as follows: If a commodity's price closes up or down limit for three consecutive days in three or more contract months during a business year, or all contracts in a business year if there are less than three open, the variable limits policy increases daily price limits to 150 percent of the normal levels for the next three consecutive business days. Those limits remain in effect until at least three contracts in the commodity, or all contracts in a business year if there are less than three open, fail to close up or down the limit during that period. Limits then revert to their original levels.

Appendix G: Worksheet: Estimating the Impact of Monetary and Economic News Reports on Interest Rate Behavior

1. Monetary Aggregates

	Recent Week	Four-week Average	Twelve-week Average
Growth of M_1 and M_2			
Current Federal Reserve growth targets	M_1	M_2	
Excess or shortfall of twelve-week average to Fed targets			

	Tightening	Easing	Stable
Response of FOMC to recent money supply change			

2. Market Interest Rates

Current federal funds target rate_____In effect for (no. of weeks)_____

Direction, amount and dates of last three changes
in fed funds rate _____ _____ _____

Results of latest Treasury bill auction:
Average rate, 13-week _____, 26-week bills _____
Change from previous week _____, previous month _____

Weekly change in 90-day commercial paper rate from _____ to _____

Weekly change in 90-day CD rate from _____ to _____

3. Economic Growth

	Recent Quarter	Six-Month Average	Twelve-month Average
Rate of GNP growth			

	Recent Month	Month Earlier	Three-months Earlier
Change in leading economic indicators			

Also, current trend in industrial production, unemployment and monthly retail sales figures measured against month earlier and latest twelve-month average.

4. Inflationary Trends

	Recent Monthly Change (Annual Rate)	Annual Rate Year to date	Projected Annual Rate	Projected Change Current Month
Consumer price index				
Producer price index (Wholesale prices)				

5. Demand for Credit—Private Sector

	Weekly Change	Month Earlier	Six months Earlier
Commercial and industrial loans 10 large New York City banks			

	Projected for Current Month	Month Earlier	Six months Earlier
Amount of corporate bond offerings			

	Current Month	Month Earlier	Six months Earlier
Consumer credit			

6. Demand for Credit—Government

	Projected	Change from Earlier Estimates
Federal budget deficit (surplus)		

	Current Month (Dollars)	Balance of Fiscal Year (Dollars)	Change from Year Earlier
Projected Treasury borrowing			
Projected agency borrowing			
Projected State and Local borrowing			
Estimated effect of legislative or policy changes on receipts or expenditures			

INDEX

427